WORLD ® AIR POWER

J O U R N A L

Aerospace Publishing Ltd
AIRtime Publishing Inc.

Published quarterly by
Aerospace Publishing Ltd
179 Dalling Road
London W6 0ES
UK

ISSN 0959-7050
Aerospace ISBN 1 86184 006 3
                (softback)
                1 86184 007 1
                (hardback)
Airtime ISBN   1-880588-07-2
                (hardback)

Published under licence in USA and
Canada by AIRtime Publishing Inc.,
USA

Editorial Offices:
WORLD AIR POWER JOURNAL
Aerospace Publishing Ltd
3A Brackenbury Road
London   W6 0BE   UK
E-mail: info@aerospacepbl.co.uk

Publisher: Stan Morse
Managing Editor: David Donald

Editors: Robert Hewson
        E-mail: rob@aerospacepbl.co.uk

        David Donald
        E-mail: dave@aerospacepbl.co.uk

Sub Editor: Karen Leverington

Editorial Assistant: Tim Senior

Origination by Universal Graphics
                Pte Ltd Singapore
Printed in Italy by Officine Grafiche
                de Agostini

Correspondents:
General military: Jon Lake
USA Washington: Robert F. Dorr
USA Southwest: Randy Jolly
Europe: John Fricker
Russia/CIS: Yefim Gordon
Asia: Pushpindar Singh
Canada: Jeff Rankin-Lowe
Argentina: Jorge Nunez Padin
Chile: Patrick Laureau

The editorial team at *World Air Power Journal* can
now be contacted, via e-mail, on the individual
addresses opposite. General queries should be
addressed to info@aerospacepbl.co.uk

The *World Air Power Journal* web site can
be found at:
http://www.airpower.co.uk

The authors and publishers gratefully acknowledge
the assistance given by the following people:

Northrop Grumman and Rick Burgess for their
assistance with the E-2 Hawkeye article.

Commandant Kevin Byrne, Irish Air Corps Press
Officer, for all his research and support for the
Irish Air Corps feature. Thanks are also due to
Mr M. V. Unen.

Mr Rob Lea for his important contribution to the
Second-generation Harriers feature.

Sheila Dewart, Marketing Communications
Manager, Pilatus Britten-Norman for timely
assistance with several photographs.

Paolo Gianvanni, of *JP4* magazine, Italy, for his
invaluable help with the Cuban section of the Air
Power Analysis. Thanks also to Mr Paolo Poggi
and Mr Tulio Soto.

Photographs supplied for the US Navy Warfighters
feature are from a forthcoming book, 'Warfighters
III – The Story of the US Navy Strike and Air
Warfare Center', by Rick Llinares and Chuck
Lloyd/Dash 2 Aviation Photography, to be
published in 1998.

**World Air Power Journal is
published quarterly and is
available by subscription and
from many fine book and hobby
stores.**

**SUBSCRIPTION AND BACK
NUMBERS:**

**UK and World (except USA and
Canada) write to:
Aerospace Publishing Ltd
FREEPOST
PO Box 2822
London
W6 0BR
UK**

**(No stamp required if posted in
the UK)**

**USA and Canada, write to:
AIRtime Publishing Inc.
Subscription Dept
10 Bay Street
Westport
CT 06880, USA
(203) 838-7979
Toll-free order number in USA:
1 800 359-3003**

**Prevailing subscription rates are
as follows:
Softbound edition for 1 year:
       $59.95
Softbound edition for 2 years:
       $112.00
Softbound back numbers
(subject to availability) are
$16.00 each, plus shipping and
handling. All rates are for
delivery within mainland USA,
Alaska and Hawaii. Canadian
and overseas prices available
upon request. American Express,
Discover Card, MasterCard and
Visa accepted. When ordering
please include card number,
expiration date and signature.**

**U.S. Publisher:
    Mel Williams
Subscriptions Director:
    Linda DeAngelis
Charter Member Services
Manager:
    Janie Munro
Retail Sales Director: Jill Brooks
Shipping Manager: E. Rex Anku**

WORLD AIR POWER ®
JOURNAL

CONTENTS

Military Aviation Review

International

German cabinet clears the way for EF 2000

German aerospace industry hopes of an early cabinet decision on Eurofighter production funding when the Bundestag reconvened after its summer recess in early September were initially unrealised. Finance Minister Theo Waigel then confirmed that German EFA procurement had become possible from Bonn's most recent funding plans, despite drastic cuts in public spending.

Defence Minister Volker Ruehe revealed that Bonn's 1998 military budget now included DM847 million ($472 million) for the Eurofighter production phase. On 8 October 1997 German cabinet approval was finally given to the EF 2000 production documentation, confirming the decision to go ahead with production. The matter then passed to the parliamentary defence and budget committee for final approval, hopefully in November. At time of writing the German Ministry of Defence stated that it expected to have a signed memorandum of understanding for full production go-ahead on 12 December 1997, but this date was by no means certain. However, it seems clear that despite almost rabid opposition to the EF 2000 among some of Germany's political parties, particularly the powerful Green party and opposition Social Democratic Party, Eurofighter production will be approved on the grounds of safeguarding jobs and industrial base.

Given parliamentary approval, this would allow Bonn to go ahead with its commitment to Germany's DM23 billion ($12.8 billion) EFA programme for 180 EF 2000s, including 40 with additional ground-attack capability, within a few weeks from the final decision. Earlier in 1997, Luftwaffe chief of staff Lieutenant General Bernhard Mende said that the necessity for a new fighter was undisputed, since air superiority was a question of sovereignty, and added that "the price of the aircraft was no longer an issue."

Some parliamentary opposition to final approval of Eurofighter production was still evident, however, particularly from the Federal Audit Office, which proposed restricting EF 2000 procurement to only 100 aircraft. The FAO claimed that the Eurofighter still had technical problems, and its funding was at the expense of other military equipment projects.

Tiger production go-ahead

Formal agreement was finally reached in mid-1997 between the Defence Ministers of France and Germany on the production phase of the joint Eurocopter Tiger attack helicopter project. This followed settlement of major defence budget problems in both countries, accompanied by 10 per cent cuts in Tiger programme costs. Initially,

80 Tigers each will be bought from 1998 contracts, although the overall programme requirements remain unchanged at 427 helicopters. Deliveries will be made from discrete French and German production lines, at up to 22 per year by 2005.

Germany will receive the first of its 80 dedicated anti-tank Tigers, now known as the multi-role UHT (Unterstutzungs Hubschrauber Tiger), at a joint training school at Le Luc in 2001, while, for budget reasons, France has stretched its initial deliveries to 2003. They will comprise 70 HAP (Helicoptère Appui-Protection) versions, equipped for helicopter escort/fire-support roles.

French army aviation (ALAT) will now not receive its first 10 HAC (Helicoptère Anti-Char) anti-tank Tigers until 2011, with only pod-mounted cannon armament if required, to begin replacing over 150 currently-operated HOT-armed SA 342Ms. Official programme costs of France's first 80 Tigers are now quoted as some FF12 billion ($2 billion).

Recent air firings from the Tiger HAC/UHT of the Euromissile HOT 2 anti-tank missiles are being followed by the first helicopter launches of the TriGAT ATM, as the definitive anti-armour weapon, from an AS 565 Panther. Long-term French orders are now expected for 115 HAP and 100 HAC Tigers, to meet its full programme commitment, while Germany's overall total of 212 UHTs will be equipped solely for anti-tank use.

UHT armament, however, will include four GD Stinger defensive AAMs, with which five firings of eject test vehicles were successfully completed in April from the PT5 Tiger prototype, as well as up to eight HOT 2s or TriGATs. By the end of 1997, the five MTR 390-powered Tiger prototypes were expected to complete about 2,000 hours of flight development that has been ongoing since 1991. For export, a multi-role version of the Tiger is being offered as the HCP (Helicoptère de Combat Polyvalent).

MoD invites new transport aircraft bids

While confirming the UK's decision to follow the example of France, Germany, Italy, Spain and Turkey, as full partners, in issuing RFPs through the embryo Airbus Military Company (AMC) for the European Future Large Aircraft, Defence Secretary George Robertson has encouraged the FLA group to follow Britain's lead in seeking alternative bids to meet national airlift needs.

He committed the UK to endorsement of the European Staff Requirement and Statement of Principles governing commercial FLA management, but gave no indication of any British government intention of formally rejoining the consortium. UK FLA

Above: In October 1997 the last Cessna L-19 Bird Dog was withdrawn from Austrian air force service. A total of 20 L-19A/Es was supplied between 1958 and 1960.

Below: Two Luftwaffe Airbus A310-304s (this example is still wearing vestigial Lufthansa colours) are due for conversion to MRTT tanker/transport standard.

participation is currently limited to British Aerospace, although the other five main partners all have government as well as industrial support. Belgium and Portugal have associate status in the consortium.

The RFPs will initiate pre-launch activities for the FLA, including further wind-tunnel tests and preliminary design of structure and systems, plus powerplant selection from between the 10,000-shp (7460-kW) BMW Rolls-Royce BR700-TP and the SNECMA/FiatAvio/MTU M88-derived M138 of similar output. They will also allow the AMC to put forward formal detailed technical and commercial proposals to partner nations, covering specifications, firm prices, delivery timescales, performance guarantees and support package details.

This will permit the UK and its partners to assess for the first time the FLA's detailed performance characteristics and the full cost by November 1998, for a possible 1999 programme launch. The MoD made it clear that the RFP did not imply any formal British FLA commitment. That decision, it said, could only be taken once RFP responses had been considered.

Its statement was significant, however, in opening the door to US and other aircraft manufacturers to bid for the RAF transport requirements, which include 25 replacements for its remaining 30 Lockheed C-130Ks from about 2003. About 21 multi-role tanker/transports will also be needed around that time to replace the RAF's current air tanker and long-range transport

support force of BAe VC10s and Lockheed TriStars.

Airbus has high hopes for its A310 MRTT, now being developed for Germany, for this programme. Robertson's 'best estimate' of possible UK requirements for 40-50 FLAs, however, could indicate that they were intended to replace the RAF's entire transport and tanker fleets. Other national FLA requirements are quoted as France, 50; Germany, 75; Italy, 44; Spain, 36; and Turkey, 20-26. Another 12 would be required by Belgium, plus nine by Portugal. The first of them is currently planned to fly in 2003, and enter service in 2004.

For the intense 11-month period of pre-launch activities accompanying the RFPs issued by six of the eight FLA countries to Airbus Industries, Alenia and Turkey's TAI, a 30-strong Joint Wing team from the four Airbus Industrie partners is being formed at Filton to work on the basic hybrid composite mainplane. Final wing assembly would be at Chester.

RFP responses will cost the FLA partners about $85 million, promised by all except Germany by late 1997, as a follow-on to about three times that total already spent by industry on pre-liminary and pre-definition studies. FLA R&D is currently estimated at about $5 billion, and target fly-away unit sales price for a 300-aircraft programme is still put at about $75 million. This compares with a sticker price for the first and considerably smaller Lockheed Martin C-130Js of some $40 million.

Europe

BULGARIA:

Base closures and long-term storage of 80 combat aircraft

In late August 1997 the Bulgarian air force revealed plans for the implementation of 10 per cent cuts to its current strength of 20,000 personnel, closure of four air bases, placement into long-term storage of up to 80 combat aircraft, and introduction of a temporary system of training operational pilots. The severe lack of funds necessary for normal flying operations and the maintenance of all air bases and aircraft has caused a dramatic reduction in flying hours and in the number of serviceable aircraft in the last two to three years. According to the new Bulgarian air force C-in-C, Lieutenant General Stephan Popov, 50 per cent of the CFE-allowed combat aircraft are out of service due to lack of spares.

Lack of funds and the need for rationalisation have prompted the gradual closure over two to three years of four front-line air bases. They comprise the MiG-23MLD/UB-operating Gabrovnitza AB and the MiG-21bis/UM-operating Baltchik AB, which are under the control of the Corpus Protivovazdushna Otbrana (Air Defence Corps); the MiG-21bis-operating Uzundzhovo AB, controlled by the Corpus Taktich-eska Aviatzia (Tactical Aviation Corps); and the L-29-operating Straclevo AB, a training base of the VVVU Georgy Benkovsky Higher Aviation School.

Temporary changes to the training of front-line pilots were also announced. The number of active flying pilots will be reduced to between 70 and 100. They will be the most experienced pilots and will undertake 50-60 flying hours in 1997 – a level that will maintain operational proficiency and instructor qualification. The other pilots will be grounded for most of the year, but during the summer months will fly several hours. Their training will be restored as soon as sufficient funds can be provided from the country's defence budget.

The Bulgarian air force C-in-C rejected a report in a Sofia popular newspaper that the country's Ministry of Defence is intending to sell up to 14

of its 21 Su-22M4/UM3 strike/reconnaissance aircraft to an unspecified country because of the high cost of 'Fitter' operations.

Refusal of MiG-29SM deal

Bulgarian President Peter Stoyanov officially declared in mid-June that the country has refused MAPO's offer to sell 14 MiG-29SM fighters, valued at $450 million. The President said the refusal was due to Bulgaria's extremely poor economic situation. He did promise to assist with the long-discussed delivery of Russian-made spare parts, which are necessary to improve the service condition of air force front-line units. Talks – which have carried on for three years – deal with the delivery of vital aircraft parts and the completion of overhauls in return for the write-off of the $50 million trade debt owed to Bulgaria by Russia, and have not yet been finalised. A separate offer from MAPO included the establishment of a MiG-21/23 upgrade centre, which could also undertake MiG-29 main overhauls.

According to Bulgarian government officials, refusal of the second offer could be justified by a lack of guarantees that the upgrade centre would be profitable, and fears that the Russians would be not able to compel enough MiG-21 operators to upgrade their aircraft in Bulgaria. Another reason for the refusal of both offers is the desire of Bulgaria to join NATO around 2000. In this light, large-scale acquisitions of Russian weapons like the MiG-29SMs are not the right steps toward NATO membership. The first attempt to introduce Western aircraft into service – two C-130B Hercules offered by the US government in 1994 – failed due to

the refusal of the then-ruling Socialist government. At the time, the reasons given were maintenance and serviceability problems that would make the Hercules too expensive to operate.

CZECH REPUBLIC:

Gripen air base evaluation

A British Aerospace team of military operations and engineering specialists made a recent evaluation visit to the Czech Republic's Caslav fighter base as part of BAe/Saab's joint marketing efforts for the multi-role Gripen in Eastern Europe. Caslav will be among the first air bases there to operate next-generation combat aircraft now being evaluated by the Czech Republic for its fighter replacement programme, and the BAe team made a detailed analysis and survey of its facilities.

L-159 first flight

A successful 50-minute initial flight of the two-seat prototype Aero L-159 Advanced Light Combat Aircraft (ALCA), which reached 15,000 ft (4572 m) and 330 kt (378 mph; 609 km/h) from Vodochody on 2 August, included an unusual intentional shutdown and relight of its AlliedSignal/ITEC F124-GA-100 turbofan. In three more flights, on 4 August, the L-159 was demonstrated to Czech staff officers before being flown to Kbely for further ground tests on 1 September. For the 72 single- and two-seat L-159s ordered by the Czech air force, the FIAR division of Alenia has received a $60 million contract from Boeing/Rockwell, as prime avionics contractor, for 70 Grifo-L multi-mode radars.

Above left: Bulgarian Su-22M-4s have been the subject of persistent rumours that the air force is attempting to dispose of them to another, unnamed, 'Fitter' operator as a cost-cutting measure.

Above: This enthusiastically splinter-camouflaged MiG-21MF was seen on display at Hradec Králové in September 1997, but is normally stationed at Cáslav.

Left: The Luftwaffe test unit WTD 61 continues to operate several Su-22M-4 'Fitter-Ks' (as seen here) and two-seat 'Fitter-Gs' from those inherited from East Germany in 1990.

FRANCE:

Defence economies continue

Reductions of 3 per cent in the 1998 defence budget from the previous year, as part of further cuts in government spending planned by the new Socialist administration, will decrease overall military spending to FF238.2 billion ($40 billion). Procurement allocations within this total will be 8.7 per cent lower at FF82 billion ($13.8 billion), with corresponding cuts in major equipment programmes.

For the French air force (AA), the main effect is cancellation of the multi-year (1997-2002) procurement of 48 Dassault Rafale advanced combat aircraft approved in principle by the previous government, which industry had hoped would have included 10 to be made available for export by 2001. Orders for only two Aéronavale Rafale Ms will apparently be funded in the 1998 defence budget, increasing overall procurement to 15, with nothing allocated in that year for AA Mirage 2000Ds or 2000-5s. Delivery timescales are otherwise unaffected, as are the Eurocopter Tiger and NHI NH-90 helicopter programmes.

First Mirage 2000-5 nears completion

Formal qualification of the volume production standard (SF1) for the Dassault Mirage 2000-5F (France) on order for the AA was recently confirmed by the aircraft programmes department of the French defence procurement agency (DGA/SPAe). Thirty-seven AA Mirage 2000C air defence fighters are currently being converted by Dassault with new avionics to

Left: This Iryda – dubbed the M-96 – is the first to be modified with a new extended tail fin, redesigned wing profile and French-supplied cockpit/mission avionics. All existing Polish AF M-93K Irydas will be brought up to this standard.

Below: PZL inherited the An-28 design from Antonov in 1978, and has proceeded to develop the type at its Mielec factory. The latest version is the M-28.03/4 Skytruck Plus.

multi-role 2000-5F standards. They will replace the Mirage 2000Cs of Escadres de Chasse 1/2 and 2/2 at Dijon-Longvic, initially for air superiority and air defence roles, from December 1997.

The Mirage 2000-5F upgrade, in which Dassault Electronique and SNECMA are also involved, includes Thomson-CSF/RCM RDY radar and other new digital avionics. They allow operation with MATRA/BAe MICA for air defence, as well as ASMs for attack roles at a later stage.

More C-135FRs arrive

The French air force has taken redelivery of the first aircraft of its second batch of three Boeing C-135FRs following its re-engining by Boeing at Wichita, KA, with new CFM56-2 (F108-CF-100) turbofans. The Armée de l'Air has supplemented its 11 original C-135FRs with three more ex-USAF KC-135As upgraded to similar standards by Boeing Defense & Space Group's Product Support Division. Prior to re-engining, the KC-135As for France underwent depot maintenance at the USAF's Air Logistics Center at Tinker AFB, OK.

GERMANY:

Airbus tanker conversion

Daimler-Benz Aerospace and Lufthansa Technik have received a German Defence Ministry contract to convert two Luftwaffe Airbus A310-304s for cargo and air refuelling. They were owned by Lufthansa between 1987 and 1996, until bought by the Luftwaffe, and will now become prototypes of the A310 multi-role tanker/transport (MRTT), long proposed by Airbus.

DASA Airbus subsidiary Elbe Flugzeugwerke will undertake the first A310 MRTT conversion at its Dresden facility, involving a large freight door on the port forward-fuselage, and floor modifications for freight or passenger interchanges. Lufthansa Technik will undertake similar work on the second A310 at Hamburg-Fuhlsbuttel, for delivery by 1999. Provision for a remotely-operated telescopic refuelling boom beneath the rear fuselage, plus two underwing hose and drogue pods and associated fuel system modifications, will allow incorporation from kits at a later stage to add an aerial tanker capability.

Alpha Jets retired

Formal retirement took place at Fuerstenfeldbruck on 30 June 1997 of the last 11 Alpha Jet trainers in Luftwaffe service. Most of the 175 Alpha Jets originally delivered by Dornier to the Luftwaffe from March 1979 were operated by three light fighter-bomber wings (JBG 41, 43 and 49) until 1993. Two then disbanded and their Alpha Jets were withdrawn from service, leaving 34 for crew-training roles, now being undertaken in the USA.

Army EC-135 order

Fifteen seven-seat Eurocopter EC-135 helicopters have been ordered from the German defence procurement agency (BWB) for army aviation (Heeresflieger) pilot training roles. EC-135 certification was approved by the LBA in Germany in 1996 with either Pratt & Whitney PW206B or Turboméca Arrius 2B turboshafts, but powerplant selection for the German EC-135s was still undecided when the order was announced. The first seven EC-135s will begin to arrive at Bueckeburg in 1998, to replace Alouette IIs, followed by the remaining eight in 1999.

GREECE:

F-4E upgrade contracts

Following reduced bids by both contending groups – DASA teamed with Elbit and Hughes Radar Systems, and Boeing North American – the Greek government has selected the former for the avionics upgrade of 39 F-4Es. As prime contractor, DASA will integrate most of the upgrades from its similar ICE programme for 110 German air force F-4Fs. This includes licence-built APG-65 radars and digital avionics to allow operation with the AIM-120.

Elbit will supply new mission computers and cockpit colour MFDs for the Greek contract, while DASA is responsible for the required software development. An associated Greek government contract has also been placed with Hellenic Aircraft Industries for structural upgrades of 70 F-4Es to extend their useful operating lives until at least 2015.

HUNGARY:

High-level Gripen flight

A personal flight evaluation made by air force C-in-C General Attila Kositzky at Linköping on 9 September 1997 reflected continued Hungarian interest in Sweden's Gripen multi-role fighter for its new combat aircraft requirements. Saab test pilot Ola Rignell accompanied General Kositzky for his front-seat evaluation flight in a two-seat JAS 39B combat trainer.

IRELAND:

Police Defender delivered

The Garda Síochana, the Irish police force, has taken delivery from Pilatus Britten-Norman of the first production Defender 4000. Based at Baldonnel, this radar-equipped -4S development of the BN.2T forms the fixed-wing element of the Garda's new multi-role air support unit, with pilots and technical support provided by the Irish Air Corps. In addition to routine police operations, it performs transport and communications, coastal patrol, and contraband interdiction throughout the Irish Republic and its offshore areas.

MOLDOVA:

MiG-29 sale surprise

The US Air Force has acquired 21 MiG-29s from Moldova, for a reported cost of $41 million. Moldova inherited 38 'Fulcrums' from Soviet naval aviation's 119 Fighter Division/86 Fighter Regiment at Markuleshty, on 23 March 1992. Since then several attempts have been made to dispose of the remaining servicable aircraft. The USAF has acquired six MiG-29As, one MiG-29UB and 14 MiG-29Cs, plus R-13, R-60, R-27 and R-73 missiles. The MiGs were flown by C-17s to Wright-Patterson AFB in late October/early November and their arrival may well lead to the establishment of a new USAF unit to operate them.

NORWAY:

New fighters sought

New military equipment sought in Norway's next long-term defence plan from 1999-2002 will include 40 combat aircraft. Delivery would be from 2003 onwards, to replace the RNoAF's 24 recently-upgraded F-5A/Bs and balance F-16 attrition. Funds are also sought for six C-130J-30 transports.

Over the shorter term, a $3 million contract has been received by the Applied Technology Division of US Litton Industries to provide 25 upgrade kits for the lightweight APR-39A radar-warning systems it previously supplied for 18 Bell 412SPs of the Royal Norwegian air force.

POLAND:

New Skytruck unveiled

WSK PZL-Mielec has unveiled a new version of its popular PZL M-28 Skytruck STOL transport, the Skytruck Plus. The first public presentation took place during celebrations of the company's 60th anniversary, as well as at Air Day at the end of August. Two derivatives will be built, designated M-28.03 and M-28.04, but the 'prototype' aircraft is a non-flying machine and will be used for ground and handling tests, installations template and presentation for potential customers.

The original 23.53-m (77-ft 2.5-in) fuselage was lengthened by 1.84 m (6.04 ft) by adding two plugs, just aft of the cockpit and before the rear door. Two horizontal plugs of 0.25 m (0.82 ft) were inserted on each side along the whole fuselage, increasing height. The new Skytruck will be capable of carrying up to 30 passengers or three LD-3 containers. Other optional interior configurations include two cargo pallets, an internal fuel tank that increases the aircraft's range to 3000 km (1864 miles), military configuration for 30 paratroopers or other equipment, and a medevac version.

The M-28.03 and M-28.04 will have differing rear fuselages. The first will have rear clamshell doors like those on current models; the other will be equipped with a side cargo door capable of taking an LD-3 container. Both will be powered by two Pratt & Whitney Canada PT6A-65Bs – like other Skytrucks – but each engine will be uprated to 862 kW (1,157 hp), an increase of some 73 kW (98 hp). The engines will drive five-bladed Hartzell propellers.

Portugal's air-defence-optimised Block 15 OCU F-16s have adopted an attack role that was previously the preserve of the FAP's A-7s. Note the USAF titles on the AGM-65.

Both models will be offered with optional avionics from Bendix/King or Collins, facilitating full day and night VFR and IFR operations. A six-screen EFIS system will be fitted in the cockpit. GPS, double VOR, LOG/GS, DME and ADF are to be installed, as well as a laser gyro platform supplying data to the three-axis autopilot. Weather radar and emergency locator transmitter will be also offered in a standard package.

Future development of the type may lead to changes, such as retractable undercarriage and a single fin.

Mielec is in the process of gathering funds for tests and certification. Three prototypes are required for static, fatigue and flight tests. The maiden flight of the first prototype is expected in mid-1998, with certification at the beginning of 1999. Deliveries should start soon after certification.

Development of new models of the Skytruck does not hamper production of the basic model, 10 examples of which will be rolled out in 1997. The military version, known as Bryza and powered by two locally manufactured PZL-10s, is under production for the Polish air force and navy.

Modified Iryda

Mielec and the Polish air force are carrying out tests of the first fully modified PZL I-22 Iryda jet trainer. The aircraft incorporates all the modifications previously tested on other Irydas, such as a new higher fin, LERXes and Sextant Avionique avionics. The Iryda, numbered 204, also has a redesigned wing with front and rear flaps. In the early autumn, the second example – 401 – should be ready, followed by an additional five units, all of which will be new-build.

Earlier in 1997, Mielec reported the possibility of a new order for additional I-22s (probably eight units). They would enter service with the Polish Air Force Academy at Deblin and with naval aviation, where Irydas will replace MiG-21s.

MiG-21 redistribution

The 32nd Tactical Reconnaissance Aviation Regiment (32 Pulk Lotnictwa Rozpoznania Taktycznego) of the Polish Air and Defence Force was disbanded at the end of 1997 when the unit's home base at Sochaczew closed. The unit operated 12 MiG-21R 'Fishbed-Hs' together with four MiG-21US 'Mongol-Bs' and four PZL TS-11 Iskras, although the last operational sortie was flown on 30 June 1997. All of the MiGs had been transferred to other units, with 11 MiG-21Rs and three MiG-21US going to 3rd Fighter Aviation Regiment Poznan (3 Pulk Lotnictwa Mysliwskiego Poznan) at Poznan-Kresiny. There they will join approximately 20 of the MiG-21PFMS

Right: This Il-76TD is operated by Russia's state agency for emergency and disaster relief and is capable of delivering an air-droppable, inflatable field hospital and then parachuting a medical team into a disaster area.

'Fishbed-Fs' which are the oldest version in Polish service. The remaining MiG-21R and MiG-21US have been relocated to the Test Group (Grupa Doswiadczalina) of the 45th Aviation Squadron (45 Eskadra Lotnicza) at Modlin. All of the aircraft had their unit markings removed, and the MiG-21Rs had been stripped of their reconnaissance capability. Both the MiG-21R and the MiG-21PFM are scheduled to be withdrawn from service before the end of 1998.

No other types are capable of assuming the MiG-21R's operations and a limited number of MiGs may yet be kept operational, but the decision has not yet been made. Another solution is to introduce a reconnaissance-dedicated variant of the PZL I-22 Iryda. The model, known as I-22R, was proposed to the air force three years ago but lack of financing meant that no orders were forthcoming.

ROMANIA:

UAV procurement order

New procurement as part of Romania's 10-year armed forces' modernisation plans include its first unmanned air vehicles (UAVs) for battlefield surveillance. They will comprise a unit of Shadow UAVs from the US AAI Corporation, for which a $23 million contract was recently finalised through the Pentagon's new Defense Export Loan Guarantee Programme. Formerly equipped almost entirely from Soviet and national sources, the Romanian armed forces are now seeking NATO-compatible weapons and systems to support plans to join the alliance.

RUSSIA:

Forces reorganisation plans

A merger of the currently independent air defence forces (PVO) with the air forces (VVS) in the coming year is one of several moves resulting from reorganisation plans announced in July 1997 by newly-appointed Russian Defence Minister General Igor S. Sergeyev. This is associated with scaling down the armed forces from about 1.5 million to 1.2 million personnel by late 1998, to meet planned defence spending reductions from 5 per cent to 3 per cent of GDP by 2000.

Rationalisation started earlier in 1997 with absorption by the independent Strategic Rocket Forces of both the missile defence organisation, formerly part of the Air Forces, and the independent Space Forces. From 1998, the Russian armed forces will therefore comprise four major commands, in the form of the Ground, Naval, Air and Strategic Rocket Forces, eventually to be manned only by non-conscripts.

New Sukhoi fighter

According to Russian ITAR-Tass news agency reports, Sukhoi has flown the prototype of its S-32 forward-swept wing, advanced technology fighter. The maiden flight took place on 25 September 1997, from the Gromov Flight Research Institute, Zhukhovskii. The pilot was named as Igor Votintsev, who also made two subsequent test flights in the aircraft. Western reports gave 1 October as the date of the first flight.

The new twin-turbofan AVPK Sukhoi project, which has been under development over the past decade (and has also been referred to as S-37), is said to be dimensionally similar to the Su-35, with a maximum take-off weight of 34000 kg (74,957 lb). Its powerplants are claimed (by some sources) to be either Lyul'ka AL-41Fs, as in the MiG 1.42, or the MiG-31's Perm D-30F6s. Western reports stated that the aircraft is powered by Lyul'ka Saturn AL-31Fs, as fitted to the Su-27.

Preliminary details of the S-32, which first appeared in late 1996, indicated unusual features of forward-swept composite wings, with sharply-cranked leading-edge profiles, twin vertical fins and stabilators, and swept canard foreplanes. Sukhoi claims that the aircraft is a technology demonstrator, rather than a fully-fledged prototype.

MiG-29 production totals

Figures released by VPK MAPO at the recent Zhukhovskii air show indicate that 1,257 MiG-29s had been produced to that time. Only 478 have been delivered to the Russian air forces, the remainder being operated by 18 other CIS and foreign countries.

Attack helicopter plans

While Mil is continuing flight development of the Mi-28N night-attack helicopter, which first flew on 14 November 1996 and was later joined by the competing Kamov Ka-50N, Russian army aviation C-in-C Colonel General Vitaly Yegerov has admitted that funding for new aircraft procurement. Finance is even insufficient to overhaul or upgrade about 1,000 of the older Mi-24s and Mi-8s, although eight Ka-50s are still being evaluated at the army aviation's Torzhok combat training centre. Their flight development was supplemented from 25 June at Lyubertsy by the prototype two-seat Ka-52 Alligator, which will match the RPKB Ramenskoye-integrated Mi-28N night-attack avionics by adding a Phazotron FH-01 Arbalet multi-mode millimetric-wave radar. This may be installed in the fuselage nose, however,

Left: During the last week of September the first Gripen squadron of the Flygvapnet (2 Div, F7) was declared operational during an off-base exercise to prove the Gripen and its ground crews can operate from Sweden's wartime road strips.

rather than mast-mounted. Its avionics also include systems and displays from Thomson-CSF and Sextant Avionique in France, matching the Ka-50N's T-CSF/UOMZ FLIR that supplements its Shkval-V navigation/attack system.

Rosvoorouzhenie is now offering the Ka-50 for export, and has reported firm interest from Myanmar and Slovakia in 15 and 12 'Hokums', respectively. Production is planned of about a dozen Ka-50s in 1998 at the Arseneyev Progress factory, which, with Myasischchev, recently joined the VPK MAPO group, supplementing the Kamov OKB as an existing member.

New engine for MiG-AT

While development of the MiG-AT advanced trainer is well advanced with SNECMA/Turboméca Larzac 04R20 turbofans, a new indigenous engine is planned for Russian air forces (VVS) requirements. Soyuz engine design bureau chief Roald Nusberg said in Moscow that the RD 1700 turbofan would develop slightly more thrust than the Larzac, at 16.67 kN (3,748 lb) for take-off. Development is jointly

with Klimov, for production by the Chernychev plant, also in the MIG MAPO group. RD 1700 bench-running will start in about 18 months' time.

With RD 1700 availability not expected for several years, the first 15 MiG-ATs now being built, including the 10 ordered by the Russian air forces for fly-off evaluation from late 1997, will be Larzac-powered. SNECMA received an initial contract in November 1996 for 10 Larzacs for these aircraft, and, through its ELECMA electronics division with Russia's EGA, is also supplying a full-authority digital engine control (FADEC) for improved operation and maintenance. MIG MAPO, SNECMA, Turboméca and Sextant Avionique have signed a framework agreement for joint worldwide promotion and marketing of the MiG-AT, for which the Larzac will continue to be available for export versions.

SLOVAKIA:

Yak-130 procurement plans

As third partner with Russia and Italy in the trinational Yakovlev Yak-130 consortium, Slovakia supplies its Povazske Strojarnye DV-2S turbofans;

the country now plans to acquire up to 40 of these aircraft to replace older ex-Soviet and Czech trainers, and some combat types. Prototype evaluation has already taken place in Slovakia, which is also interested in the proposed Yak-131 single-seat fighter derivative, with Phazotron Super Kopyo radar. It will supplement the standard digital avionics developed by Leninets and the Scientific and Production Association Elektroavtomatika in St Petersburg, in conjunction with FIAR in Italy.

Italy's $130 million government investment in the programme is accompanied by strong AMI interest in its possible acquisition as a replacement for its Aermacchi MB.339s at Lecce in about 10 years' time. Discussions have also been reported with AlliedSignal's ITEC subsidiary concerning possible installation of its F124 turbofan in derated form in export Yak-130s.

From its original design by the Zaporozhye-based Progress Design Bureau for the Russian air forces, the DV-2S as developed by Povazske Strojarnye is designated RD-35 by the VVS, and will power the 10-15 per cent smaller pre-production Yak-130/AEMs ordered for evaluation. They are now being built by the Sokol factory at Nizhni Novgorod, where the first is due to fly in mid-1998.

SLOVENIA:

NATO ambitions

Although spending only about $380 million per year on defence, the former Yugoslav state of Slovenia is proposing a 10-year armed forces expansion and modernisation programme, as part of its plans for NATO membership. They

include acquisition of a squadron of advanced combat aircraft, for which refurbished ex-USAF F-16s are favoured, plus a dozen or so attack helicopters. Talks are already in progress with Bell Helicopter Textron on possible AH-1W procurement for the latter requirement.

TURKEY:

New US procurement plans

Consideration is being given by Turkey to extending beyond 1999 the procurement and co-production of 240 F-16s through the Peace Onyx programmes now being completed by Tusas Aerospace Industries. Another 24 F-16C/Ds are planned for TAI production as THK attrition replacements, from contracts now being finalised.

While the Turkish government is still negotiating with the US to acquire attack helicopters, Ankara has also renewed informal requests to purchase 10 CH-53As formerly operated by the USMC. They would be upgraded to CH-53-2000 standard with IAI assistance from Israel. The Turkish navy also hopes to add another four Hellfire-armed S-70Bs to the four ordered in February 1997 at a cost of $113 million, for delivery by 2000. The navy has a total requirement for 28 shipborne helicopters.

UNITED KINGDOM:

Reservist combat pilots

Part-time combat service for RAF aircrews ended with the 1957 disbandment of the Royal Auxiliary Air Force fighter squadrons. Recent trials with reservists, however, to offset declining numbers of regular personnel in operating Hercules, Nimrods and Pumas, have met with some success. These trials are now being extended until 30 September 1998 to evaluate the feasibility of using reservist pilots and navigators for part-time service with the RAF's Tornado F.Mk 3 squadrons.

Up to 60 reservist aircrew are being recruited by the MoD, including those for transport and support aircraft. Tornado F.Mk 3 crews must have had recent type experience, and also be available for mid-week RAF continuation training and service to complete about 100 flying hours per year. This is a high requirement for part-time civilian volunteers to complete, although only about half the normal total required from regular RAF Tornado aircrews.

Many of the regulars are continuing to leave the RAF for better-paid airline jobs, for which they are particularly welcome. The extra flying required from reservists, however, may conflict with the CAA-regulated annual maximum of some 900 flying hours imposed for commercial pilots. In addition, it is not expected that reservists could maintain even a limited combat-ready status for more than two or three years.

Following unification in April this year of the former RAF Volunteer Reserve and the Royal Auxiliary Air Force, under the latter name, its establishment is being doubled to about 3,000. Most are for ground jobs in support elements and the RAF Regiment, although a few RAuxAF pilots, navigators, loadmasters and air electronics officers continue to fly in RAF Hercules, Nimrods, Pumas and other aircraft. Reservist pilots also provide most of the aircrew for the RAF's Air Experience Flights, which share the 85 civilian-supported BAe Bulldog basic trainers of the University Air Squadrons to fly Air Training Corps cadets throughout the UK.

Hughes UK gains contracts

After the Lockheed Martin F-22 and the same company's Popeye-based AGM-142, yet another 'raptor' has joined the aerospace scene. Hughes UK Ltd has received a £55 million MoD contract to supply eight reconnaissance airborne pods ('RAP') for the UK's Tornado ('TOR') GR.Mk 1s. RAPTOR incorporates Hughes Danbury Optical Systems DB-110 sensor with dual band electro-optical and infra-red imagery over ranges of up to 24 nm (27 miles; 44 km), providing a high-/medium-level reconnaissance capability to the RAF's Tornado GR.Mk 1As. Two ground processing stations are in the contract, although the pod also incorporates video recording facilities.

This was the second MoD order awarded within a month to Hughes UK. In August, Hughes received a £5 million contract for programme definition and risk-reduction studies for its proposals to meet the SR(A) 1239 requirements for a new beyond-visual-range air-to-air missile (BVRAAM). These proposals were originally based on its ramjet-boosted Future Medium-Range AAM, but lower-cost and less ambitious projects are now being studied to meet reduced budget targets.

RAF helicopter changes

Two Westland Wessex HCC.Mk 4 helicopters of the RAF's No. 32 (The Royal) Squadron are due for retirement in early 1998. At the request of the Royal Family, the Wessexes are being replaced by a single new helicopter leased from a civil contractor, although flown by RAF personnel. The type of replacement helicopter had still to be selected, but will achieve substantial savings over the £4 million annual running costs of the two Wessexes.

Nineteen Westland Sea King HAR.Mk 3s of the RAF's search and rescue force are to be equipped with Racal Avionics' control display and navigation units (CDNU) from a new £2 million Defence Ministry contract. Incorporating embedded P(Y) code GPS, the CDNU will include a range of specific SAR functions.

Above: This Swiss air force Mirage III was painted up in special Fliegerstaffel 17 markings during June 1997, to mark that squadron's transition from the Mirage to the F/A-18 Hornet. FISt 17 should become operational with the F-18 on 1 January 1998.

Below: This CASA 212 (T.12D) testbed is operated by Spain's National Institute of Aerospace Technology and is flown by Ala 54/CLAEX, based at Torrejón.

Middle East

EGYPT:

New equipment plans

Planned procurement by Egypt of a recently-notified $332 million FMS arms package will include another four Boeing CH-47D Chinooks. With spare Textron Lycoming T55 engines, plus airframe spares and support equipment, the new CH-47Ds will cost some $149 million and supplement earlier deliveries of 15 EAF CH-47Cs. Other new FMS procurement includes 32 AGM-84G Harpoons costing $51 million for its F-16s, and 84 Mk 46 homing torpedoes worth $32 million for its frigates and 10 Kaman SH-2G(E) Super SeaSprite ASW helicopters.

The first of these helicopters from a $150 million FMS order recently completed flight qualification and performance testing for USN production approval, and Egyptian acceptance in mid-October 1997. Deliveries are following at one per month, with the first three SH-2G(E)s initially sent to NAS Pensacola for Egyptian pilot training with the USN. In-country deliveries will follow in April 1998. Powered by new GE T700-401 engines, the SH-2G(E)s have new digital avionics and equipment, including AlliedSignal AQS-18A dipping sonar in place of the original MAD systems.

ISRAEL:

Fighter force expansion

While still awaiting delivery of its 24 MDC F-15I advanced strike aircraft, due from January 1998, the Israeli Defence Force/Air Force (IDF/AF) is finalising follow-on requirements for more new F-15Es or F-16s. IDF/AF combat aircraft orders are expected to total 50-100 by about 2001/02, during which Israel is also planning to upgrade a large part of its 42-strong AH-64A Apache attack helicopter force to AH-64D Longbow standards.

An Israeli Defence Ministry cockpit avionics improvement contract worth an initial $12.5 million has already been awarded to Elbit Systems, through its EFW Inc. subsidiary in Fort Worth, TX, for F-15A/B and C/D of the IDF/AF. The planned Baz 2000 digital upgrade programme will mainly involve installation of a flat-panel cockpit MFD, plus associated equipment and software.

KUWAIT:

Longbow Apaches sought

Recent US Foreign Military Sales aircraft requests by the Pentagon to Congress have included one from Kuwait for 16 AH-64D Longbow Apache attack helicopters. The $800 million Kuwaiti procurement package also includes four spare General Electric T700 engines, 384 AGM-114A Hellfire missiles, 19,918 Hydra 70 rockets and launchers, 30-mm cannon ammunition, plus related spares, equipment, training and technical support. If approved by Congress, it would represent the first sale of the advanced Longbow radar system to the Middle East, where such Apache operators as Egypt, Israel and Saudi Arabia have been restricted to procurement of the AH-64A.

OMAN:

Jaguar upgrade contract

Britain's Royal Air Force and the Ministry of Defence have achieved their first aircraft export upgrade contract following a Letter of Arrangement signed last September by Defence Secretary George Robertson with the Omani Defence Affairs Minister in Muscat. It covers a planned £40 million

This rarely seen Egyptian air force Falcon 20F-5 is one of three such aircraft in service for VIP duties.

upgrade contract for the 18 or so Royal Air Force of Oman (RAFO) Jaguar ground-attack fighters, to equip them with updated digital avionics, a new navigation system and a thermal imaging capability (TIALD), to new RAF Jaguar 97 or GR.Mk 3/T.Mk 4 standards. This will allow them to designate and deliver precision-guided munitions.

The RAF Jaguar 97 upgrade, developed and now in progress at the Defence Evaluation and Research Agency site at Boscombe Down, in Wiltshire, involves several major sub-contractors, including British Aerospace, GEC-Marconi Avionics, Hunting Aviation and Ultra Electronics. These companies will also provide services and equipment for the RAFO Jaguar upgrade. In addition to the BASE TERPROM ground proximity warning system, new Jaguar 97 avionics include a wide-angle head-up and colour multi-function cockpit display, a modified 1064C INS with integrated GPS, helmet-mounted sight and HOTAS controls.

The RAFO bought three batches of single-seat SEPECAT/BAe Jaguar OS/GR.Mk 1s totalling 21 aircraft, plus four two-seat OB/T.Mk 2 combat trainers between 1977 and 1986, of which about 15 and three, respectively, are thought to remain in service. Under joint RAF/RAFO management, the upgrade is due for completion in Oman mainly by RAFO personnel by late 2000, for service for another 10 years or more.

QATAR:

Mirage 2000-5s accepted

Formal handover by Serge Dassault took place at Bordeaux-Merignac on 8 September of the first three of 12 multi-role Dassault Mirage 2000-5s. Ordered by the Qatar Emiri air force in July 1994 at a package cost of some $1.25 billion, they were completed earlier in 1997 and comprised two of three 2000-5DDA two-seat combat trainers (QA86 and QA87), plus the first of nine single-seat 2000-5EDAs (QA90). On the following day, QEAF C-in-C General Ali Sayeed Al Marri made his first Mirage 2000-5 flight in one of the two-seaters, with Dassault test pilot Denis Garnier.

Qatar's Mirage 2000-5s are expected to re-equip the QEAF's No. 7 Air Superiority Squadron by late 1998, replacing 14 Dassault Mirage F1EDA and two-seat F1DDA interceptors, six of which have also been sold to Spain. The first QEAF Mirage 2000-5s will remain in France for initial pilot conversion at Mont-de-Marsan, while about 100 Qatari technicians undergo training with Dassault and the French air force on the new Mirages, their SNECMA M53-P2 engines, and Magic and MICA AAMs.

QEAF Mirage 2000-5s are the first to be qualified for ground-attack roles, for which Qatar is planning to acquire French PGMs and ASMs at a later date. It has not yet been nominated, but MATRA/BAe Dynamics displayed an export version of its APACHE stand-off missile, designated the Black Pearl, at the Bordeaux ceremony.

SAUDI ARABIA:

AB 412 order expected

Long-term Saudi armed forces orders for about 100 Agusta-Bell helicopters since the mid-1960s were expected to be followed in late 1997 by a $160 million contract for 40 AB 412EPs to meet search and rescue roles. The AB 412EP is powered by Pratt & Whitney Canada PT6T-3D twin-

This is the first SH-2G(E) Seasprite for Egypt, which was handed over in a ceremony on 21 October 1997. Nine more will be delivered over the following 12 months.

turboshafts, which are uprated for operation in tropical conditions.

UNITED ARAB EMIRATES:

Mirage 2000-5 proposals

A further upgraded version of the Mirage 2000-5, designated 2000-9, is reportedly being offered to the UAE for its pending order for up to 60 new and advanced multi-role combat aircraft. No details have yet been revealed of its changes, although they are mainly believed to involve radar and avionics upgrades to allow the use of long-range air-launched cruise missiles such as the UAE's Al Hakim family, developed by GEC-Marconi.

Dassault is seeking to improve its chances in current UAE evaluations of such contending types as the F-16 in Block 50 or proposed Block 60 variants, new variants of the MiG-29 and Sukhoi Su-30MKI/-35/-37, and the later generation Rafale and Eurofighter. A decision on the short-term UAE requirement was expected by late 1997, although it may be confined to a short-list for final evaluation.

US missiles requested

New ship-launched missile equipment recently requested from the US by the UAE has included 72 RIM-7M (Build F1) Sea Sparrow ShAMs costing $27 million, and 24 RGM-84G-4 Harpoon anti-ship missiles ($90 million).

Africa

ANGOLA:

C-130K transfers proposed

Six RAF C-130K Hercules from those which Lockheed Martin is taking back in part exchange for the 25 new C-130Js ordered by the UK were being offered to the Angolan air force through FMS auspices in late 1997. Although State Department approval had been given for this transaction, some opposition was being encountered from Congress at that time.

ERITREA:

MB.339CE deliveries begun

Eritrean air force (ERAF) acceptance began at Asmara, in East Africa, in April 1997 of the first two of six Aermacchi MB.339CE jet trainers ordered on 7 November 1995. Like the MB.339CD/CBs delivered to Italy and New Zealand, those for Eritrea have comprehensive digital avionics, although the AMI's 15 examples also have a fixed air-refuelling probe for operational training. The ERAF MB.339s, finished overall in desert sand and dark green camouflage, carry the national roundels and a fin flash towards the tail. Aermacchi's Eritrean contract involves helping to establish an ERAF pilot and technician training centre.

ETHIOPIA:

MiG-21 upgrade contested

Strong competition has been reported between Russia's VPK MAPO and an Israeli/Romanian and Ukrainian consortium for the upgrade of a squadron of Ethiopian air force MiG-21bis fighters. In Moscow, First Deputy Director of the Russian State Research Institute of Aviation Systems (GosNIIAS), Pavel Pozniakov, claimed that MAPO's MiG-21-93 upgrade, with its Phazotron Kopyo multi-mode fire-control radar, plus Vympel R-73 (AA-11 'Archer') close-combat and R77 (RVV-AE/AA-12 'Adder') long-range active radar-homing AAMs, represented an unbeatable 'Fishbed' combination. MIG MAPO has already received an Indian air force contract, in conjunction with Russia's Sokol Aircraft Plant, to upgrade 125 IAF 'Fishbeds' to MiG-21-93 standard. This has reportedly been delayed, however, because of payment problems.

SOUTH AFRICA:

Rooivalk delivery plans

With the first production Denel CSH-2 Rooivalk of 12 on order now out of its fuselage jigs for equipment installation, No. 16 Squadron will be the first South African air force unit to operate this new attack helicopter. Rooivalk deliveries to Bloemspruit air base will start in early 1999 for the reformed squadron, which operated Alouette III and Oryx helicopters until its 1991 disbandment. Completion will then continue of only four aircraft per year for the SAAF, to allow earlier availability of eight Rooivalks from a Malaysian order now being finalised. Interest has also been expressed by Australia in the Rooivalk, which recently completed successful day and night firing trials with Euromissile HOT-3 anti-tank missiles.

Since 25 April 1997, Denel Aviation's CSH-2 Rooivalk attack helicopter and Oryx transport helicopter have had the formal backing of Eurocopter, through a joint agreement for their future development, production and engineering support. An initial batch of 12 Rooivalks is being built for the SAAF, and the sale of a similar number to Malaysia is also being discussed, while Denel has upgraded or built from new over 40 Oryx helicopters for the South African defence forces. Both projects are now being offered for export.

Both Denel helicopter types will be supplied by Eurocopter with the dynamic components already being produced for the Cougar Mk 1. The Oryx fuselage has also been redesigned with similar features to the AS 532, while incorporating weight-reducing composite components, and improved cockpit avionics. An increase in maximum take-off weight from the 16,315 lb (7415 kg) of the original Puma to 18,518 lb (8417 kg) raises the maximum slung load of the Oryx from 7,055 lb (3206 kg) to 9,920 lb (4509 kg), with

overall performance improvements of up to 25-30 per cent.

The new joint agreement also includes collaboration on the SAAF's Light Utility Helicopter (LUH) programme, to replace a number of Aérospatiale Alouette IIIs still in current South African service from at least 120 or more originally delivered. Eurocopter's submission for the LUH requirement is the twin-turboshaft EC 635, which is the military version of the seven-seat EC 135.

SAAF deliveries

The SAAF has acquired a Pilatus PC-12M single-turboprop pressurised light utility transport, costing some $2.4 million. It will also supplement 12 SAAF Cessna Caravans, two Cessna Citations, and three Beech King Airs.

ZIMBABWE:

SF.260 trainer contract

The Air Force of Zimbabwe (AFZ) has given Aermacchi its first SIAI-Marchetti SF.260 contract since it took over the former company's trainer programmes last year. Six SF.260Fs will replace some of the SF.260C/Ws lost in accidents from 31 originally received by the AFZ between 1980-84. Twelve of the remaining examples have been converted locally with Allison 250-B17D turboprop engines to SF.260TP standards.

Southern Asia

INDIA:

Su-30MKI prototype flies

Sukhoi's prototype Su-30MKI long-range multi-role combat aircraft, which made its initial flight on 1 July 1997, is the first of the two-seat Su-27 series to fly with canards. The 40 being produced by the Irkutsk Aviation Industrial Association for an Indian air force order will also have customised digital avionics from France's SAGEM. Prototype and initial production Su-30MKIs lack the planned vectoring nozzles on their Lyul'ka AL-31FP turbofans and integrated fly-by-wire control systems to be installed in the last 10 IAF examples from 1999.

Earlier IAF deliveries, including six of the eight original Su-30Ks which recently arrived at the Lohegaon/Pune air base for training, will start returning to Russia in the next couple of years for retrofit installation between 2002 and 2007 of the full range of Su-30MKI modifications, including canards, new avionics and TVC. A second batch of 10 Su-30MKs is due by late 1998, and another 22, including the first 10

definitive Su-30MKIs, by mid-2000. Su-30MK and MKI models displayed by Sukhoi at Zhukhovskii showed the former to lack canards, as well as vectoring nozzles. The Su-30MKI maximum take-off weight of 26000 kg (57,320 lb) quoted by Sukhoi includes an 8000-kg (17,637-lb) combat load.

The IAF is reportedly planning to include Russian Zvezda-Strela Kh-31 (AS-17 'Krypton') rocket/ramjet-propelled multi-role Mach-4.5 long-range air-to-surface missiles among its Su-30 weapons fit. It is also seeking funds to acquire up to four Il-78 'Midas' tanker/transports for Su-30 support.

Harrier T.Mk 4s ordered

British Aerospace has received a £16.5 million Indian navy contract for two refurbished ex-RAF Harrier T.Mk 4 conversion trainers. They will be attrition replacements for the four T.Mk 60s operated by the Indian navy alongside 23 Sea Harrier FRS.Mk 51s since 1983. Work on the former RN T.Mk 4s at BAe's Dunsfold factory in

Surrey is due for completion in 1999, with delivery in the same year.

MiG upgrades falter

After prolonged negotiations, a $600 million VPK MAPO contract for Hindustan Aeronautics Ltd to upgrade in India the nav/attack avionics of about 135 HAL-built IAF MiG-27M ground-attack fighters had been placed on hold in mid-1997 by the Defence Ministry in Delhi because of military budget economies. New Russian avionics, plus associated advanced PGMs, were envisaged in the contract, although India's Defence Research and Development Organisation considered

Egypt has one transport regiment of 19 C-130Hs, plus three C-130H-30s, based at Cairo. This C-130H was observed passing through Lajes in September 1997.

that indigenous equipment could reduce costs to about $380 million.

HAL is believed to have built about 165 MiG-27s for the IAF, although fewer than half this number are reportedly in current service. Another 30 or so have been lost in accidents since the early 1990s, and many have been grounded pending upgrade. VPK MAPO's Rs15 billion ($420 million) contract to upgrade 125 IAF 'Fishbeds' to MiG-21-93 standard was also reportedly stalled in late 1997 because of Indian funding problems.

Far East

BRUNEI:

More CN.235Ms

Recent Brunei government arms orders have included an additional three CN.235M tactical transports from IPTN. Five have already been delivered for the air wing of the Brunei armed forces.

CHINA:

US Congress assesses Russian acquisitions

In its latest report on world arms exports, which the US led in 1996 with a total of nearly $11.3 billion, the Congressional Research Service (CRS) stated that Russia has sold China at least 72 Sukhoi Su-27 'Flankers' to date, and has approved a PRC licensing agreement for it to co-produce as many as 200 more. Negotiations have also been reported for China's direct purchase of 55 two-seat Su-30MKs, including Zvezda-Strela Kh-31 (AS-17 'Krypton') ASMs among their armament. China has received 59 AlliedSignal TFE731 turbofans from the US for its NAMC K-8 Karakoram jet-trainer export programme to Pakistan and elsewhere.

According to the CRS, Russia was a close third to the UK in 1996 arms exports, with a total of $4.6 billion, although this was almost halved from its 1995 figure of $8.4 billion. Additional arms export orders worth $7.3 billion were recently claimed by the Russian Presidential Office, however,

coupled with plans for increased overseas military sales, particularly in the Far East and Latin America.

Joint AWACS development

A complex international programme, involving China, Russia, Israel and Uzbekistan, has been agreed to develop an Ilyushin Il-76-based AWACS system to meet an urgent Chinese air force (AF/PLA) requirement for an initial four airborne early warning and control

Right: Present at the 1997 Oshkosh EAA convention in August 1997 was this Mali air force Basler T-67 Turbo Dakota.

Below: To celebrate the Indian Air Force's 65th anniversary, in October 1997, an Su-30MK from No. 24 Sqn was displayed in this special scheme, based on the Indian flag.

aircraft. They are expected to result from an AWACS programme agreement between the Russian state-run Rosvoorouzhenie arms export organisation and IAI, as management agency and prime contractor. The announcement was not specifically linked to the AF/PLA requirement, but presented more as an export alternative to the

Boeing AWACS series; it is derived from Russia's Beriev A-50 'Mainstay' development of the Il-76, with mainly Western avionics and systems.

Beriev will therefore be involved in the programme, together with its related Taganrog Aviation Complex, which will apparently undertake the structural modifications of the Il-76, centred on

Flypasts to celebrate the IAF's 65th anniversary, held on 8 October 1997 at Palam, included this Canberra and Hunter formation – billed as both types' last flying appearance.

the large dorsal radome. The aircraft involved will come from the Tashkent Aircraft Production Organisation (TAPO) factory in Uzbekistan, which apparently has up to 45 unsold Il-76s available.

The first A-50I for the new contract is due to be fitted in 1998 by IAI in Israel with Elta Electronics' Phalcon active phased-array surveillance radar in a triangular configuration within a fixed radome to provide 360° coverage. After three years or so of development, a follow-up contract is expected for at least three more A-50Is for China, costing up to $250 million each.

China has also had prolonged negotiations with GEC-Marconi for possible acquisition of GMAv's Argus AEW radar system, although its relationship with the new Russian/Israeli AWACS programme is unclear. The AF/PLA already operates at least 15 Il-76 transports acquired from TAPO in the past few years, which offer technical support commonality with the A-50Is.

INDONESIA:

Su-30s in arms package

Following the June 1997 US veto on Indonesia's purchase of nine F-16A/Bs built for the Indonesian air force because of alleged human rights infringements, the Jakarta government has turned to Russia. According to announcements in August by Russia's Presidential Assistant Boris Kuzik and Indonesia's State Minister for Planning and Development, a $1 billion arms package negotiated with Rosvoorouzhenie and AVPK Sukhoi will include further export orders for the Su-30K.

In addition to 12 Su-30s and associated weapons, eight Mil Mi-17-1V armed assault helicopters are also being ordered from the Kazan Plant, through Rosvoorouzhenie, as well as air defence missiles, spares and support equipment. The Mi-17-1V is powered by two uprated Klimov TV3-117VM turboshafts, for improved hot-and-high performance. Apart from hard currency, payment will reportedly involve a 50 per cent barter element, including rubber, palm oil and coffee supplies to Russia.

JAPAN:

FY98 aircraft requests

Defence budget requests totalling 4,491 billion yen ($37 billion) for FY98 were unchanged from the current fiscal year, which started in April 1997. R&D funding requests by the Japanese Defence Agency dropped by 17.6 per cent to 143.4 billion yen ($1.186 billion), having peaked for the Mitsubishi F-2 and Kawasaki OH-1. Funding is being sought, however, for a new XAAM-5 close-combat thrust-vectored air-to-air missile. Overall procurement funding requests were also slightly reduced by 2.3 per cent to 2,750 billion yen ($22.74 billion). This includes 52 new aircraft costing over $2 billion requested for the Japanese Self-Defence Forces, comprising 26 costing $1.3 billion for the JASDF, 11 for the JMSDF ($445 million), and 15 for the JGSDF ($348 million). By service, they comprise the following, with current year's procurement authorisations in parentheses where applicable.

Air SDF: Mitsubishi (MHI) F-2A/B, nine (eight); Kawasaki (KHI) T-4, 10 (13); Raytheon Hawker/BAe U-125A, three (four); Gulfstream U-4, one (one); Beechjet T-400, one; Sikorsky/MHI UH-60J, two (three). Maritime SDF: Sikorsky/MHI SH-60J, eight (seven); Sikorsky/MHI UH-60J, two (two); Fuji (FHI) T-5, one. Ground SDF: Sikorsky/MHI UH-60JA, five (four); FHI/Bell AH-1S, one (one); KHI OH-1, three (three); FHI/Bell UH-1J, four (three); KHI/Boeing CH-47J, one (two); Beech LR-2 King Air 350, one (two).

Hawkeye upgrade plans

Northrop Grumman has teamed up with Kawasaki Heavy Industries and Toshiba for a $400 million structural and avionics upgrade programme for the JASDF's 13 E-2C Hawkeyes. Delivered between 1982 and 1993, the JASDF E-2Cs are of the original Group 0 standard, with APS-138 radar. This will now be replaced by the longer-range APS-145, plus such other changes as JTIDS, GPS and Litton ALR-173 passive detection system, to the current E-2C Group II standard. Northrop Grumman recently completed the first of 36 new-build E-2C-IIs

ordered for the US Navy, to follow the first of 12 similar upgrades from 18 Group I USN Hawkeyes completed late in 1996.

Further E-2 upgrades are planned by Northrop Grumman, mainly from replacement of the earlier Litton L-304 mission computer by a Raytheon Model 940, and a new Advanced Control Indicator Set with flat-panel displays and a track-ball controllers, among other changes. They include new workstations, satellite communication systems and provision for air refuelling, now being test-flown for development of the new Hawkeye 2000. Deliveries will start in 2001, while longer-term development is also planned of the Hawkeye 2005, incorporating electronically-scanned radar, IRST, and other improvements.

SOUTH KOREA:

KTX-II go-ahead

After delays from budget economies, the Seoul government finally renewed its backing in July 1997 of the MoU between Samsung Aerospace and Lockheed Martin for joint development of the tandem-seat KTX-II supersonic advanced trainer and light combat aircraft. In agreeing to fund 70 per cent of the $2 billion R&D programme, the Seoul government effectively launched its full-scale development from 1 October 1997, to allow RoKAF deliveries of the first 94 production KTX-IIs from 2003-09.

As partner with Samsung as prime contractor in the current co-production of 120 F-16s for the Korean Fighter Programme, Lockheed Martin will fund 13 per cent of the remaining KTX-II R&D, with the Korean company providing the last 17 per cent. Apart from component production, the LMAS share includes development of the avionics, flight-control system and mainplanes at its Fort Worth facility, plus continuation of design and technical collaboration with Samsung.

No KTX-II funding is expected in South Korea's $17 billion 1997 defence budget, which already faces cuts of 10 per cent, and will defer planned purchases of eight more P-3Cs, and up to 20 C-130Js. Funding is also frozen for four air-refuelling tanker.

E-767 for RoKAF AWACS

Formal notification was made to US Congress by the Pentagon in September

The static line-up at the IAF anniversary ceremony included this No. 47 Sqn ('Black Archers') MiG-29 armed with an R-27 (AA-10 'Alamo').

1997 of a South Korean request for a $3.2 billion FMS arms package, which mainly comprised four Boeing E-767s for the RoKAF's long-standing AWACS requirement. They were selected in preference to rival offers from IAI, Airbus, Saab-Ericsson and Rosvoorouzhenie for the A-50, and are expected to be similar to those ordered by Japan. Powered by two GE CF6-80C2 turbofans, the E-767s are fitted with Westinghouse AN/APY-2 radar in a dorsal radome, and will be available for delivery from around 2000.

Popeye for ground attack

The RoKAF has selected Lockheed Martin/Rafael's AGM-142 Popeye medium-range ASM for its main ground-attack armament, in preference to the Boeing (formerly Rockwell) AGM-130. Initial orders comprise 116 1360-kg (3,000-lb) AGM-142As costing some $125 million to arm 30 modified RoKAF F-4Es. Purchase is also sought of the lighter (1115-kg/2,450-lb) AGM-142B, for RoKAF F-16s

LAOS:

Russian helicopter and maintenance contracts

Recent signing of a defence co-operation agreement in Moscow has been followed by a Laotian government order for 12 Mil Mi-17-1Vs from Russia. They were due for almost immediate delivery, to supplement earlier receipt of about 10 Mi-8S variants.

A $1.1 million air force maintenance contract has been awarded by the Laotian government to HAL in India. It is for the technical support of the 29 MiG-21 fighters operated by the Laotian air force, and is the first contract of its kind to be received by HAL.

SINGAPORE:

KC-135 tanker order

Singapore placed a firm FMS order in September 1997 for four Boeing KC-135Rs. They are ex-USAF aircraft which are being refurbished and upgraded by Boeing Wichita before delivery, which is expected to start in late 1998.

TAIWAN:

More US helicopters sought

Recent Pentagon FMS requests to Congress have included 13 Bell OH-58D Kiowa Warriors for Taiwan, costing $172 million. This includes similar numbers of Rolls-Royce Allison T703-AD-700 engines and AGM-114A Hellfire missile launchers, plus mast-mounted sights, Hydra 70 rockets and launchers, and ammunition. The OH-58Ds will also supplement unarmed Bell TH-67 training helicopters already operated by Taiwan's air force, and follow recent $479 million Taiwanese army orders for another 21 AH-1W SuperCobras, increasing overall purchases to 47.

Having operated 10 frigate-based Sikorsky S-70C(M)-1 Thunderhawk ASW helicopters since 1990-91, the Republic of China navy (RoCN) has finalised an FMS follow-up contract for another 11 S-70C(M)-2s, plus spares and support equipment.

THAILAND:

Chakri Naruebet delivered

Delivery of the 11,500-tonne V/STOL carrier *Chakri Naruebet* to the Sattahip naval base in August 1997 also brought the Royal Thai navy its seven ex-Spanish navy McDonnell Douglas AV-8A and two two-seat TAV-8A Harriers. Six recently-delivered Sikorsky S-70B Seahawks will also be embarked for maritime patrol, SAR and general support roles.

VIETNAM:

'Fitter' upgrade contract

As one of 17 countries which received some 1,800 Sukhoi Su-20/22 'Fitter' strike-fighters from 1964 onwards, Vietnam has recently contracted with

VPK Sukhoi and the Komsomolsk-on-Amur Aviation Production Association for their avionics upgrade. The VNAF operates 32 late-production Su-22M4s and a pair of Su-22UM3 trainers, which already featured a PrNK-54 digital nav/attack system with a central computer, and will now receive a Pha-

Above: This beautifully decorated Fuji T-1A is attached to 13 Hiko Kyoikudan (13th Flight Training Wing), based at Ashiya. It was painted for the 1996 air show at that base but has kept its dazzling special scheme.

Right: Three Raytheon Hawker U-125 navaid calibration aircraft are based at Iruma, with the JASDF's Hiko Tenjentai (Flight Check Group).

zotron Kopyo X-band multi-mode pulse-Doppler radar.

Also included will be TV and FLIR sensors with read-outs on two cockpit LCD MFDs and a wide-angle HUD, ring-laser gyro INS with integrated satellite navigation, HOTAS and other digital systems to operate with a range of advanced air-to-air and PGMs. Vietnam is also taking delivery in 1997 of six Sukhoi Su-27SK fighters from an overall requirement for 24.

Australasia

AUSTRALIA:

F/A-18 radar evaluation

The RAAF has bought two Hughes APG-73 radars, as installed in the new F/A-18E/F Super Hornet, for evaluation by its Aircraft R&D unit at Edinburgh, near Adelaide, and the Defence Science and Technology Organisation's Microwave Radar Division in Salisbury. The new radars are being evaluated for inclusion in a follow-on FMS contract for the RAAF's planned upgrade of its 70 or so F/A-18A/B Hornets.

RAN Seahawk upgrade

Hawker de Havilland Victoria Ltd, in conjunction with Telstar Systems of Melbourne which has software responsibility, has been awarded a $A200 million ($145 million) contract to upgrade the avionics of the Royal Australian Navy's 16 Sikorsky SH-70B-2 Seahawks. New equipment will include a version of the Hughes AN/AAQ-16 FLIR, plus Israeli Elisra Electronic Systems AES-210 electronic support and countermeasures defensive sub-systems. Programme completion is planned between 1999 and 2002.

Similar equipment is expected to be selected for the RAN's recently-ordered initial batch of 11 Kaman SH-2G(A) SeaSprite ASW helicopters, from overall requirements for 23, for which evaluations are also being made of the Elta EL/M-2022 and Telephonics APS-143(V)3 maritime surveillance and targeting radars. This will allow operation of the Kongsberg Penguin anti-ship missiles selected for use by the RAN SeaSprites.

NEW ZEALAND:

Brand-new SH-2s for RNZN

The Royal New Zealand Navy has opted to acquire four new-build SH-2G Seasprites instead of the zero-timed, upgraded SH-2Fs originally planned. Fears have been expressed about the potential of fatigue/lifespan problems with the older, rebuilt airframes which, if they did occur, would have a profound effect on the RNZN's small SH-2 fleet. The Westland Wasps that the Seasprites are replacing had a service life of 30 years and the SH-2s will be expected to have the same. The added expense of the new aircraft will mean that they will now only have a conventional (SH-2F-style) avionics fit.

South America

BRAZIL:

Army S-70 order

Orders for four Sikorsky S-70A Black Hawks, plus a five-year training/maintenance contract, were placed in mid-1997 by the Brazilian army for short-term delivery. Equipped with GPS, HF radio, weather radar and a rescue hoist, they will perform peace-keeping roles along the Ecuador and Peruvian borders to replace four similar US Army-operated UH-60s based at Patuca in Ecuador.

CHILE:

Air refuelling for F-5s

An estimated $5 million contract to supply air-refuelling probe and fuel system modification kits for the Chilean air force's 16 upgraded F-5E/Fs has been received by the Tiger Century company in California. The kits are being installed in Santiago by ENAER, to allow the F-5s to join Chile's Mirage M5MA Elkans in operating with the FACh's 707-300C tanker. This was converted by IAI's Bedek Aviation Division in 1996 with two underwing pods and a fuel system.

COLOMBIA:

Helicopter reinforcements

US FY98 foreign military aid funding includes $50 million for four UH-60s to replace UH-1Hs used for narcotics control roles by the National Police. Seven Colombian Bell 212s and three UH-60s are also fitted with 0.5-in (12.7-mm) GAU-19/A machine-guns.

Bell Helicopter Textron is finalising a contract with the Colombian government to upgrade up to 14 UH-1s from over 32 used by the armed forces and police, mainly for drug interdiction. They are planned to be modified in Colombia, in partnership with that country's Industrial Aeronautical company. Improvements would include uprated AlliedSignal T53-L-703 engines, combined with Bell 212 main and tail rotors, plus transmission systems, for about $1 million each, to UH-1HP Huey II standards.

PARAGUAY:

Taiwan F-5 offer

As a follow-on to 1996 transfers of two Bell UH-1Hs, the Taiwanese Defence Ministry has reportedly offered 10

Left: Kawasaki T-4 trainers are now being allocated to front-line JASDF units, as well as the six training squadrons of the Koku Kyoku Shudan (Air Training Command). This aircraft wears operates with the Nyutabaru-based 202 Hikotai.

Below: This Myanmar Tamdaw Lay (air defence force) Mil Mi-17PM was a most unusual visitor to the Thai '97 aerospace and defence exhibition, in late October 1997. The type is a very recent addition to Myanmar's intensely secretive air arm.

surplus Northrop F-5Es and two-seat F-5Fs to the Paraguayan air force. This is apparently in recognition of Paraguay's unique (in Latin America) diplomatic recognition of Taiwan, but the national defence budget may be insufficient for F-5 operation. Current Paraguayan air force combat equipment comprises only seven ex-FAB EMB-326 Xavantes and half a dozen of the world's last North American T-6G Texan armed trainers remaining in military service.

URUGUAY:

New aircraft for the FAU

Formal acceptance of the six Westland Wessex HC.Mk 2s formerly operated by No. 28 Squadron, RAF, was made by General Cesar Borucki, commanding the Uruguayan air force (FAU), after their farewell flypast from Kai Tak, in Hong Kong on 3 June. Escuadrón

Aéreo Nº 5 of the Fuerza Aérea Uruguaya received them in July 1997. The Wessexes arrived at Montevideo harbour aboard the SS *Artic Dream*, which also carried spare parts and ground equipment. The Wessexes were reassembled on the dock and then flew the short distance to Carrasco airport, home of Brigada Aérea 1. Wessex ex-RAF XT605/E made the first flight, over Base Aérea Carrasco,

escorted by two Bell UH-1H Hueys and one Bell 212 of Grupo 5, plus a civil-registered Bell 206 JetRanger III. Another four helicopters (XR522/A, XR515/B, XT675/C and XT673/G) arrived between 14 and 15 July, and the last (ex-XT678/H) on 16 July.

The FAU plans to retain four Wessex HC.Mk 2s in service, for these helicopters will provide an important transport capability and augment the

meagre Uruguayan helicopter fleet, which also includes two Bell 212s and three Bell UH-1H Hueys. The Wessexes were delivered with Spectrolab Nitesun searchlights. At least one aircraft will be detached for SAR duties to Base Aérea 'Teniente Parallada' (Durazno) to support Escuadrón 1 (IA-58 Pucará) and Escuadrón 2 (T-33/A-37) operations.

The Fuerza Aérea Uruguaya has recently purchased two Eurocopter AS 365N2 Dauphins under a US$9.5 million contract. These helicopters will be used mainly as VIP transports, with medevac facilities. The Dauphins, the first Eurocopter-built helicopters in Uruguay, will be supported by Helibras (airframe) and by Turboméca do Brasil (Arriel engines). The first example was scheduled to be delivered to Escuadrón Aéreo 5 during August 1997.

Finally, the Uruguayan air force concluded its selection of light transport/liaison aircraft to replace the current mixed fleet. Under a US$3.6 million programme, the FAU is purchasing 10 six-seat Cessna 206H Stationairs powered by a single 300-hp (224-kW0) Lycoming IO-580, and two six-seat Raytheon (Beech) Model 58 Barons powered by 300-hp Continental IO-550C engines. All aircraft are to be delivered during 1998 to the Escuadrilla de Enlace at Base Aérea 'Teniente Parallada' (Durazno). The unit is now flying the last four Cessna U-17A-CEs delivered in 1965, plus single examples of the Cessna 182D, Cessna 206, Cessna 210 and Piper L-21.

North America

CANADA:

CF-18s deployed to Bosnia

Canadian CF-18 Hornets joined other IFOR air arms at Aviano, Italy and undertook the Canadian Forces' first fighter combat missions since the Gulf War. One hundred and twenty personnel from 4 Wing at CFB Cold Lake, Alberta supported six 416 'Lynx' Squadron CF-18As on a three-month deployment called Operation Mirador. 416 Squadron deployed the aircraft in mid-August 1997 to carry out combat air patrol, detection of incursions into the 'No-Fly Zone' and protection of over 1,200 Canadian Land Forces Command troops stationed in the Balkans. The Hornets were armed with Loral NITE Hawk FLIR pods, GBU-12 Paveway II LGBs, AGM-65G Mavericks, AIM-7 Sparrows and AIM-9 Sidewinders. This marked the first combat operations for Canada with PGMs, which have been acquired for the Hornet force within the last 12 months.

Canada has also operated several rotations of CP-140 Auroras for naval blockade-running detection, CH-124 Sea Kings aboard naval vessels, and major tactical airlift work with CC-130 Hercules in the Bosnian theatre.

CC-130 upgrade contract

CAE Aviation of Edmonton, Alberta, which for many years has specialised in Lockheed C-130 repair, maintenance and overhaul, has received a Canadian Air Command order as prime contractor for the avionics upgrade of its 32 CC-130 Hercules. They comprise 19 C-130E and 13 C-130H models with four different cockpit configurations, now to be standardised by 2000 with a new Rockwell Collins digital avionics suite. As well as an FMS-800 flight-management system, this will include five EFIS cockpit displays with twin attitude and heading reference (AHRS) and air-data systems, updated GPS/INS, plus flight-data and cockpit voice recorders.

Super Tucano contract

Following selection of the EMBRAER EMB-312H Super Tucano for the basic stages of the NATO Flying Training in Canada programme, the Canadian government is finalising an order for 25 examples. Powered by a 1,600-shp (1193-kW) Pratt & Whitney Canada PT6A-68 engine, the Super Tucano will also undertake some

NFTC advanced training requirements, and may also be used for special mission and light combat roles. The 100 Brazilian air force ALX drug interdiction versions on order have an Israeli Elbit mission avionics package, including a central computer, cockpit MFDs and HUD, and digitised nav/attack systems.

T-33 upgrade contracts

Kelowna FlightCraft has announced a $C20 million ($14.4 million) contract to upgrade 18 Bolivian air force (FAB) Lockheed T-33s. Bolivia received 20 Canadair-built T-33ANs from Canada between 1973 and 1977, plus 18 generally similar Lockheed T-33SFs transferred from the French air force in 1985; the remaining 18 still equip both first-line and advanced training units. The Canadian Air Command also operates about 45 CT-133s on electronic warfare, target facilities and advanced training roles, and they are already receiving avionics, cockpit and structural upgrades with Kelowna to extend their operating lives until at least 2005. This will be 52 years since they first entered Canadian air force service.

In addition to depot-level inspection and repairs, similar Bolivian T-33 upgrades will include Honeywell Primus II radios, H764 laser-gyro attitude and heading reference system (AHRS), radar altimeter and air-data computer. EFIS instrumentation with LCD

screens will also be supplied by Rogerson Kratos. Kelowna is looking for further upgrade contracts, from a potential market for at least 100 aircraft.

UNITED STATES:

Boeing 737 for US Navy

The Boeing 737-700 beat out the MD-90, now another Boeing product, to become the replacement for the US Navy's C-9B Skytrain II and DC-9 transports. Boeing won a $111 million contract for an initial two aircraft, both to be delivered by December 2001.

The C-9Bs, military versions of the Douglas DC-9 airliner, are assigned to the Navy Reserve and perform the NUFEA (Navy Unique Fleet Essential Aircraft) mission. The US Navy has 29 of these aircraft, 17 new-build C-9Bs purchased between 1973-82 and 12 used DC-9s purchased in 1984. Included in the differences are the C-9B's liquid oxygen system compared to the DC-9's gaseous oxygen system. The C-9B had a Crash Position Indicator system installed, not found on Navy DC-9s. Some of the C-9Bs have a different flight director system than the DC-9s. A recognition feature is the shape of the aft upper part of the fin tip: the C-9B is square-shaped and the DC-9 is rounded. For the time being, the US Navy's replacement plans are limited to no more than three 737s, which would replace its oldest C-9Bs.

RAH-66 tests

The US Army resumed flight testing of its sole RAH-66 Comanche (94-0327) on 27 August 1997, after the programme was interrupted for several months for a series of modifications. While the helicopter was not flying, engineers installed a new transmission that allows the RAH-66 to operate at full power. A problem discovered in 1996 on the transmission limited flight tests to 86 per cent of engine power and restricted the Comanche's top speed to 149 kt (171 mph; 275 km/h).

F-22 first flight

Lockheed Martin's F-22 Raptor fighter (91-0001) made its maiden test flight on 7 September 1997, spending an hour in the air at speeds up to 285 mph (459 km/h). The flight was made from Dobbins AFB adjacent to the manufacturing plant in Marietta, GA. Much of the flight took place at 15,000 ft (4572 m), followed by a brief period when pilot Paul Metz retracted the gear and climbed to 22,000 ft (6705 m). Flying chase in two F-16s were Lieutenant Colonel Steve Rainey, scheduled to be the first USAF pilot to fly the F-22, and Lockheed Martin test pilot Jon Beesley.

The USAF and Lockheed decided to cut the Marietta test effort from three flights to two. The F-22 was scheduled to be trucked – rather than flown aboard a C-5, as planned – to the Air Force Flight Test Center at Edwards AFB, CA, in the spring of 1998. The first aircraft will undergo about 50 test flights before delivery of the second to Edwards in mid-1998.

The USAF is scheduled to receive 339 F-22s to replace the F-15C, at a cost of $43 billion. The maiden flight came nearly four months after originally scheduled. The USAF's goal for IOC (initial operating capability) has now slipped six months, to April 2005.

Boeing Joint Strike Fighter

The Boeing Corporation revealed on 10 September 1997 that the Joint Strike Fighter (JSF) programme had successfully passed the conceptual demonstrator initial design review stage, enabling the company to commence fabrication of components and assembly of the two X-32 JSF demonstrators. The review encompassed significant aspects of the design including the airframe and its sub-systems, weight of the aircraft, the preferred propulsion system, the most suitable weapon system concept, planning of the manufacture, flight simulation planning, and details of the first flight.

The designers have trimmed the air vehicle weight to below that which Boeing originally announced in January 1997. A series of propulsion system tests has highlighted the compatibility of the JSF direct lift system components and the high-speed inlet/forebody compression system. Boeing was awarded a Concept Demonstration

Phase contract valued at $662 million at the end of 1996 to build and flight test two X-32 demonstrators. Lockheed Martin is also seeking to win the lucrative JSF competition with its X-35 design. The latter was expected to begin parts production at the Skunk Works in Palmdale, CA sometime in 1998. Following a fly-off between the two designs, the competition winner will be selected in 2001; production of test and evaluation airframes is due to commence soon afterwards, leading to delivery of operational aircraft in 2008.

Last T-1A delivered

The Raytheon Aircraft Company delivered the 180th and final Beech T-1A Jayhawk tanker/transport aircraft to Air Education and Training Command (AETC) on 23 July 1997. The T-1A is in service with four flying training wings to perform flying training for aircrew who are destined to crew transport and/or tanker aircraft. They consist of the 99th FTS, 12th FTW at Randolph AFB, TX, 48th FTS, 14th FTW at Columbus AFB, MS, 86th FTS, 47th FTW at Laughlin AFB, TX, and the 32nd FTS, 71st FTW at Vance AFB, OK, which is a joint pilot training unit catering for aircrew operating multi-engined types with the US Navy and Marine Corps as well as the USAF. The entire fleet of 180 T-1As is operated exclusively by AETC, and no Class A or B mishaps have occurred during 5.5 years of service involving more than 182,000 flight hours and 370,000 landings. By the summer of 1997, almost 700 students had graduated after receiving training on the Jayhawk.

50th anniversary marred by accidents

The week preceding the 50th anniversary of the date the US Air Force became an organisation independent of the Army was marred by a series of

A type unique to the Chilean navy is this ENAER Namcu, which has recently entered service. The Namcu (eaglet) is a two-seat all-composite Chilean design, first flown in 1986.

unrelated aircraft accidents which forced the Department of Defense to issue a safety stand-down while procedures were reviewed. The first major accident occurred on 13 September 1997 and involved 305th AMW C-141B (65-9405) on a flight from Windhoek Airfield in Namibia, where it had delivered US Army mine-clearing equipment. The aircraft was heading for Ascension Island to refuel when it is believed to have collided off the African coast with Luftwaffe Tu-154M (11+02), which was on a flight from Niamey in Niger to Windhoek. The C-141B was carrying a crew of nine, while the Tu-154M had 10 crew and 14 passengers, none of whom survived. The location of the accident was some 60 nm (69 miles; 111 km) off Cape Fria, Namibia. A small amount of wreckage from both aircraft was subsequently discovered in the same location, indicating a mid-air collision.

The F-117A fleet assigned to the 49th Fighter Wing at Holloman AFB,

NM was grounded for inspections following the loss of 81-10793 at the Chesapeake air show staged at Baltimore Martin State Airport, MD on 14 September 1997. The pilot ejected safely, although four spectators suffered minor injuries. The aircraft suffered a structural failure of the port wing, reportedly due to high g loading. Checks revealed the fault was an isolated incident, enabling the fleet to resume normal duties soon afterwards.

On the same day, an F/A-18C of VFA-15 flying from the USS *John F. Kennedy* (CV-67) crashed 75 miles (46 km) northeast of Raysut in Oman when the pilot Lieutenant Jason E. Jakubowski flew into the canyon wall and was killed, in an area known as 'Star Wars Canyon'. An F/A-18D of VMFA-224 operating from MCAS Beaufort, SC was lost the following day close to the Piney Island Bombing Range on Pamilco Sound, NC. The aircraft was on a night bombing exercise when it crashed, killing both crew.

On 16 September an F-16C and an F-16D, both of the 119th FS from Atlantic City, NJ, collided approximately 30 miles (18 km) off the coast of New Jersey. The crew of the F-16D

The Fuerza Aérea de Chile has introduced two new types to its VIP transport unit. In 1996 this ex-USAF C-20B (Gulfstream III) was acquired (below). A more recent addition is this Raytheon Beech 300 Super King Air (right).

Left: The Mexican air force recently introduced this Schweizer SA 2-37A ultra-quiet surveillance aircraft into service for anti-narcotics patrols. It is unclear whether this aircraft is an ex-US Coast Guard RG-8A Condor.

ejected and was rescued from the sea by helicopter soon afterwards. The pilot of the F-16C managed to nurse his damaged aircraft back to Atlantic City for a safe landing.

The loss of five aircraft in as many days resulted in the Pentagon ordering a 24-hour halt to all military flying training for a safety review. Each service was to be permitted to decide when to hold the stand-down, over a week-long period beginning on 26 September. However, even before the suspension of flying could be implemented, the USAF lost B-1B 85-0078 of the 37th BS, 28th BW from Ellsworth AFB, SD, which crashed onto the Powder River Military Operating Area, 25 miles (15 km) from Alzada, MT. The aircraft was completely destroyed and the four crew killed. Following the accident ACC brought forward its planned stand-down by four days, to 22 September.

An earlier accident, which did not capture the headlines as dramatically, was that of 55th Wing EC-135C 63-8053 which suffered an undercarriage collapse upon landing at Pope AFB, NC on 2 September. There were no fatalities, although 11 of the 14 crew were treated for minor injuries. The aircraft was badly damaged, with the spine being cracked forward of the tail and various antennas on the underside of the fuselage being ripped off. It is unlikely that the aircraft will be repaired, for the Looking Glass fleet is due to be retired within the next 12 months.

USAF changes calendar of events

The Air Force has taken the unprecedented step of cancelling or delaying many of its flying competitions which were due to take place during 1997 or 1998, and has restructured others. The biennial Gunsmoke competition due to have been staged at Nellis AFB during the autumn of 1997 has been moved to November 1998, and the William Tell gunnery meet at Tyndall AFB, FL, which was to have been held in the autumn of 1998, will now take place in 1999. Thereafter, these two competitions will take place every three years instead of every two. The air readiness exercise Longshot at Nellis AFB will be delayed from 1998 until the summer of 1999. The Air

Above: The 55th SOS 'Night Hawks', AFSOC's primary MH-60 unit, based at Hulburt Field, has repainted some of its MH-60Gs in an overall grey camouflage, as already applied to the MH-53J.

Below: The Texas ANG's 182nd Fighter Squadron is attached to the 149th Fighter Group. The 'Lone Star Gunfighters' painted up this Block 15 F-16A for their 50th anniversary in 1997.

Warrior exercises, which are flown from Nellis AFB to practice close air support with the US Army at the huge Fort Irwin range in eastern California, will be reduced from 22 annually to 15. The Checkered Flag series of deployments, which began in 1979 to provide realistic deployment training for US-based units, has been terminated altogether since the high level of worldwide responsibilities, combined with the number of exercises, provides sufficient opportunities for most units to maintain their readiness to deploy.

Reasons cited by the Air Force for the changes are 'operational commitments'. The predicted shortfall of some 350 pilots required for FY 1998 may have a bearing on the decision, and is due in part to an increase in the requirement for qualified pilots by airlines. The high volume of deployments overseas for operational duties has resulted in

low morale due to personnel being away from home for long periods.

NC-141As in Europe

Two rare NC-141A StarLifters of the 412th Test Wing from Edwards AFB visited Europe during the summer of 1997. The first pre-production StarLifter (61-2775) made brief visits to RAF Brize Norton and RAF Lakenheath on 17 June before continuing to Ramstein AB, Germany. Sister ship 61-2776 arrived at Mildenhall on 6 August, having been forced to divert due to technical problems while on a flight from the USA to Bitburg AB, Germany (with a refuelling stop at Lakenheath) while transporting a cargo of F-16 test equipment for the 52nd Fighter Wing. Maintenance personnel at Mildenhall were unable to rectify

the fault, resulting in an AMC C-141B being retasked to ferry the cargo on the final leg of its journey. Following repairs, the NC-141 finally departed for Dover AFB, Delaware on 30 August. These C-141s are the only two of the three pre-production StarLifters still in operational service, as 61-2777 had been retired to the AMARC at Davis-Monthan AFB, AZ by October 1995. The 412th Test Wing's only other NC-141A 61-2779 had joined the AFFTC Museum at Edwards AFB around the same time. All four aircraft have spent their entire service career on test and evaluation work, and have retained the white and grey colour scheme which was introduced to the airlift fleet by MAC in the late 1960s.

12776 is named *Desert Rat* due to the amount of time the aircraft spent supporting test programmes in the southwestern USA when stationed at Wright-Patterson AFB, OH with the 4950th Test Wing during the 1970s and 1980s. The aircraft has the unofficial nickname 'The Electric StarLifter' because it has a glass cockpit and fly-by-wire flight controls. Lockheed Martin modified the aircraft with electrically powered flight control actuators which are similar to those that will be installed in an F-16 demonstrator as a proof of concept for the Joint Strike Fighter/Integrated Subsystem Technology (J/IST) programme. The C-141 received the new flight controls during 1996 and has been flying routine airlift sorties on behalf of AMC in order to amass 1,000 hours to test the reliability of the actuators. This has required the aircraft to visit a variety of airlift centres around the world, including Mildenhall. At present, the StarLifter is the only transport aircraft which has been fitted with electrically powered flight control actuators which are coupled to the FBW flight control computer.

AFTI/F-16 to test electric flight controls

Lockheed Martin has received a contract to produce the first fighter aircraft equipped with electric flight controls. The Advanced Fighter Technology Integration/F-16, better known as the AFTI/F-16, will be the proof-of-concept vehicle for the Lockheed Martin JSF, with modification work due to commence at Fort Worth, TX during the autumn of 1997. The aircraft involved in the AFTI/F-16 programme is the sixth full-scale development single-seater (75-0750). Once the installation of the electrically actuated flight controls has been completed, an extensive series of trials will be undertaken by the manufacturer to evaluate planned reductions in maintainability, weight, and lifecycle costs compared with conventional hydraulic flight controls.

Deliberate Guard bolstered

The Pentagon announced on 4 September that it would increase the number of USAF aircraft assigned to Operation Deliberate Guard for duties over Bosnia for the period 8 to 22 September while municipal elections were being held. The polls opened on 13 September, and the additional hardware was sent to the region as a precaution against Serbian disruption. An Air Expeditionary Force composed of six F-16Cs from the 52nd FW from Spangdahlem AB, Germany (but temporarily in residence at Bitburg) was deployed to Aviano on 5 September, supported by additional KC-135Rs of the 351st ARS, 100th ARW detached from RAF Mildenhall and C-130Es of the 37th AS, 86th AW from Ramstein AB.

Deployed to Brindisi, Italy in time for the elections were three EC-130E Commando Solo versions of the Hercules from the 193rd Special Operations Squadron at Harrisburg IAP, PA. The aircraft were flown to Italy to monitor and if necessary to jam Serbian radio and television broadcasts, which in the period leading up to the elections had been conducting a campaign to encourage disruption and violence. The three aircraft should have arrived at Brindisi shortly before polling day on 13 September, although at least one encountered mechanical problems during a refuelling stop in Gander.

The 192nd Airlift Squadron from Reno-Cannon IAP, NV sent one of its 'Furnish Breeze' photo-reconnaissance C-130Es to Aviano on 29 August 1997. The aircraft is one of three which have large focal length cameras mounted in the fuselage to conduct photographic missions from a safe distance. No further details were made available about the use of this aircraft in the region.

First F-15 Eagle with APG-63(V)1 radar upgrade

The first F-15 Eagle fitted with the upgraded Hughes APG-63(V)1 radar was flown for the first time by McDonnell Douglas on 18 July 1997 at St Louis, MO. The upgrade is in kit form and comprises tactical software from the APG-70; it offers substantial improvement in the air-to-ground mode, while providing improved reliability and maintainability as well as enabling considerable growth in processing and ECM capability. The kit is compatible with the existing APG-63 radar antenna and display consoles and entails only minor modifications to the aircraft interface. The F-15E and late production F-15C/Ds are equipped with the APG-70, although there are estimated to be over 100 F-15A/B models and approximately 400 F-15C/Ds which are still fitted with the APG-63, along with some F-15s operated by overseas air arms. Low-rate initial production commenced in August 1997 for installation as aircraft are cycled through for overhaul. Full production is expected to be achieved by early 1999.

Above and right: Lockheed Martin has been undertaking extensive research into maintenance-free 'paintless' aircraft, primarily as part of its JSF development. The most recent example of this work is this F-16, which was flown with 600 sq ft (56 m²) of its surface area – including all upper wing and fuselage surfaces – covered in a lightweight, adhesive, black film. The remainder of the airframe was painted gold, in a similar fashion to other special schemes worn by ANG F-16s for the USAF's 50th anniversary. The F-16 involved was supplied by the F-16 CTF at Edwards AFB, and flew in late 1997. Previous 'paintless' tests have been made with an S-3 and a C-130.

FY 1998 US defence budget

The US House of Representatives approved the Fiscal Year 1998 defence budget at $248.3 billion. Among the acquisitions are plans for another nine B-2A Spirit 'Stealth Bombers', although the aircraft have not been requested by the Department of Defense. Their inclusion will almost certainly prompt strong debate between the House and Senate, for the latter has vehemently opposed any further B-2 acquisition. Additional items in the bill include funding for nine C-17A Globemaster IIIs ($1.9 billion); four E-2C Hawkeyes – one more than requested ($304 million); 20 F/A-18E/F Hornets ($2.1 billion); 30 H-60 Black Hawks – 12 more than requested ($309 million); and seven V-22As – two more than requested ($661 million). A further $175 million has been allocated for Kiowa Warriors, and $282 million has been made available for development of the RAH-66 Comanche. The allocation of $309 million to Sikorsky for 30 H-60s is part of a multi-year procurement contract for the acquisition of 108 helicopters over a five-year period. Included are 58 UH-60L Black Hawks for the US Army, 42 of the new CH-60 versions for the Navy's fleet combat support role, and eight HH-60G Pave Hawks for the USAF's combat search and rescue.

B-2A Spirit news

Following the granting of an Initial Operational Capability earlier in 1997, the 509th Bomb Wing is working toward having the 393rd Bomb Squadron fully equipped with its complement of eight aircraft available for operational duties, plus an additional number available for the 394th Crew Training Squadron. At present, the US Air Force has a total active inventory of 19 B-2As, which includes aircraft assigned to operations, training, test and maintenance, as well as those in reserve or under modification. However there are only nine primary aircraft authorised at present, which is the gauge for the performance of operational missions.

A highly controversial and well publicised General Accounting Office (GAO) report issued in August 1997 alleged that moisture and extreme weather conditions can have an adverse effect on the B-2's 'stealthy' qualities, requiring extensive field maintenance. During each sortie some low-observable materials deteriorate, requiring rectification in the environmentally controlled shelters at Whiteman AFB. This has resulted in maintenance hours rising to 124 hours for each flight hour, which is 2.5 times the original projection of 50 hours. To enable the Air Force to fulfil its missions, all B-2 sorties will be flown from Whiteman AFB, with the majority being non-stop and supported by tankers pre-positioned at various locations. The GAO report also confirmed that the cost of the B-2 programme appeared to have stabilised at $45 billion. This included the cost of acquisition, planned upgrades, and test and development. The report raised caution that the programme cost could rise if the flight test programme, which was originally planned for four years and which has already lasted for eight, was extended beyond March 1998. In addition, the cost could be affected if any further deficiencies were to arise.

The eight-year development and test programme for the B-2A at Edwards AFB was largely completed by the end of June 1997. The third B-2A, 82-1068 (AV3), will be retained by the 412th Test Wing for the time being to continue software development. When this aircraft departs for upgrade to Block 30 configuration at Palmdale in the spring of 1998, it will be replaced by a B-2A on loan from the 509th BW. The 420th Flight Test Squadron at Edwards AFB, which has been responsible for all aspects of the B-2 development programme, was due to have been inactivated late in 1997, with the 419th Flight Test Squadron planned to expand its role to include all bomber testing with the B-1B, B-2A and B-52H.

55th Wing news

WC-135W: The 55th Wing at Offutt AFB, NB detached its WC-135W, serial 61-2667, to Mildenhall on 26 July 1997 for three weeks until 16 August. During the stay, 12667 performed at least two local sorties, one of which was for crew training, although the other was believed to have been an operational mission. This latter mission involved the aircraft being airborne for 12 hours, and heading in a northerly direction after departure. This route was similar to that which the RC-135s flew during the Cold War but which has been seldom flown in recent years. The aircraft is a former WC-135B which was operated by the Air Weather Service to gather weather reconnaissance data. As a WC-135B, 12667 was fitted with air scoops on the side of the fuselage to ingest particles and radiation samples; the air was also used to keep onboard electrical equipment cool.

With the merger of Boeing and McDonnell Douglas the V-22 Osprey programme has now become the responsibility of St Louis-based McDonnell Aircraft and Missile Systems. It now oversees all fixed- and rotary-wing aircraft and missile projects previously underway with both corporations. Thus the V-22 now finds itself as a stablemate with the CH-46, F-15, F-18, RAH-66, AH-64, AV-8B, SLAM and JASSM. Here the Nos 8 and 9 airframes, which have been built to production (MV-22) standard, are seen at Arlington in late 1997.

Right: This C-141A is the aircraft now undergoing a 1,000-hour flight evaluation with fully electrically-powered flight actuators.

Below right: The USAF, and manufacturer Teledyne Ryan, are progressing towards the first flight of the Global Hawk (Tier II Plus) high-altitude, long-endurance UAV. Global Hawk was rolled out on 20 February 1997. The craft is 44.4 ft (13.53 m) long and has wing span of 116.2 ft (35.41 m). The maiden flight will take place at Edwards AFB, and was scheduled for the fourth quarter of 1997.

When the requirement was reduced, several WC-135Bs were reassigned to other duties, with the weather reconnaissance equipment being removed. The role of atmospheric sampling was incorporated into the mission of the B-52H under a programme called Giant Fish, involving the installation of a pod containing air scoops mounted in the forward section of the weapons bay. However, it was later determined that the B-52 was too costly to operate in this role, with the result that the weather reconnaissance equipment was reinstalled into the WC-135W. 12667 spent a short time based at Mildenhall as an aircrew trainer with the 10th ACCS. Upon reassignment to Offutt AFB when the 10th ACCS was inactivated, 12667 became a TC-135B, before being redesignated as a WC-135W in 1996. 12667 is assigned to the 45th Reconnaissance Squadron alongside the OC-135B, RC-135s and TC-135s, whose fin markings are a black stripe.

RC-135X Cobra Eye: The unique RC-135X Cobra Eye 62-4128 has been in store with E-Systems (now Raytheon E-Systems) since 1993 while the Air Force considered its future role. With an ever-increasing requirement for the RC-135 fleet to perform tactical as well as strategic reconnaissance, there was a need for additional assets. To partially satisfy the requirement, the Air Force funded the conversion of two additional Rivet Joint RC-135Ws. However, the Air Force has now decided on a role for the Cobra Eye, and is funding the conversion of the RC-135X to a configuration known as Cobra Ball 2, abbreviated simply as CB2. It will

involve the installation of the optical sensors on both sides of the forward fuselage instead of on the starboard side only, as on the RC-135S. To continue the Cobra tradition and 'mystique', CB2 will have one wing painted black, even though the sensors will be installed on both sides, and there is no real need for this as sun glint is no longer a problem.

The majority of mission sensors on the two RC-135S Cobra Ball aircraft are located on the starboard side, and are positioned behind four windows on 61-2662 and behind three on 61-2663. The window nearest the cockpit houses the Medium-Wave Infra-Red Array (MIRA) designed and built by Textron Systems. The next two windows contain the Real Time Optical System which records visible light images

through a combination of five tracking and eight acquisition sensors. The fourth window accommodates the Large Aperture Tracking System (LATS) with a 12-in focal length long-range telescope for fine resolution of small targets. A powerful laser range-finder has recently been installed just aft of the right wing trailing edge. A large flat panel aft of the nose contains arrays for collecting electronic signals, while three elongated horizontal fairings below the sensor windows contain frequency antennas for acquiring additional signals from missiles. These windows, fairings and sensors will be installed on both sides of 24128, although the long-range LATS telescope may not be installed in CB2 initially, as it is possible it could be mounted in a turret to provide 360°

observation, thereby eliminating blind spots. Work is expected to be completed by the middle of 1998. The aircraft is officially still on the strength of the 55th Wing and will be returned to Offutt AFB once installation work has been completed.

Despite SALT treaties being implemented, the testing of Russian strategic missiles has continued, since there is a healthy export market and the Russian military itself needs to upgrade its defence systems. The weapon which is of greatest interest to the West is the Russian SS-X-27, which is considered by some to be the most advanced ICBM in the world. This weapon is believed to be undergoing testing at present which could lead to an IOC as an upgrade to the existing land-based strategic missile force. The three Cobra Ball aircraft are considered to be vital assets to detect and monitor such weapons, with potential upgrades being studied. Included among them is the Snake Eye radar enhancement to improve all-weather capability, particularly blowing sand or haze which can hamper data collection within certain frequency bands.

Exercises and deployments to Europe

F-16s to Iceland: Five F-16Cs of the 523rd FS, 27th FW from Cannon AFB, NM arrived at Keflavik, Iceland on 30 June 1997. The aircraft were present to perform patrols of the Icelandic Air Defence Zone as part of the ongoing commitment to have an air defence capability at Keflavik following the withdrawal of the F-15s of the 57th FS. The commitment to defend the zone has been carried out by F-15 Eagles of the Air National Guard and Air Combat Command rotated from their home bases; the 27th FW deployment was the first to involve the F-16.

F-16s to Denmark: Ten F-16C/Ds of the 120th FS from Buckley ANGB, CO were flown to Karup AB, Denmark on 19 August 1997 under Coronet Blade to participate in air defence exercise Tactical Fighter Weaponry '97. The F-16s were teamed with F-15Cs of the 53rd FS, 52nd FW from Spangdahlem AB to form the 3rd Air Expeditionary Group. Four aircraft from the deployment flew to Brnik Airport in Slovenia on 29 August for a three-day goodwill visit. The F-16s were included in a local exercise with the 9th Rocket Brigade of the Slovenian

F/A-18E/F testing continues apace, despite some aerodynamic problems that have been encountered in certain areas of the flight test envelope. Here the F2 development aircraft is seen making the type's first AGM-65 shot.

Defence Force at Pocek, as well as providing a number of high-ranking Slovenian Armed Forces personnel with the opportunity of familiarisation flights. The complement returned home over the weekend of 6/7 September. Earlier in July 1997, eight F-16C/Ds of the 457th FS, 301st FW deployed to Karup AB for four weeks to participate in exercises. During their stay the F-16 pilots were engaged in dissimilar air combat training against MiG-29 'Fulcrums' of the German air force flying from their base at Laage, which is home to JG 73.

C-17s to Kazakhstan: The 437th AW participated in exercise Centrazbat '97 commencing on 14 September 1997. Eight C-17As departed from Pope AFB, NC with 500 paratroops from the 82nd Airborne Division for a non-stop flight to a drop zone in Kazakhstan. While deployed, the troops were engaged in peacekeeping exercises in both Kazakhstan and Uzbekistan between 15 and 21 September, before returning home.

Carriers on the move

The USS *Kitty Hawk* (CV-63) will replace the USS *Independence* (CV-62) as the only aircraft-carrier with a home port outside of United States territorial waters. Currently, the USS *Independence* is stationed at Yokosuka in Japan, but is due to return to the USA for decommissioning. Carrier Air Wing 5 (CVW-5) is assigned to the *Independence* when embarked, but resides at Atsugi Air Base, Japan while the ship is in port. The *Kitty Hawk* will depart from San Diego, its current home port, on 15 July 1998 and head for Pearl Harbor where the vessel will officially assume its new duties. The aircraft, helicopters and personnel of CVW-5 will also embark aboard *Kitty Hawk* at Pearl Harbor in time to participate in exercise RIMPAC '98.

The USS *Nimitz* (CVN-68) left its home port at Puget Sound Naval Shipyard in Bremerton, Washington on 1 September 1997 to commence an around-the-world cruise, visiting various ports in Asia, before assignment in the Arabian Gulf. At the completion of duties in the Middle East the ship will transit the Mediterranean before arriving at its new home port at Norfolk, VA. *Nimitz* is then due for a three-year overhaul and refit of the nuclear core.

Unit news

22nd FS: Aircrews from 22nd Fighter Squadron, 52nd FW at Spangdahlem have begun training to perform the Suppression of Enemy Air Defences (SEAD) role with their Block 50 F-16C/Ds. Squadron aircraft have the facility to carry the podded AN/ASQ-

Left: This F-16 of the 944th FW, 302nd FS, Arizona Air Force Reserve was painted in these special markings to echo the squadron's lineage with the 332nd FG, 302nd FS – the famous all-black 'Tuskegee airmen' of World War II.

Below left: The 192nd FW, 149th FS of the Virginia ANG celebrated the USAF's 50th anniversary, in August 1997, with this special scheme.

213 HARM Targeting System. Sister squadron the 23rd FS has performed the role for at least three years.

422nd TES: The 422nd Test and Evaluation Squadron at Nellis AFB, NV was reassigned from the 57th Wing to the 53rd Wing (with headquarters at Eglin AFB, FL) on 1 August 1997. Aircraft of the 422nd TES have remained stationed at Nellis AFB, but now sport a green-and-black fin-tip marking together with the 'OT' tailcode in place of 'WA', and the familiar black-and-yellow checkerboard fin band.

46th TW: The 46th Test Wing at Eglin AFB continues to operate NC-130A 55-0022, which is the oldest Hercules in the USAF inventory, although the aircraft resides at Duke Field for convenience. It is assigned to the 40th FTS alongside a single UH-1N and a mixed complement of F-15s flown on test duties. The 39th FLTS operates the F-16s.

507th Wg: The 507th Wing at Tinker AFB, OK was redesignated as an Air Refueling Wing on 1 August 1997

with the KC-135R, under Air Force Reserve Command. Prior to the change the 507th had been a composite unit responsible for the tankers as well as the air and ground personnel crewing E-3 Sentries on an associate basis. The wing was composed of the 507th Operations Group and the 465th Air Refueling Squadron with the KC-135R, together with the 513th Air Control Group and the 970th Airborne Command and Control Squadron with personnel operating E-3s drawn from the 552nd ACW.

HMT-204: HMT-204 (Heavy Lift Squadron 204) 'White Knights' has been designated as the first US Marine Corps unit to operate the MV-22A Osprey. Deliveries are expected to commence in 1999, and IOC is scheduled for 2001.

News in brief

4,000-hour F-16C: 56th Fighter Wing F-16C 83-1164 of the 62nd Fighter Squadron became the first USAF

Fighting Falcon to achieve 4,000 flying hours, during a sortie from its home base at Luke AFB, AZ on 30 July 1997.

C-5 maintenance: The Warner Robins Air Logistics Center at Robins AFB, GA has won a seven-year contract valued at $434 million to perform major overhaul and depot-level maintenance on C-5 Galaxies. The first arrived in October 1997 and an annual turnover of 20 Galaxies is anticipated. The work previously had been carried out by the San Antonio Air Logistics Center at Kelly AFB, TX, which had the contract since the early 1970s; the facility is scheduled for closure as part of the drawdown process. The bid from the WRALC was successful against other tenders submitted by Boeing and Lockheed Martin.

AFSPC: US Space Command is studying an option to lease civilian helicopters to support missile wing operations by ferrying personnel from home base to the numerous ICBM silos at each facility. At present AFSPC has the following complement: the 30th Space Wing at Vandenberg AFB, CA with five UH-1Ns; the 90th Missile Wing at Francis E. Warren AFB, WY with seven UH-1Ns; the 91st MW at Minot AFB, ND with five HH-1Hs; the 321st MW at Grand Forks AFB, ND with six HH-1Hs; and the 341st MW at Malmstrom AFB, MT with 10 UH-1Ns.

The 321st MW is scheduled to inactivate in September 1998, with its HH-1Hs being retired prior to this date. Two options are being considered, the first being a full wet lease of aircrew and ground personnel, and the second a scaled-down version whereby USAF crews would continue to operate the new leased helicopter type.

BRIEFING

Shooting at Oulu

Once a year the Suomen Ilmavoimat (Finnish Air Force/FAF) has its annual shooting camp at the civil airport of Oulu, 200 km (125 miles) south of the Arctic Circle, near the Gulf of Bothnia. In 1997, the camp was held from 9 to 12 June, much less than the three weeks it took in the previous years. The reason behind this was the introduction of the F-18 Hornet into FAF service. As the FAF comprises three fighter units, each squadron previously participated in the shooting exercise for one week, bringing its own fighters, so that one MiG-21 and two Draken detachments normally visited Oulu. In 1997, Haittalentolaivue 21 (HavLLv 21, Fighter Squadron 21) of the Satakunta Air Command at Pirkkala air base in southern Finland did not participate in the shooting camp. This unit was the first FAF squadron to convert to the F-18 Hornet, in September 1996, and held its own weapons

exercise with the F-18s in the spring of 1997. The remaining two fighter squadrons both participated in the shooting camp in the same week. HavLLv 11 of the Lapland Air Command came from its northern base of Rovaniemi with Drakens and Hawks, while HavLLv 31 of the Karelian Air Command from the eastern base of Rissala brought MiG-21s and Hawks. In total, 40 pilots and 160 support crew were present at Oulu.

HavLLv 11 of the Lapland Air Command, based at Rovaniemi, brought five Saab Drakens and a number of Hawks. The Drakens comprised three Saab 35Ss assembled by Valmet (now renamed Finavitec) and three Saab J 35Fs acquired from Swedish air force stock. The Rissala-based HavLLv 31 flew seven MiG-21s to Oulu, which represents almost half of the operational MiG fleet. Of them, six were MiG-21bis 'Fishbed-Ns' and one was a locally modified recon-

naissance version, the MiG-21bis/T (Tiedustelu/reconnaissance). A few years ago six MiG-21bis/Ts were operated in the reconnaissance squadron at Tikkakoski but, due to the decreasing number of operational MiG-21bis fighters at Rissala, the six MiG-21bis/Ts were returned to Rissala last year. Externally, the Finnish reconnaissance version can be identified by the small wingtip pods, an additional antenna with two small cylindrical fairings extending from the rear of the tail, and a small dome underneath the fuselage just behind the wingroot. The reconnaissance task, if still performed by these MiGs, apparently does not interfere with the combat task since the MiG-21bis/T flew standard missions with the 21bis versions.

The Karelian Air Command was also in charge of two target-towing Learjet 35A/As and one Mi-8T rescue helicopter. In addition to the MiGs, HavLLv 31 flew in sev-

eral Hawks of the Rissala training flight. Of the seven Hawks present, four Hawk T.Mk 51As wore the new overall grey colour scheme, while three Hawk T.Mk 51s wore their original brown/green camouflage. Several transport and liaison aircraft also attended the shooting camp. Transport of pilots and other personnel was performed with one Piper Chieftain, two Piper Arrows, two Valmet Vinkas, two Valmet Redigos and a Fokker 27.

Lieutenant Colonel Kari Janaunen, commander of HavLLv 31, detailed the procedures of the shooting camp: "A shooting day starts with a flight by a fighter to check the weather over the range. Later, a target-towing Learjet uses its radar to check for air traffic and vessels in the range, which extends 175 km (109 miles) west of Oulu into the Gulf of Bothnia. Any aircraft present is told to leave the range, and if ships are present then firing takes place in another area of the range. The Learjet is equipped with two underwing target banner pods, a sort of sock made out of orange ropes 3 m (9.8 ft) long. The targets are towed 1 km (0.62 miles) distant in a profile whereby the Learjet orbits at 500 mph (310 km/h) at an angle of 30°, and an altitude of 5,000 to 10,000 ft (1525-3048 m). For gunnery missions, pairs are formed of MiG-MiG, MiG-Hawk, Hawk-Hawk,

Left: Finland acquired Falcon AAMs with the ex-Flygvapnet J 35FS Drakens it purchased in 1975 and 1984. This aircraft is carrying the Rb 27 (AIM-26B) SARH version.

Below: A sight unique to Finland is the BAe Hawk carrying Russian weapons – in this case R-60 AAMs.

Above: Gunnery target-towing facilities are provided by the Learjet 35As of the 1st Flight, Air Support Command, based at Tikkakoski.

Above right: This Draken is armed with the thin-bodied, IR-homing Rb 28 (AIM-4D) Falcon missile.

Right: This HavLLv 31 MiG-21bis is carrying the K-13M missile, known to NATO as the AA-2 'Atoll-D'.

Draken-Draken or Draken-Hawk. The MiGs use the GSh-23 23-mm canon, the Drakens the 30-mm ADEN canon and the Hawks the centreline podded 30-mm ADEN canon. Hits are counted by means of air pressure differences, using a microphone located in the front of the banner. The banner is shot at in turn by the two fighters in a pair, one of which is inside the circular flight profile of the Learjet and the other outside. After the shooting run, the circle is crossed and the fighters switch places. Before actual shooting is performed the pilot makes one to three aiming runs, followed by about eight shooting runs."

Oulu is a civil airfield, so the crossing runway was closed during the exercise and was used as a ramp for the Learjets and liaison aircraft. The fighters were parked on a small flight line in the wooded area on the south side of the airfield. After the arrival of the aircraft on the afternoon of Monday 9 June, the shooting camp got under way. Over 100 gunnery missions were flown in 1.5 days, with mission times varying from 18 to 40 minutes. First take-offs were made at 08.00 and flights continued into the early evening. Due to Oulu's northerly position in 'the land of the midnight sun', it does not get dark at this time of year.

On Wednesday and Thursday more than 50 missile missions were flown, and the Learjet 35A/A flew again to check the range. The missiles need a type of target different to the towed banner, which

This MiG-21bis carries the little-seen radar homing version of the AA-2, the R-3R or 'Atoll-C'. This missile has a range of 8 km (5 miles).

this time was carried under the wing pylon of a MiG-21bis. The M-5 looks identical to a standard 100-kg Russian practice bomb but is a large magnesium flare which descends slowly on a parachute. Over the range, three fighters fire missiles at the live M-5, observed by two Hawks. First, two IR missiles are fired at the flare; the third, a radar-homing missile, homes in on the reflection of the parachute.

During the following days the MiG-21s carried the Russian equivalent of the Sidewinder, the R-13M (AA-2D 'Atoll') and the small R-60 (AA-8 'Aphid') infrared missile. In the last two days, the long radar-homing R-3R (AA-2C 'Atoll') semi-active radar missile was shot by the MiGs. The Drakens shot both versions of the Swedish-

built AIM-4 Falcon missile: the IR-homing AIM-4D/26 (known in Sweden as Rb28) and the larger semi-active radar homing AIM-4 (Rb27). The Drakens are capable of firing the AIM-9J Sidewinder but were noticed carrying the Russian R-13M (AA-2D 'Atoll') IR missile instead. The Hawks can carry the R-13M (AA-2D 'Atoll'), AIM-9J Sidewinder and R-60 (AA-8 'Aphid'), but only carried the latter during this shooting camp. By 11 June the shooting programme of the Drakens and Hawks of HavLLv 11 had finished, and the aircraft departed for their home base of Rovaniemi. HavLLv 31 stayed one day longer at Oulu and returned to Rissala in the late afternoon, following the completion of the programme.

The shooting camp for 1998 will be different, as the HavLLv 31 MiG-21s will be taken out of operational service later in 1997. Current plans foresee the use of two MiGs for carrying the M-5 target at the next shooting camp. The first F-18s are already at Rissala and early next year the first Hornet flight will achieve IOC. Late in 1997, the Drakens will be taken out of service at Pirkkala in favour of the F-18 then equipping both fighter flights of HavLLv 21. The Drakens of HavLLv 11 at Rovaniemi, however, will be in service until 2005 when they are replaced by the last Hornets. So, the shooting camp of 1998 is expected to attract Hawks, Hornets and Drakens.

René van Woezik

MAKS-97

Moscow Aerospace Salon 1997

On 19 August 1997, the third Moscow International Aerospace Salon opened in Zhukhovskii, south of Moscow. That is, the third as far as officials are concerned; curiously, the organisers stubbornly disregard MosAeroShow '92, which was Russia's first 'real' major air show. The 'international' part of MAKS-97's official name is an appellation open to doubt; quite a few foreign companies were represented in the display stalls, yet, characteristically of the Moscow air show, very few Western aircraft were on display, and they were invariably civil aircraft. Journalists and military aviation experts (both Russian and foreign) had been looking forward to the show because the latest products of Russia's aerospace industry were expected to be there. They should have included, first of all, the Mikoyan MFI fifth-generation fighter (*mnogofunktsional'nyy istrebitel'*/ multi-role fighter), alias Product 1.42 as per advanced project documents. The prototype, designated Product 1.44, has been around for several years but the lack of some systems components means it still

has not flown. Also, everyone was hoping to see, at least in model form, the much-discussed Sukhoi next-generation fighter formerly known under the false designation of S-32 (which was really the manufacturer's designation of the Su-17 'Fitter-B'/'C'); now believed to be designated S-37, the forward-swept-wing aircraft made its first flight in September.

Discussions in Russian aerospace industry circles indicate that the companies, especially MAPO-MiG, were willing to display their latest products. However, the Defence Ministry had different views and refused to declassify the new fighters. As at MAKS-95, Mikoyan had wanted to display the 1.44 but the military had said no.

Much to the disappointment of the foreign visitors, even the Su-30MKI prototype (tactical code 'Blue 56'), which made its first flight recently, was barred from the show. The Su-30MKI is the export version for the Indian air force with canards and two-plane vectoring nozzles. Some sources claim that India had objected to the aircraft

being displayed; however, there were no official comments.

The organising committee found itself in a tight spot. The decision to run the show had come too late, leaving the committee almost no time to arrange things properly. Then, given the ministerial thumbs-down for the fighters which were expected to be the stars of the show, the organisers had to find something – at least a couple of 'show-stealers' which would attract public attention and save the day. Still, many foreign visitors felt deceived.

The Myasischchev bureau displayed its twin-boom M-55 high-altitude research aircraft in formation with two M-101T Ghzel light aircraft.

Below: Star of the show for most observers was the second prototype Antonov An-70, which made its first flight on 24 April 1997.

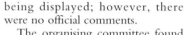

The two-seat Kamov Ka-52 Alligator was a MAKS-97 debutante, and flew at the show. The Ka-52 was first shown in public in November 1996.

What did the Russian military hardware designers have to offer in the absence of the Mikoyan and Sukhoi fifth-generation fighters? The MAPO defence industry group – which includes the Mikoyan, Kamov and Myasischchev bureaux – was the biggest exhibitor, displaying primarily the MiG-31M heavy interceptor with a full range of armament, the attack version of the MiG-AT advanced trainer (with Russian avionics), the Ka-50N and Ka-52 attack helicopters.

The seventh prototype MiG-31M, 'Blue 057' (c/n N72100106137), had been in the static park two years ago, but then the Defence Ministry had vetoed the display of its

armament. This time the aircraft was displayed with 10 hardpoints and carried new Russian air-to-air missiles: four Vympel R-77/RVV-AE on the wing pylons and six R-37s semi-recessed in the fuselage. The latter missile is something of an enigma, since Russian specialists claim that it does not yet have an official designation and that the R-37 designation was 'invented in the West'. Whatever its real designation is, it is probably the most powerful AAM in its class and can take out a bomber/fighter-bomber target at up to 300-km (186-mile) range. MAPO top officials had forbidden close-up photography of the MiG-31M's ventral missile installations, and Mikoyan representatives on site were very active in enforcing this veto. Nonetheless, pictures taken from a few yards away were more than enough for specialists to see what they wanted to.

The static park also included the prototypes of the night-capable Ka-50N (*nochnoy*) and its two-seat spin-off, the Ka-52 Alligator 'Hokum-B' prototype ('White 061', c/n 01012). The latter made only a single demo flight in all six days of the show, leading five Ka-50s. One can hardly blame Kamov for this; the Alligator has only just begun its test programme and the company cannot risk losing the sole prototype. Incidentally, the large cylindrical FLIR chin turret, ventral binocular periscope and Arbalet (Crossbow) mast-mounted sight (MMS) which were present at the time of roll-out had all been removed for initial flight tests, resulting in a smooth nose reminiscent of the mock-up displayed two years ago.

Kamov is known to have signed a contract with Thomson-CSF for the delivery of French thermal imaging systems to be tested on the 'Hokum'. A podded version was carried on the port inboard wing station by the 10th flying Ka-50

Victor Pugachev flew one of his trademark displays in the T10K-6 (Su-27K or Su-33) development aircraft.

Above and right: The highlight of the Sukhoi bureau's presence at MAKS-97 was an aerial refuelling demonstration between an Su-27PU and an Su-24M equipped with the UPAZ-A 'buddy' pod.

('White 020', c/n 01003, Le Bourget code H318) during MAKS-95. Later the Thomson-CSF FLIR was temporarily integrated into the Samshit-E (Boxwood) combined TV/IR/laser sighting system developed by the Ural'sk Optical and Mechanical Plant and fitted in 1996 to the Ka-52 prototype.

A similar Samshit-50 system incorporating a Thomson-CSF Victor FLIR was fitted to the Ka-50N prototype unveiled in March 1997. Unlike the Ka-52, the 640-mm (2 ft 1 in) ball turret housing the gyro-stabilised Samshit system has four windows instead of three (one large window and three small ones). Originally it was mounted dorsally above the optically-flat window of the Shkval-V (Gale) daytime TV/ laser targeting and ranging system. At Zhukhovskii, however, the Ka-50N was shown in modified form with the Samshit turret mounted ventrally, resulting in a sharp nose profile more similar to the production day version.

The night mission equipment enables the Ka-50N to detect a tank-sized target at 4.5-5 km

(2.8-3.1 mile) range. Like the Ka-52, the Ka-50N is to be equipped with the Arbalet MMS; it was fitted to the prototype as originally rolled out but was removed by the time of the air show. The MMS not only serves for target location and navigation, but is integrated into the defensive avionics suite, warning the pilot of attacking enemy aircraft or incoming missiles. The helicopter is equipped with a GPS receiver, and the automatic PA-4-3 moving map display with a paper scroll map is due to be replaced by a colour liquid-crystal display (LCD).

The armament of the Ka-50N is the same as the day version. Since

the FLIR of the Samshit-50 is linked to the Shkval-V laser tracker/ rangefinder, the 9A4172 Vikhr (Whirlwind)/AT-9 laser-guided anti-tank missiles can be fired both day and night. Like the Ka-52, the Ka-50N can carry Kh-25ML air-to-ground missiles with semi-active laser guidance, as well as R-73 and 9M39 Igla-*V* (Needle) AAMs for self-defence.

The Ka-50N prototype was converted in early 1997 from the first production Ka-50 (the eighth flying example, 'White 018') and first flew on 5 March. Kamov is prepared to export both the day and night versions of the 'Hokum',

The MiG-29SMT is something of a cross-breed between the MiG-29SM (Product 9.13) and the still-experimental MiG-29M (Product 9.15). It features the revised air intakes with downward-hinging anti-foreign object damage (FOD) grilles replacing the solid anti-FOD doors of the standard MiG-29; extra fuel is housed in the leading-edge root extensions (in the style of the MiG-29M) and the fatter-than-average fuselage spine.

The MiG-29SMT can carry 1800-litre (396-Imp gal) drop tanks, and a strap-on refuelling probe can be fitted if customers wish. The maximum ordnance load is 4500 kg (9,920 lb). All weapons carried by the standard MiG-29SM can be used, including the R-77 (RVV-AE), R-27R, R-27R1, R-27T, R-27T1 and R-73E AAMs, Kh-29T, Kh-29TE and Kh-31A AGMs, Kh-31P anti-radar missiles and KAB-500KR guided GP bombs.

A new multi-mode fire control radar is fitted which can engage both air and ground targets, along with a MIL-STD 1553B tactical information exchange system (datalink). The cockpit features two large colour LCDs; a cockpit mock-up was displayed at Le Bourget in June 1997. The MiG-29SMT also has a new HOTAS control system.

Normal take-off weight is 16000 kg (35,273 lb); MTOW in overload condition is 21000 kg (46,296 lb). Top speed and rate of climb are unchanged, and range has grown to 3500 km (2,174 miles) with no refuelling probe or 6700 km (4,161 miles) with a single top-up if a refuelling probe is fitted. MAPO is targeting foreign customers with the MiG-29SMT and will manufacture aircraft to customer specifications.

Incidentally, another 'fatback fighter' with a similar designation – MiG-21SMT 'Fishbed-K' – was not a particularly successful aircraft. It was overweight, and most were converted to MiG-21ST standard with a smaller fuselage spine (as in

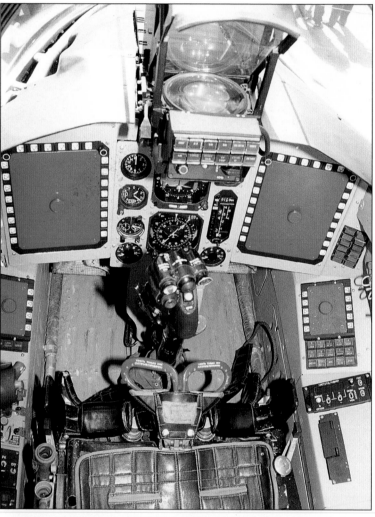

Above and left: MAPO MiG caused a minor stir when it unveiled the MiG-29SMT, a 'new' variant with increased fuel tankage and upgraded avionics. The cockpit (left) resembles that of the MiG-29M with some refinements, and far fewer switches.

along with the reconnaissance/strike Ka-52; this is facilitated by the possibility of installing Western components (e.g., French avionics) at the customer's request. In the spring of 1997 press reports started appearing regarding an impending delivery of eight day 'Hokums' to Slovakia as Russian foreign debt payments. If the deal materialises, Slovakia will be the first foreign operator of Kamov army helicopters.

The first prototype Ka-31 ship-board AEW helicopter ('Blue 031') did not attract much interest, since it stayed on the ground throughout the 1997 show, unlike MAKS-95.

A minor surprise from MAPO MiG came in the shape of the MiG-29SMT; the official designation (T, *toplivo*/fuel) had been allocated immediately before the show. The aircraft was really a mock-up hastily converted from the retired last pre-production MiG-29, as revealed by its tactical code 'Blue 25' and the original narrow-chord rudders. Surprisingly, the aircraft carried a late c/n (25975) – obviously bogus and intended to pass it off as a new aircraft.

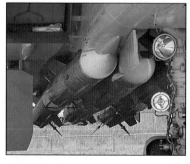

Above and left: An armed MiG-31M was on show carrying Vympel R-77 (AA-12) missiles under the wings and the more sensitive, very long-range 'R-37' AAM, a development of the R-33 AA-9 'Amos'.

the MiG-21bis 'Fishbed-N') and less internal fuel to improve performance.

MAPO exhibits also included the MiG-29SD ('Blue 357', Le Bourget exhibit code 353) with a strap-on refuelling probe and N-019ME radar, which has become a seasoned air show visitor. Also in attendance was the long-retired first prototype MiG-29K shipboard fighter ('Blue 311', c/n 2016188) which was refurbished for static display. The second prototype ('Blue 312', c/n 27579) is being readied for renewed trials, possibly as an avionics testbed for the MiG-29M.

Kamov announced the Ka-60, a light troopship and assault version of the civil Ka-62 helicopter (itself a Eurocopter SA 365N Dauphin II lookalike with tailwheel landing gear, which was expected to fly in late December 1997). The Ka-60 is viewed as a possible replacement for the Mi-8/Mi-17 'Hip', large numbers of which are in service with Russian army aviation.

Another potential 'star of the show' was the prototype MiG-ATS, the trainer/attack version of the MiG-AT. Coded 'Blue 83' and painted light grey with sky blue undersurfaces, the aircraft (actually the second airworthy MiG-AT built) sported two wing pylons and a centreline pylon, as well as a compact Phazotron Moskit (Mosquito) radar in the nose (the basic MiG-AT has none). In addition to R-60 AAMs, B-8M1 unguided rocket pods and an UPK-23-250 gun pod, the weapons array included a powerful Kh-31A anti-shipping

missile, indicating that MAPO is taking this 'pocket fighter' seriously.

The Sukhoi OKB's display was a pale shadow of its presence at previous shows. The thrust-vectoring Su-37 ('White 711') took part mostly in the flying display, appearing in the static park only on the last-but-one day. In addition to the Su-27K 'Flanker-D' (called Su-33 by Sukhoi), which was really the ninth prototype (T-10K-9, 'Blue 109', c/n 49051003604) and was displayed previously in 1995, the static display featured the Su-39, as the production version of the Su-25TK is officially designated. The tactical code 'Blue 21' and c/n 01005 implied it was one of the first production aircraft, possibly the second ('White 20' was displayed at MAKS-95).

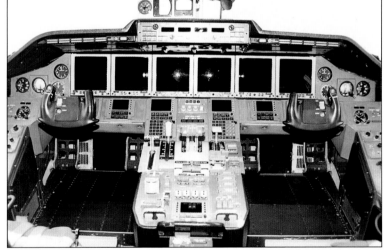

The Su-34 tactical bomber (obstinately called Su-32FN by Sukhoi) was likewise familiar ('White 44' from this year's Le Bourget), and gave a pleasing flying display with a full load of dummy Kh-31 missiles. Sukhoi test pilot Igor Votintsev illustrated very clearly how nimble the aircraft is – apart from being able to perform the Pugachev Cobra, perhaps.

The Mil OKB's display was likewise disappointing. The new Mi-28N could have generated interest but did not show up, ostensibly because of a tight test schedule but suggesting another MoD veto. Visitors had to make do with the fourth prototype day-version Mi-28A ('Yellow 042') which made some demo flights. The most inter-

esting item was an upgraded Mi-24V or D (unidentifiable as the wingtips had been lopped off) sporting a FLIR/laser ball turret on the starboard side of the nose, and Mi-28-style eight-packs of 9M114 Shturm (AT-6 'Spiral') missiles.

Mil's civil component included a new version of the Mi-26T 'Halo' (RA-06089, c/n 34001212499) fitted with a port-side rearward-facing pilot's gondola and a precision hovering system for flying crane operations, as well as the Mi-34S 'Hermit' light helicopter, which has now received its type certificate and entered production in Arsenyev.

The two major factories producing the Mi-17 presented their latest variations on the 'Hip' theme. The Kazan plant displayed yet another version of the Mi-17MD (designated Mi-8MTV-5 for the local market). In its latest guise, the unmarked helicopter (ex-RA-70937, c/n 95448) featured a redesigned one-piece rear loading ramp replacing the earlier Mi-26-style arrangement with upper clamshell doors and a small ramp. The Ulan-Ude plant revealed the sinister-looking Mi-8AMTSh, dubbed 'Terminator' by the Russian popular press. However, this machine (RA-25755, the third Mi-8 to use this registration) was not new, having made its debut at Farnborough in 1996.

The show did have one real star – the Antonov An-70 transport, the world's first aircraft to fly solely on propfan power. The unregistered

The tour ended with a non-stop flight from Trencin back to Zhukhovskii. The prototype had made its 100th flight in Italy and was getting close to 120 flights by the time MAKS-97 opened. Further test flights will be undertaken at Russian air force and Aeronautica Militare Italiana (AMI) bases. During the show the Yak-130 made low-speed/high-Alpha passes and high-speed dashes; despite being brief, the flights were impressive.

Unable to display its latest military designs, the Tupolev bureau had to make do with the Tu-22M3 ('Black 9804', c/n 4898649) with a Kh-22M anti-shipping missile and bombs, and the 'Tu-160SK' ('Blue 342', c/n 84704217, f/n 04-01) displayed at Le Bourget with a crude wooden mock-up of the Burlak sub-orbital launcher rocket. Also present were the three UAVs shown in 1995: the Tu-141 Strizh (Swift) and Tu-243/VR-3 Reys (Flight) reconnaissance drones, the latter on an eight-wheeled self-propelled launcher, and the Tu-300 strike UAV. Tupolev also went to great lengths to promote the very capable Tu-204 airliner on which the Tu-204P maritime patrol and ASW aircraft (now under development) is based. Tupolev has been reticent about the latter aircraft, and the programme has only become publicly known in Russia via several articles published by Russian Naval Aviation C-in-C Vladimir Deyneka.

Specialists visiting MAKS-97 got ample proof that Russia is actively developing helicopters for the armed forces. Aircraft factories have their own design bureaux, and they have also joined the race. The Kazan Helicopter Plant displayed the Ansat twin-turbine light helicopter (the name Ansat means 'light' or 'airy' in Tatarian). The example on display (c/n 001) was the static test airframe; the real prototype (c/n 002), powered by twin P&W/Klimov PK206As, was due to fly by the end of 1997. The Russian Federal Border Guards are reported to have placed an order for 100 aircraft, but this will call for time and money.

In addition to the R-37 (or whatever it is called) AAM, new weapons displayed included the Vympel K-74ME short-range AAM similar in size and layout to the R-73E but with better performance. Also present were the APR-2E and APR-3E anti-submarine missiles (looking more like guided torpedoes) and the C3B (KAB-250-100) anti-submarine guided bomb, all of which are developed by the Region State Research and Production Enterprise.

first prototype had begun flight tests in December 1994 but crashed on 10 February 1995 on its fourth flight after colliding with its An-72 chase plane. The second prototype, UR-NTK (c/n 01-02), converted from what was originally the static test airframe, made its first flight on 24 April 1997. It was to have been the star of Le Bourget but did not get there due to bureaucratic obstacles. Until MAKS-97 Antonov had been very careful to avoid any damage to the aircraft. At the show, however, the An-70 made almost daily demonstration flights. In the air the big aircraft (the An-70 is larger than a C-130) looked and sounded impressive, demonstrating high manoeuvrability and extremely good field performance; it even taxied backwards by reversing the contra-rotating props. Unlike the C-17A, the An-70 can operate from dirt strips.

The Russian AF is very interested in the An-70 to replace its ageing An-12s, but very little funding has been allocated by Russia. Antonov spokesmen said Antonov has raised 90 per cent of the money for the design and test programme by flying cargo charters on company-owned An-124s. The An-70 now has no competitors in the CIS, as the Tupolev design bureau has no funds to complete the Tu-330 transport prototype, and Ilyushin's Il-106 likewise remains a 'paper aeroplane'.

The Yakovlev OKB showed only the familiar Yak-130 trainer prototype – curiously, bearing the civil registration RA-43130 – which Yakovlev chief test pilot Andrey

This modified Mil Mi-24M was on show with a newly added FLIR turret, and associated displays in the rear cockpit. The similar night-attack-capable Mi-35M is under development for the Russian army.

Sinitsin (bearer of the Hero of Russia title) confidently took through the flight display routine. The Yak-130 recently completed another stage of the flight test programme, when, on 11-31 July this year, Sinitsin took the prototype on a demonstration tour of Italy and Slovakia. The implications are obvious: Aermacchi has partnered with Yakovlev in refining, Westernising and marketing the trainer, and Povazske Strojarne of Slovakia manufactures the trainer's Lotarev DV-2 (RD-35) turbofans. The Italian part of the tour included five test flights and two demonstration flights at Aermacchi's home base of Venegono, to where the aircraft was flown from Zhukhovskii via Brest. Aermacchi chief test pilot Plinto Cecconello, who had successfully flown the aircraft in Russia, participated in all seven flights, taking

the Yak-130 to the current limits of its flight envelope: 32° Alpha, Mach 0.9 and 10000 m (32,808 ft).

Once again, Italian aviation experts, high-ranking MoD and economics ministry employees praised the aircraft's performance. The Italian government has allocated about $100 million to the Yak-130 programme. South African Defence Minister Joe Modise was one of the officials watching the demonstration flights, since the type is one of the contenders for the SAAF's new multi-role combat aircraft and advanced trainer. Two combat-capable versions of the Yak-130 (a single-seater and a two-seater) are under development as the Yak-131. The configuration is as yet uncertain, but up to nine hardpoints will be provided: three pylons under each wing, two wingtip missile rails and a centreline pylon.

On 28 July the Yak-130 was flown to Slovakia, performing three demonstration flights at Trencin AB. Slovakian AF/Air Defence Chief of Staff Major General Stefan Gombik and another Slovak pilot had the chance to fly the aircraft. The Slovakian air force's high opinion of the type was confirmed when Defence Ministry officials handed over its specific operational requirement. Slovakia intends to purchase up to 40 Yak-130s in combat trainer and attack versions to replace its MiG-21s, Su-22M-4Ks and Su-25Ks.

The Ka-52 flew just once during the show, having only recently made its maiden flight. The Ka-52 is intended as an answer to those who doubt the efficacy of the single-seat Ka-50.

Avionics manufacturer Phazotron presented the RP-35 X-band phased-array radar developed for the MiG-35, capable of engaging both air and ground targets, the Sokol (Falcon) X-band phased-array radar intended for the Sukhoi S-54 light-weight fighter, and finally the Moskit slotted-array radar. The latter is now being offered for upgrading the Indian air force's SEPECAT Jaguar GR.Mk 1s armed with Sea Eagle ASMs for anti-shipping strike.

If the static park was a disappointment, then the demonstration flights were a success. The spectators applauded the performance of the Russian air force's many display teams: the 'Russian Knights' (Russkiye Vityazi) and 'Fighters' (Istrebiteli) flying Su-27s, the 'Swifts' (Strizhi) flying MiG-29s, and 'Russia' (Rus) – a little-known team from Vyaz'ma – flying Aero L-39C Albatros trainers.

An estimated 500,000 visitors attended the show during its six days. Unlike previous occasions, this included top government officials: President Boris Yeltsin formally launched the show, and Prime Minister Viktor Chernomyrdin was present at the closing ceremony. Moscow Mayor Yuri Luzhkov was also there.

Such close attention from the government indicates that, in spite of everything, the aerospace industry is a high-priority issue in Russian economic policy. It is one of Russia's few competitive industries which can generate much-needed hard currency, and accounts for 56 per cent of Russian arms exports.

Above and right: Kamov had five Ka-50s flying at MAKS-97, and the Ka-50N night-attack variant was also on show. Approximately 10 Ka-50s (including the aircraft seen right) have been delivered to the Russian army and are based at the helicopter pilot training school, in Torzhok.

Given that few major deals are signed in Zhukhovskii, MAKS-97 came as a pleasant surprise. For example, the Russian Ministry of Economics signed a contract with Airbus Industrie regarding broader co-operation in research, design, production and certification of civil aircraft. The MAPO group and Mikoyan signed two protocols with SNECMA and Sextant Avionique regarding joint worldwide marketing of the MiG-AT and commercial interests in the programme. Some noteworthy deals concerning space flight were also struck, such as Aérospatiale and the Russian Space Agency agreeing to start work on a hypersonic research vehicle which will be used in a new-generation space shuttle programme. An agreement has also been signed with NASA on possible US funding for joint US-Russian high-Alpha research programmes.

President Boris Yeltsin had to listen to quite a few complaints from Russian aerospace industry leaders, and promised state funding for the industry so that new programmes could be completed. To quote Economics Minister Yakov Urinson, who spoke at the closing press conference, "Russia has again demonstrated its ability to develop and produce state-of-the-art aerospace products."

Yefim Gordon and Dmitri Komissarov

BRIEFING

Eagle's Talon '97
Exercising for the new NATO

Poland, Hungary and the Czech Republic will join NATO in July 1999. To work toward integration, NATO and these countries have held regular exercises under the Partnership for Peace (PfP) programme. Between 9 and 18 September, the Polish and US air forces held a large bilateral exercise in Poland, known as Eagle's Talon '97. Twenty US tactical aircraft deployed to Poland and flew with fighters from the Polish air force (PAF) against a mixed force of PAF fighters, fighter-bombers and SAM sites. The most obvious barriers to the integration of these countries into NATO are differences in communication, infrastructure and

procedures. Moreover, trust, respect and mutual understanding between the former adversaries have to be developed – which is not an easy task. Procedures and prejudices became well established during the years of the Cold War, and NATO and the three 'new' countries have a long way to go before complete interoperability is achieved. With this in mind, it is not surprising that the objectives of Eagle's Talon include removing these barriers and developing interoperability, in particular for peacekeeping/enforcement operations. The scenario for the exercise was one of contingency operations like those that have been conducted

since the beginning of the 1990s; the conflict in the former Yugoslavia is the most obvious example.

For the purposes of the exercise, the fictional country of Baltica had split into the independent states of Pyrland, Eastland and Northland. The latter threatened to overtake Pyrland. Heightening this tense situation, Eastland was sympathetic to Northland. Consequently, Pyrland leaders asked the North Atlantic Council (NAC) for assistance to deter Northland aggression. The NAC responded by sending the 52nd Combined Air and Space Expeditionary Wing (CASEW) to defend Pyrland. Temporarily based at Powidz Air Base, the CASEW (Blue Force) comprised six F-15Cs, six F-16CJs (Block 50s for defence suppression) of the 52nd Fighter Wing at Spangdahlem, six F-16C

Block 30s of the 183rd Fighter Wing, and two C-130Hs of the 182nd Airlift Wing. The latter two both report to the Illinois Air National Guard. Powidz is home of the 7. Bomber Reconnaissance Air Regiment, equipped with some 30 Su-22M4/UM3 'Fitter-K' fighter-bombers, 12 of which were made available to the 52nd CASEW. Other Pyrland fighters were four MiG-23MF 'Flogger-Bs' normally based at Slupsk-Redzikowo (28. Fighter Regiment), four MiG-21bis from Zegrze Pomorskie (9. Fighter Regiment) and four MiG-29As from Minsk-Mazowiecki (1. Fighter Regiment). These 12 fighters formed a composite squadron at Poznan-Kresiny Air Base, located just south of the city of Poznan.

The MiG-29 and Su-22 are the only Polish combat aircraft equipped with Western-style Identification Friend or Foe (IFF) equipment. The MiG-21 and MiG-23 will not be fitted with this system because they are too old, and costs would be too high. That is one of the reasons that all intercepts took place under Visual

Left: Polish air force aircraft acting as part of the Pyrland Blue Force wore white recognition bands with small black 'Republic of Pyrland' titles, in handwritten script.

Below: Six F-16s of the US Air National Guard's 183rd Fighter Wing made a historic deployment to Powidz air base to participate in Eagle's Talon '97.

Right: The unofficial designation F-16CJ is being applied to the SEAD-capable F-16C Block 52D aircraft of the 52nd FW.

Below: Su-22M4s of the 7. Pulk Lotnictwa Bombowo-Rozpoznawczego/Bomber-Reconnaissance Aviation Regiment faced Red Force Su-22s from its sister unit, the 3rd PLBR. This aircraft carries a KKR reconnaissance pod.

Right: This former 6. PLMB Su-22UM had left its previous base at Pila to take up residence at Powidz, and participated as part of the Blue Force, giving 'famil' and orientation rides to US Air Force personnel.

Identification (VID) rules, meaning that fights only started after the adversary was visually identified. Because both sides flew similar aircraft, Pyrland had painted a large white stripe over the fuselage of its aircraft to ease identification.

The US also brought in the 1st Combat Communications Squadron from Ramstein and the 463rd Airlift Control Squadron from Little Rock AFB, Arkansas. The 606th Expeditionary Air Control Squadron (EACS) from Spangdahlem AB was based at Kresiny. The USAF had moved about 400 personnel and 523,000 tons of cargo by road and transport aircraft, including a C-17 Globemaster III. A KC-135 of the 108th Air Refueling Squadron arrived at Powidz for the final stage of the exercise, but only supported the concluding air power demonstration. The tanker/transport took a portion of the Illinois ANG personnel and equipment back to the US. It was not coincidence that men and women of the Illinois ANG came to Poland. This US state has a special PfP exchange programme because the city of Chicago, in particular, has a large number of immigrants from Poland.

The adversaries (Red Force) had available four MiG-29s of 1. Fighter Regiment at Minsk-Mazowiecki, 12 Su-22M4s of the 3. Fighter Bomber Division (Swidwin-Smardzko AB, Miroslawiec AB),

12 MiG-23MFs of the Slupsk-based 28. Fighter Regiment, 12 MiG-21MFs of 41. Fighter Regiment at Malbork AB, and 12 MiG-21bis of 9. Fighter Regiment at Zegrze Pomorskie. Additional Polish units included SAM sites along the coast, several command and control units, and a liaison team of the 4th Air Corps.

The CASEW had tactical command of Blue Force. Brigadier General Victor Renuart, commander of the 52nd FW, was the Combined Force Air Component Commander (CFACC), with PAF Colonel Marek Ciszewski as co-commander. The 3rd Air Defence Corps/Red Force commander was Brigadier General Baszuk at Bydgoszcz. All air tasking was conducted by a Combined Air Operations Centre manned by 21 US and Polish officers.

The conflict in the former Baltica was fought in the northwest of Poland where the majority of PAF air bases are located. Eastland was the eastern part of Poland, while the western part was equally divided between Northland in the north and Pyrland in the south. The exercise was more firmly organised than multilateral PfP exercises, but

the participants still operated at a cautious pace in the early stages. The Americans used the first two days for familiarisation. During this period they flew pre-planned routes over emergency airfields, trained with Polish SAM regiments, got acquainted with the Nadarzyce air-to-ground range, and reviewed the flying procedures in the exercise area and at Powidz Air Base. On the third day, Polish and American fighters flew together for the first time, although only the 'Fulcrums' were really integrated with the F-15s. The other fighters operated separately. "That day was intended for us just to become used to each other," said 'Fulcrum' pilot Major Andrzej Rogucki of the 1st Fighter Regiment 'Warszawa', who was based at Kresiny for the duration of the exercise. "But soon we were really dogfighting." The air operations took place under Ground Control Intercept (GCI) conditions, using the Polish air defence system augmented by USAFE personnel and equipment. The latter was provided by the Spangdahlem-based 606th ACS. An ACS is a mobile control and reporting centre: with its own

radars and other equipment, it can build a detailed air picture, exchange data and provide GCI anywhere in the world. An ACS is specifically prepared for out-of-area operations. The Polish and American operators worked side by side, although both parties did C^2 primarily for their own fighters. They learned a lot about each other's tactics. A month before the exercise, the Poles had gone to Spangdahlem for familiarisation training. A large portion of the Polish controllers and pilots can speak moderate to good English – a prerequisite for NATO integration.

The second phase of the exercise included the establishment of a buffer zone to protect Pyrland and the demonstration of resolve by overflying Northland as a 'show of force'. Missions were flown in the morning and afternoon, each divided into sub-phases A and B. Sub-phase A involved air policing in which MiG-29s and F-15s established defensive counter air (DCA) combat air patrols while MiG-21s and -23s launched from Strip Alert to intercept any aggressors. Sub-phase B was the 'show of force' phase: packages of Su-22s and F-16Cs escorted by F-16CJs for Suppression of Enemy Air Defences (SEAD) flew routes near SAM sites for training, and visited the Nadarzyce range for practice bombing. The C-130Hs practised airdrops on the Drawsko Pomorskie range where Polish and US armies were conducting an exercise called Brave Eagles. The transition to the high-intensity phase came with a massive air attack on Pyrland by Northland aggressors.

Phase three, held on Saturday and Sunday 13 and 14 September, was also called the peace enforcement phase. Pyrland's intent was to establish a 'No-Fly Zone' over all of Northland and to undertake retaliatory air strikes on Northland. On Sunday morning a large attack was expected from Northland. "Our squadron is responsible for the air defence of the west, while the MiG-29s and F-15s are responsible for the east," said Major Jerzy Serwa of the 3. Air Fighter Regiment that was added to the composite fighter squadron at Kresiny. "But

we do not know when and from which direction the attack will come. That is why we have put a number of aircraft on Strip Alert. They can take off within four minutes of the alert. The MiG-29s and F-15s are to fly combat air patrols." Minutes later, the first 'Fulcrums' and 'Floggers' did indeed taxi out swiftly to counter the attacks. Jerzy Serwa could not resist pointing out that the US aircraft could not start up and take off in such a brief period, which is typical for Russian combat aircraft.

Sunday afternoon was reserved for offensive counter-air operations by 'Fitters' and F-16s. They launched a massive air attack on Northland, including live bomb drops on the Nadarzyce range which had once been used by the Russian air force. The F-16s dropped Mk 82 bombs, while the attacks of the 'Fitters' included dropping fire bombs and strafing the targets with their twin 30-mm guns. Major John Patterson, an F-16 pilot from the Illinois ANG, has fond memories about the exercise. "I am the first American to drop live bombs (here) since World War II." Range time was strictly scheduled, and the Polish and American pilots were managed by their respective range controllers. Personnel were flown to the range in an An-2, a type still in widespread use by the PAF for liaison duties.

One excellent way to create trust, respect and mutual understanding is to fly orientation flights in each other's aircraft. Major Patterson was one of those who

had the opportunity to fly in a PAF combat aircraft. His flight in the Su-22UM3 recalled memories of his time in the F-4 Phantom. "The 'Fitter' has very much the same construction and flight controls. It has good acceleration, much better than I had expected." Poles got the opportunity to fly in the US aircraft. "Most of them like to fly with the sidestick of the F-16," Patterson remarked. "At first they were a bit wary, but they learned quickly." Although the Americans were open with their former Warsaw Pact colleagues, some Poles were a little disappointed. "They can see everything of ours," a 'Fulcrum' pilot said, "but they do set their restrictions." For example, the US flight line was guarded by US guards carrying M16 rifles, and some cockpits were 'for US eyes only'. For Americans, it was still 'business as usual'.

The expected challenges of the

exercise were in the fields of C^2 structure, interoperability, logistics and common procedures. "The principle challenge was to integrate two command and control systems that had been very different for many years," says US spokesman captain Mark Shavers. "Over the course of the exercise we were able to bridge that gap through an open exchange of ideas and experiences." Complete interoperability was not achieved, needless to say. "That will take additional training," Shavers added, "but we feel we have made great progress." For the USAF it proved that long logistic lines of communications were a challenge, but the C-130Hs of the Illinois ANG kept those lines open and maintained a daily shuttle to Spangdahlem. Having the Polish and American pilots, controllers and planners work so closely together also proved fruitful. The importance of liaison officers,

interpreters and translators was emphasised, and the use of liaison officers at every level of command enhanced the effectiveness of the CAOC.

In total, Blue Force flew 160 sorties of the 208 planned, which would have comprised 48 'famil' flights, 17 SEAD, 84 interdiction, 54 defence counter air, and five airlift. Red Force flew 274 sorties. Saturday 13 September was the only day on which all flying activity was cancelled due to bad weather. According to the USAF, Eagle's Talon will be the benchmark for future exercises between NATO and prospective new members.

Without a doubt, this exercise also served as a marketing effort for American hardware. Poland is on the verge of buying Western fighter aircraft. Additionally, a wide variety of other systems need to be procured. During the concluding air power demonstration for VIPs, press and personnel on 16 September, the solo F-16 demonstration was flown by Lockheed Martin pilot

Bland Smith. Curiously, his aircraft, an F-16C of the 52nd FW, was not parked on the guarded American flight line but on the 'Fitter' flight line at the other side of the base, far away from the audience. The majority of Polish pilots are more impressed with the F/A-18 Hornet than the F-16. Still, they are not totally persuaded by Western fighters. A 'Fulcrum' pilot disclosed that he and many of his colleagues would rather see their country buy Su-35s because of the type's agility and versatility. This pilot was nevertheless pragmatic enough to realise that the F-16 was the most likely candidate because of its costs and NATO interoperability.

Meanwhile, phase-outs of aircraft and restructuring of the Polish air force continue. According to MiG-23 pilots, the 'Flogger' will

be phased out of service within two years, when the airframes have reached their maximum flying time. The MiG-21s of the regiment at Poznan are scheduled for retirement in 1998, and some may have been withdrawn by the end of 1997. The MiG-21R reconnaissance variant of the 32. Fighter Reconnaissance Regiment at Sochachew was retired in July 1997. The Su-20 squadron of 7. Bomber Reconnaissance Regiment

retired in May and its reconnaissance task was transferred to the regiment's Su-22M4s. 6. Fighter Bomber Regiment at Pila is being disbanded and the 'Fitters' are being transferred to the remaining three regiments based at Swidwin, Powidz and Miroslawiec. A number of these 'Fitters' had already been operating from Powidz. The latest 'Fishbed' variant, the MiG-21bis, will remain in service for at least another 10 years.

The most potent aircraft in Poland's air force are the MiG-29s of 1. PLM 'Warszawa' – which will ultimately be the first Polish squadron to be declared to NATO.

It remains to be seen how well and how quickly Poland can integrate its old and new hardware and infrastructure with those of NATO, but the lessons learned in Eagle's Talon '97 will surely be valuable.

Gert Kromhout

Right: The lead aircraft in this 9. PLM MiG-21bis two-ship is carrying an R-60 AA-8 'Aphid' acquisition round.

Below: 52nd FW Eagles were tasked with maintaining defensive counter air patrols, along with MiG-29s. Unlike the F-16s, the F-15s had no live weapons exercises.

Lithuania

Karinés Oro Pajégos

Following their independence from the USSR in the early 1990s, the three Baltic States – Estonia, Latvia and Lithuania – established their own armed forces. The Lithuanian Air Force (Karinés Oro Pajégos) is currently the largest air arm in the region, and after its first lustrum is struggling to accomplish its missions with limited funding. More personnel and equipment, and increasing participation in international exercises, are necessary to prepare the KOP to enter the next century – which may include membership in NATO.

Since August 1940, Lithuania had been one of the 15 republics of the USSR, although it was briefly occupied by the Nazis between 1941-44, and together with Estonia and Latvia fell under the Baltic Military District of the Red Army. On 11 March 1990, the Lithuanian Supreme Soviet dominated by the Sajüdis (the 'Movement' calling for independence) declared Lithuania an independent republic, implementing the constitution established on 16 February 1918, which had not lost its validity over the years. The Soviets responded to the independence declaration with massive troop movements around Vilnius for intimidation purposes, but this was scaled down after 2½ months when Sajüdis leader Vytautas Landsbergis agreed to postpone independence for 100 days, and in the meantime to hold talks with the Soviet government regarding independence. Nothing resulted, and on 13 January 1991 Soviet military troops and police stormed various strategic locations in Vilnius, including the central TV tower where 14 people were killed. Although intended to support a Communist coup against the Sajüdis, the action had an adverse effect and was condemned in the West. The situation thereafter remained quiet, until the 19 August 1991 *coup* in Russia against Mikhail Gorbachev. Estonia and Latvia almost immediately called for their independence (Lithuania had done so earlier), and this status was recognised by the West, followed by the Soviet Union on 6 September. On 17 September, the Baltic countries joined the United Nations.

Military aviation

The Karinés Oro Pajégos (Lithuanian Air Force) was established on 1 March 1993, with its headquarters in Kaunas. Earlier, the Ministry of Defence (Krasto Apsauga Ministerija) created an initial form of military aviation (Karo Aviacija) on 2 January 1992 by acquiring 25 An-2 transport aircraft in the same month. The first commander of the KOP was Colonel Zenonas Veg-elevicius, a former VVS pilot – and is still commander today. He finished his flying training at the Chernigov air academy in Ukraine in 1973, whereafter he was a flying instructor on the L-39 Albatros for four years at Chernigov and other Ukraine-based air academies. Then he went to a test unit at Emba near Akhtubinsk in Kazakhstan,

flying the MiG-21 and testing various types of air-to-air and air-to-ground missiles and equipment. In 1990, he finished his service with the Soviet air force and returned to Lithuania as a teacher. One year later, after independence, he joined the Ministry of Defence as an aviation engineer.

Deputy commander of the KOP is Colonel Stasys Murza. "I also finished the Air Academy at Chernigov, but in 1968. I stayed as an instructor, where the present KOP commander later became my student. Throughout my career, from 1964 until 1992, I served in military aviation training units: first in Chernigov, then in Charkov, and thereafter in Lugansk. My main aircraft was the MiG-21. From 1983 I was regiment commander of an L-39C regiment. Later I became deputy commander of the Chernigov academy, flying the MiG-21, MiG-23 and L-39.

"During the first two years at the academy, student pilots fly the L-39. During the third and fourth year, they fly the MiG-21 and MiG-23. Because I was also chief of the flying section, I flew all types."

Albatros acquisition

The KOP began its operations at the small airfield of Barysai, near Siauliai, which acted as a diversion airfield for the large nearby Zokniai base. The Lithuanians bought four Aero L-39C Albatros aircraft from Kyrgyzstan for US$13,000 each, which arrived in Kaunas on 6 February 1993, nearly one month prior to the establishment of the KOP. The air arm had set a requirement for 16 aircraft, but eventually only those four aircraft were obtained from the Lygovaya School near Biskek where a number of aircraft had become superfluous after the break-up of the former USSR. The four Albatrosses formed I. Naikintuvu Eskadrile (I. NE – 1st Fighter Squadron), and the 25 An-2s mentioned earlier formed I. Transporto Eskadrile (I. TE – 1st Transport Squadron). Both units were stationed at Barysai.

Major Alvydas Kazakevicius, chief engineer of special equipment and head of the environmental commission at the KOP HQ in Kaunas, clearly remembers the first flying day of the Albatrosses, on 22 April 1993: "The first day the L-39s flew from Barysai, the Soviets were very surprised and seemed to be unaware of the fact that Lithuania

had acquired jet aircraft. The L-39s were closely monitored by some Su-24s, flying overhead at 15,000 ft altitude, but made no actions."

During the first half of 1993, several units of the VVS were still based on Lithuanian soil, and operated alongside the KOP. This situation posed no major problems, however. According to Colonel Murza, "There were some limitations set for Soviet military aviation in Lithuania; they did not have the opportunity to fly freely over our country." An agreement with Russia included that all flights had to be reported in advance to the Lithuanian authorities, including transit flights from and to the Russian enclave of Kaliningrad. Furthermore, it was (and is) prohibited to carry any kind of armament while over Lithuania. During a brief period, both the Soviet and the Lithuanian air forces had units stationed at Pajouste air base near Panevezys. Murza recalls a peculiar incident: "I once landed at Panevezys air base with an L-39 while diverting from Siauliau due to an emergency. After landing, I was immediately arrested! Obviously, there was no permission from the Soviets to land on their base. It was a very interesting sight: the L-39 standing there guarded by Lithuanian soldiers with assault guns, next to the Soviet aircraft which in turn were guarded by Soviet troops with their assault guns!"

The L-39s of the KOP are of the basic C model and have only two underwing hardpoints. On these stations, they can carry two UB-16-57UMP rocket pods containing 16 57-mm rockets for use against aerial and ground targets. No guns can be carried. During mid-1997, only two Albatrosses were operational; the other two were grounded awaiting engine overhaul. It was expected that all four aircraft would be operational again by the end of 1997. Expanding the budget will mean more flying hours; budget restrictions have resulted in the addition of only eight to nine flying hours annually per airframe.

It is also the intention to have one aircraft stand by on a 24-hour QRA status, able to be airborne in five minutes. "After Mathias Rust landed his Cessna on Red Square in Moscow, the Russian military commanders decided that the best aircraft to intercept a Cessna would be an L-39," joked Murza. "Presently (mid-1997), there is no official government decision to undertake QRA tasks. If such a decision is made – most probably before the end of 1997 – one L-39 will be prepared for this duty. There is only one limitation: the L-39 can't intercept aircraft at speeds faster than 450 km/h. We have some unauthorised flights into Lithuanian airspace, such as illegal immigrant transports and drug smuggling by light aircraft like An-2s and Cessnas, which we will be able to cope with."

The last Soviet troops left Lithuania on 31 August 1993. Two months before, they abandoned their base at Zokniai, which then was immediately taken over by the KOP as it moved its aircraft from the cramped ramp space at Barysai. Subsequently, Zokniai became I. Aviacijos Bazé (1st Air Base) instead of Barysai. In mid-1997, I. NE was redesignated 11 Squadron. Currently, only the far northwestern area of Zokniai is occupied by KOP units, which can operate from two parallel runways orientated east-west. A large part of the base's infrastructure, including taxiways and shelters, was at least partly demolished and left unusable, as would be the case in Pajouste (2nd Air Base).

The KOP has a variety of transport aircraft on strength. Two Let L-410UVP Turbolets were taken over from the German air force, which in turn had inherited these aircraft from the former East German NVA. They have been taken on charge by I. Transporto Eskadrile (I. Transport Squadron, now redesignated 12 Squadron), previously based at Siauliau-Barysai but moved to Zokniai along with the rest. They arrived in Lithuania on 3 March 1993, and after a quick conversion course were manned by KOP aircrew. They can be used for a variety of tasks such as (VIP) transportation flights, communication flights and paradropping.

Similar tasks can be performed by the 10 An-2s of 12 Squadron, although, due to lack of funds and maintenance, very few aircraft remain airworthy. Originally, 25 An-2s were obtained and based at Barysai, from where these aircraft had operated since 1978, although in civil colours. Ten were transferred to II.TE (now 22 Squadron) which was created at the II. Aviacijos Bazé (2nd Air Base) at Panevézys-Pajouste after the departure of the resident Soviet units in August 1993. The status of the unit's An-2s is similar to that at Zokniai. Only three aircraft remained operational in 1997, the other seven aircraft having been placed into open storage and needing considerable overhaul to become airworthy once more.

Also based at Pajouste are three Antonov An-26V transports which form part of 22 Sqn. The An-26s were obtained from Lithuanian civil sources in November 1994, and sported a white colour scheme with a green cheatline. They are now being camouflaged. At the time of writing, two aircraft were temporarily stored at their home base awaiting engine overhaul, but were expected to return to service during the second half of 1997.

The same unit also used a single An-24V, but it was retired in 1996 since lack of funding precluded its mandatory major inspection, including engine overhaul. It was donated to the aviation museum at Kaunas-Aleksotas airfield, a former Soviet army air base, where it is now stored.

The KOP also operates a few helicopters for various duties. One camouflaged Mil Mi-8MTV and two Mi-8T helicopters sporting a white scheme belong to 13 Squadron at Zokniai. These helicopters were acquired after similar examples were demonstrated for military officials during 1992, and were delivered one year later. In addition to their transport tasks, the sole Mi-8MTV and one of the Mi-8Ts are equipped with a hoist over the port forward door for SAR operations; the first was converted in March 1996. In the same year, five Mi-2s were donated by the Polish air force and are presently being operated by 23 Squadron at Panevezys-Pajouste. The KOP's helicopters are overhauled by the Aviabaltica company in Kaunas, which is a former Soviet helicopter maintenance facility but which has come under the control of Lithuania.

Current organisation

In the present KOP command structure, the KOP commander (Colonel Vegelevicius) controls the general staff at the air force HQ in Kaunas, as well as the three base commanders and the airspace surveillance and control base near Kaunas. The latter controls four radar sites in Lithuania: the main base is near Kaunas, and three addi-

Above: Lithuania's four L-39Cs were acquired from Kyrgyzstan via the Lygovaya School, at Biskek. This aircraft is the only one in service to carry a sharkmouth, and it also wears a slightly modified camouflage scheme.

Above and right: There are three active An-26s in the air force inventory, all with yellow codes (above). A further two aircraft are in storage (right) still wearing the last vestiges of their Lithuanian Airlines colour scheme – from whom they were all obtained.

Left and below: At one time the Lithuanian Air Force had 25 An-2s in service, but this number has been greatly reduced and soon only six will remain in everyday use. Aircraft that have been withdrawn from use are stored at Zokniai, a former Soviet Su-24 overhaul base and operational MiG-27, MiG-29 and An-12 regiment base.

tional radar sites are situated near Rokai, Juodkrante and Deguciai. The radar companies are equipped with P-18 (A-band), P-37 (E/F-band), P-40 (E/F-band), Jawor-2M (E/F-band), Koren-As (D-band SSR) and PRV-16 (H-band) equipment, mainly supplied by the Czech RDP Group. There are plans to buy surface-to-air missiles in the near future; their units will fall under KOP command. The 1st Air Base is home to one fighter squadron (11 Sqn – L-39), one transport squadron (12 Sqn – An-2 and L-410) and one helicopter squadron (13 Sqn – Mi-8), while at the 2nd Air Base one transport squadron (22 Sqn – An-2 and An-26), one helicopter squadron (23 Sqn – Mi-2) and one fighter squadron (no aircraft) can be found. 3rd Air Base currently houses neither units nor aircraft.

KOP's current peacetime missions are defined as: (a) air space surveillance, control and defence; (b) air support for the other military services – army, navy and home guard; (c) air transportation; (d) search and rescue operations; (e) activities according to applications of other government organisations such as forest fire spotting, police support and radioactivity monitoring; (f) training aircrew and aviation specialists for other organisations like the Vilnius Aviation Institute and the Latvian air force. Recently, it has been decided to establish a Regional AirSpace Control Centre (RASCC) for all of the Baltic States, which will be situated near Kaunas. Furthermore, an additional SAR detachment will be maintained near the Baltic coast.

SKAT border guard

Lithuania's Home Guard (the Savanoriskoji Krasto Apsaugos Tarnyba/SKAT) operates two squadrons with a variety of support aircraft (An-2, Yak-18T, Yak-52, Yak-55, PZL-104 and Piper Tomahawk), mainly for border patrol. These units are based at Silute (Silutes Eskadrile) near the Baltic Sea and Kyviskes (Vilniaus Dariaus Ir Gireno Eskadrile) near Vilnius. The latter airfield is also used by the Vilnius Aviation Institute. Although the Home Guard is not part of the air force, they co-operate very closely.

Lithuania's participation in international exercises is increasing. The country signed NATO's Partnership for Peace treaty during the Brussels Summit in January 1994. Observers were sent to Exercise Co-operative Zenith '97 from 6 to 17 May 1996, and to the bilateral US-Lithuanian peacekeeping exercise Guardex '96, both held in the United States. Full participation first occurred between 1 and 12 October 1996 during Exercise Baltic Circle: 25 officers and four aircraft (An-26, L-39C, Mi-8T and L-410UVP) joined this event. Some 800 foreign personnel from peacekeeping forces have been transported to and from former Yugoslavia so far. During 1997, aircraft, crew and/or observers were scheduled to join Exercises Co-operative Zenith '97 (Canada), Co-operative Baltic Eye (Sweden), Co-operative Chance (Netherlands), Co-operative Bear (Sweden), Co-operative Safeguard (Iceland) and Baltic Challenge '97 (Estonia). Participation in these exercises, and in air shows in the region, has resulted in closer international contacts. Lithuania's future membership of NATO will possibly be discussed during a summit in 1999.

On the topic of co-operation with Lithuania's neighbouring air arms, Colonel Murza said, "We are training pilots for the Latvian air force; they

undergo conversion here to the L-410. With Poland and Estonia, we don't have close links. The Poles only trained our pilots in flying the Mi-2 helicopters they donated. For them, we are not interesting since we are very small and do not encounter the same problems (as they do)."

Pilot training

KOP pilots were recruited from various sources. Said Murza, "There are two categories of pilots within the Lithuanian Air Force. One group has flown as agricultural pilots on An-2s in the past, about 20 men. The other group came from Soviet military units, trained in military schools. New pilots start their training at the Lithuanian Aviation Institute in Vilnius. The course in this civilian institute lasts for four years. During the first two years they fly Cessna 152s and 172s. In their third year, they make one familiarisation flight in an L-39. Then, in their last year, they continue training on the L-39 to become solo. Three pilots have finished this course so far and joined 11 Sqn at Zokniai."

It is not likely that the KOP will establish its own *ab initio* pilot training programme. "That will be too expensive," Murza explained. "In the Aviation Institute, future pilots receive their aviation training, while on the weekends and after lessons they visit the military academy to follow a small military course. After finishing at the Institute, they receive tactical training in our squadrons. At the Lithuanian military academy, there is no aviation training, so we use this method. We understand that this course is too short to create well-trained military pilots, but we have good contacts in Denmark, Sweden, the United Kingdom, the USA and Germany, and I think that our future military pilots will have to take their courses in these countries. Presently, we have two pilots in training at the United States Air Force Academy at Colorado Springs, Colorado while Lieutenant Colonel Majekis, our chief of aviation services, is currently following a staff course at the German general staff academy. One pilot finished military training in Germany last year.

"A final decision has to be made by our government about the future status and strength of the Lithuanian Air Force. Depending on that, the exact number of pilots needed will be set. So far, we don't have a shortage. Another problem is that our pilots have to learn the English language. One step is taken to encourage this: if someone wants promotion to major or higher ranks, learning English is now compulsory."

New hardware

Future procurement of new equipment will depend on a number of factors, of which money will be the key one. Referring to reports that Poland offered a squadron of second-hand MiG-21s, Colonel Murza said, "This is a big problem. I would like to receive MiG-21s from Poland or the Czech Republic because they are cheap to operate and are still very potent. We have some problems with Russia regarding flights over Lithuania, but it is presently a political problem. About 80 per cent of our pilots have flown the MiG-21, which would reduce problems like training; it would take little time to prepare our pilots. Buying another type – like, for example, the F-16 – means we have to spend more time to prepare. Anyway, I think we have to do something. The MiG-21s are still on offer by Poland."

Other reports suggested that Sweden offered Saab 105s (Sk 60s) to establish a joint Baltic training unit. "For us, the Saab 105 is a very interesting aircraft. Getting these aircraft would allow us to phase out the L-39s in five to seven years. However, like the MiG-21s, this is a problem for the politicians. If we can use these aircraft in Lithuania, it would cost less than if we would have to set up a training programme in Sweden.

"If you ask me what type of aircraft I would like more of, I can say that I personally like the Gripen very much. All new types are very expensive, but, regarding philosophy, I like the Gripen more than the F-16 or Mirage 2000. Secondly, after the year 2000, the F-16 will probably be out of production. If we were to use it, the F-16 would soon be an old type. Why should we buy an old aircraft with all its accompanying problems?"

Decisions for the future

The KOP is not opting to buy new hardware in the near future, other than the offered MiG-21s, according the deputy commander. In 1998, one transport aircraft will be configured for medevac duties. Furthermore, KOP aircraft will be equipped with new navigation equipment and ATC transponders to enable them to co-operate with other NATO countries. The Lithuanian defence budget totals one per cent of the GNP. Of this, about 10 per cent is allocated to the air force. Some 650 personnel including 79 pilots serve in the air force. "In the near future, we will have funding for 950 personnel. More money also means more flights and better training for our aircrew, like training our L-39 pilots for multi-role tasks. The main problem we encounter today is that, although we have new radars and communication equipment, we don't have the personnel to man them permanently. And then, of course, these systems don't work," Murza concluded. **Emiel Sloot**

Karinés Oro Pajégos (Lithuanian Air Force)

KOP HQ, Kaunas

I Aviacijos Bazé (1st Air Base), Siauliai-Zokniai

11 Squadron (NE)	L-39C (4)
12 Squadron (TE)	An-2 (10), L-410UVP (2)
13 Squadron (SE)	Mi-8T (2), Mi-8MTV (1)

II Aviacijos Bazé (2nd Air Base), Panevezys-Pajouste

21 Squadron (NE)	(no aircraft assigned)
22 Squadron (TE)	An-2 (10), An-26 (3)
23 Squadron (SE)	Mi-2 (5)

III Aviacijos Bazé (3rd Air Base), Kazlu Ruda
(no units assigned)

Savanoriskoji Krasto Apsaugos Tarnyba

Vilnaus Dariaus ir Gireno Eskadrile, Kyviskis
Yak-18T, Yak-52, Yak-55, An-2, PZL-104 Wilga, Piper PA-38

Silutes Aviacijos Eskadrile, Silute
Yak-52, An-2, PZL-104 Wilga, L-13, LAK-12, Jantard Standard 3

(The Savanoriskoji Krasto Apsaugos Tarnyba is a voluntary border guard/home guard unit)

Additional material by **Tieme Festner**

...ove: This strangely ...mouflaged An-2 is a SKAT ...rcraft, based at Silutes.

Below: The KOP took delivery of two former East German LET L-410UVPs in 1993.

...ove: This SKAT Yak-55 ...robatic trainer still wears ...old DOSAAF colours.

Below: Yak-52s form part of both SKAT flying units, at Kyviskis and Silute.

Above: This Transport Squadron An-2 wears a well-executed tiger badge, which also appears on the Mi-2s. All Pajouste-based aircraft wear yellow codes.

Right: This black An-2 is attached to the SKAT unit at Kyviskis.

Below: Five Mi-2s were acquired from the Polish air force.

Left and right: The PZL-104 serves as a glider tug for the SKAT glider fleet which includes the locally-built LAK-12 and Czech L-13s (right).

Below right: This KOP Mil Mi-8T crash-landed on 24 July 1997, reducing the active fleet to two.

...e Yak-18T is a four-seat cabin monoplane derived from the original tandem ...o-seat trainer design. This is a Kyviskis-based SKAT example.

E-2 Hawkeye

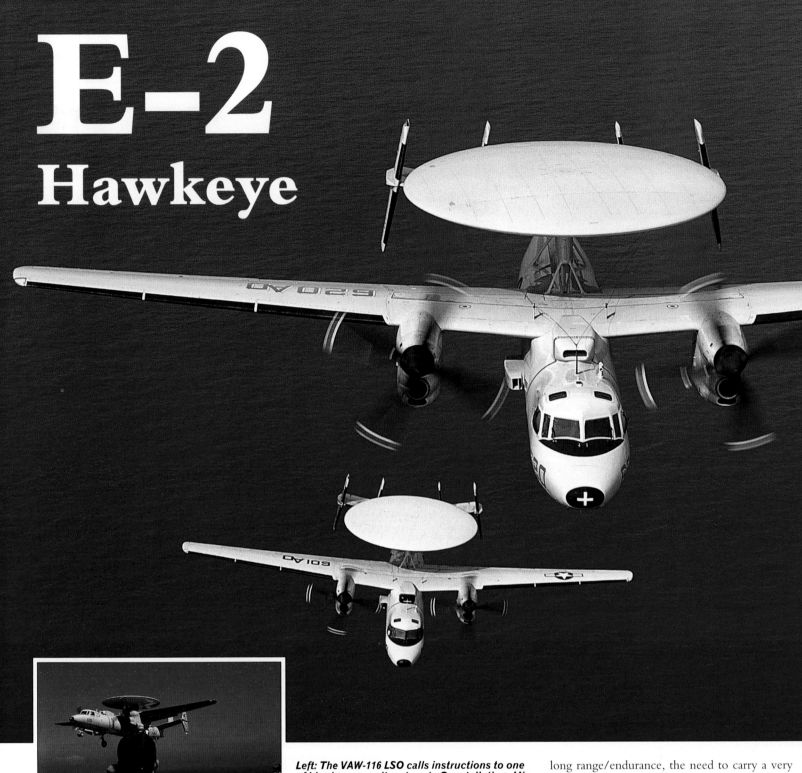

Left: The VAW-116 LSO calls instructions to one of his charges on its return to Constellation. *His tunic reflects the nicknames for the E-2 ('Hummer') and the LSO ('Paddles'), the latter harking back to the days when LSOs used bats to transmit landing instructions.*

When the Grumman G-173 Hawkeye first flew on 21 October 1960, there could have been few witnesses present who would have bet money on the aircraft still being in production nearly 40 years later. Since 1964 the Hawkeye has protected US Navy carrier battle groups and shepherded their aircraft, tasks which it still performs today and most likely will do well into the next century. It has been used operationally in numerous conflicts, and has outlasted all of its contemporaries.

It has seen deck companions come and go, but for over 30 years its traditional haunt at the base of the carrier's island has never been threatened by a replacement. At the time of writing, the envisioned replacement (the Common Support Aircraft) could not realistically be expected in service until around 2020.

Grumman (now Northrop Grumman, and in 1997 itself a likely candidate for a merger with Lockheed Martin) has a long history of integrating airborne early warning systems into carrier-borne aircraft, beginning with the TBF-3W Avenger with APS-20A radar, followed by the AF-2W Guardian (with APS-20E), WF/E-1B Tracer (with APS-82) and finally the W2F/E-2 Hawkeye, which in its initial versions featured the APS-96 radar. The Hawkeye's strange configuration was a result of dramatically conflicting requirements: aerodynamic efficiency for long range/endurance, the need to carry a very large radar in a position where it had a relatively unobstructed 360° view, low carrier approach speed, and the ability to fit onto carrier decks and lifts. Apart from the very similar unflown Yak-44 'Russian copy', the E-2 remains the only aircraft ever designed from the start for the AEW mission

As a result, the aircraft features high aspect ratio (9.27) wings with high-lift devices for long range and low approach speed, a dorsally mounted rotodome to house the radar, a pressurised cabin to house the operators, and efficient T56 turboprop engines. To fit the confines of the hangar deck, the rotodome could be lowered by around 2 ft (0.61 m) when not in use. The height restriction also dictated the use of four vertical fins as a means of providing sufficient keel area, and yaw authority during an asymmetric take-off, without the height exceeding that of the hangar roof; the E-2's height is a remarkable 5.58 m (18.31 ft). The slender wings were fitted with a folding system which hinged the wings back while rotating them through 90° so that they lie parallel to the

Arguably the least glamorous of the aircraft on the US Navy's carrier decks, the E-2 nevertheless has a vital role to perform, one which is central to the carrier battle group's ability to project power on a global basis. No air wing operation could be conceived without the Hawkeye acting as airborne sentinel, watching for hostile action while directing friendly aircraft. In addition to its traditional blue-water defensive role, constant development has allowed the Hawkeye to adapt to other roles which have become increasingly important – littoral and overland operations and theatre missile defence.

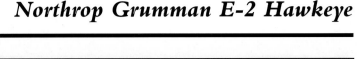

In service for over 30 years, and scheduled to serve for at least 20 more, the Hawkeye remains a vital part of the US Navy carrier air wing. Although the E-2 has changed little externally – highlighting the basic soundness of the original design – its systems have been aggressively updated throughout its career, a process which continues unabated in the 1990s. The result is an aircraft which is set to maintain its position at the forefront of AEW&C technology into the next century.

Above: Representing the original Hawkeye design is W2F-1 (E-2A after 1962) BuNo. 148712, the fifth aircraft built and seen here testing the fuel dump system. Note the original rounded nose profile which distinguished the E-2A/B models from the E-2C.

Below: The propellers of this E-2C leave spiral vortices behind them as they bite into the moist air. The Hawkeye regularly launches ahead of the rest of the carrier air wing, is aloft during the course of two launch/trap cycles, and then lands last after marshalling returning aircraft.

fuselage. With wings folded, the E-2 has a span (across the propeller blades) of 10.68 m (35.04 ft), compared to 24.56 m (80.58 ft) with the wings spread. At 17.60 m (57.75 ft) long, the E-2 is only marginally longer than an F/A-18, and about 6 ft (1.8 m) wider in folded span.

Fully equipped for life on board a carrier, the Hawkeye was tailored for its role with a host of new features, which included an advanced autopilot for flying precise orbits, and an unusual rudder-only turn feature, which made good use of the widely-spaced fins and was employed to keep the radar level during orbits.

E-2As entered service with the Pacific Fleet's VAW-11, and in late 1965 undertook their first Southeast Asia combat cruise. In 1969 the first E-2B conversion was flown, representing a major improvement over the A by virtue of its Litton L-304 digital mission computer. This was swiftly followed by the E-2C, which was dubbed Hawkeye II, so wide-ranging were its improvements. All subsequent US Navy production aircraft have been designated E-2C, but the latest aircraft are very different from the aircraft which first entered service with

VAW-123 in November 1973. Today, this initial batch is known as the Basic E-2C.

Basic 'Charlies' were readily identifiable by a lengthened, reprofiled nose housing antennas for the ALR-59 PDS (Passive Detection System) and a large airscoop added aft of the flight deck, necessary to increase cooling for the new mission equipment. Uprated T56-A-425 engines were installed, with ASN-92 CAINS (Carrier Aircraft Inertial Navigation System) and ASN-50 heading and attitude reference system fitted for accurate overwater navigation. Mission system improvements included doubling the number of L-304 computers and the installation of the APS-120 radar. The new sensor included many features of the APS-111 tested on one E-2A in the late 1960s, the most important of which was the improvement to manual overland tracking by the employment of 'double-delay' technology, which analysed three successive returns from a target to isolate it from the background. The radar was augmented by an APX-72 or -76 IFF system, and was itself raised to APS-125 standard from 1976 with moving target Doppler filters which

effectively provided automatic overland target tracking. Communications was handled by five UHF and two HF radios.

Basic E-2Cs were the mainstay of the fleet until 1980, when an improved version of the Hawkeye started to enter service. When upgraded variants began to appear in a two-stage programme in the late 1980s (known as Group I and Group II), the 1980-standard Hawkeye was retrospectively christened the Group 0. This standard introduced four important features which significantly upgraded its operational effectiveness.

Reducing the sidelobes

Most importantly, the APS-125 radar was replaced by the APS-138 with a TRAC-A (Total Radiation Aperture Control – Antenna). The new antenna design largely rectified a major problem suffered by previous Hawkeyes – large sidelobes which rendered the radar considerably less effective against small targets, especially over land. The TRAC-A antenna allowed the APS-138 system to increase its detection range of small overland targets to

A Group II Hawkeye from VAW-116 floats over Constellation's churning wake. The Hawkeye is relatively docile during the approach but its wide span makes alignment with the centreline crucial to avoid hitting obstacles to either side.

around 120 nm (138 miles; 222 km). The more sharply focused beam made the APS-138 far less prone to enemy jamming.

Other elements of the Group 0 1980 upgrade included the replacement of the elderly ALR-59 PDS with the ALR-73, which provided much greater angular accuracy for the passive detection of targets way beyond radar range, and the expansion of the computer memory to 16K. Communications were enhanced by the addition of ARC-182 Have Quick jam-resistant radio. Group 0 aircraft (although not then known as such) ruled the roost for most of the 1980s, and are still in service today, although

Although it is a relatively large aircraft, the Hawkeye is very manoeuvrable on deck. The angle of the nosewheel here gives some idea of the turning circle achievable.

plans to upgrade them to Group II standard were terminated as the cost of the modification (which included a full structural relifing for carrier service to at least 2020) were not far short of a new aircraft. Fifty-five aircraft were built to the Group 0 standard.

In 1988 the first of 18 Group I aircraft appeared, and this type entered service with VAW-112 in August 1989. The Group I had new engine flight deck instruments and revised lighting, a cooling system with 12-ton (as opposed to 10-ton) capacity, an SCADC (standard central air data computer) and improved APS-139 radar. The radar was augmented by a vastly improved mission computer system which, although still based on the L-304, had high-speed processors that effectively quadrupled the number of tracks it could follow compared to the E-2C Group 0, which could handle 400. For the pilots, however, the main difference was the installation of the T56-A-427 engines. Rated at 5,250 eshp (3916 ekW), the Dash 427 provided a significant power increase,

combined with increased reliability and reduced fuel-burn. To make it more attractive to land-based operators, the Dash 427 incorporates a low-speed ground idle setting, which had hitherto been considered unnecessary as the E-2 had been designed only with carrier operations in mind. Although the new engines had been flown in a Hawkeye as early as 1986, it was not until 17-19 December 1991 that they were given an impressive public outing when a Group I Hawkeye (BuNo. 163535) was used to set a series of 20 time-to-height, closed-circuit speed and altitude records.

Group II Hawkeye

Significant though the improvements introduced by Group I were, they merely provided a springboard for a far more advanced Hawkeye – the Group II. This entered service in June 1992 with VAW-113 and consists of both new-build aircraft and conversions from 12 Group I aircraft. Having initially equipped the Pacific Fleet with Group IIs (leaving the Atlantic Fleet with Group 0s), the US Navy is progressing rapidly towards an all-Group II fleet. What follows is a detailed description of the Group II's systems.

At the heart of the E-2's mission avionics system is the L-304 computer processing system, also known as the OL-77/ASQ. It takes inputs from the radar, IFF, PDS and navigation systems, processes the data and presents it on the three main displays. The L-304 can also receive and output data into the communications suite. The mission can be preplanned and loaded into the L-304 by the TAMPS (Tactical Aircraft Mission Planning System), and there is a recorder incorporated for subsequent analysis of the data input. The whole mission system has an IFPM (In-Flight Performance Monitoring) system for self-test, which operates every three to four seconds.

New to the Group II is the phenomenal Lockheed Martin APS-145 ARPS (Advanced Radar Processing System) with its fan beam antenna. The latter is the Randtron APA-171 antenna array/rotodome assembly, which incorporates the IFF system. The radar provides fully automated operation with continuous coverage

The Schoolhouse

For much of the Hawkeye's career there were two training units: VAW-110 at Miramar ('NJ', below) for the West Coast and VAW-120 at Norfolk ('AD', right) for the East Coast. Today the latter is entrusted with all Hawkeye training, operating a sizeable number of aircraft. It also handles C-2 Greyhound training with a handful of aircraft using AD-63x Modex numbers.

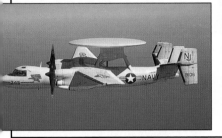

from the surface to high altitude. It has a single operating mode that offers simultaneous detection/tracking for both surface (maritime) and airborne targets. The radar works in 10 channels, which are automatically monitored and selected for optimum performance (to avoid interference) or to combat jamming, and incorporates an AMTI (airborne moving target indicator). A major advance is the triple-PRF operation, also known as blind-speed control, which cancels the clutter encountered at certain frequencies by earlier two-PRF radars and which caused gaps in the radar's coverage. Furthermore, the rotodome can operate at variable speeds between five and six rpm (previously operated at a fixed six) for greater options.

Environmental processing

Naturally, the radar incorporates advanced ECCM (electronic counter-countermeasures), and it has an advanced environmental processing operation. The latter breaks down the radar scan (or at least that part of the scan that grazes the surface) into around 4,000 processing cells, each 5.6° in angular width and typically 4 miles (6.43 km) in length. The system identifies the type of terrain that is contained within that cell (sea, flat terrain, rough terrain, etc.) and gates itself automatically to remove the ground clutter (high clutter from rough terrain, very low from a calm sea surface). Previously, this job had been done manually.

Height-finding of targets is accomplished by using DTOA (differential time of arrival) techniques rather than by an elevation scan. Each target gives two radar returns: one which reflects straight back to the E-2's radar and another which bounces down off the surface and then up to the radar. The position of the target is known accurately because of the radar plot, so, by measuring the time difference between the straight and reflected returns, it is a simple geometric exercise to compute the target's altitude.

Equally impressive is the new IFF system with Hazeltine OL-483/AP airborne interrogator. It operates co-directionally with the radar (as opposed to operating half a revolution behind as on the E-3), making it much easier to solve multipath anomalies. It has an increased throughput compared to earlier IFF systems, enabling it to operate effectively in a difficult airborne environment with many targets. It has an overlapping 'degarbling' function to handle multiple targets with small range separations. As it is fully integrated with the mission computer, the IFF data is therefore fully integrated with traces from the other primary systems (radar and PDS), and the traces can be recorded for later playback. It, too, has an IFPM function for self-test.

For passive detection the ALR-73 PDS remains unchanged from previous Hawkeyes. With antennas in the nose of the aircraft and in the outer endplate fins, the PDS offers 360° coverage, and operates simultaneously in four frequency bands. Up to 250 passive tracks can be followed. The PDS receives signals from a wide range of emitters, and analyses them to determine PRF (pulse repetition frequency), frequency, PW (pulse width), scan rate and modulation type. The PDS has a preloaded threat library which stores the individual intelligence 'I-files' of many known radar systems. The precise location of emitters can be computed using triangulation (that is, by measuring the bearing of the emitter from different positions along the Hawkeye's flight path).

As can be imagined, a huge amount of data from the radar, IFF and PDS has to be assimilated by the L-304 computer. In the Group II aircraft this has EHSP (Enhanced High-Speed Processing) which allows the computer to follow over 1,600 'live' tracks, that is those produced by the radar and IFF. In addition, the system can handle an additional 800-plus GRP (geo, remote, passive) tracks. Geo tracks correspond to fixed land points (such as airfields) while passive tracks are those generated by the PDS. Remote tracks are those received through datalinks and are generated by offboard sensor systems. The system can also handle over 20 simultaneous intercept solutions.

Secure voice and datalink

Communications are handled by a comprehensive suite which incorporates two HF radios for secure voice and Link-11 air-to-ground tactical data (ARQ-34), three VHF/UHF Have Quick secure voice radios and three UHF radios which handle the functions of secure voice transmission, communications relay, Link-4A air-to-air and Link-11 air-to-ground

Deck crew clear the cat as a VAW-126 'Hummer' waits for launch. The blast deflector is raised, the nosewheel tow strut attached to the catapult shuttle and the aircraft is moments from launch. The glazed panel on the underside of the nose protects the aircraft's twin landing lights and 'traffic light' landing indicator set.

Northrop Grumman E-2 Hawkeye

Pacific Fleet Hawkeyes

VAW-112 was one of several Pacific Fleet Hawkeye squadrons established on 20 April 1967 from the various detachments of VAW-11.

VAW-115 is the Hawkeye squadron for CVW-5, forward-deployed in Japan with a shore base at Atsugi. Here a 'Sentinels' E-2C flies past Mount Fuji.

VAW-113 became the first Group II squadron, receiving its first aircraft in June 1992. In 1993 it undertook an evaluation cruise in Carl Vinson.

VAW-116 was one of several E-2 squadrons which operated during Desert Storm. It then flew from Ranger, but is now assigned to Constellation.

VAW-114 'Hormel Hawgs' was officially disbanded on 31 March 1995 along with the remainder of Air Wing Fifteen.

VAW-117 was a late-comer to the Pacific Fleet, not standing up until 1 July 1974. It is currently assigned to Air Wing Eleven.

data transmission (ARC-150). Finally, the Group II Hawkeye introduces the Link-16 JTIDS (Joint Tactical Information Distribution System).

A crew of five operates the Hawkeye, comprising two pilots and three weapon systems operators. The pilots of the Group I/II aircraft welcome the extra power of the Dash 427 engines, which provide a cross-bleed start facility, better single-engine climb performance and, to the delight of Navy 'bean-counters', a 13 per cent reduction in fuel-burn. The ASN-92/ASN-50 navigation suite is retained from earlier aircraft, but the Group II aircraft also incorporate GPS (global positioning system). GPS data are displayed on joint JTIDS/GPS display units on both the flight deck and in the cabin.

The three systems operators occupy the main cabin, seated side-by-side facing to port. With the consoles installed, together with seats and the racks of electronic equipment, there is little spare room. In Hawkeye parlance the cabin is known as the CIC (Combat Information Center) and has three consoles. At the centre console sits the CICO (Combat Information

Center Officer), who is the mission commander. Although the pilots are responsible for navigation and safety, it is the CICO who chooses the location, altitude and orientations of patrols to fulfil the tasking. The CICO is also responsible for assigning tasks to the operators sitting to either side, and controlling the workshare in the CIC. Communications with command authorities at land bases or in the carrier's own CIC would largely fall to the CICO.

To the CICO's right sits the RO (Radar Operator), whose initial task is to turn the equipment on, usually before the aircraft has taken off. Traditionally it was the RO's job to monitor and adjust the equipment to maintain optimum performance of the system, but the high level of automation has largely removed this requirement. He/she now acts as an airborne controller, albeit junior to the other two operators.

On the CICO's left is the ACO (Air Control Officer). The initial task in this seat is to establish communications links with other air defence elements such as interceptors and the carrier's CIC. Again this is accomplished on

deck or land. When 'on task', the ACO joins the RO and CICO in monitoring aircraft and controlling friendlies.

New displays

In Hawkeyes up to and including Group I, each WSO had a round monochrome main display, but in the Group II this has been changed for an 11-in (27.94-cm) square screen with colour symbology, known as the EMDU (Enhanced Main Display Unit). This provides a graphic representation of the main computer's processed data. Each operator can choose which information is displayed to suit their particular tasks.

A base map is often displayed, showing coastlines, political borders and special areas (for instance, 'No-Fly Zones' or missile engagement zones). GRP tracks can be overlaid, showing the positions of airfields and radar sites. On top can then be overlaid the radar/IFF data, using different symbology for various types of vehicle. Simple geometric shapes are used to denote fighters, commercial aircraft, ships and the like. Using the IFF equipment allows each target

symbol to be displayed in a colour according to its status (for instance, blue for friendly, orange for unknown and red for hostile). The use of colour greatly eases the rapid interpretation of the tactical display.

Each symbol is also annotated with course, speed and altitude. Using a lightpen, a controller can 'hook' a specific target to a friendly fighter, and the computer will automatically work out an intercept vector. For suitably-equipped fighters (notably the F-14 Tomcat), a datalink transfers the local situation display and intercept information straight into the F-14's rear cockpit without the need for voice transmissions. A key feature of the new EMDU is its 'windows' approach. This allows information to be displayed in a small window on the main screen, and can also show magnified areas of the display for detailed analysis or control work. The main display remains behind the windows. Of course the main display itself can be changed in magnification, available range scales being 25, 75, 125, 200, 300, 400, 500 and 1,000 nm.

Each WSO has a central EMDU which is flanked by software, display and range scale controls to the left, and alphanumeric data entry panels to the right. Above the EMDU is the upper main display which has video distribution and intensity controls. Below the EMDU is the ADU (Auxiliary Display Unit) which displays alphanumeric track information, system status and initialisation parameters for the avionics system. A software function select panel allows each WSO full access to the hundreds of options available.

Individual controls

At the central console, the CICO has main control of the voice communications suite, and his/her console is flanked with UHF/VHF radio controls, although any of the three WSOs can access the radios once they have been tuned to the correct frequencies. Further to the right are the controls for the radar and IFF, traditional responsibilities for the RO. To the left of the CICO's console are the HF and datalink controls, operated by the ACO. Included in them is the new MFCDU (Multi-Function Control Display Unit) which is the dual Link-16 JTIDS and GPS display mentioned previously. Another MFCDU is installed on the flight deck, and the pilots have the use of one of the three UHF/VHF radios carried. Each WSO console has individual lighting, clocks and ventilation, while instruments for basic aircraft information (heading, altitude, airspeed) are repeated above the CICO's console.

Easy access to all of the systems controls, including communications and intercom, makes crew co-ordination much easier than with a larger AEW system, while the system is fully automated to make good the lack of personnel. Although there exists a difference in experience between the three systems operators, there are no specialisations, and each can undertake all facets of system initialisation and operation.

Unlike that of the E-3 AWACS, the E-2C's system is fully operational at take-off, and the aircraft can be 'on task' as soon as it is airborne.

TRAILING WIRE ANT.

In the defensive role the primary reason for having an AEW aircraft in the first place is to extend the radar horizon, so that low-flying (less than 100 ft/30 m) aircraft can be detected a long way from the carrier. Within three minutes of take-off the Hawkeye can reach 10,000 ft (3048 m), from where the radar horizon is already 125 nm (143 miles; 231 km). After eight minutes it has reached 20,000 ft (6,097 m) with a horizon of around 180 nm (207 miles; 333 km), and after 18 minutes reaches its initial operational cruise height of 30,000 ft (9146 m), from where the horizon is 220 nm (253 miles; 407 km) away. A standard

patrol can last for six hours, during which time the aircraft slowly climbs as it burns off fuel. A six-hour mission will 'reach the top' at about 37,000 ft (11280 m), by which time a second E-2 will be on station during continuous operations. A defensive patrol close to base could be extended to 10 hours with a single inflight refuelling, although at present the US Navy has only a trials aircraft fitted for receiving.

Similarly, the Hawkeye is very valuable for vectoring tankers and receivers to smooth the refuelling process, and in a search and rescue operation can provide radar top cover.

In peacetime the Hawkeye has a valuable drug interdiction role, although its full-time use by the US Coast Guard in this role (taken over from the US Customs Service) has ended due to high cost. Nevertheless, US Navy E-2s are still tasked with anti-smuggling missions as and when required. Surface surveillance can also be targeted against smuggling, and in a combat scenario it provides a useful warning against potential raids, especially by small coastal craft.

Interrupted production

Production of 139 E-2C Hawkeyes at the old Grumman plant at Calverton, New Jersey, came to an end in 1994 following budgetary cuts in FY 1992. Work continued, however, at the Fort Augustine plant in Florida, where retrofits from Group I to Group II were undertaken. The first of 12 aircraft was redelivered to the US Navy on 21 December 1995, and this work ended in 1997. All of these updated aircraft went to the Atlantic Fleet. By this time low-rate Group II production had been reinstated at Fort Augustine and the plant expects to turn out four aircraft per year for the US and future export machines. Engineering work is handled by Northrop Grumman's Electronic and Systems Integration Division at Bethpage, New York.

Capable though the Group II is, development has far from stopped on the aircraft, which is expected to lead to the next generation E-2, known loosely as the Group II Plus, or Hawkeye 2000. Already flying in some aircraft is a new navigation system, CAINS 2, while a Standard AFCS (Automatic Flight Control System) is also installed.

For offensive operations, or defensive patrols further from base/carrier, the E-2 has an unrefuelled time on station of 4 hours at 300 nm (345 miles; 555 km) from base or just over an hour at a 600-nm (690-mile; 1111-km) radius, these figures rising to 7½ hours and 4½ hours respectively with one refuelling. At extreme range a refuelled one-hour station can be undertaken at 1,000 nm (1,151 miles; 1852 km) radius. During maximum intensity operations the E-2 can be turned round and airborne again in under 15 minutes, including a crew change and refuelling.

Far-sighted radar

At its operating altitude the Group II Hawkeye has an impressive reach. As previously noted, low-flying fighter-size aircraft can be detected at more than 220 nm (253 miles; 407 km) distance (the effective horizon), while aircraft at altitude can be seen at about 300 nm (345 miles; 555 km). Low-flying cruise missiles show up at more than 120 nm (138 miles; 222 km), while helicopters can be tracked from about 100 nm (115 miles; 185 km) distance. In the simultaneous maritime surveillance role, detection range for small patrol boats is more than 125 nm (143 miles; 231 km). Altogether, the scan volume of the APS-145 encompasses six million cubic miles of airspace.

This capability can be put to effective use in a number of ways, many of which can be performed simultaneously. The primary role is defensive – providing early warning of approaching aircraft using radar, IFF and the PDS. The Hawkeye system can then be used to direct appropriate reactions, being able to vector interceptors accordingly. A datalink can be maintained with a ground/carrier-based command centre and a real-time picture can be presented to commanders.

On offensive operations the Hawkeye is used to provide AEW cover for the attack force, warning of hostile fighters and assigning targets to the fighter escort, and also providing airspace management to ensure deconfliction among friendly units. The PDS provides a useful Elint system to monitor hostile air defence radar activity and warn of its presence. The recovery of a large strike package can be a potentially dangerous time, and the Hawkeye will effectively manage the traffic entering the pattern to avoid mid-air accidents and to regulate the spacing as aircraft return to the carrier.

Hawkeyes in the Atlantic Fleet

Like those of the Pacific Fleet, the Atlantic Fleet Hawkeye detachments (from parent squadron VAW-12) were raised to squadron status, on 1 April 1967. VAW-121 was one of the initial tranche of three units which stood up on that date.

VAW-124, established on 1 September 1967, was aboard John F. Kennedy during its 1996 Atlantic cruise, the highlight of which was a visit to Ireland.

VAW-122 'Steeljaws' was the unlucky Atlantic Fleet E-2 squadron when the fleet reduced from six to five air wings. It was assigned to CVW-6.

VAW-125, established on 1 October 1968, took a leading role in Desert Storm, when one of its aircraft directed two Hornets to shoot down two Iraqi F-7s.

VAW-123 aircraft feature a huge spiral marking on top of the rotodome. The unit was one of the initial three Atlantic units to stand up.

The last of the Atlantic Fleet E-2 units, VAW-126 was formed on 1 April 1969. This is the current incarnation of the squadron's 'Seahawk' nose marking.

Far more important is the next logical step in Hawkeye evolution – the MCU (Mission Computer Upgrade). With Group II the Litton L-304 computer had reached saturation point, despite the integration of the latest in high-speed processors. To enable the E-2 to continue to develop its potential, a new computer was required. The unit chosen was the Raytheon Model 940, which is a modification of the Digital Equipment Corporation 2100 Model A500MP system and similar to that used in the E-8C J-STARS. This is a commercial computer, modified for Navy use under the E²COTS (Extended Environment Commercial Off-The-Shelf) programme, which uses Ada language as opposed to the previous Assembly. The computer offers greater memory and faster processing compared to the L-304, and its open architecture offers large potential for improvement and expansion in the future. Furthermore, the new computer is considerably lighter, and takes up a lot less precious room in the E-2's cramped cabin than the old equipment.

Accompanying the MCU are new workstations produced by Lockheed Martin/APL. Dubbed ACIS (Advanced Control Indicator Set), the new displays have a 19-in (48-cm)

square screen. Each ACIS is a single LRU (line-replaceable unit), as opposed to four LRUs with the old displays. ACIS and MCU first flew in a trials modification aircraft on 24 January 1997 and were evaluated at Patuxent River. New production E-2s will incorporate the MCU/ACIS, while retrofit kits will be manufactured for existing aircraft. An important facet of the Group II Plus is its increased capability in the TMD (Theatre Missile Defence) role, which has become increasingly important with the proliferation of 'Scud'-type weapons. Detection, tracking and classification of such missiles can be accomplished far more quickly with the new system, providing the opportunity for a realistic defence.

Sensor fusion

Another improvement being developed for the Hawkeye 2000/Group II Plus is the incorporation of CEC (Co-operative Engagement Capability), the US Navy's multi-platform sensor fusion system. This allows vessels to share sensor information about threats from a variety of platforms. The E-2 will become the airborne node of the CEC, giving the fleet a far deeper field of vision. Incorporation of CEC will

require the addition of a large ventral antenna. CEC is expected to fly in a test Hawkeye in early 1998, the same aircraft also featuring fully integrated satellite communications antennas (some aircraft have a satcom installation already). The satcom systems offers secure dual-band voice transfer, with full datalink capability expected to be funded at a later date. All the additional equipment will require a new cooling system to provide greater capacity. The Allied Signal vapour-cycle hardware provides the opportunity to switch to an 'environmentally-friendly' non-freon coolant (R134a). CEC, satcoms and the new cooling system are expected to enter fleet service in 1999, while the full-up Group II Plus is expected to attain IOC in 2000 following Navy evaluation in 1999. All Hawkeye 2000 aircraft will be upgraded from current Group II production.

In addition to the main elements of the Hawkeye 2000 upgrade, Northrop Grumman is planning to add a passive IRST (infra-red search and track) sensor (considered and rejected some years ago). A development contract was awarded for this in 1996 and test hardware was due to appear in 1997. The IRST will be podded, and mounted front and rear to provide 360° cover-

Left: A VAW-116 E-2 takes the No. 2 wire. All five Hawkeye squadrons of the Pacific Fleet are equipped with the Group II version, as was VAW-114 before its disbandment.

Below: The Roman 'II' on the nose identifies the lead aircraft of this pair as the first E-2C Group II (BuNo. 164108). This followed 100 Basic/Group 0 and 18 Group I aircraft (of which 12 were upgraded to Group II). Before E-2C production was shut down in 1994, 21 Group IIs were built for service with the Pacific Fleet. With manufacture reinstated at Fort Augustine, at least 14 further Group IIs have been funded, to bring the total of the latest variant so far to 47.

age. An upgrade to the PDS is also being studied. In 1997 the US Navy fitted an E-2C at the NAWC-AD Patuxent River with an inflight-refuelling probe. It is mounted above the flight deck with pipes carrying the fuel around the forward fuselage back into the centre-section fuel tanks.

Beyond Group II Plus, Northrop Grumman is studying further enhancements. A radar modernisation programme is in place to continue the improvement of the radar's abilities. Key features of this are a solid state transmitter, hi-dynamic range receivers, a new ADS-18A phased-array antenna and the adoption of STAP (Space/Time Adaptive Processing) technology.

Another study involves a 'tactical cockpit' with a missionised co-pilot's position. The latter will make the co-pilot more involved with the surveillance tactics in addition to his/her normal flight duties.

Overseas sales

The above describes the US Navy Hawkeye variants and their operations, but Grumman (and its successors) has also been successful in selling the Hawkeye abroad, and is actively involved in promoting the system (with or without the E-2 platform) to new customers. All of the customers so far (with the exception of France) have bought the aircraft for land-based operations, despite efforts early in the Hawkeye's career to sell the aircraft to the Royal Navy (when it still operated conventional fixed-wing carriers) and France.

Unsurprisingly, the first customer was Israel. It purchased four Hawkeyes in 1977/78, all to Basic E-2C standard (now also known as 'pre-Group 0'). These aircraft were flown by 192 Squadron at Hatzerim, and had the local name Daya (Kite) bestowed on them. Israeli E-2s saw some action, notably during the brief 1982 air war over the Beka'a Valley, in which they guided F-15s and F-16s to a claimed total of 85 kills over Syrian fighters. They also provided warning to strike aircraft, keeping Israeli losses to a minimum, and generally policed the flow of traffic into and out of the warzone. It is also likely, although unconfirmed, that 192 Sqn played its part in the raids on the Osirak nuclear plant in Iraq in 1981 and the raid on the PLO headquarters in Tunis in 1985. In the early 1990s the E-2Cs acquired inflight-refuelling probes, but by 1997 their operational status was unknown. Their recent use has been described as 'sporadic', while other sources suggest they have been put into storage pending disposal. The development of indigenous AEW systems such as the Phalcon may have rendered the aircraft surplus to requirements.

Between 1982 and 1985 eight E-2Cs to Group 0 standard arrived at Misawa for service with the JASDF's 601 Hikotai, a direct-reporting unit. Five more aircraft were added in 1992/93 to bring the total to 13. The sale to Japan had been a long and at times bitter affair, but once in service the E-2s rapidly established their value by extending coverage to the north. The choice of Misawa as the Hawkeye base was

Naval Reserve

From 1970 until recently the US Naval Reserve manned two full air wings, each with an AEW component (E-2 from 1973). VAW-78 operated with the East Coast CVWR-20 while VAW-88 flew with the West Coast CVWR-30. Both used E-2Bs for some time after the E-2C became front-line equipment, although both received 'Charlies' in the 1980s. When the Reserve was cut back to just one air wing, the West Coast unit was deactivated, along with its constituent squadrons. Although this saw the demise of VAW-88, the Reserve then stood up a Hawkeye unit (VAW-77) at Atlanta. The squadron's E-2Cs are not assigned to carrier operations, but instead undertake anti-drug smuggling patrols, operating over the southern United States and the Caribbean. In this role the unit has replaced the Hawkeyes previously operated by the US Coast Guard.

VAW-78 'Fighting Escargots' is the USNR carrierborne AEW squadron, based at Norfolk.

The 'Cottonpickers' of VAW-88 were based at Miramar, and flew as part of Reserve Air Wing 30.

Above: Painted in high-visibility markings, this E-2C Group II is the flagship of the training unit, VAW-120. The squadron operates a mix of Groups 0, I and II, in addition to its C-2 Greyhounds.

*Right: VAW-117's CAG-bird Group II Hawkeye leaps from the deck of **Kitty Hawk**. The extra power of the T56-A-427 engines and the extensive high-lift devices make the latest Hawkeye a sprightly performer around the deck, and greatly increase the single-engined safety margins.*

far from coincidental: located in the north of the island of Honshu, it is conveniently located for providing radar coverage to the north of Japan, near to Russia. Throughout the 1980s the Japanese faced increasing probing flights from Soviet aircraft, and on several occasions were presented with large formations of Tu-16/22/22Ms flying attack profiles towards Japanese territory, breaking away close to their airspace. The Hawkeyes provided vital early warning of these mock attacks, enabling interceptors to be in the air much earlier than a ground-based defence would have allowed.

Despite having procured four Boeing E-767 AWACS platforms, Japan is now considering the upgrade of its E-2s to Group II standard with APS-145 radar. Although able to function as the primary AEW vehicle, the E-2C is also a very effective 'gap-filler' in a larger air defence system, and its proven ability to work directly with fighters in large-scale intercept situations is of great attraction to nations facing real threats from many directions.

Defending the republic

Singapore is just such a nation. A major economic stronghold situated at the crossroads of Southeast Asia, the tiny state has built a powerful defence force since it chose independence in 1971. Not blessed with long borders along which to position ground radars, Singapore required an airborne radar platform as its only effective means of providing warning of any attack. Accordingly, four E-2C Group 0 Hawkeyes were purchased for service with No. 111 Squadron. The aircraft remained in the United States after their initial handover to allow crew training, and did not become operational at Tengah until March 1987. Like Japan, Singapore is actively evaluating an upgrade programme. It would certainly go as far as

Group II as part of a phased modernisation, but may even go straight to the forthcoming Group II Plus configuration.

In the Middle East, Israel was joined by Egypt as a Hawkeye operator, taking delivery of five Group 0 aircraft in 1986 for service from Cairo West. They were joined by a sixth aircraft in 1993. The aircraft have been updated to a unique Group 0/II ('Group I½') hybrid status, employing the square colour EMDU displays and new IFF system of the Group II, but retaining APS-138 radar. In 1997 a decision was expected to complete the upgrade with the APS-145 radar.

Taiwan joined the Hawkeye club in 1995, when it received its four aircraft. In so doing the RoCAF became the first customer to use refurbished US Navy aircraft (in this case E-2Bs). The rework programme, which resulted in the new designation E-2T (for Taiwan), raised the aircraft to full Group II standard, with APS-145 radar. The Hawkeyes achieved IOC with 78 Sqn at Pingtung in 1996, and now provide a welcome extension of radar coverage across the Formosa Strait. 78 Squadron is part of the 6th (439th) Troop Carrier and Anti-Submarine Combined Wing, and its aircraft are

Specification
Northrop Grumman E-2C Hawkeye
Powerplant: two Allison T56-A-427 turboprops, each rated at 5,100 eshp (3803 ekW) and driving Hamilton Standard Type 54460-1 four-bladed constant-speed propellers
Dimensions: wingspan 80 ft 7 in (24.56 m); length 57 ft 9 in (17.60 m); height 18 ft 3¾ in (5.58 m); wing area 700 sq ft (65.03 m²); tailplane span 26 ft 2½ in (7.99 m); rotodome diameter 24 ft 0 in (7.32 m); wheel track 19 ft 5¾ in (5.93 m); wheelbase 23 ft 2 in (7.06 m)
Weights: empty 40,484 lb (18363 kg); maximum take-off 54,426 lb (24687 kg); maximum usable fuel 12,400 lb (5624 kg)
Performance: maximum speed 389 mph (626 km/h); maximum cruising speed 374 mph (602 km/h); carrier approach speed 119 mph (191 km/h); stalling speed 86 mph (138 km/h); minimum take-off run 1,850 ft (564 m); landing run 1,440 ft (440 m); service ceiling 37,000 ft (11275 m); ferry range 1,773 miles (2854 km)

thought to regularly operate from fighter bases such as Ching Chuan Kang. The entry of the Hawkeye into service coincides more or less with that of three new fighter types: AIDC Ching-Kuo, Dassault Mirage 2000-5 and Lockheed Martin F-16. More E-2s may be purchased at a later date.

At the time of writing only one other firm

Above: Japan operates a force of 13 E-2Cs with 601 Hikotai. Since the first deliveries in 1982 the steadily-growing fleet has been busy monitoring Soviet/Russian activity around the northern approaches to Japan.

Left: In 1997 this E-2C (BuNo. 164109 – the second Group II and MCU/ACIS testbed) was fitted with an inflight-refuelling probe, positioned centrally above the flight deck and with a conduit leading aft to the centre-section fuel tanks.

Below: Much of the new equipment under development for the US Navy's Hawkeye fleet is evaluated by the Force Test squadron of the NAWC-AD at Patuxent River. BuNo. 163029, seen here, was built as the first Group I aircraft, but was subsequently upgraded to Group II standard and fitted with additional internal test equipment (painted orange to avoid confusion with fixed kit).

customer order was outstanding, that being for France's Aéronavale. Sporadic attempts to sell Hawkeye to the French were going on since the early days of the E-2's career. The Armée de l'Air evaluated the aircraft in 1980, and the navy evaluated it in 1991, leading to the current order. The $562 million contract for two E-2C Group II Plus aircraft was eventually signed on 28 April 1995. Hawkeyes have been procured as part of a major three-pronged effort to radically modernise the French navy's carrier capabilities. A new nuclear-powered aircraft-carrier, the FNS *Charles de Gaulle*, is due to enter service in 1999, equipped with Dassault Rafale Ms as its primary fighter asset. Hawkeyes are an essential part of the ability to provide a wide-reaching air defence for the new carrier.

Training of French crews began in June 1997, with the first delivery slated for the end of October. The second aircraft is expected to be delivered in January 1998. The two aircraft are scheduled to remain in the United States for training and carrier qualifications in November 1998, followed by the ferry flight to their new shore base at Lann-Bihoué. In March 1999 a 4 Flottille Hawkeye is due to make its first landing aboard *Charles de Gaulle*. The Aéronavale has signed for two more E-2Cs, although the future of these two aircraft is in some doubt, especially since the election of the budget-cutting Jospin government.

Possible customers

Numerous other nations are currently studying the procurement of AEW platforms, and naturally the Hawkeye is a major candidate. In Europe, Greece, Italy, Spain and Turkey are in the middle of major studies, while elsewhere Malaysia, Thailand, South Korea and a combined Gulf Co-operation Council force are being eyed as highly potential Hawkeye customers. With the replacement of the US Navy fleet by Group II aircraft, numbers of Group 0 aircraft have become available for modification and export at noticeably less cost than all-new machines. The cost problem of relifing the aircraft for US Navy service reflected only their continued use from carrier decks, and the Group 0 aircraft have a long fatigue life ahead of them provided they are used in the benign arena of land-based operations, for which they have a 20,000-hour life. The basic unit being offered consists of four aircraft (three for 24-hour coverage and a spare), backed by a comprehensive training and support package.

World Hawkeye population, 1997

United States Navy
The United States Navy currently operates 89 E-2Cs. All of the Pacific Fleet squadrons operate the Group II, while the Atlantic Fleet operates Groups 0, I and II. The Hawkeye 'roadmap' envisages a fleet of 75 all-Group II aircraft.

Unit	Fleet/shore base	Assignment	Modex
VAW-112 'Golden Hawks'	Pac/Miramar	CVW-9/*Nimitz*	NG-60x
VAW-113 'Black Hawks'	Pac/Miramar	CVW-14/*Abraham Lincoln*	NK-60x
VAW-115 'Sentinels'	Pac/Atsugi	CVW-5/*Independence*	NF-60x
VAW-116 'Sun Kings'	Pac/Miramar	CVW-2/*Constellation*	NE-60x
VAW-117 'Wallbangers'	Pac/Miramar	CVW-11/*Kitty Hawk*	NH-60x
VAW-120 'Cyclones'	Norfolk	Fleet Readiness	AD-60x, 61x, 62x, 64x
VAW-121 'Bluetails'	Lant/Norfolk	CVW-7/*John C. Stennis*	AG-60x
VAW-123 'Screwtops'	Lant/Norfolk	CVW-1/*George Washington*	AB-60x
VAW-124 'Bear Aces'	Lant/Norfolk	CVW-8/*John F. Kennedy*	AJ-60x
VAW-125 'Tigertails'	Lant/Norfolk	CVW-17/*Enterprise*	AA-60x
VAW-126 'Seahawks'	Lant/Norfolk	CVW-3/*Theodore Roosevelt*	AC-60x
VAW-77 'Night Wolf'	Atlanta	US Naval Reserve	AF-0x
VAW-78 'Fighting Escargots'	Norfolk	CVWR-20/US Naval Reserve	AF-60x
Naval Force Warfare Aircraft Test Squadron (NFWATS)	Patuxent River	test and trials	–

Unit disestablishments have been VAW-110 'Firebirds' (West Coast FRS/NJ-6xx), VAW-111 'Graywolves' (CVW-10/NM-60x), VAW-114 'Hormel Hawgs' (CVW-15/NL-60x), VAW-122 'Steeljaws' (CVW-6/AE-60x), VAW-127 'Seabats' (CVW-13/AK-60x) and VAW-88 'Cottonpickers' (Naval Air Reserve CVWR-30/ND-60x)

Egypt	'EW Sqn', Cairo West – 162791/1, 162792/2, 162823/3, 162824/4, 162825/5, 164626/6 – (six)
France	4 Flottille, Lann-Bihoué (*Charles de Gaulle*) – 2 from 1997/98, requirement for 2 more
Israel	192 Squadron, Hatzerim (service status unknown) – 941, 942, 944, 946 – (four)
Japan	601 Hikotai, Misawa (Keikai Kokutai – AEW Air Group) – 34-3451, 34-3452, 34-3453, 34-3454, 54-3455, 54-3456, 54-3457, 54-3458, 34-3459, 34-3460, 34-3461, 44-3462, 44-3463 – (13)
Singapore	111 'Hawkeye' Sqn, Tengah – 011/162793, 012/162794, 014/162795, 015/162796 – (four)
Taiwan	78 Sqn, Pingtung – 2501, 2502, 2503/151724, 2504 – (four)

Indeed, for a typical four-aircraft package the actual aircraft only constitute about 42 per cent of the programme cost.

At the time of writing the most likely next customer for an AEW system was Australia, which issued an RFP in late 1996. The Northrop Grumman Australian proposal, made in conjunction with Lockheed Martin (and now made easier by the merger between LM and NG), highlighted a very important facet of the Hawkeye system, namely its ability to be 'transportable' between platforms. Hawkeye-type systems have already been flown in the P-3 Orion and C-130 Hercules, including the EC-130V used briefly by the US Coast Guard for drug traffic monitoring and now in use for test range control at Hill AFB. Unable to meet the RAAF range/endurance requirements with the Hawkeye airframe, the proposal integrates the Group II system with the C-130J airframe (the result inevitably being dubbed the 'Herkeye'). The 'transportability' of the system could be attractive to many other C-130 operators, and could also be a key factor when the time comes to eventually replace the E-2 airframe some time in the next millennium.

For the moment, that day is probably more than 20 years away, and it is quite conceivable that Grumman's E-2 will notch up over 60 years of front-line service. From the outside it may well look the same, but the notional Hawkeye of 2020 will doubtless be as radically different in its capabilities compared to today's service machines, as the latter are when compared with the first E-2As which joined the fleet in 1964.   **David Donald**

Above: Singapore's costly commitment to protecting its independence is epitomised by the procurement of four E-2s to provide early warning. The aircraft will almost certainly be upgraded to at least Group II standard.

Below: Egypt's six-aircraft fleet is currently in the unique 'Group I½' configuration, with upgrade to full Group II likely. The aircraft retain their BuNos under the tail but wear a single Arabic numeral (in this case '3') on the nose.

Above: Despite their E-2T designation and E-2B ancestry, the Taiwanese Hawkeyes are in fact virtually identical to an E-2C Group II. As well as the RoCAF serial, the aircraft wear their original BuNos (in this case 151724) under the tail. This 78 Squadron aircraft stands next to its unlikely stablemate within the 6th TC&ASC Wing, a Fairchild C-119 still in use as a transport.

Left: Israel's Hawkeye fleet has seen much action since it was delivered in 1978. The aircraft were supplied with APS-125 radar but may also have featured triple-PRF and AMTI functions. Although no details have been released, they have almost certainly been modified, and this aircraft sports an additional fairing along the fuselage side. In the early 1990s they were fitted with refuelling probes, as illustrated by this 192 Sqn example demonstrating its new-found capability with a KC-130 Hercules. The four aircraft are now reportedly in storage.

Force Aérienne Belge
Belgische Luchtmacht

*A Belgian Air Force photo feature
by Antoine Roels*

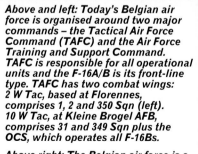

Above and left: Today's Belgian air force is organised around two major commands – the Tactical Air Force Command (TAFC) and the Air Force Training and Support Command. TAFC is responsible for all operational units and the F-16A/B is its front-line type. TAFC has two combat wings: 2 W Tac, based at Florennes, comprises 1, 2 and 350 Sqn (left). 10 W Tac, at Kleine Brogel AFB, comprises 31 and 349 Sqn plus the OCS, which operates all F-16Bs.

Above right: The Belgian air force is a bilingual force and all unit designations are applied in French and Flemish. Thus, a squadron is both an Escadrille and a Smaldeel. These F-16As are from 23 Esc/Sm and 31 Esc/Sm, wearing 'devil' and 'tiger' special schemes.

Above centre: Transport assets are controlled by the 15th Wing, at Melsbroek. 20 Esc/Sm operates the C-130H. The 727 flies with 21 Esc/Sm.

Right: These two Alpha Jets are attached to 11 Esc/Sm. One wears the now-standard grey scheme adopted by all Belgian Alpha Jets. The other wears a special scheme to commemorate the squadron's 75th anniversary, in July 1993.

Belgian Air Force

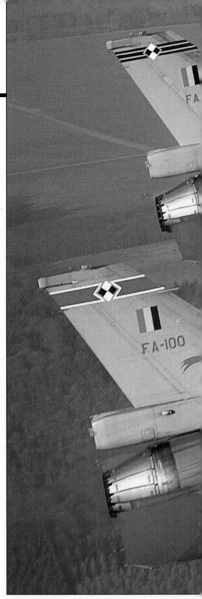

Above: The first F-16 to be delivered to Belgium was an F-16B, which arrived in January 1979. Belgium was one of the four European NATO air forces that ordered the F-16 as an F-104 replacement in the 'sale of the century'. An initial total of 96 F-16As and 20 F-16Bs was acquired between 1979 and 1985. The air force Operational Conversion Squadron which today operates all two-seat F-16s recently moved from Beauvechain to Kleine Brogel.

Below: When Belgium decided to retire its Mirage 5 fleet a partial replacement arrived in the shape of 40 additional F-16As plus four F-16Bs, delivered between 1987 and 1991. The three F-16As seen here are from 31 'Tiger' Esc/Sm, 10 W Tac, based at Kleine Brogel.

Right: Today Belgium has a total of just 72 active F-16A/Bs, with an operational reserve of 18. The aircraft in service are a mix of Block 10 and 'big tail' Block 15 Falcons. These aircraft carry the thistle badge of 1 Esc/Sm and the comet badge of 2 Esc/Sm. In June 1993 the decision was made to join the European F-16 MLU project, and update 48 Belgian F-16s. In January 1997 funding was released for the remaining 42 in a two-phase programme, lasting until 1998.

Below right: Belgium has a tradition of decorating aircraft to mark squadron anniversaries, or simply just for air shows. This trio of 2 W Tac F-16s, from Nos 1, 2 and 350 Sqns, was painted for the Florennes air show (September 1997) – the first air show to be held in Belgium after the tragic crash involving the 'Jordanian Falcons' team at Ostend in July.

Above and below: A total of 31 Alpha Jets is operated by 7 Esc/Sm and 11 Esc/Sm, part of 1 Wing, Transport and Training Command, based at Beauvechain. Primary flying training is undertaken on the 34 SF.260M/Ds of 5 Esc/SM, which moved during 1997 from Gossoncourt to Beauvechain.

Left: 1 Esc/Sm can trace its lineage back to 1910, but the unit's existence was not formalised until 1917 – hence these 80th anniversary marks.

Below: Eleven Fouga CM.170 Magisters still serve with 33 Esc/Sm, at Beauvechain AB, on training and liaison tasks. To celebrate the air force's 50th anniversary, four Magisters were painted in the scheme of the former 'Red Devils' aerobatic team, which was disbanded in 1977.

Above: The 'Swallows' display team was reformed with two SF.260Ms in 1995, and in 1996 they gained special markings to celebrate the modern Belgian air force's 50th anniversary. The 'Swallows' were originally established in the early 1970s, and were preceded by the 'Penguins', a two-ship display team flying Stampe SV-4Cs during the 1960s.

Right: The first Airbus A310-222 was 'delivered' to 21 Esc/Sm on 29 September 1997. Until the withdrawal of the Boeing 727, this unit will operate six aircraft types.

Below: All Belgian Alpha Jets have been repainted in this overall grey scheme, replacing the early green/ brown camouflage. The Alpha Jet was acquired to replace the T-33 and Magister, from 1978 onwards.

Above: The Swearingen Merlin IIIA serves with 21 Esc/Sm, based at Brussels-Melsbroek. Five, of six delivered in 1976, remain in service.

Above left: Five Westland Sea King Mk 58s serve with 40 Esc/Sm, based at Coxyde. This squadron is a joint air force and navy SAR unit.

Left: In 1995 the air force acquired a single Dassault Falcon 900B long-range executive jet, for VIP duties. The Falcon 900B is based alongside the other specialised transports of 21 Esc/Sm.

Right: An unusual type in the transport fleet is this Hawker-Siddeley HS 748 Srs 288, one of three delivered in 1976. Belgium is the only military operator of the famously reliable HS 748 in Europe, and one of very few remaining in the world.

Below: Until the arrival of the Airbus A310, the largest aircraft operated by 21 Esc/Sm was the Boeing 727. Two 727-29Cs were acquired from SABENA in 1976/77, replacing a pair of DC-6s. By January 1998 the 727s will have been replaced by (ex-SABENA) A310s. The first A310 had arrived by mid-August, though it did not officially enter service until September.

Above: Belgium has a *C-130H* force of 11 aircraft, based at Brussels-Melsbroek, as part of 20 Esc/Sm. Twelve Hercules were delivered from 1972 onwards, but one was lost in 1996. In 1992 Sabena Technics was awarded a contract to undertake an avionics upgrade programme (*AUP*) for the *C-130Hs*. Each aircraft was retrofitted with a Honeywell *EFIS* cockpit and flight management system, *INS* and *GPS* navigation systems, colour weather radar and an associated chaff/flare self-defence system. The first *AUP* aircraft was reflown in May 1995, and the programme is continuing.

Right: Two Dassault Falcon 20Es (Mystère 20Es) were acquired by 21 Esc/Sm in March and May 1973 for *VIP* missions. At the same time, the air force was also acquiring a large fleet of Dassault Mirage 5s.

Below: In 1990 Sabena Technics initiated a life extension programme for the Belgian *C-130s* to extend their operational lives by an additional 15 years. This involved dismantling and replacing all outer wing sections, using kits supplied by Lockheed Martin. The process was completed by May 1994, and preceded the *AUP*.

Harrier II
AV-8B/Night Attack, AV-8B Plus, GR.Mk 5 & GR.Mk 7

The story behind the genesis and deployment of the first-generation Harrier was outlined in *World Air Power Journal* Volume 6 just as the RAF's Harrier GR.Mk 3s were being withdrawn from service, and as the new GR.Mk 5, GR.Mk 7 and AV-8B were working up. These second-generation Harriers have now matured, having overcome early teething troubles, and represent some of the most advanced and effective attack aircraft in service today. At first sight, first- and second-generation Harriers look very similar, but, in fact, the new aircraft enjoys considerably greater capability, flexibility and effectiveness, and has assumed new roles and responsibilities.

The basic RAF Harrier GR.Mk 1 had never been intended to be much more than an interim STOVL fighter-bomber, originating after the cancellation of the supersonic, all-weather P.1154. The aircraft emerged as a timely, slick, glib, clever, compromise combination of the prototype P.1127/Kestrel airframe, with some elements of the cancelled aircraft's nav-attack system. The basic airframe/engine combination was unsophisticated, making the Harrier little more than a VTOL Hunter. Unlike aircraft like the Hunter and A-4 Skyhawk, however, the Harrier's limitations and high vibration levels made it certain that it would have only a relatively short service life, and Hawker Siddeley (later BAe) never stopped looking at more advanced Harriers as potential replacements for the original aircraft. Despite its limitations, the Harrier's unique capabilities made it a useful combat aircraft, and the type won a vital export order from the US Marine Corps. In service, the Harrier was a slightly frustrating enigma, pointing clearly to what might be possible, while being itself too constrained by its limitations. On Europe's Central Front, the Harrier's ability to operate from forward sites made it a useful CAS/BAI tool, and won it the affection of its pilots. Nonetheless, it was never very capable, carrying too small a warload over too short a radius of action. It was often dismissed (sometimes with good humour) as a VTOL Hunter.

UK/US plans for the future

By 1975, the Harrier GR.Mk 1 and the US Marines' AV-8A were looking decidedly tired, their primitive avionics severely limiting operational capability. The addition of a Ferranti LRMTS and a radar warning receiver to produce the GR.Mk 3 was no solution to the underlying

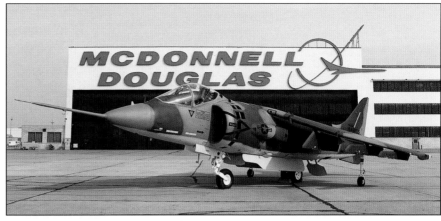

(80 miles; 130 km) short of the A-4's normal radius, but with less than half of the Skyhawk's 4,000-lb (1814-kg) payload. The Skyhawk did require much more of an airfield, however. Comparisons with the lightweight Skyhawk revealed that what was actually needed was a VTOL or STOVL strike fighter with the payload and range of aircraft like the F-105 or A-7, or perhaps even the F-111. The era of fast-jet CAS was coming to an end, and future jet fighter-bombers would need to strike further behind the front line.

The search for a 'Super Harrier'

Hawker Siddeley had examined a plethora of advanced Harrier designs, most notably the P.1184 'Super Harrier' with increased thrust and wing area giving improved payload capability. McDonnell Douglas had explored an advanced Harrier for the US Navy under the designation AV-8C (later reapplied to a simple SLEP-type upgrade to USMC AV-8As). Finally, in 1973, Hawker Siddeley and McDonnell Douglas teamed to examine Harrier derivatives, primarily to meet the US Navy Air Systems Command HIPAAS (High Performance Attack Aircraft System) requirement for a new STOVL or VTOL strike fighter. The aircraft was also intended to fulfil an RAF requirement for a Harrier replacement, a US Marine requirement for a Skyhawk and first-generation Harrier replacement, and to serve aboard the Royal Navy's new through-deck cruisers and the US Navy's projected Sea Control Ships. A Joint Management Board was established in 1972, with co-chairmen, project managers, financial and engine specialists from both countries. A 26-volume, jointly financed, eight-month project definition phase began on 12 April 1973 and was presented to the two governments on 13 December 1973. A Phase I specification was set out in 1974.

Above: The first of four FSD AV-8Bs is seen here outside its St Louis birthplace, where it was rolled out on 16 October 1981. The years leading up to this had been fraught with difficulty for the AV-8B programme as pro- and anti-Harrier factions battled over funding in the US Congress. The Harrier's 'foreign' origins, and somewhat biased criticism of the AV-8A's performance, led to a long drawn out debate as to whether the programme should proceed – despite the fact that the AV-8B under discussion would be far superior to the earlier Harriers. The coming to power of the Reagan administration cleared away many of the funding obstacles as the AV-8B no longer had to compete for cash against other acquisition programmes.

Below: The arrival of the radar-equipped AV-8B Harrier II Plus in 1995 brought with it an even greater transformation than that from AV-8A to AV-8B.

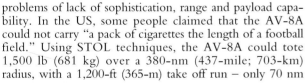

problems of lack of sophistication, range and payload capability. In the US, some people claimed that the AV-8A could not carry "a pack of cigarettes the length of a football field." Using STOL techniques, the AV-8A could tote 1,500 lb (681 kg) over a 380-nm (437-mile; 703-km) radius, with a 1,200-ft (365-m) take off run – only 70 nm

Below: The AV-8B (Night Attack) variant of the Harrier was originally referred to as the AV-8D and featured several important changes over earlier versions. The most important, and obvious, change was the addition of a FLIR sensor above the nose.

In 1969 McDonnell Douglas had been granted a licence to manufacture the Harrier in the United States when the USMC placed its first order for the aircraft, and in 1971 Pratt & Whitney received a similar licence for production of the Pegasus engine. In fact, the USMC's 112 AV-8As and eight TAV-8As were all built at Kingston (as were the 10 AV-8S and two TAV-8S Matadors delivered to the Spanish navy) and were merely assembled by McDonnell Douglas. Although the option of building Harriers in the US was not exercised, the same agreement had provided for

collaboration between Hawker Siddeley and McDonnell Douglas in future V/STOL and Harrier developments.

The aim of the study was to produce a minimum-change, minimum-cost derivative of the Harrier, taking advantage of the new 24,500-lb (108.99-kN) Pegasus 15 engine and a new advanced wing design to produce what became known as the AV-16A Advanced Harrier. The unofficial AV-16A designation was applied to indicate the programme's objectives, which were to develop a Harrier with twice the payload/range capability. Specifically, the partners sought a VTO gross weight of 21,500 lb (9752 kg), or 25,000 lb (11340 kg) with a 320-ft (97-m) deck run, with a VTO payload of 2,000 lb (907 kg) over a 300-nm (345-mile; 555-km) radius, or of 4,000 lb (1814 kg) over the same radius after a short take-off (STO).

The new aircraft was also known as the AV-8X. It would have a wider fuselage to accommodate the new engine, with its increased diameter fan (2¾ in; 7 cm larger), bigger intakes, a raised cockpit, strengthened undercarriage and new avionics. Although the Pegasus engine's huge fan and 'four-poster' nozzle configuration gave it a huge frontal area, factions in the US and the UK continued to press for a supersonic Harrier, although the aircraft's inherently large frontal cross-section made such a development difficult, if not unlikely. A supersonic version, known variously as the AV-16S-6 or P.1185, was drawn up at much the same time as the AV-8X, incorporating Plenum Chamber Burning and relatively minor airframe improvements.

An engine demonstrator using only the fan of the proposed Pegasus 15 had run at 24,900 lb (110.74 kN) in 1972, revealing that increased thrust was quite possible. Similar McDonnell Douglas and Hawker Siddeley wing designs were evaluated and tunnel tested for the new design. Both proved to have superior drag and lift co-efficient characteristics to the original Harrier wing, despite their lower sweep, wider span, extra hardpoints and thicker skins.

UK pull-out leads to AV-8B

The AV-16A was finally halted in 1975, when the British government pulled out of the project, ostensibly because there was insufficient common ground between the USMC, USN and RAF requirements, but also because the Pegasus 15 engine promised to be too expensive to develop, requiring, as it did, a new high-pressure section and an estimated $250 million (or even $500 million) R&D programme. The overall costs of the AV-16A programme

were estimated at $31 billion or more, and this was simply too much for the politicians in both countries to bear. It was a bad time for any advanced military programme, with the oil crisis in full flow, and with a massive need for public expenditure cuts.

McDonnell Douglas continued to work on an advanced Harrier, although it, the AV-8A Plus (later AV-8B), was less ambitious than the AV-16 – to the delight of the US Marines, who wanted the Harrier to be kept simple, serviceable and survivable. The US Navy turned away from

the project altogether, looking instead to the Rockwell XFV-12. Powered by a Pegasus Mk 105 (derived from the Sea Harrier's Mk 104, with a Digital Engine Control System), the new Harrier II combined the raised cockpit of the AV-16 (itself developed from the raised Sea Harrier cockpit) with the McDonnell Douglas-designed, increased-span, increased-area, supercritical wing, of mainly composite construction, albeit with metal tips, leading edges, pylon and outrigger attachment points. It was the largest single airframe component ever manufactured in

Above: The AGM-65 is an important AV-8 weapon and the Marines employ a unique version of the missile – the AGM-65E – to meet their special (close air support) requirements. Unlike previous versions of the Maverick, which relied on TV or imaging infra-red guidance, the AGM-65E has a laser seeker head. Though the AV-8B cannot self-designate a target, it can attack targets designated by Marines on the ground. This allows the Harrier/ Maverick combination to operate very close to the forward line of troops but with a much reduced risk of fratricide. It also gives the Harrier pilot a measure of stand-off distance and even allows him to attack targets he cannot see.

Left: The addition of APG-65 radar should have opened up a whole new range of weapons to the Harrier II Plus. In principle, the aircraft is now capable of carrying a BVR missile, like the AIM-120 AMRAAM, and long-range air-to-surface weapons, like the AGM-84 Harpoon. However, integration of these weapons has proceeded at a very slow pace and none is yet cleared for use on the Harrier II Plus. As a result, the most capable Harriers in the world are still using the old fashioned ordnance of earlier versions, such as the dumb bombs seen here on these VMA-223 aircraft.

epoxy resin composites and promised to be corrosion-proof, fatigue resistant and 400 per cent stronger than an equivalent alloy wing. It demanded new construction techniques, in which laminated sheets were heated to 500°F (260°C) in an autoclave, under 200 psi (1379 kPa) pressure. The new wing was fitted with massive single-slotted positive circulation flaps, which lowered to 61° and added 7,600 lb (3447 kg) to STO lift.

The new wing had a 4° reduction in sweepback but had increased span and a higher thickness/chord ratio, going from 8.5 per cent to 10 per cent. This thicker wing provided increased internal fuel tankage, equivalent to 30 minutes more of on-station time. Portions of the upper wing skin were detachable for servicing, but the whole lower skin was fixed. It was 330 lb (150 kg) lighter than an equivalent metal wing.

Pegasus developments

The new Pegasus engine for the AV-8B was developed from 1980 by Rolls-Royce at Patchway, with assistance from Smiths Industries and Dowty. The DECS was fitted to a GR.Mk 3 (XV277) and successively improved systems and development engines were flown in the aircraft between 11 March 1982 and 1987. Software was refined and fine-tuned to solve the problem of slow throttle response, and the engine was able to reliably provide 100 per cent thrust on take-off (on earlier Pegasus engines there was a tendency for thrust to stagnate at 92 per cent). An important by-product of the DECS was that it allowed engines to be changed without requiring full-power run-ups, making engine changes in the field easier to accomplish. A development Mk 105 Pegasus 11-21 with DECS was ready in time to be installed in the first development Harrier GR.Mk 5, ZD318, which first flew on 23 April 1985.

The need to provide a 'deck alert' capability made McDonnell Douglas determined to improve VTO and hover performance; the company designed a new retractable air dam which helped trap a cushion of air between the gun pods or newly designed ventral strakes. They were closely based on new Lift Improvement Devices

(LIDs) designed by Hawker Siddeley (like the big flaps) but not adopted by the British company during the period in which increased thrust seemed to offer the best way forward. The LIDs trapped a cushion of air below the fuselage, and helped prevent reingestion of recirculated air from the nozzles, adding the equivalent of 1,200 (5.34 kN) of extra lift. The company also reduced aircraft weight, by making extensive use of composites in the wing and forward fuselage.

YAV-8B into the air

Naval Air Systems Command demanded a 'full-scale' wind tunnel model of the new AV-8B wing, and a simple boilerplate replica of the new wing, intakes and flaps (together with an instrumented Pegasus 3) were fitted to the grounded second AV-8A (158385) for tests in NASA's vast 80 x 40-ft (24.4 x 12.2-m) wind tunnel at the Ames Research Center. These tests were successful, and flight-worthy examples of the new wing were fitted to two more AV-8As (158394 and 158395) which became the YAV-8B prototypes. The first made its maiden flight on 9 November 1978, and the second followed on 19 February 1979. The second aircraft was subsequently lost on 15 November, when the pilot ejected following a flame-out. As well as the new wing, the two YAV-8Bs were fitted with the new YF402-RR-404 engine that featured distinctive extended zero-scarf forward nozzles, which were more fully enclosed and which prevented the jet efflux from 'splaying outwards'.

The YAV-8B proved to be much 'draggier' than the original AV-8A, even after modifications to the wingroot fairing, intake cowl, and inboard underwing pylons. This made the aircraft significantly slower, although it did have much better payload/range characteristics. The USMC finally could look forward to a Harrier which could fly more than a '20-minute sortie'. Brief consideration was given to retrofitting the new wing to existing AV-8As, but this option was soon rejected, since it gave an unacceptable increase in tailplane loads. The new LIDs were incorporated in 47 AV-8As, which underwent a SLEP to become AV-8Cs.

The enhanced performance of the YAV-8Bs was sufficient to prompt the US DoD to fund a Full Scale Development batch of four Harrier IIs in FY79. They were powered by F402-RR-404 engines. The F402-RR-404 or Pegasus 11 had a nominal short lift wet (brief take-off/hover rating, with water injection) of 21,500 lb (95.62 kN), or a dry rating of 20,500 lb (91.17 kN). Either is available for only 15 seconds per flight, and in standard operations a normal lift rating of 19,500 lb (86.72 kN) for up to 150 seconds per flight is more significant. In conventional wingborne flight the engine is limited to 16,750 lb (74.49 kN) (for up to 15 minutes), with a maximum continuous rating of 13,500 lb (60.04 kN). McDonnell test pilot Charlie Plummer took the first FSD AV-8B on its initial hover check on 5 November 1981, by which time the British had signed up to buy the aircraft, as described below, so they all had British-built rear fuselages.

Wing and fuselage changes

These aircraft also introduced MDD's entirely new nose and revised, extended centre fuselage. The new forward fuselage was of composite construction, and weighed 25 per cent less than the equivalent section of the AV-8A. The pilot's seat and cockpit floor were raised, giving more internal volume for systems and equipment, while a new rear-view canopy covered the raised cockpit, with a wrap-round windscreen in front. The rear fuselage was extended to compensate for extra weight forward, and the tailplane was redesigned, with an aluminium leading edge and a detachable trailing edge of honeycomb construction.

From the second FSD aircraft, all AV-8Bs were fitted with the smaller '70 per cent' version of the British-designed LERX, although, interestingly, the larger 100 per cent LERX eventually was adopted on later aircraft. Four of the seven pylons were plumbed for the carriage of auxiliary fuel tanks.

Although McDonnell Douglas had pressed on alone to develop the AV-8B, the programme was never given an easy ride in Washington, DC. Its British origins were always a major stumbling block, while the limited payload range characteristics of the AV-8A were dragged up again and again. Throughout the life of the programme, various politicians repeatedly attempted to withhold funds from the AV-8B, usually in favour of further production of the F/A-18 Hornet.

Such opposition was not really justified, as test results started to show. During one early FSD sortie, for example, Charlie Plummer carried seven 500-lb (227-kg) bombs over a range of 422 miles (679 km) after a 700-ft (213-m) take-off run, returning to Patuxent River with 1,800 lb (816 kg) of fuel. He then flew a CAS profile with 12 500-lb

bombs, taking off after a 1,200-ft (365-m) roll and attacking a target 185 miles (298 km) away, returning for a vertical landing with 600 lb (272 kg) of reserves. By comparison with the AV-8A, the new version carried double the payload with much enhanced accuracy.

When the USMC procured its first-generation Harriers it did so on the basis that the aircraft was an 'off-the-shelf' item, and while some systems were replaced during service

The Harrier GR.Mk 7 upgrade brought the RAF Harrier force up to the same standard as the USMC's AV-8B (NA)s. These No. 20(R) Sqn aircraft are seen recovering from an attack training mission over Scotland.

Second-generation Harriers

Above: The GR.Mk 7 Harrier is fitted with a GEC-Marconi 1010 FLIR in a new overnose housing. The same system is being fitted to the Tornado as part of the GR.Mk 4 upgrade and to the Jaguar if that part of the GR.Mk 3 upgrade is approved. This aircraft is carrying two AIM-9L Sidewinders and two 500-lb bombs.

Above right: The Canadian-built Bristol CRV-7 rocket system is now replacing the earlier SNEB rockets long associated with British Harriers. This aircraft is firing a full LAU-5003 pod of the 2.75-in rockets, in a 30° dive over the Holbeach range, in Lincolnshire.

Opposite right: This No. 20 (R) Squadron is seen dropping a load of four (inert) 1,000-lb bombs, from 150 ft (45 m), over the Tain range, on Dornoch Firth in northeastern Scotland. These bombs are fitted with the Type No. 117 retarding tail unit, which was specially designed for UK 1,000-lb bombs. It features a 1.9-m (6.23-ft) diameter ribbon parachute and four metal airbrakes which pop out from the tail section. On release, a timer is triggered by a lanyard. The timer deploys the retarding system which is pulled into place by aerodynamic force. The system is linked to the bomb's fuse, ensuring that the weapon only becomes live when correctly deployed – an essential safety measure for low-level operations.

to optimise the aircraft for its USMC role, others had to be retained until the advent of a 'clean piece of paper' in the shape of the Harrier II. They included the aircraft's INAS (the Marines preferring to use TACAN), the use of LOX (instead of an OBOGS) and the need for a laser designator. The USMC was particularly keen to replace the Harrier's twin 30-mm cannon, since they were logistically difficult to support (using ammunition which was unique in the US forces) and were not adequately protected against electromagnetic interference onboard ship. For the AV-8B, McDonnell Douglas replaced the twin ADEN guns with a single GAU-12/A Equalizer 25-mm Gatling gun. The gun was housed in the port cannon pod, with ammunition (300 rounds of linkless Oerlikon KBA) layered in the starboard pod, and supplied to the gun across a 'bridge' which doubled as a lift enhancer. The new gun enjoyed a very rapid rate of fire, being driven by engine bleed air at up to 9,000 rpm and firing 3,600 rpm. The new gun was optimised for strafing ground targets.

AV-8B systems

Unlike the AV-8A and AV-8C, the AV-8B featured almost from the start the Hughes AN/ASB-19(V)-2 Angle Rate Bombing System, proven in the A-4M Skyhawk. It was optimised for dive attack profiles and was linked to the new AN/AYK-14 mission computer and the SU-128/A HUD. The first two FSD aircraft initially flew with 'solid' noses and extended test instrumentation probes, but later aircraft had the distinctive glass nose associated with ARBS.

Inside the cockpit, the AV-8B was a very different aircraft to any of its predecessors. Whereas the original Harrier cockpit had been entirely analog (unkindly described by some as an ergonomic slum), the AV-8B used a cockpit based on that designed for the F/A-18 Hornet, which in the 1980s was regarded as the benchmark modern fighter cockpit with its HOTAS controls and large MFDs.

The Harrier II was made easier to fly in an effort to reduce the high attrition rate. Advances in technology allowed the use of a sophisticated three-axis Sperry Stability Augmentation and Attitude Hold System (SAAHS), linked to a Departure Resistant System (DRS), minimising pilot workload in the hover and during the transition to and from the hover. The SAAHS even allowed hands-off vertical landings to be made, demonstrated by Bill Lowe in February 1983.

A USMC report entitled "Frosty Nozzle" had addressed the EW and secure communications shortcomings of the original AV-8A, and as a result the AV-8C had incorporated a KY-28/TSEC secure voice radio, AN/ALE-39 dispensers, ALR-67 RWR, and provision for the ALQ-126C DECM pod. These systems were used from the start by the AV-8B, which was also planned to use the troubled ASPJ jammer.

The first FSD aircraft was used primarily for the evaluation of general flying characteristics, and the second for engine and intake testing, proving of the fuel system and inflight refuelling. The third FSD aircraft undertook avionics and weapons testing, and subsequently underwent spin testing, while the fourth (closest to the intended production standard) concentrated on the new gun.

A pilot production batch of 12 F402-RR-404A-engined AV-8Bs was ordered in FY82, the first of which flew on 29 August 1983. Like the four FSD aircraft, the pilot production AV-8Bs were originally delivered with a double row of suction relief doors on the intake lips, but they were deleted when the intake was refined to improve airflow. Early aircraft were subsequently retrofitted with the new single row of intake doors. FY83 saw a limited production batch of 21 aircraft, towards a planned total of 328 aircraft, a number that was soon reduced to 286, including the FSD aircraft and three aircraft transferred to Italy. The pilot production aircraft were the last delivered with F402-RR-404A engines, subsequent aircraft (delivered from mid-1985) being powered by the F402-RR-406 (Pegasus 11-21).

The F402-RR-406 cured early surge problems, and gave a longer life, with a hot-end inspection at 500 hours and a TBO of 1,000 hours. The engine had a maximum lift rating of 22,800 lb (101.40 kN), though a combat rating gave a maximum rating of 24,500 lb (108.96 kN) in level flight. The new engine's turbine section ran about 10°-20°F cooler, improving component life.

The Harrier II attained its Naval Preliminary Evaluation in June 1982, opening the way for an Initial Operational

Test and Evaluation (IOT&E) by VX-5. The AV-8B began to enter service in December 1983, initially with VMAT-203, the Harrier training unit, which received the first of the pilot production batch on 12 January 1984. The first of eight front-line ('gun') squadrons, VMA-331, was formally commissioned on 30 January 1985.

Early DACT training showed a tendency to depart if the aircraft was pushed past its brochure limits, and from BuNo. 162081 the SAAHS was refined. Only lingering fuel leak and AN/ARC-182 radio problems prevented the squadron from beating the USMC maintenance requirements of 15.9 MMH/FH, a 1.9 hour mean repair time, and a 75 per cent mission ready rate.

TAV-8B for the Marines

Although the Marines had suffered from a high accident rate during Harrier pilot training before the introduction of the TAV-8A, the service initially decided that it had no need for a dedicated trainer version of the AV-8B. This decision was quickly reversed, but it was still three years between the introduction of the first VMAT-203 AV-8Bs and the induction of the squadron's first TAV-8B. In the interim, trainee Harrier pilots first flew in the all-analog 1960s cockpit, then transitioned to a first solo in the digital cockpit of the AV-8B. Apart from the radical difference in operating environment, the new variant also had dramatically different handling characteristics, justifying design and development of a two-seat Harrier II – the TAV-8B. The first TAV-8B was the 65th Harrier II, and first flew (in the hands of Bill Lowe) on 21 October 1986.

Second-generation Harriers

The TAV-8B features a lengthened forward fuselage (by 3 ft 11 in/1.19 m to 50 ft 3 in/15.32 m) housing stepped tandem cockpits for the student (front) and instructor (rear). They are fitted with full dual controls. The aircraft has a taller fin (by 17 in/43 cm) with a 'filled in' leading edge, giving increased chord and area for improved directional stability, and the environmental control system is modified to cope with the demands of two cockpits. Unlike the TAV-8A, the new trainer does not have an extended tailcone. The TAV-8B was not designed to have an operational front-line role, so it has only two external hardpoints, intended principally for the carriage of auxiliary fuel tanks, training weapons or practice bombs. Twenty-four TAV-8Bs were ordered, two for Italy and the rest for VMAT-203.

From 1986, production Harriers began to receive a new digital engine control system developed by Dowty Smiths Industries. Engines fitted with DECS received an A-suffix to their designations. The TAV-8B prototype (162747) was actually the first aircraft to be so-equipped. The second TAV-8B was delivered to VMAT-203 on 24 July 1987.

Britain orders the AV-8B

After pulling out of the AV-16A, it was certainly not a foregone conclusion that Britain would produce a STOVL or VSTOL aircraft to replace the Harrier. The future of the McDonnell Douglas Harrier II was by no means assured, and a successful Kingston second-generation Harrier could even sell to the USMC. Air Staff Target 403 (AST.403) drew competing proposals from BAe at Warton (the STOL P.96) and from Kingston, which proposed a new STOVL type with a PCB Pegasus and a ventral intake. This eventually led to the Eurofighter, but a new Harrier began to take shape in response to Air Staff Requirement 409 (ASR.409).

Britain's original plan for a second-generation Harrier was to modify existing Harrier GR.Mk 3s with Kingston's new 'big wing', which differed from the new McDonnell Douglas wing primarily in its composition, being of conventional alloy construction and thus known as the 'tin wing'. This derisive nickname was unfortunate, since the wing was aerodynamically very advanced and reflected BAe's advanced wing design experience gathered in the Hawk and Airbus programmes. Opponents of the indigenous design averred that the McDonnell design was 'more advanced', and that the Kingston 'big wing' was in some way 'inferior'. This was a gross over-simplification, and the American wing was probably less advanced, except in its use of advanced (and arguably less battle damage tolerant) materials. In many respects, during the early and mid-1970s, the upgrade of existing Harriers with a new metal wing made more sense than the production of an all-new design with a carbon-fibre wing.

Utilisation of the RAF's GR.Mk 3s continued apace, and it soon became clear that to rewing the aircraft (some of which had amassed 4,000 flying hours by 1988) would not be cost-effective. Ever optimistic, BAe suggested producing new-build big-winged aircraft as Harrier GR.Mk 5s, making extensive use of GR.Mk 3 or Sea Harrier production tooling, and incorporating a Sea Harrier-type forward fuselage, with its raised cockpit. By this time the GR.Mk 5(K) incorporated the YAV-8B's revised intakes, zero scarf nozzles and AV-8B type LIDs (known in the UK as CADs). The Kingston wing would almost certainly have given lower drag than the McDonnell Douglas wing at high speed, and, despite its heavier weight, the GR.Mk 5(K), as it became known, would have been faster than the AV-8B. It would also have enjoyed an equivalent or better low-level radius of action and payload capability. The company eventually hoped to retrofit Sea Harriers with the new 'big wing', though this improvement died when the RAF ordered the AV-8B.

UK needs versus US reality

The RAF's requirement for second-generation Harriers was always perceived as being quite small, since it was thought that the Harrier GR.Mk 3 needed replacing only in RAF Germany, and that the UK-based squadron could soldier on with upgraded GR.Mk 3s. Unfortunately, a 60-aircraft order to equip two front-line squadrons was insufficient to launch production of the GR.Mk 5(K), particularly in the face of competition from the US AV-8B, which already had 330 firm orders. Moreover, the new British Conservative government was firmly committed to the Trident missile, and to massive Tornado procurement, and yet wanted to keep a tight reign on defence expenditure. Against such a background, the Harrier programme was not accorded a high priority. Finally, the technical merits of the lightweight composite supercritical American wing became increasingly apparent, while the low unit price of the AV-8B proved even more attractive to the politicians. It was soon considered inevitable that if the RAF were to acquire a second-generation Harrier, then that aircraft would be the American AV-8B. A Memorandum of Understanding signed in August 1981 provided for the abandonment of British 'big wing' Harrier development, and for the acquisition of AV-8Bs for the RAF. This was something of a kick in the teeth to BAe, whose Kingston Division (as Hawker) had designed the original Harrier configuration, and who would now only be expected to build some sub-assemblies and components of an American refinement of its own design, rather than its own Harrier derivative.

Fortunately, the AV-8B and the cancelled Kingston 'big wing' Harrier shared a host of common features, including a relocated outrigger undercarriage, which actually reduced

wheeltrack from 22.18 to 16.99 ft (6.76 to 5.18 m), despite its wider span. This allowed either aircraft to taxi on single track roads.

The RAF order for 62 AV-8Bs won BAe a substantial share in the programme, which initially included 336 aircraft for the US Marines and 12 for Spain. The aircraft were designated as Harrier GR.Mk 5s, reusing the designation associated with Kingston's original 'tin wing' Harrier. BAe gained the contract to build the vital reaction control system for all Harriers, together with all aft and aft-centre fuselage sections, fins and carbon-fibre rudders, and all

Left and far left: The AIM-9L Sidewinder is carried by the Harrier GR.Mk 7 as a self-defence weapon. Crews regularly practise with captive seeker heads but each pilot can expect to fire a live missile once per tour (approximately every three years). The UK's main missile firing ranges are over the Irish Sea off the Welsh coast. Trials are conducted over the Aberporth ranges using Jindivik target drones (towing flares) flown from Llanbedr. The launch seen here (left) – of an AIM-9G – was conducted as part of a Qualified Weapons Instructor course. It is a 'look-up' launch, in a head-to-head engagement, with the aircraft climbing at 30° to 40°. The view through the HUD of a second aircraft (far left) gives some idea of more typical launch parameters, at a target crossing left to right. The trail aircraft is flying at 387 kt (Mach 0.64) and a height of 5,780 ft. The aircraft is turning right in a 17° climb (approximately) while pulling 1.3 g.

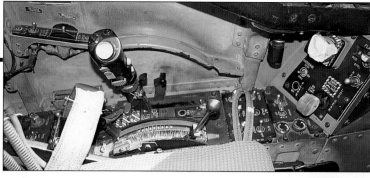

The cockpit of the US Marine Corps' AV-8B Night Attack Harrier (left) is built around the Unisys CP-1429/AYK-14(V) mission computer. The HUD (right) is a Smiths Industries SU-128/A dual combiner HUD, which can display FLIR imagery. The two CRTs are Kaiser IP-1318/A digital display indicators. The right-hand screen can show a digital moving map system – a moving map was never fitted to the Marines' original AV-8As. Allowing for its sophisticated HOTAS controls, the basic Harrier cockpit remains the same. Nozzle position and throttle controls for the F402-RR-408 Pegasus engine are located on the left side panel (above).

The cockpits of RAF GR.Mk 7s (right) and T.Mk 10 trainers (above) are identical. The T.Mk 10 retains the combat capability, uprated Pegasus 105 engines and Martin-Baker Mk 12 ejection seats of the front-line single-seat version. RAF Harriers use virtually the same systems fit as the USMC aircraft, though the AYK-14(V) mission computer is built as the Computing Devices ACCS 2000 in the UK.

The nose of the *GR.Mk 7 Harrier* is filled with the dual-mode *TV*/laser target seeker/tracker of the *AN/ASB-19(V2) Angle Rate Bombing Set (ARBS)*. Above it is the *GEC-Marconi FLIR*. Below the nose are the twin housings for the *Zeus ECM system*.

The *Night Attack AV-8B* uses the same *ARBS* and *FLIR* combination as the *RAF* aircraft, in a slightly repackaged form. The AV-8B relies on the *AN/ALR-67(V)2 RWR* and has provision for an *AN/ALQ-164 ECM* pod, which is rarely seen.

In the *AV-8B Harrier II Plus* the 'old-fashioned' *ARBS*, and its functions, have been completely replaced by the multi-mode *AN/APG-65 radar*. The addition of an all-new radome and extended nose has led to the *FLIR* system being repositioned.

McDonnell Douglas AV-8B Harrier II Plus

1 Glass-fibre radome
2 Planar radar scanner
3 Scanner tracking mechanism
4 Radar mounting bulkhead
5 Forward-Looking Infra-Red (FLIR)
6 APG-65 radar equipment module
7 Forward pitch control reaction air nozzle
8 Pitot head, port and starboard
9 Cockpit front pressure bulkhead
10 Pitch feel unit and trim actuator
11 Yaw vane
12 Single piece wrap-round windscreen
13 Instrument panel shroud
14 Rudder pedals
15 Underfloor avionics bay, air-data computer and inertial navigation equipment
16 Electro-luminescent and covert night vision goggle (NVG) formation lighting strips
17 Control column
18 Engine throttle and nozzle angle control levers
19 Instrument panel with full-colour multi-function CRT displays
20 Pilots head-up display (HUD)
21 Sliding cockpit canopy with miniature detonating cord (MDC) emergency breaker
22 UPC/Stencil lightweight ejection seat
23 Cockpit section framing, all-composite forward fuselage structure
24 Sloping seat mounting rear pressure bulkhead
25 Intake boundary layer separator
26 Port air intake
27 Landing/taxiing light
28 Levered suspension nosewheel, shortens on retraction
29 Intake suction relief doors, free floating
30 Hydraulic nosewheel retraction jack
31 Hydraulic system accumulator
32 Demountable flight refuelling probe
33 Cockpit air conditioning pack

34 Intake boundary layer air spill duct
35 Heat exchanger ram air intakes
36 Rolls-Royce F404-RR-408 Pegasus 11-61 turbofan engine
37 Full authority digital engine control (FADEC) unit
38 Upper formation lighting strips
39 Accessory equipment gearbox
40 Alternator
41 Engine oil tank
42 Forward fuselage fuel tank
43 Hydraulic system ground connectors and engine monitoring and recording equipment
44 Fuselage lift improvement device (LID), lateral strake
45 Forward zero-scarf (fan air) swivelling exhaust nozzle
46 Centre fuselage fuel tank
47 Nozzle bearing
48 Gas turbine starter/auxiliary power unit
49 Leading-edge root extension (LERX)
50 Engine bay venting air intake
51 Wing centre-section integral fuel tank
52 Starboard wing integral tank
53 Fuel feed and vent piping
54 Starboard weapons pylons

55 RWR antenna
56 Starboard navigation light
57 Roll control reaction air valve, upper and lower surface vents
58 Wingtip formation lights
59 Fuel jettison
60 Starboard aileron
61 Outrigger wheel fairing
62 Starboard outrigger wheel, retracted position
63 Slotted flap
64 Articulated flap vane
65 VHF/UHF antenna
66 Anti-collision beacon
67 De-mineralised water tank
68 Engine fire suppression bottle
69 Water filler
70 Rear fuselage fuel tank
71 Electrical system distribution panels, port and starboard
72 Chaff/flare launchers
73 Heat exchanger ram air intake
74 Rudder hydraulic actuator
75 Starboard all-moving tailplane

76 Formation lighting strip
77 Fin conventional light alloy structure
78 MAD compensator
79 Temperature probe
80 Broad-band communications antenna
81 Glass-fibre fin-tip antenna fairing
82 Radar beacon antenna
83 Rudder
84 Honeycomb composite rudder structure
85 Yaw control reaction air valve, port and starboard nozzles
86 Rear RWR antennas
87 Rear pitch control reaction air nozzle

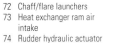

AV-8B Cockpit

When McDonnell Douglas and British Aerospace were (re)designing the AV-8B Harrier II, substantial changes were made to the forward section of the aircraft. In addition to a completely revised airframe shape, the cockpit was totally rebuilt around the new computerised navigation/attack suite and multi-function displays. The new cockpit was dubbed the 'advanced crew station'. The most obvious difference over earlier Harriers was the much improved field of vision for the pilot, courtesy of the single-piece wraparound bubble canopy. The pilot also sat much higher in the AV-8B than in the AV-8A, with an eye-line raised by some 10.5 in (26.7 cm). The new seat position also provided much improved 'over-the-shoulder' vision.

AV-8B Harrier Armament System

The gun fitted to the AV-8B is a development of the GAU-12/U 'Equaliser' 25-mm cannon, developed by General Electric. The gun was first trialled on a Harrier in 1980 and entered service with the USMC in 1984. The pods have been fitted with strakes to improve their aerodynamic effect. When the cannon are not fitted, Harriers are flown with long ventral strakes replacing each entire pod. The gun is part of a two-pod system. Each pod is 3.34 m (10.95 ft) long, 350 mm (13.7 in) wide and 470 mm (18.5 in) deep. The starboard pod contains 300 rounds of ammunition on a linear linkless feed system which is connected, at the rear, to the cannon breach system in the port pod. The rotary cannon is driven by a pneumatic system that uses engine bleed air. The motor spins at 9,000 rpm but this is geared down for the cannon. The cannon can speed up to its maximum rate of fire, 3,600 rounds per minute, in 0.4 seconds. The GAU-12 can fire a range of high-explosive incendiary, armour-piercing and armour-piercing (discarding sabot) rounds.

AV-8B Harrier II Plus
VMA-542 'Flying Tigers'
Marine Air Group 14
2d Marine Air Wing
MCAS Cherry Point

AN/APG-65 multi-mode radar for the Harrier II Plus
When the AN/APG-65 radar (developed and built by the Hughes Aircraft Company) was introduced in the F/A-18 Hornet, it revolutionised airborne radar technology. The new radar offered a combination of multi-mode, all-digital performance in the air-to-air and air-to-ground roles coupled with an extremely compact size. AN/APG-65 possesses a velocity search function which provides the maximum detection range against (fast) oncoming targets. A range-while-scan mode displays all-aspect targets within a shorter range bracket. A track-while-scan mode provides any aircraft fitted with AN/APG-65 to 'fire-and-forget' radar-guided BVR missiles such as the AIM-7 Sparrow and AIM-120 AMRAAM. Single-track target, and gun modes are also provided. For close-in air combat manoeuvring the AN/APG-65 has three 'dogfight' modes. The radar can 'look' at an area equivalent to that seen through the pilot's HUD and lock the gunsight onto any target found within a given range. The radar can scan vertically within a narrow beam, lock onto the first target found and provide sighting cues. Finally, the pilot can 'boresight' the radar to lock onto a specific target at which the aircraft is pointing directly. For air-to-ground missions the range of APG-65 modes is equally impressive, and the radar performs with ease over both land or water. The radar can update the aircraft's onboard navigation system, provide terrain avoidance information for low-level flight, locate moving targets on the ground, provide precise range to targets, and also has a specific sea surface mode to locate ships in all weather conditions. The success of APG-65 has led to an even better radar for the Hornet, the AN/ APG-73. Now that this newer set is being retrofitted to US Navy F/A-18Cs, the surplus APG-65s are being used as part of the AV-8B Harrier II Plus upgrade for the US Marine Corps. A $181 million radar integration and production contract for the Harrier II Plus programme was signed between McDonnell Douglas and British Aerospace in January 1991. This covered the conversion of a prototype for test and development work plus the 27 new-build Harrier II Plus aircraft authorised as part of the FY91 budget. The II Plus prototype first flew in September 1992 and the aircraft is now operational with several Marine Corps Harrier squadrons.

US avionics upgrade programme
In September 1997 the US Navy awarded a $14 million COTS (Commercial-Off-The-Shelf) contract to Smiths Industries Aerospace, for an upgrade to the Weapons Management and Control System (WMCS) of the AV-8B. The upgrade is known as OSCAR (Open Systems Core Avionics Requirements) and will be conducted in association with the Boeing Company – McDonnell Aircraft and Missile Systems. OSCAR is an important part of any future advanced weapons integration for the Marine Corps' Harriers, as it will allow new air-to-air and air-to-ground systems to be more easily 'plugged in' to the WMCS.

AGM-65E Maverick
The USMC has introduced a specialised version of the Maverick missile, the AGM-65E, which is a semi-active, laser-guided version of the original TV-/IR-guided Maverick. This version was developed specifically for the Marines to be used as a precision weapon for close air support missions where friendly troops are in contact with enemy forces. AGM-65E was based on development work done during the 1970s on the AGM-65C version, which was intended for the Navy and the Air Force, but never entered production. The AGM-65E introduced a new 300-lb (136-kg) blast penetrator warhead, compared to the previous 125-lb (57-kg) shaped charge warhead, optimised for anti-armour missions. The AGM-65E entered service in 1985. All 'E-model' Mavericks are painted grey.

88 Port all-moving tailplane
89 Carbon-fibre composite multi-spar tailplane structure
90 Tail bumper
91 Lower broad-band communications antenna
92 Tailplane hydraulic actuator
93 Heat exchanger exhaust
94 Avionics equipment air conditioning pack
95 Tailplane control cables
96 Conventional rear fuselage light alloy structure
97 Rear fuselage avionics equipment bay
98 Avionics bay access hatch, port and starboard
99 Formation lighting strip
100 Ventral airbrake panel
101 Airbrake hydraulic jack
102 Port slotted flap
103 Carbon-fibre composite flap structure
104 Flap hydraulic jack
105 Exhaust nozzle shroud

106 Outboard flap hinge and vane interconnecting link
107 Port outrigger fairing
108 Port aileron
109 Aileron carbon-fibre composite structure
110 Fuel jettison
111 Port wingtip formation lights
112 Roll control reaction air valve, upper and lower surface vents
113 Port navigation light
114 RWR antenna
115 Port wing stores pylons
116 Port outrigger wheel
117 Pylon attachment hardpoints
118 Outer wing panel dry bay
119 Aileron hydraulic actuator
120 Outrigger wheel strut
121 Hydraulic retraction jack
122 Port wing integral fuel tank
123 Aileron control rod
124 Intermediate missile pylon
125 AIM-9L/M Sidewinder air-to-air missile

126 Missile launch rail
127 Wing leading-edge fence
128 Carbon-fibre composite 'sine wave' multi-spar structure
129 Rear, hot stream, swivelling exhaust nozzle
130 Rear nozzle bleed-air cooled bearing housing
131 Hydraulic reservoir, dual system, port and starboard
132 Pressure refuelling connection and control panel

133 Reaction control air ducting
134 Aft-retracting twin-wheel main undercarriage
135 Inboard 'wet' stores pylon
136 External fuel tank
137 Ventral gun pack, replaces fuselage LID strakes
138 Gun pneumatic drive unit
139 Ammunition cross-feed and link return chute
140 Ammunition magazine, 300 rounds
141 Retractable LID cross-dam and hydraulic jack
142 Cannon muzzle aperture
143 Gun gas vent
144 Forward recoil mounting
145 GAU-12/U 25-mm five-barrelled rotary cannon
146 Gun pack LID strake
147 AGM-65A Maverick, laser-guided air-to-surface missile
148 AIM-120 AMRAAM, air-to-air missile
149 CBU-89B Gator, sub-munition dispenser
150 Triple ejector rack
151 Mk 82 LDGP 500-lb bomb
152 Mk 82SE Snakeye, retarded bomb
153 AGM-84A-D Harpoon, air-to-surface anti-ship missile

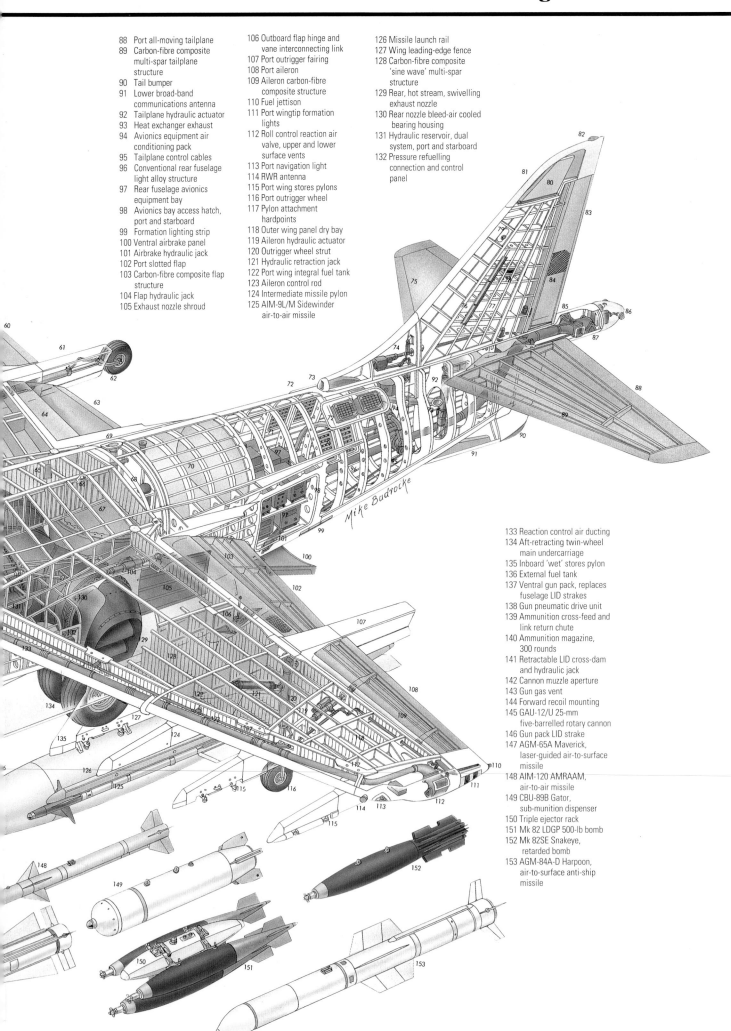

Mike Budrocke

Right: The standard RAF GP bomb is the Royal Ordnance-developed Mk 10/13/18/20 1,000-lb bomb. All basic bomb shapes are identical in appearance, but the Mk 13 has a filling of 180 kg (399 lb) of RWA 4 high explosive, while the others use slightly differing amounts of Torpex explosive. The (live) bombs seen on the GR.Mk 7 above are fitted with the No. 114 'slick' tail, while the dummy bombs seen here on this SAOEU Harrier are fitted with the No. 117 retarding tail unit.

Left: RAF Harriers employed their Paveway II LGB capability in Bosnia. In British service, the Paveway II seeker system is mated with the Mk 10 (RWA 4), Mk 13 (RWA 4) or Mk 18 (Torpex) 1,000-lb bomb body plus a No. 120 pop-out tail fin unit. RWA 4 explosive is designed to be more resistant to kinetic heating induced by low-level high-speed flight. The most recently developed Mk 20 bomb shape is also Paveway II-compatible.

Right: During Operation Warden the most commonly carried air-to-ground weapon was the US-supplied CBU-87/B Combined Effects Munition (CEM). The CEM was acquired by the RAF during the Gulf War, in preference to its own BLU 755 cluster bomb, which is optimised for low-level deliveries. The CBU-87/B carries 202 BLU-97 sub-munitions which each combine an anti-armour, anti-materiel (fragmentation) and incendiary warhead in a single bomblet.

Below: The key to the AV-8B(NA) and GR.Mk 7's all-weather attack credentials are their combination of FLIR and NVG systems. Each operator uses a slightly differing night vision goggle fit, including (from left to right): GEC-Marconi Cats Eyes (USMC), GEC-Marconi Nightbird (RAF) and Cats Eyes (Spain).

Rolls-Royce Pegasus engine

The Pegasus engine is a two-shaft turbofan, designed purely for the Harrier. It provides lift and thrust for forward flight through four swivelling exhaust nozzles. The Pegasus entered service on the Harrier in 1969, as the Pegasus 11, rated at 21,500 lb (95.64 kN) thrust. When the AV-8B entered development, an uprated version of the engine, the Pegasus 11-21, was introduced (in 1984). In addition to providing a little extra power (the Pegasus 11-21 is rated at 21,750 lb/96.75 kN), the new engine boasted much improved reliability and reduced maintenance times. From 1986 onwards all Pegasus 11-21s were delivered with FADEC (Full Authority Digital Engine Controls) systems to further improve their performance. The US designation for this engine was F402-RR-406A. The 11-21 has now been further improved to Pegasus 11-61 standard, offering 15 per cent more thrust (23,800 lb/106 kN) even at higher outside air temperatures and twice the overhaul life of the 11-21. In US service the Pegasus 11-61 is designated as the F402-RR-408A. As the leading expert on VTOL engine design and operation, Rolls-Royce is now heavily involved in the JSF programme. Rolls-Royce's American partner on the F402 programme has been Pratt & Whitney, for over 20 years. A variant of Pratt & Whitney's F119 engine (which is intended for the F-22) – the F119/JSF – has been used as the baseline powerplant in both Boeing and Lockheed Martin's competing JSF proposals. However, Rolls-Royce had a formal partnership with General Electric and Allison (which it later acquired as a US subsidiary) to develop an alternative JSF engine, based on General Electric's YF120. Whichever engine is selected by the winning JSF team, Rolls-Royce will most likely be involved – both because of its experience in the field and the important UK stake in the overall JSF competition.

ASTOVL and JSF testbed

The YAV-8B Harrier, operated by NASA's Ames Research Center, is now engaged in extensive flight test development for the USAF/USN/USMC JSF (Joint Strike Fighter) programme. Previously known as the JAST (Joint Advanced Strike Technology) programme, and before that as ASTOVL (Advanced Short Take-Off and Vertical Landing), the JSF programme seeks to provide a stealthy, affordable, single-seat fighter that would replace a wide range of US aircraft including the A-10, F-16, F/A-18 and AV-8B, while supplementing the F-15, F-22 and F-18E/F. JSF has evolved as a STOVL design and so Harrier experience will play an essential part in its development. The most important advance that can be made for any future STOVL fighter is blending the Harrier's independent, and somewhat complicated, set of lift and flight engine controls into one seamless system, allowing the pilot to translate from vertical to level flight with ease. A substantial amount of development of just such a system has already been done in the UK with the VAAC (Vectored-thrust Advanced Aircraft flight Control) Harrier – a modified Harrier T.Mk 2 – now flown by the DRA. The VAAC Harrier has been flying since 1983 with a variety of fly-by-wire control systems and other advancd controls. In the US, the NASA YAV-8B began flying in 1995 with a new HUD and flight control system that allowed pilots to make blind landing into very confined spaces, at night if necessary. The modified Harrier has been dubbed the VSRA (Vertical Systems Research Aircraft) and has been flown by pilots from the US Navy's Air Warfare Center, NASA and the UK's Defence Research Agency (DRA). The VSRA uses modified stick and throttle controls with newly devloped HUD displays to cue and control deceleration into the hover and landing.

Above: The latest model of the AGM-65 Maverick to be integrated into the USMC inventory is the AGM-65E semi-active laser homing model. AGM-65E was specially developed for the Marines to allow it to be used in close support of friendly troops.

Left: This early production AV-8B drops 500-lb bombs fitted with the Snakeye retarding tail, which is still a standard fit with the USMC and USN, but not the USAF.

Above: The Marines opted for a podded version of the General Electric (now Lockheed Martin Armament Systems) GAU-12/U Equaliser 25-mm cannon. The gun is carried to port, while the starboard pod carries 300 rounds of ammunition.

Below: This VMA-223 AV-8B is carrying four 1,000-lb Mk 83 AIR (Air Inflatable Retard) bombs fitted with the Goodyear Aerospace BSU-85 ballute tail fin.

Above: This VMA-311 AV-8B(NA) Harrier is seen here, in March 1995, carrying a heavy warload. In addition to two TERs (which are little used on the AV-8B) loaded with Mk 82 bombs, and two AGM-65 Mavericks on the inboard pylons, this aircraft is also carrying the distinctive boxy shape of a Sanders ALQ-162 defensive ECM pod. ALQ-162 operates in the 4 to 20 GHz bands.

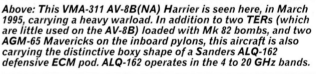

Above: Seen at MCAS Yuma, this VMA-311 AV-8B(NA) is carrying four Mk 7 dispensers, which are most commonly used in their Mk 20 Rockeye II cluster bomb form, containing 247 Mk 118 bomblets. The Mk 7 can also carry the CBU-59 APAM and CBU-78 Gator sub-munitions families.

Left: This VMA-223 AV-8B Harrier II Plus is carrying six inert Mk 83 bombs with the standard low-drag conical fins. Such heavy bombs are usually restricted to the two innermost hardpoints on the AV-8B's wing.

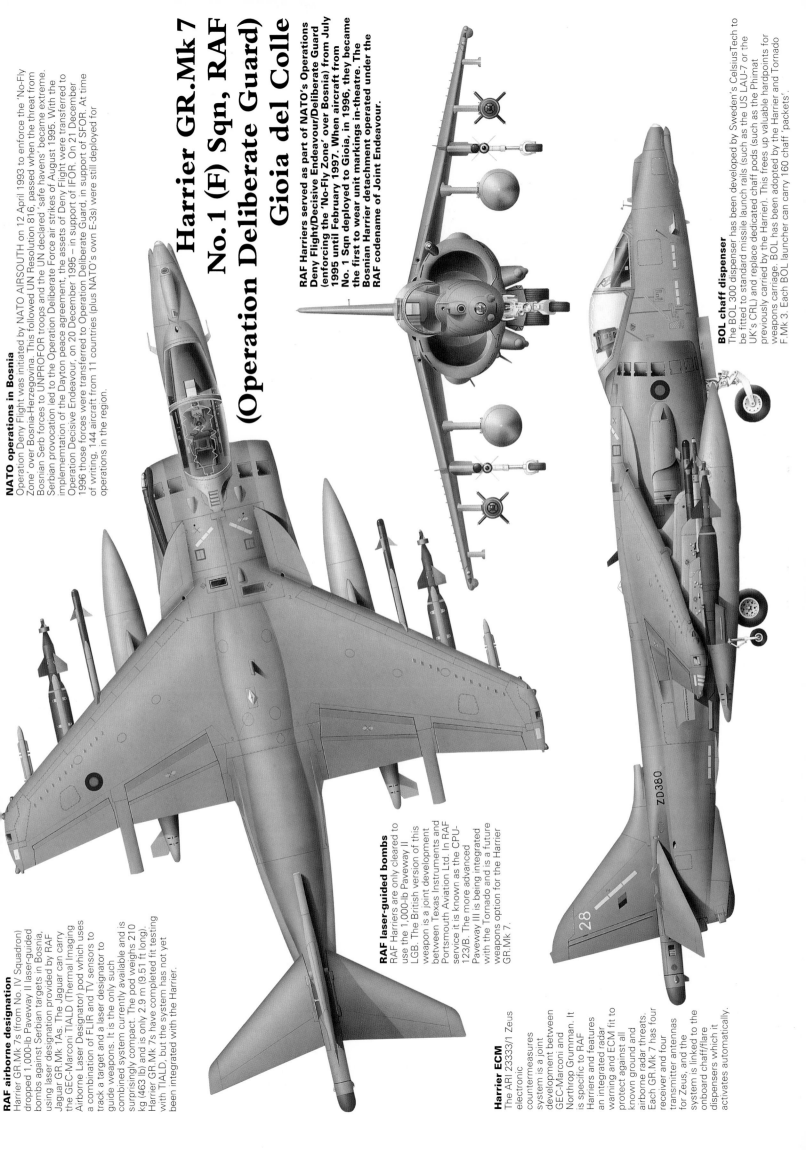

RAF airborne designation

Harrier GR.Mk 7s (from No. IV Squadron) dropped 1,000-lb Paveway II laser-guided bombs against Serbian targets in Bosnia, using laser designation provided by RAF Jaguar GR.Mk 1As. The Jaguar can carry the GEC-Marconi TIALD (Thermal Imaging Airborne Laser Designator) pod which uses a combination of FLIR and TV sensors to track a target and a laser designator to guide weapons. It is the only such combined system currently available and is surprisingly compact. The pod weighs 210 kg (463 lb) and is only 2.9 m (9.51 ft long). Harrier GR.Mk 7s have completed fit testing with TIALD, but the system has not yet been integrated with the Harrier.

Harrier GR.Mk 7
No.1 (F) Sqn, RAF
(Operation Deliberate Guard)
Gioia del Colle

NATO operations in Bosnia

Operation Deny Flight was initiated by NATO AIRSOUTH on 12 April 1993 to enforce the 'No-Fly Zone' over Bosnia-Herzegovina. This followed UN Resolution 816, passed when the threat from Bosnian Serb forces to UNPROFOR troops and the UN declared 'safe havens' became extreme. Serbian provocation led to the Operation Deliberate Force air strikes of August 1995. With the implementation of the Dayton peace agreement, the assets of Deny Flight were transferred to Operation Decisive Endeavour, on 20 December 1995 – in support of IFOR. On 21 December 1996 those forces were transferred to Operation Deliberate Guard, in support of SFOR. At time of writing, 144 aircraft from 11 countries (plus NATO's own E-3s) were still deployed for operations in the region.

RAF Harriers served as part of NATO's Operations Deny Flight/Decisive Endeavour/Deliberate Guard (enforcing the 'No-Fly Zone' over Bosnia) from July 1995 until February 1997. When aircraft from No. 1 Sqn deployed to Gioia, in 1996, they became the first to wear unit markings in-theatre. The Bosnian Harrier detachment operated under the RAF codename of Joint Endeavour.

BOL chaff dispenser

The BOL 300 dispenser has been developed by Sweden's CelsiusTech to be fitted to standard missile launch rails (such as the US LAU-7 or the UK's CRL) and replace dedicated chaff pods (such as the Phimat previously carried by the Harrier). This frees up valuable hardpoints for weapons carriage. BOL has been adopted by the Harrier and Tornado F.Mk 3. Each BOL launcher can carry 160 chaff 'packets'.

ZD380

28

RAF laser-guided bombs

RAF Harriers are only cleared to use the 1,000-lb Paveway II LGB. The British version of this weapon is a joint development between Texas Instruments and Portsmouth Aviation Ltd. In RAF service it is known as the CPU-123/B. The more advanced Paveway III is being integrated with the Tornado and is a future weapons option for the Harrier GR.Mk 7.

Harrier ECM

The ARI 23333/1 Zeus electronic countermeasures system is a joint development between GEC-Marconi and Northrop Grumman. It is specific to RAF Harriers and features an integrated radar warning and ECM fit to protect against all known ground and airborne radar threats. Each GR.Mk 7 has four receiver and four transmitter antennas for Zeus, and the system is linked to the onboard chaff/flare dispensers which it activates automatically.

Second-generation Harriers

Above: Air-to-air refuelling capability is an essential element in the US Marine Corps doctrine of rapid deployment/self deployment. As part of the major airframe changes and performance improvements of the AV-8B, the Harrier II acquired a more permanent tanking capability than the AV-8A. The early Harriers could mount an ungainly add-on refuelling probe above the port engine intake. With the AV-8B (and Harrier GR.Mk 5/7) came a retractable probe in a streamlined fairing. This probe is often described as 'bolt-on' but is virtually a permanent fixture on all aircraft. This AV-8B is a VMA-542 aircraft, refuelling from a KC-130.

Above right: The Marine Corps has four versions of the Hercules tanker: the KC-130F, KC-130R, KC-130T and KC-130T-30. The basic KC-130F was based on the C-130B, with uprated T56-A-16 engines and a new wing. It entered service in 1960. The KC-130R/T was based on the C-130H airframe, and has additional transferable fuel capacity. The KC-130T is intended as a quick-change tanker/transport. The latest version, the KC-130T-30, is the only stretched Hercules variant in US military service. Based on the KC-130T, it incorporates the 15-ft (4.57 m) fuselage stretch of the C-130H-30. The two Harriers here tanking from this KC-130F are both carrying the little-seen AN/ALQ-164 ECM pod on their centreline stations. This Harrier-specific pod has been in USMC service since 1995.

centreline stores pylons; this represented 40 per cent of the work on USMC and RAF aircraft, and BAe was promised 25 per cent of final assembly for deliveries to third countries. BAe also built carbon-fibre tailplanes for all RAF aircraft. A separate assembly line was established at Dunsfold for the final assembly of all RAF Harriers.

Even after the decision was taken to procure a BAe-built version of the US-designed AV-8B, there were pressures to change various items of equipment in order to better suit the aircraft to RAF needs, and to create more jobs for British industry. This approach has transformed the AV-8B from a cheap, fully-integrated, off-the-shelf aircraft into what was effectively a new weapons system, albeit in an existing airframe. It was probably inevitable that the RAF would require a more highly specified aircraft than the Marine Corps. USMC AV-8As had been equipped with a simpler weapons aiming computer than the RAF's Harriers, reflecting the USMC's less demanding role and more demanding maintenance requirements.

Unfortunately, the integration of many of the new RAF-specific systems did not go quite as planned, causing severe delays and cost escalation. Some people wondered why the RAF simply could not have acquired AV-8Bs to the same standards as the USMC, pointing to the cost and timescale benefits which would have accrued. This observation completely overlooked the fact that the basic USMC AV-8B simply did not meet the RAF's requirement, and that changes were not a luxury but a necessity.

UK systems for the GR.Mk 5

Although the US Marine Corps AV-8Bs were optimised for medium-level operation, the RAF expected its Harriers to continue to operate primarily at ultra-low level, and in the most dangerous threat environment in the world – the North German Plain, the inevitable battleground of the Cold War. The basic AV-8B was entirely unable to meet the RAF's stringent 1-lb (0.45-kg) bird, 600-kt (690-mph; 1110-km/h) impact requirement, and leading-edge skin thicknesses were increased, while the intake lips and wrap-round windscreen were also strengthened. The Hughes Angle Rate Bombing System (used on late-mark A-4 Skyhawks and optimised for medium-level attacks) was retained on the RAF's Harrier GR.Mk 5, although many thought that a Ferranti Laser Rangefinder and Marked Target Seeker (as used in the original Harrier GR.Mk 3, Jaguar and Tornado) would have been more useful. The ARBS uses collimated TV and laser spot trackers, and is optimised for medium-level use. The ARBS can be used to give a x6 magnification view ahead of the aircraft, presented on one of the MFDs.

For navigation at low level, the RAF demanded a moving map display, selecting a Ferranti projected map display similar to the equipment used in the Tornado, and

linking it to the Ferranti FIN 1075 INAS. The Ferranti moving map incorporated a 5.18-ft (1.57-m) film strip which was equivalent to 600 sq ft (56 m²) of charts and which was interfaced to the digital navigation computer. The system had provision for frames showing airfield approach charts, target details or FRCs. To enhance survivability, the aircraft was designed to incorporate a new Zeus internal ECM system (replacing the AV-8B's AN/ALR-67 RHAWS and podded AN/ALQ-164(V) jammer). Zeus detects and analyses radar frequencies, using an onboard library of more than 1,000 known emitters, displaying threats by direction and type, and assigning threat priorities. Threats can be jammed or countered automatically. The aircraft was also fitted with a Plessey Missile Approach Warning radar system in the tailcone, and with TACDS V-10 (AN/ALE-40) flare dispensers under the fuselage. The MAWS was essentially a small Doppler radar, and thus differed from the UV/IR-detector-based missile approach warner eventually fitted to USMC AV-8Bs. The RAF Harriers' integrated EW installation was also intended to incorporate CelsiusTech BOL chaff dispensers. They carried small packets of 160 0.3-in (8-mm) thick 'slices' of chaff, which would be ejected from the outrigger, 'blooming' rapidly in the wingtip vortices.

The RAF Harrier IIs received a new IFF transponder, replacing the Bendix AN/APX-100 used by the AV-8B with a Cossor IFF.4760, broadly compatible with the US Mk XII system. The GR.Mk 5 also introduced a GEC Avionics AD.3500 radio, giving secure voice capability.

Hardpoint changes

The RAF's brief combat experience in the Falklands had pointed to the need for extra pylons for the carriage of defensive AAMs, which otherwise used invaluable hard-points, two of which might already be required for the carriage of fuel tanks. If two more were used for AIM-9 Sidewinders, only two would be available for offensive weapons. This led the RAF to regard the standard AV-8B six-pylon wing as being wholly inadequate (the Kingston 'big wing' had incorporated wingtip launch rails). The decision was therefore taken to add two dedicated Sidewinder pylons to the wings of RAF Harriers, and the

addition of local strengthening within the wing structure for the new pylons was achieved without difficulty. The shallow new pylons did not interfere with weapons or tank carriage on the existing pylons and were neatly added to the forward end of the outrigger undercarriage fairings, which had to be fitted with a ceramic tile to protect them from damage by a Sidewinder's rocket efflux on launch.

The other underwing pylons were also redesigned to be able to accommodate the BL755 CBU, then perceived as being the RAF Harrier's primary weapon. The BL755 is heavier and bulkier than the Mk 82, around which the USMC AV-8B was designed.

The RAF's Harriers had always had a limited reconnaissance capability, with all aircraft carrying a port oblique F95 camera in the nose. No. IV Squadron in Germany and

No. 1417 Flight in Belize used a reconnaissance pod. The Harrier GR.Mk 5 was expected to retain a similar capability, and the most apparent external difference between USMC AV-8Bs and RAF Harrier GR.Mk 5s was the addition of a shallow fairing below the noses of the British aircraft. It was meant to accommodate a BAe MIRLS (Miniature/Militarised Infra-Red Linescan), adapted from the linescanner developed for the Tornado GR.Mk 1A, which was itself developed from commercial equipment. Intended to have a broad 200° field of view (from above the horizon to above the other), perhaps with a limited forward oblique coverage, the equipment was linked to a Computing Devices reconnaissance management system. It was intended that all GR.Mk 5s would be capable of carrying the equipment, but that only one squadron would be fully

The tail flash on this VMA-542 Harrier II Plus is evidence of the subtle return of squadron markings to the Marines' universally grey Harrier fleet. VMA-542 'Flying Tigers' transitioned to the AV-8B in 1986 and, in 1993, it became the first Harrier II Plus unit. The 'Flying Tigers' are one of the longest-standing Marine AV-8 units, having swapped their F-4Bs for AV-8As in June 1970.

equipped, thereby directly replacing the reconnaissance-roled Harrier GR.Mk 3s which had flown only with No. IV Squadron. In the event, the MIRLS failed to appear, and GR.Mk 5s flew with ballast in their undernose fairings.

New gun for the RAF

The original Harrier GR.Mk 3 (and the AV-8A/C) had carried a pair of 30-mm ADEN cannon. These slow-firing weapons were very different to the fast-firing but small-calibre 20-mm M61A1 used by most US service aircraft, and were bound to be replaced in the second-generation Harrier II. In designing the AV-8B, McDonnell Douglas replaced them with a single new GAU-12/A Equalizer 25-mm gun. After evaluation, the RAF decided that the new US weapon was not suitable for the RAF's GR.Mk 5, which was instead designed to carry a pair of 25-mm Royal Ordnance revolver cannons. They, it was felt, would offer a similar rate of fire (a combined rate of 1,650-1,850 rpm) to the single GAU-12, while delivering three times the kinetic energy of the old 30-mm cannon, with a muzzle velocity of 3,450 ft (1051 m) per second. Each pod contained 100 rounds of ammunition, which could include AP (armour piercing), HE (high explosive), APDS (AP discarding sabot), APHE incendiary and MP (multi-purpose) rounds, with disintegrating links. The new British weapon was thought to be more versatile, with better air-to-air performance, and the complete installation promised a weight saving of around 200 lb (90 kg). The British weapon could also fit inside slightly slimmer pods, which offered aerodynamic advantages, giving lower drag and allowing them to function more effectively as LIDS.

The RAF judged that the AV-8B's instantaneous rate of turn (about 15° per second) was inadequate (AST.409 required 20° per second). The USMC had pioneered the use of the Harrier in the air-to-air role, developing the technique of 'viffing' (VIFF – Vectoring In Forward Flight). The Corps had wired the outboard underwing pylons of its aircraft for the carriage of Sidewinders from an early stage, so it was extraordinary that it was a British invention (the LERX, first tested on the second P.1127 RAF, XV277) that transformed the turning ability of the second-generation Harrier. The LERX was originally designed for retrofit on the GR.Mk 3, and the surface adopted for the AV-8B was a smaller and less effective compromise.

It has been reported in several sources that British Harrier GR.Mk 7s dispensed with water injection, appropriating some of the weight/capacity of the water tank to increase internal fuel, but this is completely in error.

Production deliveries were originally scheduled to begin in mid-1986, with squadron deliveries beginning in 1987. Wittering did not receive a GR.Mk 5 until 1 July 1987, and operational flying began in March 1988. No. 1 (F) Squadron only reached its established strength in February 1989.

The first delay came about as the result of a freak accident to the sixth production Harrier GR.Mk 5, whose ejection seat drogue gun fired inadvertently, separating the pilot from the seat and dragging him, and his main parachute (shredding it in the process), through the broken canopy. The pilot fell to his death near Boscombe Down, while the Harrier flew on for 500 miles (805 km), and was intercepted by a USAF C-5 Galaxy during its flight. The Harriers were grounded while the cause of the accident was investigated. Doubt was cast on the seat (a Martin-Baker Mk 12H, which was one of the GR.Mk 5 specific items of equipment, replacing the US Stencel seat), leading to a prolonged grounding at a critical point in the programme. Completed aircraft awaited flight testing at Dunsfold, where they required the provision of new 'inflatable' hangars. The accident was eventually traced to a loose article which distorted the firing rod of the manual override when the pilot lowered his seat, so steps were taken to protect the rod against damage in the future.

More delays ensued because the British-specified tyres proved susceptible to 'creep', and had to be replaced. The new Sidewinder outrigger pylons initially proved impossible to use, since their nitrogen cooling bottles could not be replaced with the missile in place and the undercarriage down. Early RAF Harriers used AIM-9Gs on the pylons for publicity photos and the like, but when a powered-up missile or acquisition round was required, it was carried on a Sidewinder launch rail fitted to the outboard underwing pylon.

A slow service start

Even more seriously, the Ferranti FIN.1075 INS did not live up to expectations. Employing a floated, rate-integrating gyro platform, Ferranti's FIN.1075 was extremely advanced, but even in 1989 was insufficiently mature for service use. The equipment initially was of so little utility that the RAF were forced to equip the first batch of aircraft with the USMC-specified Litton ASN-130 INS sets. It then had to procure 32 more Litton sets to give additional aircraft (the first RAF Germany machines) a measure of operational capability. Fortunately, the FIN.1075 eventually came good, and now is regarded as a superb piece of equipment, fitted to all Harriers. From late 1992, some aircraft had GPS added, and their INSs were modified to FIN.1075G standard, with the facility to be automatically updated using inputs from the GPS. In the early days of the programme, though, many Harriers were delivered straight to storage at RAF Shawbury while the problems were addressed.

The delayed deliveries of Harrier GR.Mk 5s meant that the aircraft had a 'slow start'. A Harrier Conversion Team (with three pilots who had trained on the AV-8B simulator with the USMC at Cherry Point) was established within No. 233 OCU in February 1987, but did not begin flying

TAV-8B
1 Gruppo Aereo
Marina Militare
Grottaglie

Italy joined the Harrier club in May 1989 when it ordered two TAV-8Bs for initial pilot training, to be conducted in the United States. A front-line force of 16 Harrier II Plus aircraft followed. The TAV-8Bs were delivered in August 1991, at a reported cost of $25 million each.

TAV-8B changes

This two-seat operational trainer version of the Harrier, which has been delivered to the US Marine Corps and the Italian navy, has a forward fuselage stretch of 3 ft 9 in (1.2 m) compared to the AV-8B. To compensate for the resultant change in the centre of gravity the fin has also been extended, by 1 ft 5 in (0.43 m). Internal fuel capacity remains unchanged but the TAV-8B has only two hardpoints under each wing. The RAF's equivalent two-seat aircraft, the Harrier T.Mk 10, has eight underwing pylons and the full FLIR and night vision system fit of the GR.Mk 7 attack version.

Italy's carrier: the *Giuseppe Garibaldi*

Named for the great Italian patriot, Giuseppe Garibaldi, who led the 19th century unification of Italy, the Marina Militare's sole CVS (light aircraft-carrier) was laid down in March 1981, launched in June 1983 and commissioned in 1985. Flagship of the fleet, the *Garibaldi* is a 10,000-ton vessel, which makes it roughly half the size of the Royal Navy's 'Invincible'-class ships. The vessel is armed with Teseo Mk 2 anti-ship missiles, Aspide SAMs, 40-mm cannons and Mk 46 torpedoes for anti-submarine defence. Its air group can comprise either 16 Harriers or 18 SH-3D Sea Kings, with a mix deployed for routine operations.

Italian naval aviation

Until new legislation was passed on 29 January 1989, Italy's naval air arm was forbidden from operating fixed-wing aircraft, at the instigation of the air force. The dispute between the two services pre-dated World War II. As a result, until the arrival of the Harriers, the only aircraft embarked on modern Marina Militare vessels were SH-3D Sea Kings and AB 212s.

Electronic countermeasures

Like US Marine Corps aircraft, the Italian Harriers have provision for the Sanders AN/ALQ-164 deception jamming pod on their centreline station. The ALQ-164 combines the features of the earlier ALQ-126B and ALQ-162, allowing it to counter both pulsed and continuous-radar threats. ALQ-164 is a reprogrammable, multi-mode system that can be linked to the aircraft's onboard radar warning receiver.

Sourcing Italy's Harriers

Aircraft for the Italian navy were built from parts supplied by McDonnell Douglas (now the Boeing-owned McDonnell Aircraft and Missile Systems) and British Aerospace. For these aircraft the total US/UK workshare is divided 60:40 (for RAF Harriers it is 50:50). The wing, front and forward centre fuselage, underfuselage fences, strakes and tailplanes were sourced in the US. The rear centre and rear fuselage, fins, rudders and, of course, the complete engine control system were supplied by the UK. Italy's AV-8B II Pluses were then assembled by Alenia.

Uprated engines

The pilot production AV-8Bs and TAV-8Bs were fitted with Rolls-Royce F402-RR-404A Pegasus engines. It was two aircraft from this early batch that were transferred to the Italian navy, to allow training to began as early as possible. However, to make them compatible with Italy's Harrier II Pluses, the TAV-8Bs were later re-engined with the 23,800-lb (105.9-kN) F402-RR-408 Pegasus 11-61. Engine assembly and installation work was undertaken in Italy.

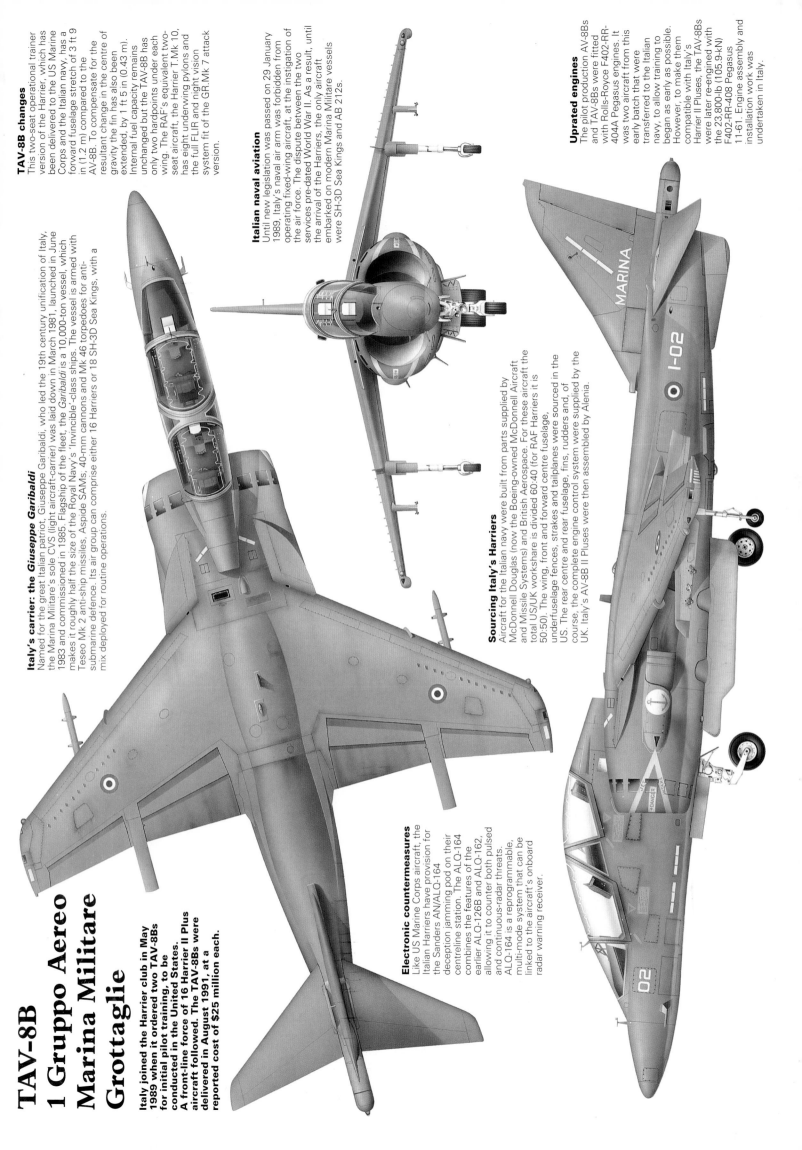

Second-generation Harriers

on the GR.Mk 5 until March 1988. The first conversion course began on 18 July 1988, using the Spanish EAV-8B simulator at Rota. The course provided eight days of ground school, teaching pilots the new aircraft's systems, followed by 16 flying sorties, five of which were range sorties using ARBS. Most of the initial trainees were long-time Harrier GR.Mk 3 pilots, who required little training, and ground began to be made up. About six flying hours were dedicated to handling, four to formation flying, and five to ARBS work plus simulated attack profiles.

Although serious, the Harrier GR.Mk 5's problems were viewed as being temporary teething troubles, and a further order for 34 more Harrier IIs was placed in early 1988. This order brought the total to 96, and promised to allow the re-equipment of all the RAF's Harrier squadrons, not just those at RAF Gütersloh in Germany. Original plans had called for the retention of the 'youngest' GR.Mk 3s at Wittering, where they were to have operated after receiving a comprehensive upgrade that would have included modifications to extend fatigue life, a small LERX, enlarged fuel tanks, twin Sidewinder launch rails, a nav-attack system upgrade, new ECM equipment and a new anti-armour weapon. However, procurement of the extra 34 Harrier IIs brought the GR.Mk 3's career to a premature close. This was perhaps just as well, since no convincing solution had been found to the problem of the GR.Mk 3's very limited remaining fatigue life, which was pegged at a modest 3,000 flying hours.

No. 1 (F) Squadron (originally to have retained GR.Mk 3s) was declared operational in the autumn of 1988, and No. 3 Squadron began its transition to the new aircraft from May 1989. Unable to drop full-scale live ground attack weapons, No. 1 (F) Squadron went on Missile Practice Camp at RAF Valley in July 1989, and mounted a deployment to Bardufoss, Norway, its aircraft wearing a temporary coat of disruptive white camouflage. No. IV Squadron (originally scheduled to have been the RAF's first GR.Mk 5 unit) soldiered on with GR.Mk 3s until 7 December 1990, when it transitioned straight to the more advanced GR.Mk 7.

As the second-generation Harrier began to enter service, it assumed a subtly different role to that undertaken by its predecessor, with more emphasis on hitting targets further behind the front line. What had been a pure CAS (close air support) mission shifted to become a BAI (battlefield air

interdiction) and FOFA (follow on forces attack) role. This alteration in role inferred operating at longer ranges, but also necessitated improved night-attack capability, since enemy reinforcements were most likely to 'move up' under cover of darkness. The new batch of aircraft (to be designated as GR.Mk 7s) were to feature additional night-attack capability, although they used different equipment to the McDonnell Douglas-developed Night Attack Harrier II for the US Marine Corps. The aircraft was not intended to operate as an all-weather, day/night attack aircraft, since its sensors were essentially clear air capable only, with even light rain severely degrading FLIR performance. Night navigation remained difficult until the introduction of GPS.

The Nightbird programme

Development of equipment for the night-attack role had gathered pace during the 1980s, most notably under the joint RAE/DRA Nightbird programme. Initially, rudimentary night-vision goggles were flown aboard a variety of aircraft, from Andovers to Hunters and Harrier T.Mk 4As. From 1988, lighter, balanced helmet/NVG combinations were developed and flown. Under a programme known as Penetrate, FLIR imagery was projected onto a raster HUD. GEC developed a terrain-referenced navigation system and a new digital map display. Under the Nightbird programme, various equipment was flown 'tactically' aboard an A&AEE Buccaneer, a Tornado, the 'Nightcat' Jaguar T.Mk 2A, and a pair of Harrier T.Mk 4As. The latter aircraft had NVG-compatible cockpits, and featured an experimental FLIR in their extended LRMTS nosecones, together with a developmental Ferranti 4510 cursive/raster HUD. The first Nightbird Harrier was initially used by the RAE's Flight Systems department, then by the SAOEU at Boscombe Down, where it was joined by the second modified T.Mk 4A. The Nightbird programme provided a steep learning curve for its participants, supplying general lessons in the limitations of NVGs,

and the difficulties imposed by poor weather, brightly lit urban areas and even a full moon. It also revealed the difficulties imposed by flying a fast jet while looking through relatively narrow field of view NVGs, and of the problems posed by monochromatic vision and the lack of depth perception. Equipment was refined, improved and even invented as the scientists reacted to the pilots' findings. For VTOL operations, RAE Bedford invented a cheap, simple night landing light system (the Bedford Experimental Lighting System), which used standard 240-V household fluorescent light tubes, powered by a 12-V battery. This made them invisible to the naked eye, but bright enough to mark the hover position to a pilot wearing NVGs.

GR.Mk 5 gives way to GR.Mk 7

The RAF's first 41 Harriers were built as GR.Mk 5s, followed by 21 built to an interim GR.Mk 5A standard. This incorporated wiring for the FLIR and certain fittings and was intended to allow easy conversion to full GR.Mk 7 standards. All but three GR.Mk 5As were delivered straight to storage at RAF Shawbury, ZD433 going to Wittering as a ground instructional maintenance trainer, ZD466 to Rolls-Royce at Filton, and the last GR.Mk 5A, ZD470, to Boscombe Down on 19 June 1990. The GR.Mk 5As were followed by the 34 production GR.Mk 7s. A total of 58 surviving GR.Mk 5s and GR.Mk 5As was retrofitted to GR.Mk 7 standards, the number being held low by attrition.

The first GR.Mk 7s were two rebuilt Development Batch GR.Mk 5s, ZD318 and ZD319, which retained the earliest grey colour scheme. ZD318 made the GR.Mk 7's maiden flight on 29 November 1989, transferring to Boscombe Down for service trials on 30 May 1990, just as the first 'production' GR.Mk 7s began rolling off the Dunsfold production line. Conversions of existing aircraft began with GR.Mk 5 ZD380, redelivered to Dunsfold on 9 January 1990, and delivered to No. IV Squadron on 21 December. The £16 million contract to update 58 GR.Mk 5/

Above: Many of the improvements integrated into the AV-8B Harrier II Plus came as a result of experience during Operation Desert Storm.

Far left: Marine Corps Harriers flew 7.7 per cent of all US combat sorties during Operation Desert Storm – 3,380 sorties were made by 86 aircraft. When Iraq invaded Kuwait the AV-8B(NA) was not yet fully operational so the squadrons that deployed to the Gulf were all equipped with AV-8Bs. The first to arrive were MAG-13's VMA-311, along with VMA-542. The Harriers travelled to Shaikh Isa air base, in Bahrain, but transferred to the King Abdul Aziz base in Saudi Arabia. VMA-231 arrived in December 1990, followed by a detachment from VMA-513. VMA-331 arrived with MAG-40, 4th MEB, embarked aboard the USS Nassau. A dark grey disruptive pattern was painted over the Harrier's basic grey camouflage, as seen on this aircraft overflying the burning Al Burgan oil fields, west of Kuwait City.

5As with FLIR, NVG-compatible cockpits and digital moving maps was announced shortly before ZD380 was delivered, on 11 November 1990. The first GR.Mk 5A to be upgraded was ZD430, which was delivered from Shawbury in September 1990, and left for No. IV Squadron on 9 April 1991. The conversion programme was completed in 1994.

GR.Mk 7 for night attack

Introduction of the GR.Mk 7 was astonishingly rapid. One distinguished analyst commented, "Not for 40 years has one mark of RAF combat aircraft so swiftly been replaced by another of the same design. No sooner had the…GR.5 entered service with 1 and 3 Squadrons and 233 OCU, then it was giving way to the GR.7." This was true, at least insofar as the physical disposition of GR.Mk 7 airframes was concerned, although it was many months before pilots worked up to become 'night combat ready' and before the new variant could actually be used operationally in its intended night-attack role.

The Harrier GR.Mk 7 is the RAF's equivalent to the USMC's Night Attack model, and is for the most part similarly equipped, although almost every individual new item of equipment is different to the equivalent item in the US variant. The new variant received a new GEC-Marconi colour map display and revised software for the Computing Devices ACCS 2000 (Unisys AN/AYK-14) mission computer. An off-the-shelf GEC Avionics FLIR is mounted in front of the cockpit, as close to the pilot's eye level as is possible without obscuring forward vision. This minimises parallax problems when the FLIR image is projected in the HUD, although the image is usually presented in the starboard MFD. To allow the presentation of FLIR imagery in the HUD, the GR.Mk 7 has a new Smiths Industries wide-angle HUD. A HOTAS button on the throttle allows the pilot to select either a hot-equals-black or reversed polarity picture. The FLIR incorporates other 'clever' features, including V-shaped arrow markers which can point towards hot spots in the picture (e.g., vehicle engines), drawing attention to what may be a target. The temperature differential required is not huge, and on the ground pilots sometimes find the FLIR markers pointing at bald ground crew, whose heads tend to give off more heat!

GEC-Ferranti Nightbird NVGs complement the fixed FLIR, allowing the pilot to 'look into a turn' or to scan areas outside the FLIR coverage, and are image intensifiers, not reliant on IR to obtain a picture. As such, the pilot can see objects which may not show up in the FLIR. Flying with NVGs is not easy, since the image is monocular, with no depth and no colour. The pilot must move his head constantly to compensate for the very narrow field of view (no more than 40°), which can be disorientating. The pilot will usually 'read' the HUD symbology through the NVGs, but glances below them to look at the moving map or FLIR picture. The NVGs are mounted on a swivel, and can be hinged upwards out of the way when not in use. When flying with NVGs, a clear visor held on with press-studs usually replaces the normal twin-visor arrangement. On the GR.Mk 7, the Martin-Baker Mk 12 ejection seat is modified to Type 12 Mk 2 standards to allow automatic jettison of the NVGs, using compressed gas, actuated by a 'pulse' of energy through the pilot's helmet 'pigtail'. If a pilot ejected with the NVGs in place there would be a strong possibility of him breaking his neck, and although it is preferable to remove the goggles and stow them prior to ejection, an automatic disconnect is provided.

Externally, the GR.Mk 7 differed from the GR.Mk 5 very little, with an almost impossibly small fairing for the

FLIR above the lengthened nose (a 9-in/23-cm extension was incorporated, giving a more graceful profile). The MIRLS fairing below the nose was finally deleted and replaced by a pair of prong-like fairings (sometimes referred to as 'tusks') on each lower 'corner' of the nose, which house forward hemisphere antennas for the Zeus ECM .

The new nose shape was, inexplicably, one of the 'slowest ships' in the package of improvements which formed the GR.Mk 7 'convoy', and delayed tests aimed at ascertaining the effect of the new nose contours on the airflow into the intakes, and especially on engine stall margins. The problem was one of plastic filler breaking off, a potentially dangerous FOD hazard. When they eventually finished, the trials demonstrated that the new nose shape had no appreciable effect on handling or intake airflow.

Although designed and built for night-attack duties, the first GR.Mk 7s entered service in the day CAS/BAI role. No. IV Squadron re-equipped with GR.Mk 7s from September 1990, trading up directly from first-generation GR.Mk 3s and becoming the first GR.Mk 7 squadron. It was 18 months before the GR.Mk 7 flew a representative sortie at night, and No. 1 (F) Squadron was destined to become the first night-attack declared RAF Harrier unit.

Flying with NVGs began (with the SAOEU at Boscombe Down) on 11 December 1990. Subsequently, the SAOEU detached three aircraft to MCAS Yuma, Arizona in March-April 1991, where they flew 150 hours with and alongside the new Night Attack AV-8Bs of VMA-211. A three-man night-attack trials cadre of Wing Commander Keith Grumbley, Flight Lieutenant Paul Gunnell and Flight Lieutenant Steve Hawkins began intensive night trials on their return, dropping practice

Above and top: The RAF's UK Harrier force is based at RAF Wittering, in Cambridgeshire, which provides a wide range of operating environments. On the northern side of the airfield a 1,000-ft x 100-ft (305-m x 30.5-m) runway is provided to practise short-strip/road operations (top). The Vigo Wood site (above) allows year-round rough field training, though operations are curtailed by wet winter ground which requires 'tin strips' to be laid. Full deployment exercises are conducted 'in the field', including weapons handling and even NBC procedures, over one/two-week stints, once or twice each year.

bombs from heights as low as 200 ft (60 m). Finally, on 19 February 1992, Gunnell and Hawkins flew a fully representative night-attack profile from West Freugh to Garvie Island, where they dropped live 1,000-lb (454-kg) bombs. One of the aircraft was equipped with a modified FIN.1075G, receiving inputs from a spine-mounted GPS, giving much enhanced navigational accuracy.

The SAOEU did much more than test the GR.Mk 7's new sensors and systems, however, developing the tactics, techniques and doctrine necessary to fully exploit the aircraft's potential. They included operating in conjunction with Tornado GR.Mk 1s, which could use their radar to shepherd Harriers through patches of poor weather.

Starting with ZG506 (the 17th new-build GR.Mk 7, and the 77th Kingston-built Harrier II), RAF Harriers finally received the larger 100 per cent LERX (100 per cent of the size of the LERX originally designed for retrofit to the GR.Mk 3). The new 7.5 sq ft (0.7 m²) LERX curved down towards its leading edge, and was deeper in cross-section, fairing smoothly into the upper wing surface contours. The original 4.85 sq ft (0.45 m²) LERX, by contrast, was a simple flat plate, which left a step down from the top of the wing leading edge. Surprisingly, retrofit

of the new LERX has been slow, and many RAF Harriers (including the T.Mk 10s) retain the early, smaller LERX. When the new LERXes are retrofitted, minor adjustments have to be made to the Honeywell AN/ASW-46(V)2 SAAHS (Stability Augmentation and Attitude Hold System) to allow the increased tailplane movement which counters the destabilising effects of the increased surface area forward of the centre of pressure.

Deliveries of the GR.Mk 7 were rapid, but the aircraft took longer to be ready for front-line service. On 30 July 1991 the entire RAF Harrier II fleet was grounded following three inflight electrical fires in a period of only two months, one having caused the loss of an aircraft. The RAF declined to accept new GR.Mk 7s while modifications were made to the RAF Germany Harriers, resulting in the delivery of only 13 aircraft in 1991, and the imposition of penalties on BAe of £40,000 per aircraft per month.

Snags in service

The cause of the inflight fires was traced to chafing of Kapton wiring insulated with carbon – a problem discovered and dealt with by the USMC in 1987. The wiring wore, causing arcing, while the rectifier was already working at maximum capacity and thus was unable to cope with power surges. Tags were added to separate wires, and lightweight Tefzel wiring was substituted for Kapton. Finally, the power-switching panel in the rectifier was improved. Half of the fleet were flying again by late September after an interim repair (priority being given to repairs to the Germany-based aircraft) and deliveries of GR.Mk 7s recommenced on 4 November 1991. New wiring looms were installed during Majors and Mk 5 to Mk 7 conversions.

As if the wiring problems were not enough, fatigue cracks to frames 31 and 32 were discovered in 1991. They were caused by acoustic stresses adjacent to the rear nozzles, but proved to be reasonably minor. Accordingly, the RAF produced its own interim repair (a metal patch which took each aircraft out of service for some three weeks), before BAe produced a definitive repair incorporated during GR.Mk 7 conversion. This involved rebuilding the affected area with thicker titanium skins and doubled stringers.

More seriously, when it entered service the GR.Mk 7 was hardly an operational aircraft, and was virtually unable to carry any meaningful weapon load. At a press facility

Above: Deployments to Norway have been routine for the RAF's Harriers for many years. As part of the Arctic Express exercises, Harriers have spent several weeks operating from Bodø, sometimes with Jaguars and Tornados. On previous Arctic deployments No. 1 Squadron has camouflaged its Harrier GR.Mk 5s with a temporary white overlay, but this has not been adopted by the GR.Mk 7s.

Left: The Harrier has been based in Germany since 1970, but in 1998 the two squadrons – Nos 3 and IV – will return to RAF Cottesmore. This is a result of the post-Cold War defence cuts and also of the virtual elimination of all low-level flying training in Germany; the latter was undertaken universally in 'the good old days' and is essential for aircrew to maintain operational effectiveness. All RAF units in Germany have been forced to transit to the UK for any low-level flying. These No. 3 Squadron aircraft are seen tanking from a VC10 tanker, in 1996, having made the trek from RAF Laarbruch to conduct a four-ship low-level exercise over Scotland. Refuelling is essential as its gives the aircraft full tanks with which to begin, and one and half hours' flying time over the lakes and mountains.

marking the Harrier GR.Mk 5's service entry, years before, the press release had stated that the new aircraft could carry Hunting BL755 CBUs, MATRA rocket pods, laser-guided Paveway II bombs, conventional HE bombs and a pair of 25-mm ADEN cannon, along with AIM-9s. In fact, few of the listed weapons had been cleared for carriage by the aircraft then, and some would not be available to the Harrier force for another 10 years. Even by February 1991 (when USMC Harriers were at war in the Persian Gulf), RAF GR.Mk 5s and GR.Mk 7s were cleared only to drop 6.6-lb (3-kg) practice bombs and to fire AIM-9Ls, although trials were reportedly then proceeding well with Phimat chaff dispensers (first carried during a March-April deployment to Norway), slick and retarded 1,000-lb bombs and MATRA 155 SNEB rocket pods. All these weapons had been cleared by BAe, but not necessarily by the RAF.

No. 1 (F) Squadron had been declared to SACEUR's Strategic Reserve (with GR.Mk 5s) on 2 October 1989, though quite how useful the aircraft could have been

remains open to question. Harrier QWIs had very little to do in those earliest days, except to long for some solutions to the problems which hamstrung their aircraft.

The problems were essentially due to poor software integration, although they were exacerbated by delays to various equipment items. The sudden appearance of Phimat, for instance, was indicative of delays to the Harrier's advanced internal EW suite, which had been intended to incorporate BOL chaff dispensers inside the outrigger Sidewinder launch rails. Their unavailability led to the interim use of the French-built Phimat pods, usually carried below the port outboard underwing pylon.

Zeus itself was not cleared for use by the first GR.Mk 7s, but underwent extensive trials at NAS China Lake. The MAWS was similarly delayed, and was extensively tested at China Lake (on a GR.Mk 5) during 1989 under Operation Horsefly. Clearance trials stretched into 1994, integrating the various elements in order that (for example) the MAWS could automatically trigger the appropriate countermeasures.

Right: An increasing emphasis has been placed on sending RAF Harriers to sea, to complement the Royal Navy's Sea Harriers which are less capable in the attack role. Experience over Bosnia has shown that the two could make a good team and the only obstacles in the way may be inter-service rivalries, rather than operational problems. As a prelude to renewed sea-going trials, three GR.Mk 7s from the RAF's Strike Attack Operational Evaluation Unit travelled to RNAS Yeovilton – home of the Sea Harrier – to use the ski-jump and simulated carrier deck.

Above: In June 1994 the SAOEU went to sea aboard HMS Illustrious. The Harrier GR.Mk 7s were cleared to operate from the carrier with weapons (and external fuel) loads of up to 13,325 lb (6056 kg), which far exceeded that of the Sea Harrier. In 1997 the first serious exercise with a combined RAF/RN Harrier group was made as part of Operation Ocean Wave '97, a major deployment to the Gulf and the Far East.

Life on the Harrier GR.Mk 7 squadrons was different to life on the Harrier force in GR.Mk 3 days. The introduction of the longer-range Harrier GR.Mk 7 allowed operations from bases further back from the front line, while the need to carry heavier loads led to increased emphasis being placed on prepared, harder surfaces. The shifts from CAS to BAI and FOFA and from GR.Mk 3 to GR.Mk 7 prompted a shift from rural to urban forward operating bases. Operations from supermarket car parks (with aircraft using large retail units as hides) had always been envisaged but could not be practised in peacetime. As Cold War tensions abated, it became increasingly difficult to use even rural sites, as environmentalists and local people began to object to the disruption caused. Moreover, from 1990 Germany imposed successively more stringent limitations on low flying, lifting the base height from 250 to 500 ft (76 to 152 m), and extending a 250-ft limit from 15 minutes to the final IP-to-target run. It then imposed a low flying ban below 400 ft (122 m), then eventually below 1,000 ft (305 m), forcing the Gütersloh-based Harriers to export most of their low-flying training back to the UK. The Tornado Turnaround Facility at RAF Leuchars was expanded to provide support to RAF Germany Harriers 'popping over for the day'. By 1994, one pilot on No. IV

Squadron worked out that pilots spent an average of 180 days away from base, most of it in the UK for low-flying training. As RAF Germany shrank in size, the Harriers moved west from Gütersloh to the clutch airfield at Laarbruch, but this did nothing to help the situation. No. 3 Squadron moved on 16 November 1992, and No. IV followed on 27 November. This was made possible by the increased range of the Harrier GR.Mk 7.

Expanded capabilities, further deployments

By late 1992, the Harrier GR.Mk 7 was a much more useful operational aircraft, capable of carrying a range of weapons, including BL755 CBUs, 1,000-lb bombs, and MATRA 155 rocket pods containing 18 68-mm SNEB rockets. During 1991, No. 3 Squadron completed re-equipment with the GR.Mk 7, and the GR.Mk 5s were concentrated at Wittering, pending their turn in the conversion process. No. 1 (F) Squadron began flying GR.Mk 7s in June 1992, and had completed conversion to the new variant by November 1992. In that month, five No. 1 (F) Squadron aircraft were fitted with GPS (like the SAOEU GPS 'prototype'), opening the door to long-distance overseas deployments, operations over featureless and unfamiliar terrain, and long-range overwater flights. This capability was exploited during a deployment by four aircraft to MCAS Yuma in April 1993, following a No. 3 Sqn deployment to Kuantan, Malaysia in September 1992.

Once re-equipped with GR.Mk 7s, No. 1 (F) Squadron rapidly transitioned to the night-attack role. Original plans had provided for the establishment of a single specialist flight (with six aircraft and eight pilots) within No. 1 (F) Squadron, but instead the whole squadron transitioned to the role, and all without down-declaring from its SACEUR Strategic Reserve Commitment. An experienced SAOEU and Nightbird Harrier pilot, Squadron Leader Mike Harwood, was posted in as OC Night, reporting to the Squadron CO. The squadron soon had six GPS-equipped aircraft (ZD431, 435, 437, 438, 463 and 464), and ZD469 was fitted with a video recorder for debriefing training flights.

No. 1 (F) Squadron's pilots worked up in their new role from the autumn of 1992, practising all types of take-off and landing, medium-level formation flying, navigation and weapons delivery, low-level lay-down, dive and rocket attack missions, and inflight refuelling (with and without NVGs). Nos 3 and IV Squadrons in Germany received 'switch-on clearance' for their night-attack systems and sensors in early 1993, but did not begin training until No. 1 (F) Squadron completed its second night-attack training session in April 1994. This was largely as a result of German

civilian sensibilities, which made night flying training in Germany virtually impossible. The period May-September was not used for night-attack training, since skies were not dark enough. No. 3 Squadron then converted to the night role, each pilot flying some 25 sorties, mainly from Wittering. Ten of the squadron's GR.Mk 7s deployed to Marham in December 1994 for intensive night-flying practice and training, and more aircraft then deployed to Leeming in December. No. IV Squadron was scheduled to undergo a similar night conversion programme in the winter of 1995-96, but a deployment to Italy to support operations over Bosnia delayed this. Thus No. IV, which had been the first squadron to receive GR.Mk 7s, became the last to actually operate in the night-attack role for which the aircraft had been optimised.

Operation Warden

In 1992 deployments had been made to Chile (for participation in the FIDAE air show) and Nellis AFB (for a Red Flag). 1993 saw an even more significant overseas deployment: Operation Warden. Although billed as an operation protecting the Kurds in northern Iraq, Operation Provide Comfort (Operation Warden being the British element of the US-led mission) did little more than monitor Saddam Hussein's breaches of the UN-declared safe area. During the GR.Mk 3 era, No. 1 (F) Squadron had always been the Harrier squadron tasked with fulfilling and maintaining 'out-of-area' commitments (especially NATO SACEUR Strategic Reserve duties), with the exception of the detachment in Belize (a purely national commitment), which was always shared between the three squadrons. When it became necessary to replace Jaguars on Operation Warden, all three Harrier squadrons were on the verge of being declared to NATO's Reaction Force (Air) and it was the RAF Germany squadrons that provided the aircraft, and the majority of personnel, for the detachment (with each of the three front-line squadrons taking a two-month turn at manning the deployment). The Jaguar force had been maintaining an almost constant overseas detachment since the build-up to the Gulf War, and needed a rest. Nine Laarbruch-based GR.Mk 7s were fitted with FIN.1075G and had their dark green camouflage over-painted in washable medium grey ARTF (Alkali Removable Temporary Finish); eight deployed to Incirlik to take over from the eight-aircraft Jaguar detachment, operating primarily in the armed reconnaissance role. A total of 18 aircraft eventually received the Warden modifications.

New reconnaissance mission

Giving the Harrier GR.Mk 5/7 a reconnaissance capability has taken many years. The originally specified MIRLS has never materialised, and the undernose MIRLS fairing of the GR.Mk 5 only ever carried ballast, and later Zeus LRUs. The Harrier force effectively lost its reconnaissance commitments in the run-up to the retirement of the

GR.Mk 3. Nos 1 and IV Squadrons lost their reconnaissance intelligence and exploitation facilities in May 1989. When the RAF's second-generation Harriers did need to carry out reconnaissance missions over northern Iraq, they had to be hastily modified to carry GR.Mk 3 pods that had been withdrawn from service. This modification required the provision of a great deal of new wiring and took 650 man-hours per aircraft. These old pods contained a fan of four F.95 cameras giving horizon-to-horizon coverage, with a single forward oblique F.135. Readoption of the reconnaissance role also necessitated intensive training for the pilots involved. During the course of the Harriers' commitment in Turkey, the old pods were replaced by newly-procured and more modern reconnaissance pods.

Operation Warden ushered in a new era for the RAF's Harrier force. The aircraft gained a much improved reconnaissance role (top). This GR.Mk 7 is carrying a test camera pod. 'W' series codes were applied (above) to signify the Warden duty. The Harriers were replaced by Jaguars in April 1995. This AIM-9L-armed Harrier (below) is seen on its last Warden flight, in 1995.

Second-generation Harriers

A number of reconnaissance pods were evaluated by the SAOEU even before the Harriers deployed to Incirlik to participate in Operation Warden. They included the Vinten Vicon 18 Series 403, a Vinten-owned flight trials pod quoted by some sources as containing a Type 753 panoramic camera and a Type 4000 linescan. The pod can contain various sensor configurations, and has flown with a number of new-generation EO- and IR-based sensors, usually with an optical panoramic camera to establish 'ground truth'. Reports that the Harrier has carried the massive Vicon 57 multi-sensor pod are entirely erroneous, for the pod is much too large for the Harrier.

Harrier recce pods

For Warden, the Harrier augmented the old GR.Mk 3 pods by using the Vicon 18 Series 603 LOROP pod (three of which were acquired for use by the Jaguars during the Gulf War, and handed over when the Jaguars left Incirlik). The Series 603 contained a single F.144 (Type 690) camera with a 900-mm/36-in (7° FoV) lens, but had no space for a panoramic camera for image cross-referencing. This meant that a 603-equipped Harrier would usually operate in conjunction with an aircraft carrying the original pod.

Later, the Harrier was cleared for use with the Vicon 18 Series 601 GP-1 pod, which contains a single Type 690 (F.144) camera with a 450-mm lens, plus a Type 900B (F.152) panoramic camera with a 3-in lens aft. Eight GP-1s were acquired to meet an Urgent Operational Requirement for additional medium-level reconnaissance capability, six primarily for use by the Tornado GR.Mk 1 and GR.Mk 1A, and two for the Harrier force. (Four more pods were subsequently acquired for the Jaguar.) Aircraft carrying the pods were either those originally modified to carry the GR.Mk 3 pods, or new aircraft with the same wiring changes.

During Operation Warden flights, Harriers usually operated in pairs, each aircraft carrying a reconnaissance pod on the centreline, with AIM-9Ls, two CBU-87 cluster bombs, a Phimat pod and two 250-Imp gal (1136-litre) external fuel tanks. They tended to launch in waves of six aircraft, with each pair assigned between 12 and 18 targets and supported by VC10 tankers. Clearances for the CBU-87 and the CRV-7 rocket (in 19-round LAU-5003B/A pods) were obtained specifically for the medium-altitude role, as practised in Operation Warden. The Harrier GR.Mk 7 could carry its load farther than could a Jaguar, but the aircraft was considerably less maintainable, and to sustain the same tempo of operations required more aircraft and more personnel.

The switch from CAS-type operations with the first-generation Harrier to longer-range interdiction missions with the GR.Mk 7 led to a requirement for enhanced mission planning equipment. This led to an order for 50 Advanced Mission Planning Aids from EDS Scicon (for a reported £50 million) similar to the system planned for the Tornado GR.Mk 4. The AMPA computer receives the incoming ATM (Air Tasking Message) and generates a provisional route, taking advantage of known enemy defences and using terrain masking where possible. The route is complete with waypoints, fuel, timings and speeds to meet the Time on Target (ToT) specified in the ATM. Pilots can view a synthetic three-dimensional view of any feature, pictured from the direction of approach and shaded realistically to simulate sun or moonlight at the planned time. The system can also store reconnaissance imagery. The pilot can amend the route as necessary, before downloading the plan into a portable electronic data store from which it would then be loaded into the aircraft.

By the mid-1990s, the Harrier GR.Mk 5/GR.Mk 7 had left many of its problems behind, though one legacy of the early difficulties (particularly the software problems) was a huge backlog of clearances for various weapons, systems and items of equipment. When he retired in 1997, the

outgoing Chief of the Air Staff, Air Chief Marshal Sir Michael Graydon, admitted that "the Harrier GR.7 is relatively new – the aircraft is still getting clearances." Three years earlier, in 1994, the clearance of new equipment was probably at its peak. When the then-CAS, Sir Peter Harding, visited Bosnia and found the RAF being sidelined because of its lack of PGM capability, his directive to provide more TIALD-carrying aircraft to fill the gap had been intended to result in the integration of the TIALD designator on the Harrier GR.Mk 7. In fact, such was the pressure and workload being experienced with integrating other equipment and weapons on the Harrier that the

Jaguar was selected to use TIALD instead, and, with supreme irony, the supposedly high-tech Harrier acted as a simple bomb-truck, toting the Paveway II LGBs which were guided to their targets by the ancient but superbly-equipped Jaguar GR.Mk 1Bs.

Harrier and Jaguar

This was perhaps unfortunate for the Harrier force, since the success of the Jaguar/TIALD combination resulted in a renaissance for that aircraft and in the launch of the Jaguar 96 and Jaguar 97 upgrades. Under these upgrades, the ageing Jaguar will become the first RAF aircraft to deploy

Above: This GR.Mk 7 is fitted with the 70 per cent LERX that is still widespread on RAF Harriers.

Below left: This VMA-331 AV-8B, on deployment to Norway, is carrying a 'live' gun pod and ALQ-164 ECM pod.

Opposite, above: The RAF's T.Mk 10 trainers are fully combat-capable, unlike the Marines' TAV-8Bs. These three clean-winged aircraft wear the markings of No. 20 (R) Sqn, the Harrier OEU.

Opposite, below: This GR.Mk 7 is carrying a centreline baggage pod and a single Sidewinder acquisition round. Harrier launch rails are now being equipped with a CRL fitted with an integral CelsiusTech BOL chaff dispenser.

Second-generation Harriers

Above: In March/April 1992 VMA-331 'Bumblebees' travelled to Norway for Exercise Mallet Blow, the second AV-8B unit (after VMA-231) to make such a trip. The Harriers transitted to the UK aboard USS Nassau, and flew to RAF Wittering while the vessel was in port. From there they departed for Norway.

Top: VMAT-203 is the Marines' Harrier training unit, based at MCAS Cherry Point. The unit made the full transition from TAV-8A to TAV-8B in November 1987. Until then trainee Harrier II pilots had to contend with the 1960s-vintage instruments of the earlier two-seat Harrier.

helmet sights, ASRAAM missiles, a PC-based mission planner with embedded TRNS, and other equipment which might otherwise have made its debut on the Harrier. Even nine years after the service introduction of the Harrier GR.Mk 5, the RAF's Harrier IIs lacked much of their planned equipment. For example, despite what were said to have been successful trials during Operation Horsefly at the Naval Weapons Center, China Lake, in 1989, the Plessey MAWS has still not been fully cleared.

Operation Deny Flight

After being relieved from the Operation Warden commitment by Tornados, from July 1995 the Harrier force found itself providing a rotational detachment to Gioia del Colle. From there, the aircraft again replaced Jaguars, this time supporting NATO's Operation Deny Flight, attempting to enforce UN resolutions which aimed to damp down the fratricidal conflict between Bosnian, Serb and Croat forces. No. IV Squadron deployed with 12 'deployment pool' aircraft (fresh from an EW upgrade at Dunsfold) to Gioia del Colle, where they became operational on 1 August 1995. This allowed most of the Jaguars to return home to Coltishall, although a detachment of two TIALD-equipped aircraft was maintained at Coltishall, on standby to operate alongside the Harriers.

Some of the aircraft operated by No. IV Squadron wore the same medium grey ARTF colour scheme they previously had worn for Operation Warden, but most wore a new two-tone dark grey colour scheme, with a very high demarcation between the bulk of the aircraft (in medium sea grey) and the darker (dark sea grey) topsides. The new colour scheme used LIR (low infra-red) polyurethane paint with a lower IR signature than 'normal' paint. Squadron markings were not carried. The detachment to Italy marked the first public appearance of the new LAU-71 missile launch rail on the dedicated 'winder pylon. Distinguished by a black domed front end, incorporating a HIPAG gas generator, the new launch rail was packed with BOL chaff packages, and this allowed the aircraft to routinely operate without a Phimat pod. The Harriers usually operated with large underwing tanks inboard, AIM-9L Sidewinders on their dedicated pylons, and CPU-123/B Paveway II LGBs on the centre underwing pylons, and with the outboard pylons empty. They could have been used to allow the carriage of two more AIM-9s had there been a significant air threat, or for the carriage of CRV-7 rockets, CBU-87s or other offensive weapons. Operating in the reconnaissance role, the Harriers carried a GP.1 or Vicon 18 Series 603 pod, sometimes with CBU-87s replacing the LGBs. Harriers also operated in the SUCAP (cab rank) role, usually with CBU-87s or 1,000-lb HE bombs, but none was dropped in anger.

Combat over Bosnia

The RAF Harrier II had its baptism of fire over Bosnia, only one month after arriving at Gioia del Colle, participating in Operation Deliberate Force, the UN's pre-prepared response to the inevitable violations of humanitarian agreements. The operation was triggered by a Bosnian Serb mortar attack on the centre of Sarajevo on 28 August. Between 30 August and 14 September, NATO flew 3,000 sorties, with another brief period of strikes flown between 8 and 10 October. The Harriers attacked an ammunition dump at Lukavica and an arms factory at Vugosca before dawn on 30 August, as part of the second wave of strikes. They tended to operate in fours, with a Jaguar GR.Mk 1B accompanying each pair.

In the CAS role over Bosnia, the Harrier GR.Mk 7s were inevitably accompanied by (or could call upon)

AGM-88 HARM-equipped USN/USMC F/A-18s or EA-6Bs. There was inevitable speculation that the aircraft might eventually gain an autonomous SEAD (Suppression of Enemy Air Defences) capability, probably with the BAe ALARM missile.

An ongoing area of concern in the Harrier GR.Mk 7 is the continued unavailability of the 25-mm ADEN cannon. By 1996 published sources were stating that the cannon were still not in use, and that the starboard pod now accommodated a GEC-Marconi ARI 23333 Zeus RF spectrum ECM system. Certainly empty (or cannon-less) pods are routinely carried in place of ventral strakes, acting as LIDs, and cannon may have only ever been fit-checked in one development batch Harrier GR.Mk 5. It is not known if the weapons have been flown on a Harrier, though no photos have ever been released showing the guns fitted to a flying aircraft. The presence of the gun is immediately obvious, since the end of the barrel projects

some way from the gun pod, unlike those of the GR.Mk 3 or USMC AV-8B.

Harrier at sea

The Harrier's STOVL capabilities make it ideally suited for shipboard operations. The earliest prototypes flew demonstrations and trials aboard a number of ships, culminating in shipboard operations by the USMC's AV-8As, and in the development of the dedicated Royal Navy Sea Harrier. RAF Harriers deployed aboard HMS *Hermes* during 1982, playing a significant role in the operation to retake the Falklands Islands. Their inclusion in the Task Force was as much due to a shortage of Sea Harriers and pilots as to any unique capability, however, and apart from a series of deployment exercise by No. 1 (F) Squadron (the first aboard *Illustrious* in 1984, another on *Ark Royal* in 1987), shipborne operations were not routinely practised by the RAF's Harrier force.

Above: AV-8Bs wear a two-tone overall grey scheme, and most of the fleet still wear toned-down markings. This AV-8B(NA) carries the ram's head badge of VMA-214 'Black Sheep'. Note also the AN/ALE-39 chaff/flare launchers in the rear upper fuselage.

Below: There are few more ear-splitting sounds than a Harrier in the hover. The column of black smoke under this 'Flying Nightmares' aircraft is a sure sign that its Pegasus -408 is working hard.

Above: The Spanish naval air arm had acquired 11 AV-8S Matadors (service designation VA.1), plus two TAV-8As (VAE.1), by 1980. In March 1983 a follow-on order for 12 AV-8Bs was placed, and the first of these aircraft was delivered in 1987. The early model Harriers have now been withdrawn from use, and sold to the Thai navy.

Right: Spain joined the Harrier II Plus programme in 1990, signing an agreement with the USA and Italy on 28 September. The first II Plus was delivered in 1996 and entered service with 9ª Escuadrilla .

Pilots from No. 3 Squadron undertook training on Yeovilton's ski-jump in early 1994; this proved to be something of a 'false dawn', although it did provide a useful indication of the aircraft's inherent suitability for carrier operations. Carrier trials of the GR.Mk 7 (again aboard *Illustrious*) were finally undertaken by the Strike Attack OEU during June 1994. Following ski-jump take-off training at RNAS Yeovilton, Wing Commander Nick Slater led five pilots in the trials, which involved three GR.Mk 7s. Flight Lieutenant Chris Norton became the first RAF pilot to land a GR.Mk 7 aboard ship on 27 June 1994, flying ZG745. The GR.Mk 7 was cleared to operate from the ship's 13° ski-jump even at maximum AUWs of 32,000 lb (14515 kg), and carrying up to 13,325 lb (6044 kg) of external stores and weapons. Such heavyweight take-offs required about two-thirds of the deck length, reaching a take-off airspeed of 105 kt (120 mph; 193 km/h), which often represented a ground (deck) speed of 70 kt (80 mph; 130 km/h), with the wind and the carrier's forward speed taken into account. These loads represented much more than has ever been achieved by a Sea Harrier. The trials

included 40 sorties lasting 44 flying hours, and established detailed clearance limits, GR.Mk 7 deck interface and maintenance requirements. They also tested for electromagnetic interference from and with the ships systems.

The RAF goes to sea

Following these trials, in 1995 the RAF formally signed an agreement to reinstate the maritime capability of its GR.Mk 7s. In early 1997 No. 1 (F) Squadron deployed four aircraft operationally aboard HMS *Illustrious* as part of Operation Ocean Wave '97. In Exercise Hot Funnel the four aircraft flew aboard on 28 February 1997, off the coast of Oman. The four pilots were each making their first deck landing, though all had made two day and two night ski-jump take-offs at Yeovilton prior to the deployment. Wing Commander Mark Leaky (OC No. 1 (F) Squadron) led a detachment of nine pilots, 60 ground crew and three engineer officers, and conducted maritime operations from the ship for two weeks, disembarking in Malaysia. Each pilot flew around 20 hours during the period, including NVG deck landings.

This was not the first time RAF Harrier GR.Mk 7s have deployed aboard a Royal Navy carrier, but it marks the start of a new era for joint-service Harrier operations, with RN Sea Harrier F/A-2s and RAF GR.Mk 7s operating together as a mixed fighter force (Sea Harrier – OCA/DCA, and GR.Mk 7 – CAS) in support of the UK's new Joint Rapid Deployment Force. The RAF aircraft bring a new level of night-attack capability and ground attack/offensive support expertise to the carrier air wing.

The four aircraft (ZD400, 461, 462 and 468) received a number of modifications to make them better suited to carrier operations. A GPS was added, and the INS was brought up to FIN.1075G standards, with new software to reduce the likelihood of toppling while the platform aligned on the (moving) carrier deck. For interoperability

Top: Spain's flagship, the carrier **Princípe de Asturias (R-11), was based on a US Navy design for the Sea Control Ship, a multi-role, low-cost ship. The US Navy abandoned the project but the Spanish navy considered it to be an ideal way to replace its vintage carrier SNS D**édalo. **A 12° ski-jump plus additional accommodation for flag staff were added, as Princípe de Asturias would function also as a command and control ship. The ship was laid down on 8 October 1979, launched on 22 May 1982 and commissioned on 30 May 1988. The maximum aircraft/helicopter capability is 29 machines, 17 in the hangar deck and 12 on the flight deck.**

Above: Italy's Harrier II Plus acquisition has given the naval air arm a modern fighter (for the first time) that is arguably more capable than anything in the air force inventory. Like the Spanish and USMC aircraft, however, the Italian AV-8B II Pluses are hampered by the lack of progress in weapons integration.

Above and top: The APG-65 radar gives the AV-8B II Plus the capability to use the AIM-120 AMRAAM and the AGM-84 Harpoon; however, to date none of these weapons has been qualified for the Harrier. A dispute is now brewing between the three countries involved as to when and whether this work will be funded. The USMC is not leading the way, for its operational priorities have changed, while Spain and Italy feel they now have aircraft not fulfilling their potential.

Opposite page: Spain's AV-8Bs are currently operated by 9ª Escuadrilla. The 10 surviving aircraft will be remanufactured to II Plus standard and joined by eight new-build examples.

Right: Italy's two TAV-8Bs were acquired from the USMC. Spain also plans to acquire two two-seaters.

with Royal Navy Sea Harrier F/A-2s and Sea King AEW.Mk 2s, the RAF aircraft were also fitted with an I-band IFF transponder. The water replenishment point was moved to inside the undercarriage bay, saving the ground crew from having to clamber onto the slippery wings on a rolling deck.

The use of the Harrier GR.Mk 7 by a number of units, in slightly different roles and locations, has led to the incorporation of a number of temporary modifications using STFs. This, in turn, has led to a certain lack of standardisation and commonality across the fleet, although the configuration remains more common than those of the Tornado GR.Mk 1 or the Jaguar. A common configuration and equipment fit is being achieved through the Mod 95 programme, which effectively gives all aircraft the 100 per cent LERX and the

RAF Germany NVG cockpit, and incorporates the operational war fit as deployed for Operations Warden and Deliberate Force. If the Harrier is to serve until its currently planned out-of-service date, the aircraft will almost certainly receive more ambitious modifications and upgrades. The medium- and high-level roles have become increasingly important since the end of the Cold War, while peace-keeping or limited war scenarios have made the avoidance of collateral damage a pre-eminent consideration. These factors have led to a growing emphasis on the use of laser-guided bombs and other PGMs. The Harrier can already carry LGBs, of course, but still cannot 'mark' or designate its own targets. Acquisition of the TIALD laser designator pod (briefly trialled, or at least fit-checked by the SAOEU) is now very likely, perhaps with Terprom or another TRN (terrain-referenced navigation) system. The Jaguar force has shown that TIALD operation is possible in a single-seat cockpit, but many believe that if it were delivered to the Harrier force, the pod would be most likely to be fitted to twin-stick T.Mk 10s. With only 12 surviving T.Mk 10s under-taking a heavy training commitment, this seems unlikely, however.

US night attack

The retirement of the Marines' last A-6Es in April 1993 left the Corps without a dedicated long-range all-weather heavy attack aircraft. The Corps, did, however, enjoy a considerably expanded medium-range night/all-weather capability with its squadrons of F/A-18Ds, and with its night-attack-capable Lot 12 F/A-18Cs. The enhanced capability of the Harrier II placed increased emphasis on longer range and night operations, in just the same way that the RAF found itself requiring greater night-attack capabilities in its Harriers, and at much the same time.

McDonnell Douglas was awarded a $2.1 million design definition contract for a night-attack Harrier in late 1985.

This aircraft was originally known as the AV-8D, although it subsequently became the Night Attack AV-8B. A trial at the NWC, China Lake, flew a podded GEC Marconi FLIR on a TA-7C, with the pilots wearing Cats Eyes NVGs. It was decided that the proposed Night Attack AV-8B would be similarly equipped.

Night Attack FLIR system

In 1989 GEC Sensors received an initial £10 million contract for FLIRs for the new Harrier variant. MDD designed a neat installation for it above the nose, allowing ARBS to be retained. The Hughes AN/ASB-19(V) ARBS is a daylight-only device, and is therefore redundant during night operations. The new US night-attack aircraft had a new expanded field of view HUD (20° azimuth by 16°, from 14° azimuth) to allow 1:1 correlation of the FLIR picture (20° azimuth by 13°) overlaid on the HUD. The aircraft also featured a new multi-purpose colour display, and a CRT-based digital map display, which retrieved data from an optical compact disc in the Hamilton Standard AN/ASQ-194 data storage set. The pilot was provided with GEC Cats Eyes Generation III NVGs (with a field of view of 40° in azimuth by 30°) giving better peripheral vision, outside the 22° cone covered by the FLIR. The Cats Eyes NVGs featured prisms below the image intensifiers. No provision is made for NVG disconnect on USMC AV-8Bs, so use during take-off and landing is prohibited.

The Night Attack Harrier also took advantage of a new engine, the Pegasus 11-61, known in the US as the F402-RR-408. This engine was developed directly from Britain's XG-15 engine technology demonstrator programme, which had been jointly funded by the British MoD and Rolls-Royce on a 70:30 basis. The new engine had improved fan aerodynamics, and single crystal turbine blades, among a host of improvements and modifications. The hot end inspection cycle was doubled to 1,000 hours, and lifecycle cost was asserted to have been reduced by 40 per cent. Engine thrust was dramatically improved, with Rolls-Royce claiming a short lift wet rating of 23,800 lb (105.85 kN), and McDonnell Douglas claiming 24,500 lb (108.96 kN). The USMC rating was 23,400 lb (104.07 kN). Despite its British origins, the 11-61 was not adopted for retrofit on RAF Harriers, though its testbed was a black-painted GR.Mk 5, ZD402. This aircraft first flew its new engine on 9 June 1989 and was subsequently used to set a series of Class-H time-to-height records. Rolls-Royce chief test pilot Andy Sephton set records of 36.38 and 81 seconds to 3000 and 9000 m (9,842 and 29,527 ft), respectively, while BAe Dunsfold's Heinz Frick reached 6000 and 12000 m (19,685 and 39,370 ft) in 55.38 and 126.63 seconds, respectively. Very significantly, the AV-8B(NA) was fitted with four extra Tracor AN/ALE-39 chaff/flare dispensers above the rear fuselage, giving the aircraft a total of 180 flares or chaff cartridges, compared to 60 on the standard, baseline AV-8B.

AV-8B(NA) deliveries to the Corps

The 87th single-seat AV-8B was built as the first AV-8B(NA) prototype, flying on 26 June 1987 and beginning a three-month evaluation at China Lake. The first production AV-8B(NA) was the 167th single-seater, the second FY89 aircraft. From then until the introduction of the Harrier II Plus, all single-seaters built were AV-8B(NA)s. VMA-214 was the first squadron to receive the Night Attack Harrier from September 1989, and all four Yuma-based units were re-equipped by September 1992. Only two units had started to transition to the variant by the time the Gulf War broke out, and, with only about 15 aircraft delivered, it was not worth sending them to the theatre of operations. Moreover, the AV-8B(NA) was then suffering from engine problems. When the engine casings cooled rapidly, but the core heated, the clearance between fan and casing reduced. If the pilot then made a high-g pull-up the fan could distort

downwards and the blade tips could touch the abrasive coating inside the engine casing. The solution was simple, and included the replacement of titanium fan blades by steel ones, alteration of the abradable inner coating, and an increase in the fan-blade clearance. While the modifications were made the AV-8B(NA)s continued in use, powered by retrofitted F402-RR-406A engines. Then the Cherry Point squadrons started to transition, beginning with VMA-223.

Harrier T.Mk 10 trainer

The introduction of the AV-8B(NA) complicated the training task for VMAT-203, but the decision was taken not to procure a night-attack-configured two-seater for the USMC, on the basis that operational role conversion could be carried out at squadron level using the single-seater and the simulator. Had the USMC not already bought its two-seat Harrier IIs, the decision might have been different. The RAF was in a different situation, since it had failed to buy a two-seat trainer version of the second-generation Harrier.

When the RAF's front-line Harrier was the GR.Mk 5, the old T.Mk 4 was adequate (though by no means ideal) for basic conversion training, demonstrating the particular techniques necessary for successful STOVL operations. A dedicated two-seat trainer was available in the shape of the TAV-8B, though this was ruled out on cost grounds. Instead, in April 1988, it was announced that no new two-seaters would be procured, and that instead a handful of T.Mk 4s would be modified to T.Mk 6 configuration.

The increasing sophistication of the RAF's single-seat Harriers and the increasing age of its first-generation two-seat T.Mk 4s led to a 1990 £200 million order for 14 two-seat

Harrier T.Mk 10s (to meet a requirement originally stated to be for 10 aircraft), similar to the US TAV-8B, but incorporating the night-attack features of the GR.Mk 7. This order was announced on 28 February 1990, although it was later reduced to 13 aircraft. Plans to convert T.Mk 4s to T.Mk 6 standard, with FLIRs and NVGs, were abandoned as not being cost-effective. The T.Mk 4s were old, and were becoming increasingly difficult to support, while the first-generation Harrier trainer was barely representative of the second-generation single-seater in its handling characteristics or in its systems, cockpit layout, and operating procedures. This became critical once the Harrier started operating by night.

The first T.Mk 10 was built at Dunsfold from components produced at Brough, Kingston and in St Louis, but the rest were assembled at Warton, moving from Dunsfold because the latter facility was full of Sea Harriers being converted to F/A-2 standards, and Harrier GR.Mk 7s. The Dunsfold-built T.Mk 10 prototype (TX-01, ZH653) made its maiden flight (planned for 16 March) on 7 April 1994. The first aircraft to be delivered to the RAF was ZH657, which went to Wittering on 30 January 1995, and the new variant was formally introduced to service on 1 March 1995.

Introduction of the Harrier T.Mk 10 simplified the Harrier conversion training programme, during which the first GR.Mk 7 sortie (preceded by T.Mk 4 and simulator work) previously required an instructor flying chase, with two more radio-equipped instructors strategically located on the airfield. Unlike the USMC's TAV-8Bs, the RAF's Harrier T.Mk 10 is fully operationally capable, with the same equipment as the GR.Mk 7 and the full quota of

eight underwing pylons (TAV-8Bs have only two). The prime user of the T.Mk 10 was No. 20 (Reserve) Squadron, with seven aircraft on charge during 1996/97. Each front-line squadron also received a single T.Mk 10.

The heavyweight T.Mk 10 is considered by some people to be short of 'grunt', and the variant would be a prime candidate for re-engining with the Pegasus 11-61, as used by Italian two-seaters. Without it, hover performance is marginal at best, especially in warmer summer temperatures.

The cancellation of rewinged A-6F Intruders and the continued non-appearance of the Bell Boeing V-22 Osprey was a significant factor in the funding of extra Harriers and Harrier upgrades. The AV-8E did not appear (it was an improved aircraft with a more powerful engine and large LERXes) largely because it was overtaken by events – and chiefly by the Harrier II Plus.

The Harrier has many detractors within the Marine Corps, most of whom point to the longer range, greater payload, and higher speed of the F/A-18, and its ability to fire radar-guided AAMs; they loudly assert that the USMC needs more Hornets, instead of the 'second-rate' Harriers. Opponents are sceptical about forward basing (which brings increased vulnerability to enemy air attack, and difficulties with security and logistics support) and are dismissive of the aircraft's relatively heavy maintenance requirements and single-engined vulnerability. Critics felt that their position was justified and endorsed by operational experience during Operation Desert Storm, during which Harrier IIs proved less flexible than the Corps' F/A-18s and a great deal more vulnerable to ground fire, especially by heat-seeking SAMs, which tended to home onto a spot between the four nozzles. F/A-18s sometimes limped home with damage to the extremities of their engine nozzles, but when Harriers were hit they were inevitably hit amidships and downed. Had the aircraft been fitted with AN/AAR-44(V) MAWS, it has been estimated that four of the five aircraft lost in the war would have survived.

USMC Harriers in the Gulf

The Harrier played a crucial role in Desert Storm, and was the first Marine Corps tactical aircraft in-theatre. The 86 aircraft deployed flew 3,380 sorties (4,112 combat flying hours) and delivering more than 6 million lb (2.7 million kg) of ordnance in 42 days of operations. During the war the Harriers operated from a disused air base, a forward airstrip

and from USS *Nassau* (LHA-6), all options unavailable to other types. General Schwarzkopf specifically named the Harrier as being one of seven weapons systems that had made a significant contribution to the quick victory. The only other aircraft mentioned were the F-117A and AH-64.

Units deployed to the Gulf were VMA-542 (recently returned from Iwakuni), VMA-331, VMA-513 and VMA-311. The bulk of VMA-231 was at Iwakuni, but sent aircraft to the Gulf after being replaced by VMF-513. VMA-211 and VMA-214 were converting to the Night Attack version (which was suffering problems with its F402-RR-408 engine) and remained in the US, and VMA-223 deployed to Rota for possible use. Thus, five of the eight

This page: Marine Corps Harriers have made several Adriatic deployments in support of ongoing NATO air operations over Bosnia. These VMA-231 aircraft are seen on board the USS Wasp (LHD-1) as part of composite squadron HMM-264 in December 1995. Note the 'EH' tailcodes and black pawn badge of CH-46F unit HMM-264, which has been applied to the Harrier detachment. In such cases, the full-strength helicopter squadron becomes the parent aviation unit of the MEU. All were active participants in the IFOR peacekeeping operation in the region.

Second-generation Harriers

'gun' squadrons were involved in the war, either wholly or in part. The Harriers flew mainly in the BAI role against targets in Kuwait, primarily using the Mk 7 CBU (and especially its Mk 20 Rockeye II anti-armour version), the Mk 77 Mod 5 napalm bomb, Mk 82 500-lb bombs, Mk 83 1,000-lb bombs and AGM-65E semi-active laser homing Maverick ASMs (with OV-10s and later F/A-18Ds providing designation). AIM-9M Sidewinders were carried singly in the early days but, with no real air threat, were discarded in favour of using the pylons for offensive weaponry. Aircraft in each formation would usually carry a Sanders AN/ALQ-164 deception jammer, which proved effective, but were in short supply.

Most of the deployed units flew from King Abdul Aziz, moving closer to the action when Sheikh Isa became too overcrowded as the US build-up continued. Even this was not as near to the front line as the Harrier force was used to, and a basic forward operating location was established at Tanajib, an oil company airfield only 45 miles (72 km) from the Kuwaiti border. It could handle 12 aircraft. The AV-8B's war was a busy one, and included CAS of engaged Marines at Khafji on 17 January. Aircraft tended to fly in pairs rather than more unwieldy four-aircraft divisions. ARBS worked fairly well most of the time, though lack of contrast was a problem, and smoke and haze could also severely degrade the system's effectiveness.

Radar-equipped Harrier

The Harrier force was unlucky not to be able to field the more advanced AV-8B Harrier II Plus in the war, since the radar-equipped Harrier might have proved more versatile and might have silenced some of the critics, although (in truth) all USMC fast jets in Desert Storm were used almost exclusively in the air-to-ground role, principally by day. Quite apart from its enhanced air-to-air potential, the Harrier II Plus was described by McDonnell Douglas as having a 74 per cent improvement in day attack capability and a 31 per cent improvement by night. One of the radar's stated purposes was to feed slant range information to the AN/ASB-19(V)2/3 ARBS, which was retained, although its nose-mounted TV tracker was obviously supplanted by the radar antenna and radar. The radar could also be used for terrain-mapping, target location, acquisition and identi-fication, and terrain avoidance.

Design of a radar-equipped Harrier began in 1988, after a joint announcement by BAe and McDonnell Douglas in June 1987 that they intended to develop a radar-equipped variant, initially as a private venture. The US Marine Corps became increasingly interested in the new Harrier derivative, as did Spain and Italy, leading to the September 1990 signature of a tripartite Memorandum of Understanding between the four nations to develop the new variant. Alenia and CASA each gained 15 per cent shares in the programme. It was announced at that stage that the aircraft would use a Hughes AN/APG-65 pulse-Doppler radar, almost identical to the radar used by the F/A-18 Hornet, albeit with a

smaller (24 x 28-in/60 x 71-cm) scanner to fit the Harrier's smaller nose contours and 34-in (86-cm) diameter radome. The software was also modified, and a new circuit card was provided for the target data processor. Some black boxes were redistributed within the fuselage, but the installation was as much like that in the Hornet as was possible. The radar could provide range and bearing information for anti-ship missiles like Harpoon or Sea Eagle. The radar had a range of air-to-ground modes for ranging, moving target indication, mapping and navigation, and nine air-to-air modes (all fairly academic until a BVR missile could be funded). In essence, McDonnell Douglas hoped to transform the AV-8B into a STOVL clone of the Night Attack F/A-18C – an understandable desire when two of the initial three customers were already Hornet operators, and since the primary operator, the USMC, was increasingly relying on the Hornet. Anything which brought increased commonality between Harrier and Hornet was useful.

Choice of radar

Had this not been a major consideration, it might have made more sense to adopt the GEC-Marconi Blue Vixen radar as used by the British Sea Harrier F/A-2, a radar already being considered as an APG-65 replacement in some proposed F/A-18 upgrades. Blue Vixen was already integrated with AMRAAM in the Sea Harrier, with test firings beginning in March 1993.

Addition of the new APG-65 radar added a 1,000-lb (454-kg) weight penalty, but this was relatively insignificant since all Harrier II Pluses were powered by the more powerful 23,800-lb (105.85-kN) F402-RR-408 (Pegasus 11-61) engine. Other changes to the II Plus included adoption of the RAF-type wing, with a 100 per cent LERX and, most significantly, four pylons per side, including the dedicated AAM pylons on the undercarriage outriggers. The combination of uprated engine and LERX, in particular, improves performance by a significant margin. Inside the cockpit, the new variant has an additional MFD to allow the display of radar data.

The Harrier II Plus was based on the Night Attack AV-8B, and retained full night-attack capability and standard night-

attack equipment, although the aircraft had a redesigned overnose FLIR fairing (of more angular and more constant cross-section) which was reportedly more aerodynamically efficient and easier to manufacture. Like the Night Attack aircraft, the II Pluses had the 100 per cent LERX, with twin Goodyear AN/ALE-39 chaff/flare dispensers on each side of the upper rear fuselage and with a lengthened ram air intake at the base of the fin. The aircraft also had a new overwing UHF antenna, which also served as the antenna for the AN/APX-100 IFF set. Provision was made for the future carriage of a reconnaissance pod on the centreline. Gross take-off weight was increased to 31,000 lb (14062 kg), with 7,759 lb (3519 kg) of internal fuel and 13,200 lb (5987 kg) of stores, while fatigue life was increased to 6,000 hours.

The second FSD AV-8B served as the aerodynamic prototype for the Harrier II Plus, and carried inert AIM-120 AMRAAMs, which have yet to be funded. The aircraft was also intended from the start to operate with a BVR anti-ship missile – AGM-84 Harpoon is the obvious choice.

MDD modified the 205th single-seater (164129) to serve as the FSD Harrier II Plus after receiving a $20 million contract from Naval Air Systems Command. The aircraft first flew on 22 September 1992, a month ahead of schedule, in the hands of McDonnell Douglas test pilot Jackie Jackson. The aircraft was delivered to the NAWC-AD for testing, before transfer to the NAWC-Weapons Division at China Lake. It was joined by the first production Harrier II Plus from 23 April 1992. The second went to VX-5 for OT&E and the third to VMA-542 after briefly undergoing carrier suitability trials.

Harrier II Plus orders

The US Navy originally ordered 27 new-build radar Harriers, and intended to order 48 more, followed by 192 conversions from earlier versions. The aim was to bring all surviving Harriers to II Plus standards. In the event, the second batch of new-build aircraft was cancelled, although the total in the first batch later rose to 31 new-build

The GR.Mk 7 served with distinction over Bosnia, gaining the first combat experience for the type in RAF hands. Those attacks were made with CPU-123 Paveway II LGBs, but the Harrier is now being trialled with the more advanced, and accurate, Paveway III. The SAOEU aircraft seen here (above) is carrying two 1,000-lb Paveway IIIs and a TIALD designator pod on the port cannon mount. The two Warden-camouflaged GR.Mk 7s (top) are carrying CRV-7 rocket pods.

airframes. The first of them was funded from the 20 FY89 single-seaters, with six more coming from the 22 FY90 aircraft. All 21 FY91 single-seaters and all six aircraft from FY92 (Gulf War attrition replacements) were also delivered with radar. The new-build Harrier II Pluses were delivered to the three front-line squadrons at Cherry Point, which initially operated a mix of old day-attack AV-8Bs and brand-new radar-equipped Harriers. In the mixed squadrons, all pilots typically fly one week per month in the new variant, usually night cycle NVG training.

Eight new-build Harrier II Plus aircraft were procured by the Spanish navy (which will have the surviving basic AV-8Bs brought up to the same standards). Sixteen were ordered by the Italian navy, 13 of which were to be assembled locally, by Alenia.

Even if the Harrier II Plus production run was cut short, large numbers of earlier AV-8Bs may still be upgraded to the same standards. Four conversions were funded in FY94, four more in FY95, eight in FY96, 12 in FY97, 13 in 1998 and 18 in 1999, against an initial requirement for 72-75 rebuilds. The rebuild programme is worth about $1.7 billion, with completion due in 2002.

The remanufacture of a standard or Night Attack AV-8B to Harrier II Plus configuration is reported to cost about two-thirds of the price of a new aircraft. It is an extremely extensive process, using an entirely new fuselage, a new -408A engine, new radar and FLIR, and brand-new cockpit

displays, and reworking of the undercarriage, tail unit, wing, gun pod and pylons. There are suggestions that APG-65s will be taken from F/A-18s, which are themselves being upgraded with the new APG-73 radar. McDonnell Douglas and the Naval Aviation Depot at Cherry Point share the work: aircraft are disassembled and inspected at NADEP, which also incorporates most of the necessary structural modifications, and McDonnell Douglas builds the new fuselage and performs final assembly work. Reused components are fatigue tested but are not zero-lifed. The first of a currently planned 73 remanufactured AV-8Bs was flown by Jackie Jackson on 29 November 1995.

Even without AMRAAM and Harpoon (often thought to be the *raison d'être* of the upgrade programme), the radar of the II Plus significantly increases the aircraft's usefulness, since it is effective in conditions that would blind the AV-8B(NA), whose FLIR cannot cope with mist, haze, rain or smoke.

Improvements to AV-8B

A number of improvements to the AV-8B have already been funded. They include the OSCAR (Open Systems Core Avionics Requirements) programme, which improves avionics interfaces, and, by using COTS (Commercial Off-The-Shelf) items, reduces costs. The programme will allow the future integration of new weapons, and saves weight. The aircraft will also receive GPS, an automatic target hand-off system (ATHS), AN/ARC-210, a new defensive aids package including AN/ALE-47, a video fatigue recorder, a digital flap controller and a flight incident recorder, and will be made JDAM and MIL STD 1760B compatible.

Further improvements to the Harrier could easily be made, though in the present funding climate major upgrades are far from certain. Among the next series of improvements required (but still not funded) are a TAV-8B performance upgrade, and provision of an anti-ship missile capability (probably with the AGM-84 Harpoon) and a stand-off PGM capability (with a laser tracker, targeting pod and the new JSOW). For the air-to-air role, a helmet-mounted sight or display, AIM-120 AMRAAM and AIM-9X are all priorities which have yet to be funded, along with a new mission planner (TAMPS) and a digital moving map (TAMMAC). HQ/SINCGARS is also planned. Interestingly, some of these systems will be featured on export examples of the Harrier II Plus, with Italy having ordered Maverick.

In the longer term, the Marines would like to see the Harrier receive a Link 16 JTIDS datalink, AN/ALE-50, AN/ALR-67(V4), IDECM (the F/A-18E/F's integrated Defensive ECM system), IHAVS, MSI and Phase II AMRAAM. None of these improvements is funded, and must be regarded as unlikely. A new safety package, updated displays with improved processing, position-keeping equipment and combat fuel tanks are reportedly 'under consideration', along with a BOL chaff/flare dispenser in a CRL. Other potential changes include new composite wingtip extensions with wingtip Sidewinder launch rails, redesigned LIDs, and a ceramic matrix composite exhaust blast shield aft of each nozzle.

RAF Harriers are equally unlikely to receive any large-scale ambitious further upgrades. Modifications to the RAF's Jaguars have demonstrated how easily and cheaply major improvements can be incorporated, if a programme is properly controlled and managed. Work already carried out and paid for on the Jaguar could allow easy integration of a computer-based mission planner better than the unit now in use on the GR.Mk 7, and perhaps of the Jaguar's Terprom navigation system, though present plans provide for it to be hosted on the existing mission planner and data

storage cartridge. A further refined Harrier GR.Mk 9 was first mooted in 1989, with Pegasus 11-61, a TRN and even AIM-120 AMRAAM. The AIM-120 AMRAAM, of course, would be of little value without a fire control radar, and that is unlikely to be funded.

With the US JSF (Joint Strike Fighter) programme now well underway, there seems little scope for a radically modernised third-generation Harrier, and instead the aircraft is likely to undergo relatively minor updates and upgrades to keep it viable until the JSF enters service. Aircraft like the AV-8SX supersonic demonstrator with the PCB Pegasus 11F-35 are thus unlikely to appear. However, in the basic Harrier GR.Mk 7, Harrier II Plus and AV-8B(NA), the US Marine Corps, the RAF and the other operators are fortunate to have such a capable and advanced aircraft with which to 'plug the gap'.

Small numbers of first-generation Harriers serve with the Royal Navy (upgraded to Sea Harrier F/A-2 configuration, with arguably the best in-service fighter radar in the world), and with the Indian and Thai navies. A handful also serve with various trials and test establishments. Their ongoing development and their deployment status will be covered in a future volume of *World Air Power Journal*. **Jon Lake**

Above and below: A furious pyrotechnics display at the 1996 Aspen air show (above) provides a dramatic background for this VMA-211 AV-8B(NA). The Harrier has now undergone its own trial by fire in several major conflicts and emerged as a reliable combat aircraft that can undertake any task required of it. The four GR.Mk 7/AV-8B operators around the world should, by rights, have been joined by many others who need the Harrier's unique capabilities. What is required is a little extra faith in those abilities and a little extra money to ensure the Harrier II's potential does not go unfulfilled.

Harrier II Operators

United States of America

United States Marine Corps

The major role of the US Marine Corps is to mount expeditionary operations from ships provided by the US Navy, to counter land forces which threaten choke-points on international shipping lanes. Its ability to operate independently of fixed bases gives the Marine Corps a vital role in limited and contingency warfare situations.

The USMC functions as a self-contained and complete force, and has a great tradition of self-sufficiency. It is a matter of pride that the USMC provides its soldiers with their own CAS, and the Harrier II plays a major part in fulfilling that 'debt of honour'. The aircraft has replaced the AV-8A and A-4M in USMC service, and equips a training unit and seven front-line squadrons. One squadron disbanded as an economy measure (though so far not the two squadrons originally planned), although early plans to establish two reserve Harrier squadrons seem to have been abandoned.

Administratively, the USMC is divided into two Fleet Marine Forces (FMFs), each with a geographical primary 'area of responsibility'. The Fleet Marine Force Atlantic includes the 2d (not '2nd', in USMC parlance) Marine Air Wing at MCAS Cherry Point, North Carolina, which in turn includes the AV-8B-equipped Marine Air Group 14. Cherry Point is very much the 'Home of the Harrier' for the Marines, with four 8,500-ft (2591-m) runways, two dispersal sites and a relief landing ground at Bogue Field, only 20 miles (12 km) away, which has a dummy LHA deck for shipboard qualification, and even a full-size dummy carrier deck with arrester gear. The Harrier II Plus is concentrated in MAG 14 (with VMA-223, VMA-231 and VMA-542).

The Fleet Marine Force Pacific includes the 3rd MAW at MCAS Yuma, Arizona, whose Harrier element comprises MAG 13, with a mix of AV-8Bs and AV-8B(NA)s in VMA-211, VMA-214, VMA-311 and VMA-513. During the Gulf War, MAG 13 (Forward Deployed) was based at King Abdul Aziz AB with VMA-231, VMA-311, VMA-542 and VMA-513 Det B, under the command of Colonel John 'Hunter' Bioty. More Harriers participated in the war in the form of VMA-331, which formed part of MAG 40 aboard USS *Nassau*. Another AV-8B operating unit is MAG 12, which has no Harriers or Harrier pilots of its own but maintains a constant AV-8B presence at MCAS Iwakuni through a rotational deployment of 'gun' squadrons.

Marine aviation exists to deploy, usually as part of a marine air-ground task force. The largest such force is a marine expeditionary force (MEF), commanded by a two-star lieutenant general with one division and a full marine air wing, including up to 60 AV-8Bs. The forward echelon of an MEF would be provided by an MEF with an infantry regiment and a MAG, including perhaps as many as 40 AV-8Bs. They would deploy in full squadrons, and would retain their unit identities. MEFs deploy aboard the new 40,532-ton (41180-tonne) 'Wasp'-class LHDs, which can embark up to 20 Harriers and six H-60s or CH-46s.

The 'Wasp' class comprises: LHD-1 *Wasp*, LHD-2 *Essex*, LHD-3 *Kearsarge*, LHD-4 *Boxer*, LHD-5 *Bataan*, and LHD-6 *Bonhomme Richard*. A seventh example is under construction.

The older 'Tarawa'-class amphibious assault ships (LHAs) are Harrier capable and can operate a standard mix of six AV-8Bs alongside CH-53Ds, CH-46D/E and AH-1Ws, as required. The 'Tarawa' class comprises: LHA-1 *Tarawa*, LHA-2 *Saipan*, LHA-3 *Belleau Wood*, LHA-4 *Nassau*, and LHA-5 *Peleliu*.

Finally, two 'Iwo Jima'-class LPHs remain in service: LPH-9 *Guam* and LPH-11 *New Orleans*. They are Harrier capable, but have been reroled as mine countermeasures vessels in recent years.

AV-8Bs can also deploy aboard the eight 'Whidbey Island'-class LSD deck landing vessels. Trials have been undertaken with British-type ski-jumps, but the USMC ships are considered as a means of getting to the operational area, where forward sites would be prepared, and not as routine operating platforms in their own right.

Next down the scale is the marine expeditionary unit, with a reinforced infantry battalion and a reinforced helicopter squadron, usually incorporating six Harriers,

The Marine Harrier force is split between two bases, MCAS Cherry Point, in North Carolina and MCAS Yuma, in Arizona.

which routinely wear the unit titles of the parent helicopter unit.

Two Special Operations-capable MEUs are permanently deployed, each with a reinforced helicopter squadron and a reinforced infantry battalion. The aviation element usually includes 12 CH-46 Sea Knights, four CH-53s, six AH-1 Cobras, three UH-1s and six AV-8Bs.

The first AV-8Bs wore much the same colour scheme as the last AV-8As, with grey and green topsides and light grey undersides. Codes and titles were in high-conspicuity white. Code letters and titles were soon toned down by being applied in matt black, but the basic scheme was unchanged. From 1985, AV-8Bs were delivered wearing a wrap-round camouflage scheme, with the grey and green topside disruptive camouflage replacing the light grey undersides. During the Gulf War, the deployed AV-8Bs received a new Harrier Tactical Paint scheme, with toned-down codes, titles and national insignia, and with stripes of light grey painted over the green portions of the standard grey-green finish to give a two-tone grey camouflage. Since the Gulf War, the Harrier force has adopted a new three-tone grey scheme, similar to that applied to the F/A-18. It has a darker grey over the middle part of the medium grey top surfaces, with lighter grey undersides. This colour scheme was evaluated before the Gulf War, being applied to VMA-331's 162069, known as the *Gray Ghost*.

The three squadrons of East Coast-based MAG 14 operate the bulk of the USMC's radar-equipped AV-8B Harrier II Plus aircraft.

US Marine Corps AV-8B Harrier II				
Variant	BuNos	Build Nos	FY	Total
AV-8B-1 (FSD)	161396-161399	1 to 4	79	4
AV-8B-2 (pilot)	161573-161578	5-10	82	6
AV-8B-3 (pilot)	161579-161584	11-16	82	6
AV-8B-4	162068-162076	17-25	83	9
AV-8B-5	162077-162088	26-37	83	12
AV-8B-6	162721-162734	38-51	84	14
AV-8B-7	162735-162746	52-63	84	12
TAV-8B-7	162747	T1	84	1
AV-8B-8	162942-162962	64-84	85	21
TAV-8B-9	162963	T2	85	1
AV-8B-9	162964-162970	85-91	85	7
TAV-8B-9	162971	T3	85	1
AV-8B-9	162972-162973	92-93	85	2
AV-8B-10	163176-163179	94-97	86	4
TAV-8B-10	163180	T4	86	1
AV-8B-10	163181-163185	98-102	86	5
TAV-8B-10	163186	T5	86	1
AV-8B-10	163187-163190	103-106	86	4
TAV-8B-10	163191	T6	86	1
AV-8B-10	163192-163195	107-110	86	4
TAV-8B-11	163196	T7	86	1
AV-8B-11	163197-163201	111-115	86	5
TAV-8B-11	163202	T8	86	1
AV-8B-11	163203-163206	116-119	86	4
TAV-8B-11	163207	T9	86	1
AV-8B-11	163419-163519	120-133	87	14
AV-8B-12	163659-163673	134-148	88	15
AV-8B-13	163674-163690	149-165	88	17
AV-8B-13	163852	166	89	1
AV-8B-13(NA)	163853-163855	167-169	89	3
TAV-8B-13	163856-163858	T10-T12	89	3
TAV-8B-13	163859-163861	T13-T15	89	3
AV-8B-14(NA)	163862-163872	170-180	89	11
AV-8B-15(NA)	163873-163883	181-191	89	11
TAV-8B-16	164113-164114	T16-17	90	2
AV-8B-15(NA)	164115-164116	192-193	90	2
AV-8B-16(NA)	164117-164121	194-198	90	5
TAV-8B-16	164122	T18	90	1
AV-8B-17(NA)	164123-164135	199-211	90	13
TAV-8B-17	164138	T21	90	1
AV-8B-18(NA)	164139-164154	212-227	90	16
TAV-8B-18	164540-164542	T22-24	91	3
AV-8B-18(NA)	164542-164547	228-232	91	5
AV-8B+-19	164548-164562	233-247	91	15
AV-8B+-19	164566-164571	251-256	91	6
AV-8B+-21	165001-165006	257-262	94	6

Gaps in the above list are accounted for by deliveries of two-seaters T19 and T20 to Italy, and of AV-8B build numbers 248, 249 and 250. 165007-165019 were the Italian-assembled MMI aircraft.

US Marine Corps AV-8B Harrier II Plus

Remanufactured Harrier II Plus aircraft for the US Marine Corps gain new identities, of which the following are known:

Variant	BuNo.	Build No.	Former identity
AV-8B+(R)-23-MC	165305	263	ex-162728
AV-8B+(R)-23-MC	165306	264	ex-161581
AV-8B+(R)-23-MC	165307	265	ex-161583
AV-8B+(R)-23-MC	165308	266	ex-162082
AV-8B+(R)-24-MC	165309	267	ex-162083
AV-8B+(R)-24-MC	165310	268	ex-162068
AV-8B+(R)-24-MC	165311	269	ex-162074
AV-8B+(R)-24-MC	165312	270	ex-162087
AV-8B+(R)-25-MC	165354	(FY96)	
AV-8B+(R)-25-MC	165355		
AV-8B+(R)-25-MC	165356		
AV-8B+(R)-25-MC	165357		
AV-8B+(R)-25-MC	165380		
AV-8B+(R)-25-MC	165381		
AV-8B+(R)-25-MC	165382		
AV-8B+(R)-25-MC	165383		
AV-8B+(R)-26-MC	165384	(FY97)	
AV-8B+(R)-26-MC	165385		
AV-8B+(R)-26-MC	165386		
AV-8B+(R)-26-MC	165387		
AV-8B+(R)-26-MC	165388		
AV-8B+(R)-26-MC	165389		
AV-8B+(R)-26-MC	165390		
AV-8B+(R)-26-MC	165391		
AV-8B+(R)-26-MC	165397		
AV-8B+(R)-26-MC	165398		
AV-8B+(R)-26-MC	165399		
AV-8B+(R)-26-MC	165429		
AV-8B+(R)-26-MC	165430		

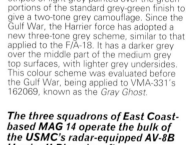

VMAT-203 'Hawks'

The introduction of the AV-8B necessitated a massive expansion of the Harrier training unit, which had hitherto had to provide pilots for a tiny force of only three front-line squadrons. An annual requirement for about 15 pilots at the end of the AV-8A era suddenly became a requirement for 90 AV-8B pilots. The AV-8B was intended to equip eight line squadrons. VMAT-203 retained a handful of AV-8As until March 1985, although the first AV-8Bs were taken on charge on 12 December 1983. TAV-8Bs were received in March 1987, and replaced the last TAV-8As in November 1987. Until then, trainee pilots had to make the mind-boggling transition from the analog 1960s TAV-8A to the digital 1980s AV-8B via the simulator. Since 1980, some pilots had

come directly from advanced training on the TA-4 Skyhawk, though all trainees have to be rated as above-average ability.

The 22-week conversion course includes 62 Harrier flights, and 60 flying hours, with 15 flights in the two-seater before soloing in the AV-8B. Ex-Skyhawk or -Phantom pilots flew 10 fewer AV-8B sorties (those concentrating on air-to-ground delivery techniques), while former AV-8A and AV-8C pilots required only 14 AV-8B flights before rejoining their squadrons. VMAT-203 played no part in the Gulf War, since the unit had no reserve combat role. The squadron's aircraft wear 'KD' tailcodes.

VMAT-203 was established in 1975 as the dedicated Harrier training unit. The first second-generation TAV-8Bs were delivered in 1983.

VMA-211 'Wake Island Avengers'

VMA-211 flew the A-4M until 27 February 1990, re-equipping with 'CF'-coded Night Attack AV-8Bs that spring, and receiving Harrier II Pluses in May 1994. The squadron did not play any part in the Gulf War, because it was working up with the AV-8B(NA) at the time. 'Avengers' AV-8Bs

usually carry diagonal candy stripes on the rudder, and a representation of the pre-war national star insignia on the nose.

VMA-211 was the last squadron to transition to the Harrier, and the second to adopt the AV-8B.

VMA-214 'Black Sheep'

Arguably the most famous USMC fighter squadron, the 'Black Sheep' traded their A-4s for AV-8Bs in 1989. The squadron subsequently became the first with Night Attack AV-8Bs, receiving its first aircraft on 1 September 1989, although it operated a mix of sub-variants (with different engines) for many years. The squadron was still working up with the AV-8B(NA) during the Gulf War, but took its Night Attack aircraft on deployment to Iwakuni in October 1991; this marked the first overseas deployment by the type. VMA-214 won the CNO Award

for safety in 1995 and 1996. The squadron uses the tailcode 'WE'. Its aircraft usually wear 13 stars on each side of the fin, following down the leading edge then looping back in a semi-circle along the fin root and up part of the height of the fin ahead of the rudder. The name 'BLACKSHEEP' is carried below the VMA-214 designator on the rear fuselage. A ram's head is carried on the nose.

VMA-214 took delivery of the first production AV-8B(NA) on 15 September 1989, while transitioning from the A-4M.

VMA-223 'Bulldogs'

The last operational East Coast A-4M squadron, VMA-223 retired its Skyhawks in July 1987 and traded up to the AV-8B in October 1987. The squadron undertook cruises aboard the USS *Nassau* (May 1989), USS *Saipan* (March 1990) and USS *Wasp* (June 1991). Six squadron jets deployed to Rota for contingency use in Desert Shield and Desert Storm, but were not 'called forward'. The deployment returned to the USA on 23 February, before the squadron deployed for a Mediterranean cruise in USS *Wasp* in June 1991 during which it covered the evacuation of US nationals from Liberia. During May 1992 the squadron deployed to MAG 12 at Iwakuni, returning before the

year's end. At the end of 1993 VMA-223 became the second unit to receive the radar-equipped AV-8B Harrier II Plus, and in 1995 two squadron aircraft were used during filming of the motion picture *True Lies*.

The squadron's aircraft wear 'WP' tailcodes (sometimes in shadow outline form) and have a sunburst design on the rudder. Most aircraft have the 'BULLDOGS' title on the rear fuselage, in front of the chaff/flare dispensers, below the squadron designation. Unusually, several squadron aircraft wear the unit's traditional Bulldog nose badge in full colour.

This 'Bulldogs' AV-8B II Plus is armed with four Mk 83 bombs and a 'live' gun pod.

VMA-231 'Ace of Spades'

A former AV-8A unit, VMA-231 re-equipped with AV-8Bs in September 1985, applying the tailcode 'CG' to its aircraft. VMA-231 deployed to King Abdul Aziz air base on 22 December 1990, flying from Iwakuni. The squadron lost one aircraft when Captain Russell Sanborn was downed by an SA-7, becoming a POW. During the Gulf War, several of the aircraft wore toned-down sharkmouths. The squadron left the Persian

Gulf on 16 March, flying to Rota, where the aircraft were shipped home aboard *Saratoga* and *Kennedy*. VMA-231 became the last of the three squadrons to receive new-build Harrier II Pluses. Squadron aircraft wear a playing card insignia under the windscreen, and have recently featured three spades on the black (or dark grey) rudders.

VMA-231 was the first of the Cherry Point Harrier squadrons and made the first deployment at sea in 1975.

VMA-311 'Tomcats'

VMA-311 flew the A-4M until July 1986, recommissioning with the AV-8B in August 1986. Under the command of Lieutenant Colonel Dick White, VMA-311 was the first Harrier II squadron to fly to the Gulf to participate in Operations Desert Shield and Desert Storm. The squadron flew from Yuma to Cherry Point on 15 August (eight days after the word to go) where its aircraft were repainted. The squadron then flew to Rota on 18 August, and to Shaikh Isa. The unit eventually moved again, to King Abdul Aziz Naval Base at Jubail, where the 7,000-ft (2134-m) runway was

disintegrating. First in to the Gulf, VMA-311 was also the last to leave, flying home on 13 April 1991. The squadron received its first Night Attack Harrier IIs in May 1992. The squadron's tailcode is 'WL', and aircraft wear a black-and-white 'standing cat' badge on the fin, ahead of the rudder. During 1995 and 1996, some aircraft wore a red dragon badge on each side of the nose, below the cockpit.

This 'Tomcats' AV-8B(NA) carries the unit's black-and-white cat badge on its fin, along with the red dragon badge of HMM-268, its parent unit while on deployment.

Harrier II Operators

VMA-331 'Bumblebees'

VMA-331 stood up as the first front-line AV-8B squadron on 30 January 1985, having previously flown A-4M Skyhawks (until January 1983). Its aircraft wear a 'VL' tailcode and a small bomb-carrying bee badge under the cockpit. The unit's initial strength was only 15 aircraft (with 21 pilots) instead of the usual 20 aircraft and 30 pilots stipulated by the USMC. Commanded by Lieutenant Colonel J. R. Cranford, VMA-331 made a shakedown cruise aboard the LPH USS Guadalcanal, and then mounted an extended deployment aboard the USS Belleau Wood between January and June 1987, flying 951 sorties. Under the command of Lieutenant Colonel John 'Mystic' Fitzgerald, VMA-331 deployed to the Persian Gulf aboard the USS Nassau as part of MAG 40 and flew 242 of the 3,380 sorties flown by the AV-8B in Desert Storm. The journey did not allow adequate training,

and one pilot, Captain Manny Rivera, was lost in a night flying accident even before the squadron arrived in-theatre. The unit would have covered any amphibious landing in the Gulf, but when none was made, the squadron did fly feints intended to persuade the Iraqis that such a landing was imminent. VMA-331 lost its first aircraft on 28 January 1991, when Captain Michael Craig Berryman was shot down by an Iraqi SAM, falling prisoner to the Iraqis. A second squadron pilot, Captain Reg Underwood, was killed on 27 February when his aircraft was downed by a SAM. The unit left the Gulf on 10 March 1991. The squadron subsequently deactivated on 30 September 1992, and formally decommissioned on 1 October 1992.

This line-up of 'Bumblebees' AV-8s is seen in here in Norway. VMA-331 was also the first Harrier squadron to TDY to Japan.

VMA-513 'Flying Nightmares'

With the conversion of VMA-331, 231 and 542 at Cherry Point completed, Yuma began transitioning to the AV-8B. The first Yuma squadron to convert was VMA-513, which stood down with its AV-8Cs in February 1987, after making the type's last deployment (aboard Tarawa). The squadron gained AV-8Bs in January 1987, and was declared operational with the new aircraft on 20 March 1988. The six VMA-513 aircraft not deployed to Iwakuni to replace

VMA-231 during the Gulf War were deployed (as Det B) to Abdul Aziz aboard the Tarawa. They re-embarked aboard Tarawa on 10 March 1991. The squadron uses the tailcode 'WF', and most aircraft wear a 'dove' badge toned-down on the tailfin.

The 'Flying Nightmares' were the very first USMC Harrier unit to form, on 15 April 1971.

VMA-542 'Flying Tigers'

VMA-542 traded its AV-8As and AV-8Cs for AV-8Bs in April 1986, after losing its last first-generation Harrier late in 1985. VMA-542 was the second AV-8B squadron to deploy to the Persian Gulf for Desert Shield and Desert Storm, initially at Shaikh Isa and then at Abdul Aziz, commanded by Lieutenant Colonel Ted 'Mongoose' Herman. VMA-542 suffered its first combat loss on 23 February, when Captain James Wilbourne hit the ground, probably due to pilot disorientation during a night attack. Captain Scott Walsh became the second pilot to be downed on 25 February, ejecting

successfully in friendly territory. The squadron returned the majority of its aircraft (via Rota) to Saudi Arabia on 16 March 1991. VMA-542 subsequently became the first squadron to operate the Harrier II Plus, with Lieutenant Colonel Kevin Leffler, the CO, delivering the first on 8 July 1993. The squadron's aircraft wear yellow triangular 'tiger skin' on the rudders, and a tiger's head badge on the nose. The squadron tailcode is 'WH'.

VMA-542 shares the famous 'Flying Tigers' appellation with the USAF's 23rd Wing and the US Army's 229th AVN (ATK).

Composite squadrons

When deploying as part of a Marine Expeditionary Unit the AV-8Bs generally operate under the auspices of a composite reinforced helicopter squadron, this usually taking the identity of the largest component helicopter squadron. The AV-8Bs usually deploy with elements from CH-53, AH-1 and CH-46 units. The AV-8B squadrons frequently deploy very small elements (typically of six aircraft) aboard the four remaining 18,300-ton (18590-tonne) 'Iwo Jima'-class LPHs, and the five 39,300-ton (39930-tonne) 'Tarawa'-class LHAs. When

This VMA-223 AV-8 wears HMM-162 titles for deployment aboard USS Wasp.

deployed, the AV-8Bs usually retain the tail markings of their parent squadron, but take the tailcode (and often the nose insignia) of the composite unit. Examples of recent composite squadrons deploying with AV-8Bs have included HMM-162 (from VMA-223, code 'YS', aboard Wasp), HMM-261 (from VMA-223 and VMA-542, code 'EM', aboard Nassau), HMM-263 (code 'EG', aboard Kearsarge), HMM-264 (code 'EH'), and HMM-365 (code 'YM').

VX-5

VX-5 was primarily concerned with the testing and evaluation of air-to-ground weapons, tactics and aircraft. As such, the unit undertook the AV-8B's Initial Operational Test and Evaluation in 1982,

and evaluated the AV-8B(NA). VX-5 disestablished on 30 September 1994, becoming part of VX-9.

This mix of AV-8B and II Plus aircraft all wear full VX-5 'Vampires' markings and titles.

VX-9 'Vampires'

The 'Vampires' at China Lake use the tailcode 'XE', differentiating them from the unit's F-14s, which wear 'XF' tailcodes and are based at Point Mugu. The AV-8Bs (which include II Pluses) have the unit's upside-down bat and twin lightning bolt badge (inherited from VX-5) on the fin-tip, between the two digits of the tailcode. The squadron was formed by the merger of VX-4 and VX-5 on 30 September 1994, when

the former VX-4 became VX-9 Det Point Mugu, and VX-5 became VX-9 Det China Lake. VX-9 undertook the IOT&E of the new Harrier II Plus, and retains a number of AV-8Bs on charge. The co-located Naval Weapons Test Squadron China Lake also flies a small number of AV-8Bs.

This anonymous Harrier II Plus is a VX-9 aircraft seen in 1996 during IOT&E trials of the new aircraft. Note the green drop tanks.

Test establishments

AV-8B Harrier IIs have served with most US test units, including the NATC at Patuxent River, and the NAWC's Aircraft Division which replaced it, including the Strike Aircraft Test Directorate. Most NAWC aircraft (which include the first Night Attack conversion) wear a black or dark grey tail

stripe, with the letters NAWC, and the words Aircraft Division below.

This TAV-8B was on charge with the Strike Aircraft Test Directorate, at Patuxent River, before that unit became the Strike Test Squadron of the NAWC-AD.

United Kingdom
Royal Air Force

The second-generation Harrier has now entirely supplanted the Harrier GR.Mk 3/ T.Mk 4 in RAF service, with the notable exception of XW175, the VAAC control technology research/demonstrator aircraft, used by DERA. RAF Wittering houses No. 1 (F) Squadron and No. 20 (Reserve) Squadron, the Harrier conversion and training unit. Nos 3 and IV Squadrons are based in Germany, but are due to return to Britain (probably to Cottesmore) during 1998. The withdrawal of British forces from Germany was prompted by the Options for Change defence review and by the increasing restrictions on operational flying imposed by the German government. If the two Germany-based Harrier squadrons do move back to RAF Cottesmore, they will be less than 20 miles from Wittering, the main British Harrier force base.

Second-generation Harrier production for Britain comprised two development batch

aircraft, ZD318 and ZD319, the former subsequently serving as the GR.Mk 7 prototype. They had the build numbers DB1 and DB2. Forty-one production GR.Mk 5s followed (ZD320-330, ZD345-355, ZD375-380, ZD400-412, build numbers P1-P41), with 19 GR.Mk 5As (ZD430-438, ZD461-470, build numbers P42-P60). Thirty-four aircraft were built as GR.Mk 7s (ZG471-480, ZG500-512, ZG530-533, ZG856-862, build numbers P61-P94). Finally, there were 13 T.Mk 10s (ZH653-665, build numbers TX001-TX013). ZG506 introduced the 100 per cent LERX, which has not been seen on the T.Mk 10.

During 1984, two RAF Germany Harrier GR.Mk 3s were used to evaluate new camouflage colour schemes. Each featured a single topside colour, with a lighter tone used on the undersides. XV809 of No. 3 Squadron had dark green upper surfaces and lichen undersides, while No. IV (AC)

This unique formation of No. 1 Sqn Harriers gathered for Operation Warden, during the brief period this huge sharkmouth was worn.

Squadron's XV738 used dark sea grey topsides and medium grey undersurfaces. The first two development batch Harrier GR.Mk 5s actually wore the grey colour scheme, but production aircraft used the dark green colours trialled by No. 3 Squadron. From time to time, aircraft deployed to Norway on exercise have received a disruptive pattern of washable white distemper over their normal camouflage, though this has been seen only rarely. From late 1992, serial numbers were raised slightly on the rear fuselage, keeping them free of the deposits of soot left by the rear nozzles.

For the predominantly medium-level role over northern Iraq, Harriers deployed on Operation Warden received a coat of grey ARTF (Acrylic Removable Temporary Finish) with toned down 'pastel' roundels and fin flashes, and with small black serials and two-letter white tailcodes, beginning 'WA'. One aircraft on Warden was briefly decorated with a huge sharkmouth, similar to that worn by a French Mirage F1

Harrier T.Mk 10s are now being allocated to front-line squadrons, such as this No. 3 Sqn example.

operating in-theatre at the same time. The ARTF finish was temporary, not least because it was applied over the existing green camouflage rather than a properly primed and prepared surface. Consequently, it had to be reapplied regularly.

The temporary light grey finish gave way to a permanent two-tone grey finish using LIR (Low Infra-Red signature) paint, with dark sea grey topsides and medium grey undersurfaces. National insignia reverted to dark blue and dark red, and serials reverted to their normal size. At much the same time, individual codes within the squadrons were replaced by a uniform, fleet-wide system which saw them replaced by two-digit numerical codes – the aircraft's BAe build numbers.

On both grey colour schemes, roundels were carried above the port wing (and on the intakes) only, not above the starboard wing. The T.Mk 10 has so far remained in the original green finish.

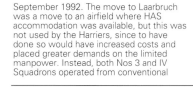

No. 1 (F) Squadron

Pilots of No. 1 (F) Squadron were converted to the Harrier GR.Mk 5 by the Harrier Conversion Team, and the unit received its first GR.Mk 5 on 23 November 1988, withdrawing the last GR.Mk 3 on 31 March 1989. The squadron redeclared to NATO on 2 November 1989. Following conversion to the GR.Mk 7 from June to November 1992, No. 1 (F) Squadron was the first front-line RAF Harrier unit to work up in the night-

attack role, from the autumn of 1989. Initially assigned to SACEUR's strategic reserve, No. 1 (F) Squadron was assigned to NATO's RF(Air), declaring on 1 January 1996. No. 1 (F) Squadron has undertaken deployments in support of Operations Warden and Grapple, and has deployed aircraft aboard HMS *Illustrious*.

A pair of No. 1 Sqn GR.Mk 7s wears the newly-adopted LIR grey camouflage.

September 1992. The move to Laarbruch was a move to an airfield where HAS accommodation was available, but this was not used by the Harriers, since to have done so would have increased costs and placed greater demands on the limited manpower. Instead, both Nos 3 and IV Squadrons operated from conventional

'flight lines'. No. 3 Squadron took over the Grapple detachment after No. IV (AC) Squadron, and thereafter the duty was rotated between the three front-line Harrier units. In 1994, No. 3 Squadron practised ski-jump take offs at Yeovilton, but as yet has not made a carrier deployment.

No. 3 Squadron

No. 3 Squadron converted to the GR.Mk 7 in 1991, but did not receive 'switch-on' clearance for its night-attack systems until early 1993, and did not begin role training until the winter of 1994. In the meantime,

Laarbruch's No. 3 Sqn continues to provide support for Deliberate Guard operations over Bosnia.

on 16 November 1992, the squadron moved from Gütersloh to Laarbruch, following a deployment to Kuantan, Malaysia, in

No. IV (Army Co-operation) Squadron

No. IV (AC) Squadron converted straight from the Harrier GR.Mk 3 to the GR.Mk 7 from September 1990, although it was 18 months before a squadron aircraft flew a representative night sortie, and the squadron was destined to be the last front-line unit to actually train for the night-attack role. The squadron moved from Gütersloh to Laarbruch on 27 November 1992, just over a week after No. 3 Squadron.

Following the withdrawal of the based No. 1417 Flight and its four GR.Mk 3s on 8 July, four No. IV (AC) Squadron GR.Mk 7s deployed to Belize from 6 September 1993 until the end of the month, demonstrating that the former colony could still be quickly and effectively reinforced. No. IV (AC) Squadron began its participation in Operation Grapple on 24 July 1995, with

the arrival of the first five aircraft at Gioia del Colle. Seven more arrived on 1 August. The detachment was reduced to nine aircraft after the initial work-up, with the squadron having brought 12 aircraft to ensure sufficient operational readiness. The squadron's aircraft flew operational sorties during Deliberate Force, primarily dropping 1,000-lb LGBs for which Jaguars provided target designation.

In August 1997 four No. 4 Sqn GR.Mk 7s made the last RAF weapons training deployment to the Decimomannu range, in Sardinia.

This No. 4 Squadron GR.Mk 7 (which is fitted with the 100 per cent LERX) is seen here at CFB Goose Bay, in September 1997.

No. 20 (Reserve) Squadron

When the RAF's historic OCUs were redesignated as reserve squadrons, the Harrier OCU took over the identity of the recently disbanded No. 20 Squadron, whose last front-line incarnation had been as an RAF Germany-based Tornado strike attack squadron. This was not the first time No. 20 Squadron's markings had appeared on a Harrier, since the unit had been the RAF's third Harrier unit, forming at Wildenrath on 1 December 1970, and disbanding on 28 February 1977 when the RAF Germany Harrier force moved to Gütersloh, reducing from three to two squadrons (though they were expanded from 12 to 18 aircraft). No. 233 OCU officially became No. 20 (Reserve) Squadron on 1 September 1992. Interestingly, although the unit applied No. 20 Squadron's markings on the noses of its

aircraft, it retained the old panther's head insignia of No. 233 OCU on their tailfins.

No. 233 Operational Conversion Unit, and later No. 20 (Reserve) Squadron, retained a pool of Harrier GR.Mk 3s for its own use, and for use in Belize. Until No. 8 Course, the first seven single-seater sorties were flown in the GR.Mk 3 (which represented an easy conversion from the T.Mk 4). The GR.Mk 3s were also used for a 10-hour familiarity course for pilots going from the GR.Mk 5 to Belize. When the Belize detachment ended (in early July

No. 20 Squadron is now the Harrier OCU. Its aircraft wear a hybrid mix of No. 20 Sqn and No. 233 OCU markings – in recognition of the unit it superseded in 1992.

1993), the need for training on the GR.Mk 3 effectively evaporated. No. 20 (Reserve) Squadron retained some aircraft for use by instructors flying 'chase' during students' early GR.Mk 5 solos, the number dwindling to two aircraft by early 1994. They remained on charge until after the Harrier's 25th anniversary celebrations, although it had

once been intended that they would retire on 31 March 1994.

The T.Mk 4 continued in use rather longer, since the first example of its replacement, the T.Mk 10, did not enter service until 1 March 1995. All first-generation Harriers have now been withdrawn from No. 20 (Reserve) Squadron.

No. 233 Operational Conversion Unit

A Harrier Conversion Team formed within No. 233 OCU on 1 March 1987, with the aim of converting a cadre of instructors for the new GR.Mk 5. The first three pilots trained with the USMC before flying began at Wittering on 30 March 1988, using GR.Mk 5s in No. 233 OCU markings. The first GR.Mk 5 had actually been delivered to Wittering on 29 May 1987, but had been used for training engineers and ground

crew. The HCT was reabsorbed by the OCU after the final course (No. 11) graduated. No. 233 OCU became No. 20 (Reserve) Squadron on 1 September 1992.

Both this Harrier GR.Mk 5 and GR.Mk 7 wear the multicoloured flashes of No. 233 OCU, which was established in December 1970.

Strike Attack Operational Evaluation Unit

The SAOEU was first formed at Boscombe Down on 1 September as an operational evaluation unit for the Tornado, becoming the SAOEU in 1987. The unit received its first GR.Mk 5 (ZD328) on 26 July 1988, and its first GR.Mk 7 on 17 August 1990. The

unit was subordinate to the Central Tactics and Trials Organisation at RAF High Wycombe (HQ Strike Command) but is now a division of the RAF's Air Warfare Centre, whose winged sword emblem has replaced the three-sword badge of the CTTO. The

SAOEU has played a crucial, if largely unsung, role in the trialling of new equipment for the Harrier GR.Mk 7, and in developing the trials and techniques which allow the front-line units to use the aircraft most successfully.

Below left: This SAOEU GR.Mk 7 wears the latest incarnation of the Air Warfare Centre's badge – a blue flash with winged sword.

Below: Calibration marks, such as those on this T.Mk 10, are a characteristic of SAOEU aircraft.

Spain

Arma Aérea de la Armada

Although Franco's Spain inevitably preferred to buy US-supplied AV-8S Matadors (known as VA.1s, EAV-8As or AV-8As in Spanish service) rather than British Harrier GR.Mk 1s, the aircraft's shipborne role led some to expect that the follow-on order would be for navalised, radar-equipped Sea Harriers (recently combat-proven in the Falklands). However, long-standing links with the USA, coupled with some continuing antipathy to Britain (dating back to Spain's Civil War and exacerbated by the continued British presence in Gibraltar) meant that Spain procured the US version. Spain signed a contract for 12 AV-8Bs in March 1983, designating its new aircraft as VA.2 Matador IIs, although the Matador name was even less commonly used than in the AV-8S era. McDonnell Douglas refers to the aircraft as EAV-8Bs. Following initial pilot conversion in the USA, the first three aircraft (VA.2-1 to

VA.2-3, BuNos 163010-163012, build numbers E1-E3) were ferried to Rota on 6 October 1987.

The new EAV-8Bs (the remainder being VA.2-4 to VA.2-12, BuNos 163013-163021, build numbers E4-E12) were delivered in an overall matt two-tone grey colour scheme, similar to that applied to contemporary US Navy carrierborne aircraft, just as the AV-8As had worn a glossy gull-grey and white scheme which echoed that applied to US Navy carrierborne aircraft of the late 1960s and early 1970s. National markings were of reduced size, while codes, serials and Armada titles were applied not in black but in a slightly darker shade of grey than the base camouflage colour.

The wooden-decked *Dedalo* (the former cruiser USS *Cabot*) was retired in 1988 (becoming a floating museum in New Orleans) and was replaced by the new

This 9ª Escuadrilla AV-8B Harrier II Plus is seen at its home base of Rota. Note the RAF Harrier GR.Mk 7s in the background.

Principe de Asturias in July 1989. AV-8Ss were cleared for operation from the new carrier's 12° ski jump by BAe test pilots Heinz Frick and Steve Thomas, and Spanish pilots were ski-jump trained at RNAS Yeovilton. This was not as astonishing as it might have seemed. With the emergence of democracy, and reduced friction over

Gibraltar, links with Britain had strengthened. The Spanish navy leased time on the Harrier GR.Mk 3 simulator at Wittering in later years, instead of sending pilots to MCAS Cherry Point. (Subsequently, the Spanish EAV-8B simulator was used by RAF GR.Mk 5 pilots, before the RAF received its first GR.Mk 5 simulator.)

EAV-8B ski jump trials were conducted later, by USMC and US Navy test pilots at Patuxent River. The smaller, older *Dedalo* had no ski jump, so such training had not hitherto been necessary. Both Spanish carriers were home-ported at Rota, only kilometres from the airfield at Rota housing the Armada Harrier squadrons.

Under the Tripartite MoU of 1990, Spain will receive eight new-build Harrier II Pluses (VA.2-14 to VA.2-21, E13-E20, 165028-165035) and a TAV-8B two-seater, and the 10 surviving AV-8Bs will be upgraded to the same standards, VA.2-8 having been lost in November 1993.

8ª Escuadrilla (Octava Escuadrilla)

8ª Escuadrilla was the original Spanish navy Matador unit, and took over responsibility for training Spanish Harrier pilots when the USMC withdrew its AV-8As. There were some expectations that 8ª Escuadrilla would

eventually take the radar-equipped EAV-8Bs, but the unit decommissioned on 24 October 1996, when the surviving seven AV-8S and two TAV-8S aircraft were transferred to the Royal Thai navy.

Spain's AV-8Bs (note the ALQ-164 pod and practice bombs on the aircraft above) are all operated by 9ª Escuadrilla. The same unit is currently responsible for Harrier II Plus operations (above right). As the Spanish navy's Harrier fleet continues to grow, the now disbanded 8ª Escuadrilla may well be reformed in the near future.

9ª Escuadrilla (Novena Escuadrilla)

9ª Escuadrilla was formed at Rota on 29 September 1987 to operate the Armada's EAV-8Bs, which were delivered between October 1987 and September 1988. The squadron underwent an intensive work-up prior to its first deployment in 1989. The squadron forms part of the Alpha Carrier Air Group with co-located Sea King and Bell 212 squadrons. Escuadrilla 008 continued to

operate the EAV-8A, with a mixed complement of four AV-8As and eight 9ª Escuadrilla EAV-8Bs typically deploying aboard the *Principe de Asturias* at the same time. Some 9ª Escuadrilla pilots were posted to the air force from late 1994 to gain experience with the F/A-18 Hornet, prior to introduction of the APG-65-equipped Harrier II Plus.

Italy

Marina Militare

The Italian navy was prohibited from operating fixed-wing aircraft by a law dating from the Fascist era (22 February 1937), and the air force owned and flew all ASW and ASV aircraft types, albeit under naval tasking. The navy only managed to operate helicopters because they were unknown when the 1937 law was drafted, and were thus not specifically mentioned. The MMI began looking at the possibility of acquiring Harriers in October 1967, when Hawker Siddeley test pilot Hugh Merewether landed one on the navy's helicopter-carrier, the *Andrea Doria*. A proposed buy of 24 aircraft became a planned offset deal which involved the supply of six British-built Harrier GR.Mk 50s, with 44 more to be licence-built or licence-assembled, while Britain would take Italian-produced Chinooks and/or an Anglo-Italian Gnat replacement. AMI opposition and funding problems killed off the plans, although when the new helicopter-carrier *Giuseppe Garibaldi* was launched in 1983, it was clearly intended to be capable of operating fixed-wing STOVL aircraft as well as helicopters. The vessel was fitted with a 6°30' ski-jump from the start, long before the MMI procured Harriers. The ski-jump was originally described as a device to protect the flight deck from excessive spray, to distract attention from the navy's ambitions. The ship hosted cross-deck deployments by USMC AV-8Bs and Royal Navy Sea Harriers in 1988.

After prolonged evaluation of the Sea Harrier and AV-8B, the MMI gained

government approval to operate fixed-wing aircraft in 1989, and immediately ordered two TAV-8B trainers (MM55032 and 55033, 164136-164137, T19 and T20) in May 1989, simultaneously dispatching a cadre of pilots to the USA for training. In 1990, construction of a runway, new hangars and other facilities began at Luni. Sixteen Harrier II Pluses were ordered (with options on eight more), and the first three of these aircraft (MM7199 to MM7201, BuNos 164563-164565, build numbers 248-250) were diverted from the USMC's allocation on 20 April 1994, being delivered to MCAS Cherry Point for training. The two TAV-8Bs were re-engined with F402-RR-408s in 1994 to improve 'hot-and-high' performance. The remaining single-seaters (MM7212-7224, BuNos 165007-165019, build numbers IT001-IT013) were assembled by Alenia, while offset work was given to Aerea (pylons), Breda (gun parts), Fiat Avio (engine components), and Magnaghi (hydraulics).

The Italian Harriers wear an unusual two-tone grey colour scheme, with the top surfaces very much darker than the undersides. Titles and codes are applied in the undersurface colour, and national insignia are of reduced size and have a lower proportion of white. An anchor insignia is carried on the forward zero-scarf nozzle fairing of the single-seaters, many of which also have markings on the rudder. The aircraft carry a three-digit code on the rear fuselage, commencing 1-01 for the two-seaters and 1-03 for the single seaters. The 'last two' are repeated on the nose.

Above: 1 Gruppo Aereo is based at Grottaglie, near the naval base at Taranto, in the southern 'heel' of Italy.

1 Grupaer's Harrier II Pluses (below) have adopted this wolf's head badge (right) and an appropriate fin 'flash' (above).

1 Gruppo Aereo (1 Grupaer)

The MMI's two TAV-8Bs were delivered in August 1991 to the new base at Grottaglie, 12 miles (20 km) from Taranto, home port of the aircraft carrier *Giuseppe Garibaldi*. The aircraft flew intensively, mounting many sorties from the ship and exploring co-ordinated operations with the vessel's helicopters. The first (US-built) aircraft were delivered on 3 December 1994, having been flown onto the *Giuseppe Garibaldi* off Mayport, departing Taranto on 21 November 1994.

One month later, on 18 January 1995, the *Giuseppe Garibaldi* sailed from Taranto

(with the three US-built single-seaters embarked) to support UN operations in Somalia. They flew top-cover and reconnaissance sorties, proving extremely serviceable and maintainable. The APG-65 was used for ground mapping, airspace control and air traffic deconfliction. The squadron returned to Grottaglie on 22 March 1995.

1 Grupaer's operational training has frequently involved co-operation with Spanish AV-8B Matadors, leading to speculation about a 'Harrier Force Southern Europe'.

Aer Chór na h-Éireann
The Irish Air Corps

Top: This Alouette III, one of the eight attached to No. 3 Support Wing, is seen over the monastic settlement at Glendalough, Co. Wicklow, founded by St Kevin in the 6th century. The first of the veteran Alouette IIIs arrived in 1963, and, according to Air Corps lore, Aérospatiale statistics 'prove' that all eight aircraft should have been lost by now, on account of their high operational tempo and longevity of service. In fact, only one aircraft has ever been seriously damaged, and that in 1995.

Above and left: Air Corps weapons training is conducted at the sea ranges near Gormanstown. This remarkable sequence of photos shows an SF.260WE Warrior firing a salvo of 68-mm rockets.

Right: Six Fouga CM.170-1 Super Magisters have served with No. 1 Light Strike Squadron since 1975/76. The squadron's black panther badge, and motto 'Beag ach Fiochmhar' (small but fierce), dates back to 1939 and the formation of No. 1 Fighter Squadron. In 1997 the Irish Air Corps celebrated its 75th anniversary and new markings were applied to the Magisters as a result.

FORFAIRE AGUS CAIRISEACT
1922 75 1997

Beag Ach
LIGHT STRIKE SQDN.
Fiochmhar.

Above and left: It is rare to see a fully-armed Air Corps Magister, though this aircraft (above) is fitted both with twin 7.62-mm machine-guns in the nose and MATRA rockets pods – similar to those carried by the SF.260WE Warriors. The Magisters play a vital role in pilot training, as part of the Advanced Flying Training School. This role, and the other invaluable capabilities that the Magisters offer to the Irish Air Corps, are now in doubt as the aircraft face retirement in 1998 with no replacement in sight.

Above: This Super Magister is seen ready for major overhaul by the Air Corps' Engineering Wing, with tip tanks removed and the covers taken away from its Turboméca Marboré engines.

This page: The Air Corps acquired five Aérospatiale SA 365F Dauphins in 1986. The Dauphins are allocated to No. 3 Support Wing, with two aircraft assigned to the Naval Support Squadron and the remainder to the Search and Rescue Squadron (above). All aircraft carry the badge of the Naval Squadron, which features the cross of St Brendan the Navigator (right). The Dauphins are all equipped to an extremely high standard, featuring a full EFIS cockpit, Bendix RDR-1500 search radar and Crouzet-Omega ONS 100A navigation system. The two 'navalised' aircraft have a deck landing system so they can operate from the Naval Service's helicopter-capable fishery patrol vessel, the L.E. Eithne. The aircraft below is seen during interoperability trials with the French destroyer Tourville, in the Irish Sea.

Left and below left: Since 1987 the Air Corps has maintained a four-ship aerobatic display team, the 'Silver Swallows', drawing on aircraft and pilots from the Light Strike Squadron. The 'Swallows' were always challenged by budgetary constraints and a lack of real official support, but were widely lauded wherever they appeared. In what many considered to be their swansong appearance, the team (without formally using the 'Silver Swallows' name) attended the 1997 Royal International Air Tattoo at Fairford, for the first time, and carried off the Lockheed Martin Cannestra Trophy for the best overseas display team. Note the new badges applied to the aircraft.

Above: The Air Corps took delivery of 10 SIAI-Marchetti SF.260WE Warriors in 1977, with another following in 1979. Three of them have been lost in accidents but the others serve with the Basic Flying Training School, Training Wing. Several of the Warriors have gained unofficial cartoon character markings on their fins.

Left: Two Aérospatiale SA 342L Gazelles were acquired in 1979 and 1981. The Gazelles are greatly appreciated by pilots for their speedy performance and good handling qualities, and both aircraft are used for pilot training as part of No. 3 Support Wing's Helicopter School.

Below: Seen over the Blessington Lakes, this Alouette III is SAR-configured with rescue hoist and emergency flotation gear. Alouettes are charged with SAR on Ireland's east coast, while Dauphins operate in the north and west.

Right and below: The Alouettes, Dauphins and Gazelles of No. 3 Support Wing are universally referred to in the Air Corps as the 'Helis', and the helicopters of the Air Corps are the most important operational element of the force. The Alouette IIIs are heavily committed to army support duties, undertaking troop transport and surveillance missions along the Republic's border with Northern Ireland. Their SAR tasking diminished with the arrival of the Dauphins, which introduced the brand-new factor of shipboard operations to the Air Corps. The Dauphins themselves have been supplanted in the SAR role by longer-range Sikorsky S-61s operated under civil contract to Ireland's Department of the Marine. This is a role that many in the Air Corps feel they should be allowed to fulfil, but a scarcity of funds and the lack of any real strategic plan for the Air Corps have hampered these, and other, ambitions. The Air Corps' recent adoption of 'true' blue uniforms, as opposed to their previous 'army' green, was another step in the Corps' establishment of a real independent identity. It is over 20 years since the Air Corps was the Army Air Corps, but it is still struggling to have its invaluable and beneficial capabilities recognised in its own right.

Above: This HS.125-700B has been in Air Corps service since 1980, and has regularly been among the highest annually timed HS.125s worldwide. It was the backbone of the VIP transport fleet for many years and is still in daily use, despite the arrival of the Gulfstreams.

Above: This is the sole Reims-Cessna FR.172K (note the undercarriage spats) operated by the Air Corps. It entered service in 1981 as an attrition replacement with the Army Co-Operation Squadron, at Gormanstown Aerodrome, Co. Meath, south of Dublin.

Right: The Air Corps main centre of operations is Casement Aerodrome, Baldonnel. One major unit is based elsewhere – the Army Co-Operation Squadron (formerly No. 2 Support Wing), at Gormanstown. This unit flies five Reims Cessna FR.172H Rockets (of eight delivered in 1972) plus one FR.172K. The Cessnas were acquired as part of the overall expansion of the Air Corps at that time, in response to the worsening situation in Northern Ireland. They undertake border patrols for army units, scouting ahead in the rough terrain of Donegal and Monaghan, and also provide the same service for Ireland's (unarmed) police for major cash shipments between towns. The Cessnas are tasked with surveillance and photo reconnaissance/survey tasks as well as target towing and air ambulance duties.

Above: A major boost to the Air Corps capabilities came with the arrival, in 1994, of the first of two CN.235MP dedicated maritime patrol aircraft. Both 'CASAs' (as they are always called) carry a Litton AN/APS-504(V)5 search radar, FLIR System FLIR 2000HP and a Litton/CASA Tactical Data Management System.

Left: Increased demands on the Air Corps' hard-working VIP transport assets brought about the introduction of a Gulfstream IV, in 1991. The GIV is flown by No. 1 Support Wing's Ministerial Air Transport Squadron (MATS).

Below left: A single Beech 200 King Air remains in MATS service. Two other King Airs were replaced in the maritime patrol role by the CN.235s, and were disposed of in 1992. The surviving transport aircraft is seen here over the Pigeonhouse power station, a well-known Dublin landmark, at the mouth of the River Liffey.

Two recently retired but important types in Air Corps history were the first CN.235M (above) and Gulfstream III (below) to be acquired. Both represented a major step forward for the Corps. The CN.235M paved the way for full-scale all-weather maritime patrol missions, in addition to providing (sorely-missed) transport capability. It was returned to the manufacturer in 1995. The GIII became the first Air Corps aircraft to circumnavigate the globe and was acquired in 1990 to support Ireland's Presidency of the European Community. It also flew Beirut hostage Brian Keenan out of captivity, to a Dublin homecoming in 1991.

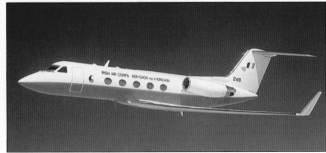

Right and below: In 1997 an Air Support Unit for the Garda Siochana (Irish National Police) was established with the assistance of the Air Corps. The ASU operates a single Eurocopter AS 355N Twin Squirrel (delivered on 22 August) and is the first operator of the advanced PBN Defender 4000 (delivered on 15 August). Each aircraft wears an Air Corps serial, is based at Baldonnel and has Air Corps flight crews and technical support. Both are equipped with FLIR and day/night TV systems. The advent of the ASU ushers in a new chapter of Air Corps operations.

Below left: The Air Corps operated DHC-1 Chipmunks as primary trainers from 1952 until the last remaining examples were replaced by Cessnas. Several Chipmunks survive, however, including this one airworthy example, which the Air Corps hopes to incorporate into a new historical collection.

Below: The Air Corps acquired six Vampire T.Mk 55s between 1956 and 1961, but this is not one of them. This is an ex-RAF T.Mk 11 obtained as an instructional airframe in 1963 and preserved in Air Corps colours at Baldonnel. The aircraft has now been moved indoors and is being restored.

Bottom: In this view along a misty Baldonnel taxiway, a CN.235 and a Dauphin return from an evening mission.

Tornado Operators

United Kingdom

Royal Air Force

Britain took delivery of 398 Tornados, including 173 ADVs (of which three were prototypes and 18 were F.Mk 2s). Four of the IDS aircraft were prototypes, and two were pre-production aircraft. The 229 remaining IDS aircraft allowed the formation of an eventual 11 front-line strike/attack and strike/attack/reconnaissance squadrons, seven (later eight) of them based in RAF Germany at Brüggen and Laarbruch. The Germany-based squadrons had a dual conventional and nuclear tasking, and were assigned to the Second Allied Tactical Air Force, which formed one half of Allied Air Forces Central Europe and which supported the NATO Central Army Group. Early plans for two maritime strike squadrons were cancelled, and the earmarked aircraft were allocated instead to RAF Germany, although the end of the Cold War eventually allowed aircraft to be relinquished for the maritime role. The UK-based Tornado squadrons are believed to have had a more strike-orientated role, being allocated to SACEUR's Strategic Reserve (Air).

The UK-based squadrons were the first to trade in their ageing Vulcans for Tornados, with No. IX Squadron reforming at Honington, and Nos 617 and 27 reforming at Marham between 1982 and 1983. Laarbruch's Nos XV and 16 Squadrons exchanged Buccaneers for Tornados in 1983 and 1984, when they were also joined by No. 20 Squadron, previously a Jaguar unit at Brüggen. The rest of the Brüggen Jaguar Wing re-equipped with Tornados between 1984 and 1985, with the conversion of Nos 31, 17 and 14 Squadrons (in that order). No. IX moved to Brüggen in 1986, while No. II converted to the reconnaissance Tornado at Laarbruch in 1989. The last of the originally planned 11 squadrons was No. 13, a second reconnaissance unit based at Honington.

The introduction of the Tornado was accompanied by a massive programme of airfield improvements, with much new hardened accommodation being provided for personnel and equipment. The bases in RAF Germany already had Phase 1 hardened aircraft shelters (HASs) from the Jaguar/Buccaneer era, and they were taken over by the new Tornado squadrons as they were, although other facilities were improved or replaced. The angular, slab-sided Phase 1 HAS can accommodate a single Tornado, and has hinging, shell-shaped doors that open outwards under an overhang, or 'porch'. Elsewhere, each

squadron was provided with a new HAS site that typically consisted of 12 HASs, a Personnel Briefing Facility (PBF) from which operations are run and in which, in wartime, the aircrew would live, with a Hardened Personnel Shelter for wartime use by the ground crew. The bulk of the PBF and HPS are protected against NBC contamination, with a comprehensive system of airlocks and a rigorous decontamination procedure to be followed by personnel entering the building. The hardened part of the facilities may be lightly pressurised, creating an overpressure which prevents any vapour contamination from migrating 'inside'. In peacetime, squadrons use 'soft' crewrooms and offices attached to the PBF, but they would be abandoned in time of war. The first UK HAS site was constructed at RAF Honington for No. IX Squadron, using semi-circular section, arched Phase 3 HASs. They had outward-sliding, externally-braced doors, and a 'lean-to' AGE (Aerospace Ground Annex) for stores and vehicles, and could accommodate two Tornados, if required. Honington was also later provided with a second HAS site for No. 13 Sqn, which used the larger Phase 4 HAS.

The Tornado force always placed high reliance on low-level tactics in order to penetrate enemy airspace but, even during the Cold War, increased restrictions on low flying (especially in Germany, where a 400-ft/121-m limit was raised to 1,000 ft/ 304 m) placed more pressure on UK airspace. The decision was taken to export some low flying to sparsely-populated Goose Bay, in Canada, and since 1983 RAF squadrons have deployed there for Maple Flag and Green Flag exercises, and for general low-level flying training. Since 1986, the RAF has maintained a semi-permanent detachment of up to nine Tornados at Goose Bay for between six and nine months each year, with squadrons rotating out to use the based aircraft.

During the 1991 Gulf War, Tornados were deployed to the region in composite units to make maximum use of combat-ready crews, and because the initial deployments were made at the height of the most popular time of year for leave. The detachments initially bore specific numbered identities, based on the squadron affiliation of the unit commander, but soon became simply the Tornado Detachment, Dhahran, the Tornado Detachment, Muharraq, and the Tornado Detachment, Tabuk. The lead squadron of the Dhahran

RAF Tornados are best known for Operation Granby, the service's contribution to the 1991 Gulf War. Here a sand-coloured GR.Mk 1A from No. II (AC) Sqn is seen after the war.

detachment was No. 31 Squadron, but the detachment also included an element of GR.Mk 1As crewed by Nos II and 13 Squadrons. The Muharraq detachment was led by No. XV Squadron, but included crews from Nos IX, 17, 27, 31 and 617 Squadrons. The Tabuk detachment was led by the OC of No. 16 Squadron, with crews from Nos IX, 14, and 20 Squadrons (the latter with ALARM missiles), and TIALD crews from Nos II, 13 and 617. The achievements of the detachments are described here under the entries relating to their lead squadrons.

Almost immediately after the war, the Tornado force was drastically pruned, with the Laarbruch wing disappearing. No. II Squadron transferred to the UK, with Laarbruch's other three squadrons simply disbanding. The two UK-based SACEUR units became maritime strike/attack squadrons, one under a new numberplate.

While the IDS force took shape, the RAF began introducing the dedicated Tornado interceptor into service. The introduction of the Tornado ADV marked more than a change of aircraft types for the RAF's home defence fighter squadrons, however, since it was but one element in a radical overhaul and transformation of the entire British air defence system, accompanying the establishment of a new air defence infrastructure, known as the Integrated UK Air Defence Ground Environment (IUKADGE), with new control centres and reporting stations and a network of mobile air defence radars. The new system did not become operational until 1992/93, and was formally commissioned on 1 June 1993. The Tornado ADV thus began its career operating under the old system.

No. 229 OCU began training instructors for the ADV force in 1985, and the first squadron began conversion at the end of 1986. Thereafter, a new squadron formed

every six months, with the last becoming operational at the end of 1990.

The RAF received seven front-line Tornado F.Mk 3 squadrons, and the additional training unit also had a reserve front-line commitment. Two of the squadrons converted from the BAe Lightning, while four were former Phantom units. The final squadron was newly formed (having last seen service as a Bloodhound SAM unit). It had once been intended that four Phantom squadrons (Nos 19 and 92 in RAF Germany, and Nos 56 and 74 in the UK) would run on beside the Tornado ADVs, but they were disbanded in the wake of the Options for Change review, together with one Tornado F.Mk 3 squadron.

Originally, five of the Tornado F.Mk 3 squadrons were controlled by SACEUR through the RAF's No. 11 Group, and were responsible for defence of the UK Air Defence Region (UK ADR), which formed the bulk of the NATO AEW Area 12. Two more squadrons were declared to SACLANT for maritime air defence duties, though they also took their turn in maintaining the RAF's QRA commitment. The F.Mk 3 squadrons were based at Leeming (a former training base which required massive construction work) and at Coningsby and Leuchars (existing fighter stations operating F-4 Phantoms, and already provided with hardened aircraft shelters). Plans first announced in 1981 were also put into effect to provide two forward operating bases for Tornado F.Mk 3s. The SACLANT-declared squadron at Leeming would use Stornoway in the Hebrides (where construction of nine HASs began in March 1989, though this was abandoned before they broke ground), while Coningsby's SACLANT-declared squadron would have Brawdy as a forward operating base.

For the purposes of fighter defence, the UK ADR is controlled from the Air Defence Operations Centre at HQ RAF Strike Command, RAF High Wycombe, with the Secondary ADOC at HQ No. 11 Group, RAF Bentley Priory. The UK ADR is divided into two parts, with Sector One (north of 55°N) controlled by the Sector Operations Centre at Buchan, and with Sector Two in the south under the control of the Sector Operations Centre at Neatishead. They have secondary SOCs (which also function as Control and Reporting Centres) at Boulmer and Ash. All four centres operate from underground bunkers, though Ash is not

Seven fighter squadrons, an overseas flight and an OCU were equipped with the Tornado F.Mk 3 interceptor, although one squadron has since disbanded.

used operationally, and houses the ground environment OEU and the training centre. The Sector Operations Centres have their own remote mobile radars, and are also 'fed' by above-ground Control and Reporting Points (CRPs) which have no direct contact with aircraft, but which have their own mobile radars, often located some way from the centres themselves. The SOC at Buchan is linked to its secondary SOC and CRC at Boulmer, and to CRPs at Benbecula, Saxa Vord and on the Faroes (the latter operated by Denmark). The SOC at Neatishead is linked to CRPs at Portreath, Staxton Wold and Ty Croes. The Northern QRA commitment was shared between the squadrons at Leeming and Leuchars, while Coningsby (together with the Wattisham Phantoms) took the Southern Q commitment.

The end of the Cold War saw a dramatic decrease in aerial contact by the RAF's Tornado squadrons, as incursions by Russian reconnaissance aircraft dwindled to an almost insignificant level. Between 6 September 1991 and 9 September 1993, for instance, there were no interceptions, while reconnaissance aircraft tracked on 9 and 17 September 1993 stayed outside the RAF's area of responsibility. The QRA commitment was steadily scaled down, and from 9 January 1992 was maintained only at Leuchars, with crews from other stations sharing the burden when necessary. A VC-10 tanker is maintained on alert at Brize Norton, ready to scramble if required, but live intercepts are rare today, and the incursion by a Tu-95 'Bear' in 1996 was front-page news.

The Phantom fleet (of four squadrons) was withdrawn prematurely, and it was decided that the F.Mk 2s would not be upgraded to re-enter service. No. 23 Squadron disbanded on 28 February 1994, and 24 RAF Tornado F.Mk 3s were long-leased to Italy.

RAF Germany disbanded on 31 March 1993, and was replaced by No. 2 Group, headquartered at JHQ Rheindahlen. This group disbanded on 8 March 1996 and stood down on 31 March, with the seven remaining flying units (four equipped with Tornados) transferring to the command of No. 1 Group in the UK. The four remaining RAF Germany-based squadrons will

apparently be further reduced to two squadrons (reportedly those now equipped with ALARM) by the end of 1998. It is still unclear whether the two squadrons not retained in Germany will disband, or whether they will be relocated to the UK. The two squadrons retained in Germany may combine with a Luftwaffe Tornado unit to form a joint strike unit.

Tornado IDS squadrons provide crews for the six aircraft maintained on a rotational deployment at Dhahran, Saudi Arabia, under Operation Jural. This is the codename given to Britain's contribution to Operation Southern Watch, the UN air patrols over the Southern Iraqi 'No-Fly Zone'. At least two of the aircraft are TIALD equipped, and all may carry the Vinten GP-1 photo reconnaissance pod. Jural began in August 1992, when aircraft and crews from Nos 14 and 617 Squadrons deployed. Crews from Nos 14 and 17 took over in December 1992, and crews from Marham, Honington and Brüggen replaced them in March 1993. No. IX Squadron manned the detachment from

June to August 1993, giving way to No. II, which in turn passed the baton to No. 31 Squadron in December 1993, staying on until March 1994. Brüggen-based squadrons have manned the detachment since then. Terrorist threats prompted a move of allied forces from Dhahran to Al Kharj late in 1996.

The Tornado force also garrisons the Operation Warden detachment at Incirlik for operations over northern Iraq. The crews man three Tornado GR.Mk 1As and three GR.Mk 1Bs, which took over from Harrier GR.Mk 7s when they were sent to Italy for operations over Bosnia in August 1995. Tornado ADVs maintained a detachment at Gioia del Colle in Italy for operations over Bosnia, policing the 'No-Fly Zone' until mid-1996. The British part of this multinational effort is known as Operation Grapple. The Tornado ADVs were withdrawn in 1996.

RAF Tornados wear colourful squadron markings in peacetime, but in time of war they would be removed, and the aircraft would carry only their serials and two-letter unit codes, the first letter indicating the

The RAF's GR.Mk 1 fleet is slowly adopting a medium grey scheme. Eleven GR.Mk 1 squadrons and an OCU were formed, although three RAF Germany units have subsequently disbanded.

squadron. Some units use these two-letter codes in peacetime, while others use single-digit codes instead. On the Tornado IDS force, two-letter codes were not initially allocated, and the code ranges beginning 'AA', 'BA', 'CA' and 'DA' were thus allocated to the Brüggen-based squadrons, with 'EA', 'FA', 'GA' and 'HA' codes for the Laarbruch units. The UK-based Tornado IDS squadrons (some of which had actually formed first) ended up with higher code ranges. The Tornado ADV squadrons were allocated codes as they formed, with No. 229 OCU taking 'AA'-'AZ' (with 'A1'-'A9' as overflows, for the Stage One Plus aircraft). and No. 29 taking 'BA'-'BZ'. No. 111 Squadron, last to form, had 'HA'-'HZ'.

No. II (AC) Squadron

No. II Squadron flew its last Jaguar reconnaissance sortie on 16 December 1988, by which time the unit's new Tornados had been delivered, though none had their reconnaissance equipment installed. For most of 1989, No. II trained in its secondary attack role, receiving reconnaissance equipment at the end of the year. No. II provided aircraft and five of the nine crews for the dedicated reconnaissance detachment based at Dhahran during Operation Desert Storm,

No. II Squadron has an 80 per cent reconnaissance tasking, using the filmless TIRRS equipment installed in the GR.Mk 1A and GP.1 external pods. The remainder of the squadron's tasking is in the overland strike/attack role.

though its crews were also involved in the TIALD detachment at Tabuk. The reconnaissance detachment was based at Dhahran from 13 January, flying the first of

128 sorties on 17 January. The squadron was granted the Battle Honour 'Gulf 1991' with the right of emblazonment. Alone among Laarbruch's Tornado squadrons,

No. II Squadron merely moved back to the UK when the wing ceased operations, rather than disbanding or transferring to a new role or type. The squadron moved to RAF Marham on 3 December 1991, marking the first step in a concentration of RAF reconnaissance assets at RAF Marham.

The Tornado GR.Mk 1A units maintain a secondary attack capability, which was demonstrated in late 1996 when a No. II Squadron aircraft was used for fit-checks of the new Brimstone anti-armour weapon. It was initially said that the GR.Mk 1A was unique in not having a nuclear strike capability, although it is suspected that the Marham-based reconnaissance squadrons may now be the only nuclear-armed Tornados until the retirement of WE177.

The No. II (AC) Squadron Tornados were allocated the codes 'HA'-'HZ', but never wore them, instead using letters which spelled out S,H,I,N,Y,T,W,O,E,R,A,C, with other codes including U, II, and IV.

No. 5 Squadron

No. 5 Squadron, the third RAF F.Mk 3 squadron, was the first to convert to the aircraft from the Lightning, gaining backseaters for the first time since its days as a Javelin unit. The first Tornado destined for No. 5 Squadron was ZE292, delivered to Coningsby on 25 September 1987, although the unit's markings had previously been applied (very small) on ZE256 during June 1987. This was somewhat premature, since the unit did not stand down from its commitments as a Lightning unit until 31 October, and continued operations until 10 December. The new, Tornado-equipped No. 5 Squadron formally stood up at Coningsby on 1 January 1988, and was declared operational on 1 May 1988. This completed the Coningsby wing. The squadron won the Seed Trophy for gunnery in 1989 and 1990. During 1990, the squadron provided four

aircraft to participate in the Malaysian air defence exercise ADEX 90-2, deploying to Butterworth with two No. 101 Squadron VC10 K.Mk 2 tankers. The squadron's initial markings consisted of a broad red band across the fin, below the RWR, with a maple leaf in a white disc superimposed. A red chevron was located on the nose, broken by the roundel. These markings were toned down following the Gulf War, with the removal of the nose chevron and the replacement of the tail insignia band by a plain green maple leaf with a yellow 'V' superimposed, flanked by small red bars. The squadron was deployed to Gioia for Deny Flight on 25 November 1993.

No. 5 Sqn has employed several unit markings since it gained the Tornado F.Mk 3. The nose chevron is applied intermittently.

Tornado Operators

No. 5 (Composite) Squadron

When Iraq invaded Kuwait, an *ad hoc* detachment of 12 Tornado F.Mk 3s from Nos 5 and 29 Squadrons was hastily redeployed from Cyprus (where it had been undertaking an armament practice camp) to Dhahran in Saudi Arabia on 29 August 1990. Because the unit was led by the OC No. 5 Squadron, it was known as No. 5

(Composite) Squadron. It later became No. XI (Composite) Squadron in September 1990.

The Tornado F.Mk 3 detachment hastily dispatched to the Gulf in August 1990 contained several aircraft in full No. 5 Sqn markings.

No. IX Squadron

A former Vulcan squadron that disbanded on 29 April 1982, No. IX Squadron, RAF, became the world's first front-line Tornado squadron when it re-emerged at Honington on 1 June 1982. The squadron participated in a Green Flag exercise in March 1985, but took some months to become combat ready; delays in receiving equipment caused disruption, and the squadron bore the burden of investigating and evaluating new equipment and tactics. The squadron enjoyed a fierce rivalry with No. 617 Squadron at Marham, with whom it shared what was almost a common history back to World War II, often sharing neighbouring airfields or even dispersals, with the same aircraft types. The two squadrons disputed which was responsible for sinking the *Tirpitz*, and a bulkhead from that ship displayed in No. 617's crewroom was a frequent target for kidnap attempts by No. IX. The squadron eventually moved to RAF Germany on 1 October 1986, as had always been intended, swapping its original aircraft for new LRMTS-equipped aircraft from Batch 4. It celebrated by winning the

prestigious Salmond Trophy (awarded to RAFG squadrons for bombing and navigation accuracy) that same year. The squadron followed up its achievement with two second placings in 1987 and 1988, before taking the trophy again in 1989.

Also in 1989, one of the squadron's aircraft (02/AZ) was painted in a special colour scheme, with yellow-edged green stripes flowing back from the cockpit, along the spine and up the fin, bisected by the squadron's full heraldic badge, and with the dates 1914 and 1989 at the fin tip.

The squadron was nominated to become the first user of the BAe ALARM anti-radar missile, and began receiving ALARM-capable aircraft even as the missile itself was being tested. Squadron aircraft establishment was raised from 12 to 18 at the same time. During the Gulf War, No. IX Squadron provided eight of its ALARM-capable aircraft for use in Operation Desert Storm, but they were destined to be flown by aircrew from No. 20 Squadron, while No. IX's pilots and navigators flew conventional bombing missions with the Tabuk and Muharraq detachments. As a result of its efforts, the squadron was granted the

Battle Honour 'Gulf 1991' with the right of emblazonment.

Following the war, the squadron settled down to the routine, peacetime introduction of ALARM, and was formally declared to NATO in the SEAD role on 1 January 1993.

On 2 November 1995 No. IX Squadron was presented with the Wilkinson Battle of Britain Memorial Sword, in acknowledgement of the squadron's

introduction and tactical development of the ALARM missile.

No. IX Squadron took the codes 'AA'-'AZ', which its aircraft continue to wear.

In the 1990s world of Tornado 'mini-fleets', No. IX Sqn is assigned the anti-radiation speciality. This Gulf veteran wears mission marks.

No. 11 Squadron

With the arrival of the Tornado F.Mk 3, the Lightning base at Binbrook in Lincolnshire was replaced by the Tornado base at Leeming, North Yorkshire. Leeming had been a training base for many years, and required massive construction work to improve its infrastructure. Like Coningsby,

Leeming was destined to accommodate an eventual total of three Tornado F.Mk 3 squadrons, the first of which was No. 11, a former Lightning operator. The original No. 11 Squadron was down-declared on 30 April 1988, and flew its last sortie (a delivery flight of two Lightnings to a warbird collector) on 30 June. Meanwhile, No. 11 Squadron (Designate) had received its first

aircraft at Coningsby on 25 April 1988, officially reforming on 1 July 1988, when the first three Tornados flew to the squadron's new home at Leeming. It was originally intended to build three HAS complexes at Leeming but the planned land for the third site proved to be unavailable, leaving room for only two HAS sites, and therefore no HAS site for No. 11 Squadron. Instead, No. 11 operated from one of the station's old C-Type hangars. It was able to do this because it took over the 'mobile' maritime defence role previously undertaken by No. 43 Squadron, this inferring wartime operation from a forward operating base (probably Stornoway, which received limited new infrastructure to allow this, not including nine HASs, which had been planned). The squadron was declared operational (to SACLANT) on 1 May 1988,

No. 11 Sqn had the privilege of being the RAF's last Lightning squadron. In the Tornado its role changed to maritime air defence in support of SACLANT, while it has been in the forefront of overseas combat deployments.

deploying to Akrotiri the same day to begin its first armament practice camp. One aircraft (ZE764) was quickly painted with a black fin for use by the squadron commander, Wing Commander David Hamilton, and wore the codes 'DH'.

During 1995 an entirely new unit was formed with the assistance of No. 11 Squadron. This was No. 555 Squadron (motto: 'With Strength We Defend') which was formed at RAF Heningley (motto: 'Firmitas et Lumen') as an elite rapid-reaction unit for contingencies overseas. Both the squadron and the station were entirely fictitious, existing only for the purposes of filming the pilot episode of a TV drama, *Strike Force*.

No. 11 Squadron was the first of the RAF's Tornado F.Mk 3 units to participate in operations over Bosnia, deploying to Gioia del Colle on the night of 18/19 April 1993. No. 11 Squadron crews were fired upon on 24 November 1994, following the NATO raid on Udbina three days earlier. One shift of No. 11 was replaced by a shift from No. 23 Squadron seven weeks later, with the remaining shift replaced one week later. Subsequent tours at Gioia were three months long.

No. 11 (Composite) Squadron

The Tornado detachment at Dhahran became No. 11 (Composite) Squadron in September 1990, receiving modified aircraft to replace the original F.Mk 3s deployed from APC at RAF Akrotiri. Crews came from Nos 11, 23 and 25 Squadrons. The unit became No. 43 (Composite) Squadron on 1 December 1990.

The modified aircraft received at Dhahran incorporated RAM on the leading edges. They wore 'Dx' codes for No. 11 (C) Sqn.

No. 12 Squadron

No. 12 Squadron finally became a Tornado operator on 1 October 1993, when the Buccaneer-equipped No. 12 Squadron disbanded, its numberplate being immediately taken over by the erstwhile No. 27 Squadron at RAF Marham. The new No. 12 converted to the Sea Eagle-capable Tornado GR.Mk 1B and moved to RAF Lossiemouth on 7 January 1994. No. 12 Squadron took the two-letter code range

commencing 'FA' (F for the fox in its badge), although this duplicated the range used by the disbanded No. 16 Squadron. Other code ranges 'freed up' by the disbandment of units were not reused.

No. 12 Sqn's fox now adorns ASuW-optimised Tornado GR.Mk 1Bs at Lossiemouth. However, overland attack remains the squadron's primary task.

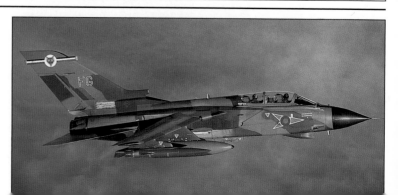

No. 13 Squadron

No. 13 Squadron was the last of the originally planned RAF Tornado IDS units, and the second operating in the reconnaissance role. Equipped with the new-build Batch 7 GR.Mk 1As, No. 13 Squadron officially reformed on 1 January 1990. The squadron worked up rapidly, and was declared attack operational on 1 January 1991. Its aircraft can carry the usual mix of IDS weapons, including ALARM. Crews from No. 13 Squadron formed part of the GR.Mk 1A-equipped dedicated reconnaissance detachment at Dhahran, but also provided four of the TIALD crews based at Tabuk, under the command of No. 617's CO, Wing Commander Bob Iveson. The squadron had previously undertaken

Two Tornado GR.Mk 1As from No. 13 Squadron display the traditional grey/green camouflage and the new all-grey scheme. Like its Marham partner (No. II), No. 13 Sqn has a primary reconnaissance tasking, although the squadron practises regularly for the tactically similar overland attack role.

the bulk of the Tornado/TIALD trial installation integration trials at Boscombe Down. Although its aircrew were spread around the Gulf Tornado force, No. 13 Squadron played a major role and was granted the Battle Honour 'Gulf 1991' with the right of emblazonment. As part of a concentration of reconnaissance units at

RAF Marham, No. 13 Squadron moved to the Norfolk base on 1 February 1994. The squadron deployed to MCAS Yuma in October 1996 for Exercise Arid Thunder, and dropped life-expired BL755 CBUs.

No. 13 Squadron uses simple single-letter codes, though it is thought to have

the full code range 'KA'-'KZ' allocated. At least one aircraft had a huge tiger's head badge painted below the raked intakes, claiming for the unit the right of participation in NATO's annual Tiger Meet events – its official badge is actually the head of a smaller cat, a lynx.

No. 14 Squadron

No. 14 Squadron was the last of the three Brüggen-based Tornado squadrons to form, but was the first of the RAF's Tornado units to receive the JP233 airfield attack weapon. (Brüggen gained a fourth Tornado squadron in 1986, when No. IX moved from Honington.) Tornados began arriving at Brüggen for what was then No. 14 (Designate) Squadron in April 1985, although the squadron's Jaguars remained operational until 1 November 1985, when the Tornado element formally came into

existence. The squadron celebrated its 75th anniversary on 3 February 1990, and marked up four aircraft for the occasion. Each received a row of diamonds across the fin, adjacent to the RWR antennas, with yellow letters immediately below. 'BA' had '14 SQN', 'BE' had '75 YEARS', 'BF' had

In 1997 the RAF Brüggen squadrons introduced new standardised markings with smaller individual unit markings and two-letter codes moved to the top of the fin.

'1915' and 'BM' had '1990'.

No. 14 Squadron's CO led the first Tornado deployment to the Gulf during Operation Desert Shield, as No. 14 Squadron (Composite), which is described separately. Before the war began, its crews had been replaced at Muharraq although No. 14 Squadron crews did play a prominent role within the Tabuk Tornado detachment during the Gulf War, winning the squadron the Battle Honour 'Gulf 1991' with the right of emblazonment.

Following the Gulf War, in late 1993, No. 14 Squadron received the lion's share

of the RAF's TIALD-capable aircraft from No. 617 Squadron, and took some TIALD pods. No. 14 Squadron still uses the code range 'BA'-'BZ'.

This No. 14 Squadron ('Bx' tailcode) GR.Mk 1 is in the standard operational finish, with new grey paint, all squadron markings removed and just the fin code remaining. Tornados currently man detachments in Saudi Arabia (Jural) and Turkey (Warden).

No. 14 Squadron (Composite)

The first Tornado squadron deployed to the Gulf was led by the commanding officer of

No. 14 Squadron, and included crews from various Brüggen squadrons and from No. 617

Squadron. The unit left Brüggen on 27 August 1990 and night-stopped at Akrotiri before flying to Muharraq, Bahrain. The unit soon lost its No. 14 Sqn identity, becoming

simply the Tornado Detachment, Muharraq. This came under the leadership of the OC No. XV Sqn, and its subsequent operations are described in the No. XV Squadron entry.

No. XV Squadron

Within RAF Germany, priority was given to re-equipping the squadrons which had been operating the Buccaneer, not least because this aircraft had already suffered a major grounding after the discovery of severe fatigue problems caused by operations in the overland role. The first RAF Germany Tornado squadron began receiving Tornados on 5 July 1983, officially forming on 1 November 1983 and being declared operational to NATO on 1 July 1984. The aircraft coded 'F' is traditionally named *MacRobert's Reply*, after one of the unit's wartime Stirlings. The squadron soon gained the Hunting JP233 airfield attack weapon, but also had a vital nuclear strike commitment. No. XV Squadron won the Salmond Trophy in 1988. In 1990 a single No. XV Squadron Tornado received a special colour scheme to commemorate the unit's 75th birthday. This consisted of a blue spine, canopy rails and fin flash, with a pair of narrow red flashes superimposed on the blue along the spine and up the fin, and with red canopy frames. The aircraft even had red and blue stripes along its leading edges.

No. XV Squadron was the lead element within the Muharraq Tornado detachment during the Gulf War, taking over the detachment from No. 14 Squadron. The detachment did also include crews from Nos IX, 17, 27, 31 and 617 Squadrons. The Muharraq detachment had a difficult war, and suffered four of the RAF's six Tornado losses (including the first three losses of the war). Nose-art was common on the

Muharraq-based Tornados, and included some shared 'flight' artwork applied to several aircraft, including 'Snoopy Airways' and 'Triffid Airways'. The Muharraq detachment flew some 400 sorties, dropping 1,700 iron bombs, 340 LGBs and 50 JP233s. The squadron's PGM missions used co-located Buccaneers for target designation, unlike the Tabuk detachment, which used TIALD-equipped Tornados. The Tabuk Tornados retained the two-letter

codes of their original operators, and there was no attempt to recode the aircraft into a uniform system. No. XV Squadron's achievements were recognised by the granting of the Battle Honour 'Gulf 1991' with the right of emblazonment.

During its time at Laarbruch, No. XV Squadron used the code range 'EA'-'EZ'.

The squadron flew home from the Gulf for disbandment on 31 December 1991, though it reappeared as the shadow identity

for the Tornado Weapons Conversion Unit on 1 April 1992, replacing No. 45 Squadron. As such it took codes in the range 'TA'-'TZ'.

No. XV Squadron was the first of the RAF Germany units to re-equip with the Tornado. It was one of three Laarbruch casualties in the post-Gulf cutbacks, although the numberplate lives on as the OCU.

Tornado Operators

No. 16 Squadron

No. 16 Squadron became RAF Germany's second Tornado squadron on 1 March 1984, after receiving its first aircraft on 13 December 1983. It was based alongside No. XV at Laarbruch, and similarly converted to the Tornado from the Buccaneer. The squadron's conventional weapons armoury included the Paveway II LGB, and not the JP233. Designation would have been provided by the Buccaneers of No. 237 OCU. Many RAF squadrons with World War I origins within the RFC celebrated their 75th birthdays as Tornado operators. No. 16 Squadron commemorated the anniversary by painting one of its aircraft black overall, with a huge yellow 'Saint' on the fin, and the legend '1915-1990'.

During the Gulf War, the Tabuk Tornado detachment was led by the OC of No. 16 Squadron, with crews drawn from Nos IX, 14 and 20 Squadrons (the latter with ALARM missiles), and TIALD crews from Nos II, 13 and 617. The Tabuk detachment suffered a single loss during the war. Nose-

Wearing No. 16 Sqn's 'Fx' codes, this GR.Mk 1 is seen prior to Operation Desert Storm. The commander of No. 16 also commanded the Tabuk detachment.

The crossed keys and 'Saint' symbol adorned No. 16's jets during their time in Germany. The unit specialised in LGB delivery.

art was common on the Tabuk-based aircraft, and several wore prominent shark-mouths. The detachment at Tabuk flew some 650 sorties (including 105 weather-related mission-aborts), among them five JP233 missions (23 sorties, 32 weapons) and 35 bombing missions (288 sorties, 1,451 bombs). The unit's total tally also included 48 laser-guided bombing missions, consisting of 192 bombing sorties (360 weapons dropped) and 95 TIALD sorties. The unit's ALARM element fired 121 missiles in 24 missions (52 sorties). No. 16 Squadron was granted the Battle Honour 'Gulf 1991' with the right of emblazonment.

At Laarbruch, No. 16 Squadron used the 'FA'-'FZ' code range. The squadron disappeared from the RAF's roll of front-line squadrons when RAF Laarbruch lost its Tornado force. No. 16 Squadron was the first of the four based Tornado squadrons to disappear, disbanding on 11 September 1991. Its historic 'numberplate' was transferred to No. 226 OCU, the Jaguar conversion unit, at RAF Lossiemouth on 1 November 1991.

No. 17 Squadron

No. 17 Squadron was the second of Brüggen's Jaguar squadrons to convert to the Tornado, forming as a Tornado squadron on 1 March 1985. To celebrate its 75th anniversary, No. 17 Squadron decorated

one of its aircraft with a black tailfin and spine. Superimposed on the fin was a large white triangle, containing the unit's mailed gauntlet in red, and the legend '1915-1990'. The same aircraft had the squadron's black and white zig-zag marking repeated above the wings. No. 17 Squadron was an early

user of the Paveway II laser-guided bomb. The squadron provided crews for the Muharraq detachment during the Gulf War and was accordingly granted the Battle Honour 'Gulf 1991' with the right of emblazonment.

No. 17 Squadron continues to form part of the Brüggen Wing, sharing the commitment to provide aircraft and aircrew for Operation Jural, the British element of Operation Southern Watch. The squadron continues to use the code range 'CA'-'CZ'.

Two views show the original No. 17 markings (left) and the new, reduced-size markings introduced in 1997 (above). No. 17 Sqn retains LGB delivery as its specialist role.

No. 20 Squadron

No. 20 Squadron had been a Jaguar squadron at Brüggen and it disbanded there on 29 June 1984, reforming as a Tornado squadron at Laarbruch (Laarbruch's third) the same day. A new HAS complex was built for the unit, with new Phase 3 HASs. Although not planned to be an ALARM squadron, No. 20 was destined to take the new missile to war, forming a discrete element within the Tabuk Tornado detachment, using aircraft borrowed from No. IX Squadron. The detachment flew 24 ALARM missions (52 sorties) and fired 121 missiles, and also contributed to the bombing missions flown from Tabuk. No. 20 Squadron was granted the Battle Honour

'Gulf 1991' with the right of emblazonment.

No. 20 Squadron was another of the Tornado units which fell victim to the defence cuts imposed in the wake of the Options for Change review, its historic numberplate being saved from extinction through reallocation to the Harrier OCU, which became No. 20 (Reserve) Squadron. No. 20 officially disbanded in May 1992, re-emerging in its new guise that September.

At Laarbruch, No. 20's Tornados were allocated codes in the range 'GA'-'GZ'.

No. 20 Sqn is unique in having operated all of the RAF's current attack aircraft (Harrier, Jaguar and Tornado).

No. 23 Squadron

Leeming's second Tornado F.Mk 3 squadron was No. 23, whose first aircraft

arrived at the Yorkshire base on 5 August 1988, prior to the official reformation on 1 November. Although the No. 23 Squadron 'numberplate' had been in use (by the four-

aircraft Phantom detachment in the Falklands), this was a reforming of a squadron rather than a conversion, since the existing No. 23 Squadron did not have its own permanent establishment, being manned by rotational deployments from RAF Germany-based Phantom squadrons. Unlike No. 11 Squadron, No. 23 moved into a new HAS complex and deployed to Akrotiri for a first APC during June and July 1989, returning to Leeming to be declared operational on 1 August 1989. This was just in time to allow the squadron to share the burden of the Northern QRA commitment, which temporarily transferred from Leuchars to Leeming while the Scottish Phantom base converted to the new aircraft. No. 23 Squadron celebrated its 75th anniversary by painting one of its aircraft

No. 23 Sqn had a single red eagle on the fin. Its official crest additionally featured a smaller bird of prey – almost identical to that of No. 29.

(ZE809) in a special colour scheme, with a red and blue fin (diagonally divided) and with the legend '(23 SQUADRON 75TH ANNIVERSARY 1 SEPTEMBER 1990)' along the spine.

In the second week of June 1993 No. 23 Squadron deployed to Italy to participate in Operation Deny Flight (the second unit to do so), but returned home to face disbandment. The Options for Change review hit the ADV fleet as well as the IDS fleet, and it was decided that one of Leeming's three Tornado F.Mk 3 squadrons would disappear. No. 23 Squadron, arguably the RAF's senior remaining fighter squadron (following the disappearance of Nos 19, 56, 74 and 92 as Reserve units), disbanded at Leeming on 28 February 1994, following a formal announcement made on 7 July 1993. The AOC had flown out to Gioia to give the squadron the bad news, only to find that Sky News had got there first. The squadron has since re-emerged as the shadow unit designation for what was the RAF's training flight for the E-3D Sentry AEW.Mk 1.

No. 25 Squadron's markings have changed subtly, but have always featured the falcon rising from a gauntlet, taken from the squadron badge.

No. 25 Squadron

Because the introduction of the Tornado F.Mk 3 originally represented part of a strengthening of No. 11 Group, some of the Tornado squadrons were new units. Only the three Coningsby- and Leuchars-based Phantom squadrons and the two Binbrook Lightning units were actually replaced, Wattisham and Wildenrath originally being slated to retain their F-4s. With the units at Leuchars and Coningsby 'staying put' even after conversion, the Binbrook units divided

between Coningsby and Leuchars. This meant that two 'new' squadrons had to form to complete the Leeming wing. One was No. 23 Squadron, as described above, but the choice of 'numberplate' for the final unit was not immediately obvious. To many, No. 25 Squadron was a surprise choice of designation for Leeming's third Tornado F.Mk 3 squadron, although it was 'still on the books' as a Bloodhound missile squadron. Cynics inferred that the unit had been selected because a former member of the squadron had reached high enough rank

to be able to influence the decision. After years 'in the wilderness' as a SAM unit, the squadron finally became a fighter squadron again, surprising all those who expected to see the re-emergence of No. 64 Squadron, No. 85 Squadron or even No. 60.

No. 25 Squadron (Designate) formed at Leeming on 1 July 1989, and officially established on 1 October, following the 30 September disbandment of the SAM unit. The squadron had received its first aircraft on 15 December 1988, and the next five were delivered on 3 July. No. 25 Squadron

was declared operational on 1 January 1990, operating from Leeming's second HAS complex.

No. 25 Squadron's anniversary ship was ZE838, which had a silver spine and black-edged silver fin flash, bearing the legend '1915 1990', broken by the unit's full heraldic badge. The following year, a squadron crew was responsible for the Strike Command Tornado aerobatic display, and their aircraft (ZE167) was similarly decorated with a silver spine and broad fin flash, though with a black tailfin, red/blue fin flash and simplified squadron badge in black silhouette form. The aircraft also had a black-edged silver anti-dazzle panel and narrow flashes running along the lower fuselage sides.

No. 27 Squadron

There were widely held expectations that No. 101 Squadron would be the RAF's third Tornado unit, having previously been the first with Canberras and one of the initial Vulcan units. Instead, No. 101 found itself with the less glamorous role of inflight refuelling, using VC10 tankers. No. 27 Squadron was the next most senior of the disbanding Vulcan squadrons, and was therefore chosen as the identity of the third Tornado unit. The Vulcan squadron had already vanished, disbanding on 31 March 1982, and the new No. 27 Squadron, which officially formed on 12 August 1983, received its first aircraft in June 1982.

No. 27 Squadron became the second Tornado squadron to take part in the USAF's Strategic Air Command's Giant Voice bombing and navigation competition. In what the RAF called Operation Prairie Vortex, No. 27 entered two two-crew teams into Giant Voice 1985, winning first and second place in both the Le May and Meyer Trophies (for individual crew high- and low-level bombing, and for the best low-level bombing damage expectancy). The

squadron also took second place in the Mathis Trophy, for the best high- and low-level team, robbed of first place by a single bomb hang-up.

When the Marham wing eventually adopted two-letter tailcodes, in March 1989, No. 27 Squadron took the range 'JA'-'JZ', choosing the initial letter J for 'Jumbo' to

reflect the unit's elephant badge. That month it borrowed two Mk 103-engined aircraft from RAFG, which were quickly painted up in squadron markings for a deployment to Malaysia (nominally for an exercise) and a courtesy visit to Indonesia. For its 75th birthday No. 27 Squadron decorated an aircraft with green and yellow

chevrons across the fin and outer wing panels, with the number 75 on each intake side. Another No. 27 Squadron aircraft ('JH') was painted black overall, but this had only a short life before being placed in storage.

No. 27 Squadron provided crews for the Muharraq detachment during the Gulf War, and was accordingly granted the Battle Honour 'Gulf 1991' with the right of emblazonment.

No. 27 Squadron's aircrew converted to the maritime role and moved to RAF Lossiemouth where they replaced the Buccaneers of No. 12 Squadron, taking over that unit's historic identity, and using the code range 'FA'-'FZ'. No. 27 Squadron's own numberplate was saved from oblivion, reallocated to the Puma and Chinook helicopter OCU at RAF Odiham, which became No. 27 (Reserve) Squadron.

Proudly wearing No. 27 Sqn markings, this is one of two GR.Mk 1s borrowed by the squadron for a Far East tour. The unit was based at Marham as part of SACEUR's strategic reserve.

No. 29 Squadron

The RAF's first front-line Tornado ADV unit was No. 29 Squadron, which had been a SACLANT-assigned Phantom squadron with a maritime defence role, and additional out-of-area commitments. They were retained following conversion to the Tornado F.Mk 3. The unit disbanded as a Phantom squadron on 31 March 1987, having stood down from its operational commitments on 1 December 1986. The first group of aircraft for the new No. 29 Squadron began training with No. 229 OCU during December 1986, and the squadron officially reformed on 1 April 1987. As a unit with out-of-area responsibilities, No. 29 Squadron was chosen to participate in Operation Golden Eagle, in which four of the squadron's aircraft circumnavigated the planet. *En route* they participated in Malaysian and Thai air defence exercises and in air shows in Sydney, Australia and Harrisburg, Pennsylvania.

In 1997 No. 29 adopted subtly different marks, with the three-'X' band being moved to the fin-tip.

After several years of wearing simple red and yellow fin markings, No. 29 adopted this more complex design.

No. 29 Squadron celebrated its 75th anniversary by redecorating the CO's aircraft. It gained a black spine, fin leading edge and tip, with a yellow band flowing up along fin behind and below the black, and with a red band behind and below that again.

The squadron's crews were involved in the initial 'emergency deployment' to the Gulf from their armament practice camp at Akrotiri. No. 29 also provided most of the ADV aircrew who flew during the war, although on each occasion they flew under

the auspices of other units, principally No. 5 (Composite) Squadron and No. 43 (Composite) Squadron. No. 29 was granted the Battle Honour 'Gulf 1991' but without the right of emblazonment, so it is not displayed on the squadron standard.

No. 31 Squadron

The first of Brüggen's Jaguar squadrons to convert to the Tornado was No. 20, which moved to Laarbruch. The first to do so and remain at Brüggen was No. 31, which officially changed over on 1 November 1984, having received its first Tornado on 13 June. No. 31 Squadron won the Salmond Trophy in 1987, knocking No. IX into second place. In 1990 No. 31 Squadron's anniversary bird was decorated with a yellow spine and fin cap, and a green fin, upon which was a large representation of the unit's mullet (a heraldic five-pointed star) badge. This aircraft also carried green underwing fuel tanks with a broad horizontal yellow stripe, on which were written the words '75th Anniversary'.

No. 31 Squadron provided the lead element of the Dhahran detachment and

crews for the Muharraq detachment during the Gulf War. The Dhahran detachment also included a reconnaissance element, flying Tornado GR.Mk 1As crewed by members of Nos II and 13 Squadron. The Dhahran detachment consisted of GR.Mk 1s from Brüggen and GR.Mk 1As from Laarbruch,

and nose-art was noticeably more restrained than on the other detachments. The unit flew 567 sorties during the war, 439 at low level. The detachment dropped 1,045 iron bombs and 14 JP233s. No. 31 Squadron was granted the Battle Honour 'Gulf 1991' in recognition of its

achievements, with the right of emblazonment.

Following the Gulf War, No. 31 Squadron became the second RAF ALARM-capable Tornado unit. In 1995, No. 31 Squadron celebrated its 80th anniversary and decorated an aircraft in a special commemorative colour scheme, with a yellow-edged green fin, yellow checkers across the fin and RWR fairings, and with the mullet on a black disc. A tiny fin flash was carried high on the fin, close to the trailing edge, above the rear hemisphere RWR antenna fairing. The unit still uses the code range 'DA'-'DZ'.

The traditional No. 31 markings have been replaced in 1997 by a much smaller nose checkerboard and fin-tip tailcodes.

Tornado Operators

No. 43 Squadron

During the Cold War, Leuchars was the RAF's most important fighter station, closest to the threat posed by Soviet reconnaissance aircraft and bombers flying down from the North Cape and through the GIUK gap. The Leuchars squadrons performed the majority of live intercepts of Soviet intruders, and the Tornado ADV had been optimised to meet the requirements of the Northern QRA role. Leuchars was destined to be the third and final station to receive the new fighter, since the need to replace the obsolete Lightning was pressing, and the main training base would inevitably be more centrally located.

Leuchars handed over the Northern QRA commitment to Leeming during 1990, by which time the conversion process was well underway. Leuchars received its first Tornado F.Mk 3 (for ground crew familiarisation) on 23 August 1989, and No. 43 Squadron down-declared on 30 June 1989, flying its final Phantom sortie on 31 July. The 'Fighting Cocks' reformed as a Tornado unit on 23 September 1989, and were declared operational on 1 July 1990.

Although declared operational, No. 43 Squadron did not immediately return to its pre-Tornado routine, and Leuchars did not regain the Northern QRA responsibility until January 1991, due to the Gulf War's impact

on crew availability. No. 43 Squadron deployed to Gioia del Colle for Operation Deny Flight from May 1994.

During 1996, one of the squadron's aircraft (ZE731/'GF') was decorated with a black spine and tailfin, on which was a flowing graphic representation of the unit's historic 'fighting cock' insignia. 'GF' is traditionally the squadron CO's aircraft, since the code letters are also the initial letters of the unit's motto – 'Gloria Finis' (Glory to the Finish). The aircraft usually has extra black and white checkers on the fin-tip to mark it out from the other squadron aircraft.

Above: No. 43 Sqn has used black and white checkers since the days of the Gloster Gamecock. The badge commemorates the aircraft's use.

Below: Carrying Sidewinders, SkyFlash and Phimat, a Tornado returns to Coningsby in March 1991 after service with No. 43 (C) Sqn.

No. 43 (Composite) Squadron

The RAF's Tornado detachment at Dhahran air base in Saudi Arabia was redesignated as No. 43 (Composite) Squadron on 1 December 1990, when OC No. 43 Squadron took command, with crews from No. 29

Squadron, and with one crew from No. 25. The unit's aircraft returned to the UK in March 1991, the commander's being specially decorated in full No. 29 Squadron markings.

No. 56 (Reserve) Squadron

One major consequence of Britain's Options for Change defence review which followed the 'end' of the Cold War was the retirement of the RAF's remaining Phantoms, which had once been expected to serve until the introduction of the Eurofighter EF2000. Ironically, the four surviving Phantom squadrons were probably the RAF's foremost fighter units, from a historical point of view, so efforts were made to save their 'numberplates'. Nos 19, 74 and 92 became shadow identities for BAe Hawk training units, but No. 56 Squadron's number at least transferred to a unit which operated a front-line fighter type, albeit not in a front-line role. No. 56 disbanded as a Phantom-equipped front-line air defence unit on 31 July 1992, reforming the next day by redesignating what had been No. 229 OCU as No. 56 (Reserve) Squadron. No. 56 Squadron was never a 'Shadow' designation for the OCU like No. 65 Squadron, and the No. 229 OCU identity disappeared. By 1993 No. 56 (R) Squadron was providing the Tornado ADV demonstration aircraft, which wore a red spine and fin. The 1995 display aircraft was ZE732, which had a red fin, red and white checkers, red taileron tips and wing flashes.

The 'Firebirds' of No. 56 Squadron now instruct Tornado F.Mk 3 crews. An important recent task has been the conversion of Italian crews to the aircraft. The OCU was the first ADV unit to form, hence the 'Ax' tailcodes.

No. 111 Squadron

The second Leuchars-based squadron to convert to the Tornado F.Mk 3 was No. 111 Squadron (known as 'Treble One') which thus became the last RAF Tornado squadron to convert to the aircraft. The squadron flew its final operational Phantom sortie on 31 October 1989, four months after No. 43 Squadron. After this, the Northern QRA commitment passed to the Leeming wing for a number of months.

Although No. 111 continued to fly training missions with its F-4Ks until the end of January 1990, a new No. 111 Squadron (Designate) began to form, flying its first Tornado sorties in May 1990, after officially reforming on 1 May. The squadron was declared operational on 1 January 1991. For its 75th anniversary, 'Treble One' decorated one of its aircraft (ZG776) with a black spine and fin. On them was superimposed a yellow panel covering much of the fin, with the squadron badge in a black circle.

Carrying camouflaged GR.Mk 1-style tanks, this 'Tremblers' Tornado F.Mk 3 displays the smart lightning flash markings of No. 111 Sqn. The complicated tail badge consists of three black seaxes in the centre of a Jerusalem cross, superimposed on crossed red swords. These symbols denote the squadron's associations with Essex, Palestine and London, respectively.

No. 617 Squadron

No. 617 Squadron reformed at Marham as the RAF's second front-line Tornado squadron on 16 May 1983, exactly 40 years after the historic dams raid in Germany. Disbanded as a Vulcan squadron on 31 December 1981, No. 617 began receiving Tornados on 23 April 1982. In 1984, No. 617 made the Tornado's first Prairie Vortex deployment to participate in the USAF Strategic Air Command Bombing and Navigation competition, Giant Voice 1984. Its two two-crew teams took first and second place in the Le May Trophy, first and third in the Meyer Trophy and second place in the Mathis Trophy.

On 25 November 1985 four of No. 617 Squadron's aircraft, accompanied by a pair of No. 229 OCU F.Mk 2s, flew to Oman for Operation Swift Sword (Saif Sareena), a convincing rapid-reinforcement exercise. On 13 January 1988 No. 617 Squadron was presented with a new standard by HM Queen Elizabeth the Queen Mother.

No. 617 Squadron's CO led the TIALD element of the Tabuk detachment and also provided crews for the Muharraq detachment during the Gulf War. The squadron was granted the Battle Honour 'Gulf 1991' with the right of emblazonment.

No. 617 Squadron was allocated two-letter tailcodes running between 'MA' and 'MZ', but they were not worn initially, two-number codes commencing 01 giving way instead to single-letter codes. The letters chosen were those used by Lancasters participating in the dams raid, albeit without the wartime 'AJ'- prefix. This continued until late 1987, when the approved 'MA'-'MZ' code range was adopted; they in turn were dropped by May 1989, replaced by the familiar single-letter codes. When squadron aircraft were sent to participate in Operation Southern Watch on 27 August 1992 they used three-letter codes based on those worn by the unit's Lancasters during the Dambuster era, with an 'AJ' prefix and a hyphen before the single letter identification. These codes rapidly spread to the whole squadron, and remain in use.

No. 617 Squadron gained TIALD immediately after the Gulf War, but converted to the maritime role in 1993, presumably losing its assignment to SACEUR's Strategic Reserve. The squadron received its first Tornado GR.Mk 1B on 14 April 1994 and moved to Lossiemouth on 27 April 1994, where it joined No. 12 Squadron and replaced the Buccaneer-equipped No. 208 Squadron, which had stood down on 31 March 1994. This completed the transformation of Lossiemouth's maritime wing to a Tornado-equipped unit, and marked the end of Marham's primary nuclear strike role. The HAS complexes used by Nos 27 and 617

No. 617 Sqn now has a secondary ASuW tasking in addition to its overland attack role. The squadron's aircraft wear 'AJ'-prefixed codes in recognition of the 1943 dams raid aircraft.

Squadrons were taken over by the reconnaissance-roled Tornado GR.Mk 1As of Nos II and 13 Squadrons.

The reroled No. 617 Squadron maintained a secondary overland role, and took over the Operation Warden commitment from Harriers on 3 April 1995, deploying to Incirlik, Turkey to enforce the 'No-Fly Zone' over northern Iraq.

In the post-Granby era, No. 617 continued to provide aircraft for UN operations over Iraq. Here one formates with a No. 20 Sqn jet.

No. 617 Squadron (Composite)

The second Tornado IDS unit deployed to the Gulf was led by Wing Commander Bob Iveson, CO of No. 617 Squadron. This unit flew to Muharraq in two elements on 19 and 27 September 1990, forward deploying to King Faisal AB, Tabuk on 9 October after a brief work-up. The unit soon lost its No. 617 Squadron identity, becoming simply the Tornado Detachment, Tabuk. It came under the leadership of the OC No. 16 Squadron, and its subsequent operations are thus presented in the No. 16 Squadron entry.

No. 1435 Flight

Following the recapture of the Falkland Islands, the area's air defence needs were initially served by a detachment of RAF Harrier GR.Mk 3s of No. 1453 Flight. From 17 October 1982 these aircraft were augmented by a detachment of nine Phantoms drawn from No. 29 Squadron, the detachment subsequently becoming No. 23 Squadron on 1 April 1983. The new Mount Pleasant airfield opened on 20 April 1984, and the Phantom detachment was reduced to four aircraft; the Harrier flight disbanded on 12 May 1985. The No. 23 Squadron detachment redesignated as No. 1435 Flight on 1 November 1988 when a new No. 23 Squadron reformed with Tornados. No. 1435 Flight re-equipped with Tornado F.Mk 3s in July 1992, with an initial four aircraft departing Coningsby on 6 July 1992. The flight has been maintained at the same strength since then, though contingency plans exist for the unit to be reinforced. The unit's aircraft bear the names *Faith, Hope, Charity* and *Desperation* – these names being echoed in the use of 'F', 'H', 'C' and 'D' tailcodes. The aircraft also have a red Maltese cross on their tailfins.

One of 1435 Flight's F.Mk 3s flies alongside a 1312 Flt VC10 K.Mk 4. Both types are detached from UK squadrons.

No. 229 OCU (No. 65 Squadron)

No. 229 OCU formed as the Tornado F.Mk 2 Operational Conversion Unit during 1984, receiving 16 aircraft between 5 November 1984 and October 1985. The unit was initially committed to instructor training, and was declared to NATO as an emergency air defence unit in December 1986, by which time the first F.Mk 3s had arrived. Training of operational squadron crews began in earnest once F.Mk 3s were on charge, allowing the conversion of the Phantom and Lightning forces, beginning with Nos 29 and 5 Squadrons, in that order. No. 65 Squadron formed as the OCU's 'Shadow' on 1 January 1987, as soon as operationally capable aircraft were available and while the first No. 29 Squadron crews were still in ground school.

No. 229 OCU took the opportunity to commemorate the 50th anniversary of the Battle of Britain in 1990 with arguably the gaudiest colour scheme ever to adorn a Tornado (ZE907). The spine, canopy frames and intake lips were red, and the tailfin was candy-striped in red and white chevrons. On the undersides, two chevrons covered the tailplanes and rear fuselage, the first one extending forward in a tapering red flash along the centreline. For the 75th anniversary of No. 65 Squadron, one aircraft received a commemorative colour scheme, with large red chevrons flanking the nose roundel, a red-edged white chevron containing the code on the fin tip, and a large representation of the squadron badge on the tailfin, together with the legend '75 Years'.

No. 229 OCU became No. 56 (Reserve) Squadron on 1 July 1992, one day after the latter squadron disbanded as a Phantom-equipped front-line air defence unit. No. 56 Squadron was never a 'Shadow' designation in the way that No. 65 Squadron had been, since the No. 229 OCU identity was lost entirely.

229 OCU's aircraft initially wore a red/yellow nose chevron, but this was replaced by No. 65 Sqn markings when this became the 'Shadow' squadron number.

Tornado Operators

Trinational Tornado Training Establishment

A trinational agreement similar to the one which established the Tornado programme set up a joint training system for the three customer nations and the four air arms involved. It was intended to provide economies of scale, and to avoid unnecessary duplication of infrastructure. There was also a stated belief that since Tornado crews from all the nations would have to fight alongside each other, they should also train together. This aim was frustrated when Germany pulled out of the establishment of a common weapons and tactical training phase, which has therefore always been a national responsibility. Although based at an RAF airfield, as a component of the RAF's No. 1 Group, under an RAF station commander, the unit is truly multinational, with senior positions (chief instructor, etc.) being rotated between the customer nations, and with aircraft from all users being employed.

Cottesmore was selected as the base for the TTTE in 1975, and personnel began to arrive from April 1978. Aircraft arrived from 1 July 1980 (British), 2 September 1980 (German) and 5 April 1982 (Italian). The first instructors (nine pilots and six navigators) trained on Service Instructor Training Courses at Manching from 5 May 1980. They then trained additional instructors at Cottesmore, before No. 1 Course arrived on

This trinational formation from the TTTE consists of two aircraft (foreground) marked with the 'S' and sword badge of the Standards squadron, and one wearing the stylised 'B' of B Sqn.

5 January 1981. The unit built up to an initial establishment of 22 German, 21 RAF and seven Italian aircraft, conforming to the 42.5 per cent, 40 per cent and 17.5 per cent funding spilt between the nations. Instructors were provided in the same ratio.

The standard Main Course lasts 13 weeks, with a nine-week flying phase providing 35 flying hours for pilots and 28 hours for navigators. The first eight hours are flown with instructors, before crews team up. By the end of the course, crews can fly an academic attack sortie, with automatic terrain following. The TTTE also provides shorter Instrument Rating Examiner courses, Senior Officer's (familiarisation) courses, and Competence to Instruct courses for TTTE instructor pilots and navigators.

Instructors and students are divided into three squadrons (A, B, and C) irrespective of nationality, and there is a separate Standards squadron (S). Aircraft are nominally assigned to the four squadrons

but are actually pooled, and a British student, for example, might well find himself with a German instructor in an Italian aircraft. The only exception to this aircraft and instructor sharing was when Saudi aircrew went through the TTTE. This was considered to be an entirely British responsibility, and only British instructors and aircraft were used for the four courses conducted by the Saudi Arabian Training Flight between October 1985 and early 1987. The places were assigned instead of RAF student places, however. A reduction in the need for new aircrew led to a 1989 reduction in the unit establishment, to 18 German, 16 RAF and five Italian aircraft.

The 200th main TTTE course graduated

on 19 February 1994. TTTE tail numbers were shared between the nations, with a nationality prefix ('B' for Britain, 'G' for Germany and 'I' for Italy). 01 to 49 were allocated to twin-stick trainers, and 50-59 and 70-99 to strike aircraft. 60-65 series numbers were briefly used by gunless reconnaissance-earmarked aircraft assigned to the unit while waiting for GR.Mk1A conversion.

In 1997 it was announced that the TTTE would disband in 1998, the Germans moving their training programme to the USA. RAF crews will be trained by an expanded No. XV (R) Sqn at Lossiemouth, which already handles weapons training on the type.

TWCU (Nos 45 and XV (Reserve) Squadrons)

Aircrew from all three partner nations (except RAF aircrew destined for the ADV) undertook a common type-conversion syllabus at the TTTE at RAF Cottesmore, before going their separate ways for operational training on the aircraft. It had originally been intended that all Tornado aircrew would train to squadron level together in the UK, but Germany was unhappy about the cost of Tornado weapons training in Britain, feeling that range charges were too high. Accordingly, that country decided to go its own way, and plans for a Trinational Tornado Weapons Conversion Unit were abandoned. RAF (and Saudi) trainees were sent from the TTTE to the purely British TWCU at RAF Honington, which had formed from 1 August 1980, with a first training course beginning on 12 January 1981. No. IX Squadron formed at Honington on 1 June 1982, and the TWCU 'geared up' to allow new squadrons to form or convert every six months.

The TWCU was originally staffed by instructors drawn from the Buccaneer, Phantom and Jaguar communities, none of whom had operational experience on the Tornado. By 1984, however, the first front-line Tornado aircrew was being posted back to the TWCU as instructors. As Tornado instructors with direct operational experience on the aircraft, they could give the unit the potential to serve as an additional front-line squadron in time of crisis or war, and as a so-called 'Shadow Squadron' during peacetime. By 1984 the squadron had 20 pilot instructors, 14 navigator instructors, and four pilots and four navigators who ran the simulator. The

unit ran courses for squadron QWIs and EWIs, and for IREs, but most students were completing basic conversion for their first Tornado tour. Their course included 35 flying hours, half flown with instructors, half as constituted crews.

The No. 45 Squadron numberplate was allocated as the Reserve Squadron identity of the Tornado Weapons Conversion Unit in 1984. (Though correctly referred to as Reserve Squadrons, such units were generally known as Shadow Squadrons in the RAF of the 1980s). This would have been used had the unit ever been transferred to SACEUR control. Reserve Squadrons could be brought up to strength and operational preparedness within a specified timescale, allowing SHAPE to plan progressive reinforcement of the front line, but were not liable to peacetime TACEVALs, which would have unnecessarily disrupted their peacetime training tasks. The TWCU took its identity seriously, taking possession of No. 45 Squadron's silver, trophies and memorabilia, painting the squadron's winged camel on its aircraft, and issuing squadron patches to its aircrew. Officially, however, No. 45 Squadron would not technically exist unless and until activated by SACEUR, and its standard could not be paraded in public.

When No. IX Squadron left Honington for Brüggen in 1988, consideration was given to No. 45 Squadron using the vacated HASs. In the end, this was not thought to be appropriate to the unit's training role, which was best met by operating from a conventional ASP and hangars.

The TWCU oversaw the conversion of the two reconnaissance units to the Tornado. Since those units had important secondary attack roles, the conversion course was unaltered, and the recce role was taught at squadron level.

Like many units, No. 45 Squadron celebrated its 75th anniversary in 1991, while equipped with the Tornado. To celebrate, the squadron painted up one of its aircraft (ZA606) in an eye-catching special colour scheme. The red and blue nose diamonds which had first appeared in the Hunter era were replaced by the squadron's older dumb-bell marking, in white on red rectangles flanking a disc containing the number '75'. The squadron's camel badge was transferred to a huge red diamond on the fin, which was painted blue all over, together with most of the rear fuselage and the spine. The tailerons had pale blue undersides (with a dark blue outline) and the same colours formed an arrowhead pointing forward almost to the radome along the centreline below the fuselage. No. 45 Squadron had previously operated a pair of specially decorated Tornados for air show use, with a blue, pale blue and red chevron on their tailfins.

No. 45 Squadron was allocated the wartime tailcodes 'LA'-'LZ', but they were rarely seen, except during the Gulf War when at least two aircraft had their codes applied. TWCU aircraft usually wore their 'last three' in yellow (outlined in white) instead of a single- or dual-letter code. No. 45 Squadron's identity was dropped on 31 March 1992, with a formal disbandment as the TWCU 'shadow'. This was a controversial move, because although No. 45 had spent some years as a second-line training unit (with Hunters and Tornados),

A few TWCU aircraft were prepared for war during 1990/91, receiving the desert pink finish and having the rarely-seen two-letter codes applied.

so had the unit whose identity was adopted in its place, and No. 45 had actually received its standard first and amassed more years of front-line service. Moreover, No. 45's peacetime career had been packed with extensive anti-terrorist and peace-keeping operations. Finally, the squadron's members were proud of their unit's traditions and were loathe to adopt those of another squadron. No. 45 Squadron's identity was effectively transferred to the Multi-Engine Training Squadron of No. 6 FTS, reforming as such on 1 July 1992. The TWCU formally adopted the new shadow identity of No. XV (Reserve) Squadron on 1 April 1992. New code letters, running between 'TA' and 'TZ', were allocated with the change of identification. The TWCU moved from Honington to Lossiemouth on 1 November 1993.

Between 1984 and 1992 the Honington training unit applied the TWCU markings to the fin and those of No. 45 Sqn to the nose.

Resplendent in No. XV (Reserve) Sqn markings and the new grey scheme, this aircraft lines up for a training mission at Lossiemouth. No. XV (R) Sqn will receive 10 more Tornados in 1998 when it adopts the initial crew conversion role upon the break-up of the TTTE.

DRA (formerly RAE)

Even before it became part of the DRA (Defence Research Agency), the Royal Aircraft Establishment was a small-scale Tornado operator. The RAE gained its first Tornado in mid-1983, in the shape of ZA326, the eighth production Tornado GR.Mk 1, damaged by a 31 July 1980 APU fire at Warton. The aircraft was repaired, repainted in the RAE's 'raspberry-ripple' red, white and blue high-conspicuity colour scheme, and assigned to the Flight Systems Department at Thurleigh, near Bedford. The aircraft was used for a number of programmes, including general swing-wing aerodynamic investigations, stores carriage, jettison and release characteristics, low-level turbulence, low-level navigation and terrain following. It remains in use with

the DRA's Experimental Flying Squadron at Boscombe Down. A Tornado F.Mk 2 was delivered to 'A' Flight of the Experimental Flying Squadron at Farnborough on 24 April 1988, which was used only briefly before being converted to serve as the TIARA testbed. This eventually made its maiden flight on 18 October 1995, when it moved to its new home at Boscombe Down, where it continued to serve with the DRA Experimental Flying Squadron. Especially at Boscombe Down, the DRA has operated a number of Tornados on short-term loan, but no others have been permanently assigned.

ZA326 has been a DRA/RAE stalwart, and is still employed on numerous trials programme. Of note in 1997 was the RAPTOR recce pod.

DERA Assessment and Evaluation Centre/Flight Test Centre (previously DTEO Flight Test Centre, previously A&AEE)

Despite a baffling succession of name changes, what was once the Aeroplane & Armament Experimental Establishment retains its traditional core role of testing and clearing aircraft, weapons and related systems for acceptance by the RAF and other British military air arms. As such, the unit employs a permanent fleet of experimental workhorse aircraft, but they are always augmented by aircraft on loan from service units and manufacturers. In recent years, the Fast Jet Test Squadron has operated two Tornado F.Mk 2s (ZA267,

the second prototype, loaned by BAe, and ZD900) and an F.Mk 3 (ZE155), as well as three GR.Mk 1s (ZA352, 358 and 402). Boscombe Down also hosts the ETPS and SAOEU as lodger units.

ZE155 is Boscombe Down's trials F.Mk 3, seen here carrying the Fast Jet Test Squadron badge on the fin. The aircraft is primarily used on armament trials, hence the SkyFlash and Sidewinder fin badge.

Empire Test Pilots' School

The ETPS gained an F.Mk 2 in 1988, but returned the aircraft to St Athan in February 1990, finding little advantage in having an example of the RAF's most numerous

aircraft type (and one often selected for student's final reviews) on its books.

The ETPS briefly operated this twin-stick F.Mk 2, applying the unit's crest to the fin and a nose chevron.

Strike Attack Operational Evaluation Unit (SAOEU)

Following the formation of the first three UK-based Tornado squadrons, RAF Strike Command established a dedicated trials unit intended to accelerate the development of tactics and operating procedures for the force. It was initially intended to have been based at Marham, and the first of four planned aircraft (ZA393) was delivered there on 11 November 1983. This was of a false start, however, and the Tornado Operational Evaluation Unit actually formed as a lodger unit at Boscombe Down on 1 September. It reported jointly to the Central Tactics and Trials Organisation at HQ RAF Strike Command, and to the A&AEE. The unit was originally planned to have a two-year lifespan, during which it was planned to develop operating procedures and techniques for the Paveway II and JP233, and to assess NVG operations and the use of FLIR. The unit had a one-year extension of its life during which it

performed ECM/EW development work and a live JP233 drop in the United States. At the end of that year, the unit gained permanent status and on 5 October 1987 was retitled as the SAOEU, receiving Harrier GR.Mk 5s in 1988, and later gaining a Jaguar, too. The CTTO was incorporated into the Air Warfare Centre when this was formed on 1 July 1993. The main effect was a change of unit insignia, with a blue chevron containing a disc with the letters AWC replacing the old insignia of three swords (hilts innermost) radiating out to form a Y shape, superimposed on a roundel. This badge was itself replaced by a winged sword within the same blue chevron.

The third, and current, SAOEU badge incarnation has a triple-winged sword in a fin chevron.

F3 OEU

A Tornado F.Mk 3 Operational Evaluation Unit (F3 OEU) was formed as an offshoot of the Central Trials and Tactics Organisation at Boscombe Down on 1 April 1987. Whereas plans to form the original IDS OEU at a Tornado front-line base had been cancelled in favour of basing the unit at Boscombe Down, the F3 OEU was established as a lodger unit at Coningsby, the primary Tornado F.Mk 3 base. Remarkably, the F3 OEU actually formed before the first front-line ADV squadron, and immediately set about its role of

developing doctrine and tactics for the ADV force, while also conducting trials to evaluate new equipment and systems. In order to keep abreast of developments, the unit has changed its four aircraft frequently, and can be relied upon to be operating aircraft to the latest standard, with the most recent radar state. When the RAF's new Air Warfare Centre formed on 1 July 1993, it incorporated the CTTO, and this led to a change of markings for the F3 OEU. The old CTTO badge of three swords forming a Y, hilts joined at the centre, was replaced by the letters AWC, carried in a red chevron on the tail-fin.

Both the SAOEU and F3 OEU wore versions of the three swords badge (above) when part of the CTTO. When the CTTO became part of the Air Warfare Centre, new markings were applied (below). One Tornado F.Mk 3 wore an 'SB' tailcode for the commander, Stuart Black.

Germany

Luftwaffe

The dark three-tone camouflage adopted by the Luftwaffe is optimised for low visibility over central Europe. Spurred by operations over Bosnia, a two-tone pale grey scheme has now emerged.

The Luftwaffe began the 1970s with five Jagdbombergeschwaderen, two Jagdgeschwaderen, two Aufklärungs-geschwaderen and a Waffenschule equipped with the F-104G Starfighter, and four Leichtenkampfgeschwaderen with Fiat G91s. All needed replacement by the mid-1970s, along with two Marineflieger F-104 units. The Fiat G91s were originally to have been replaced by the VAK-191, but that still left a requirement for some 700 Tornados to replace the F-104s one for one. It soon became clear that the Tornado would not be available until the early 1980s, and it was decided that some wings would have to be re-equipped before then. The two RF-104G-equipped reconnaissance wings were the most pressing priority, followed by the air defence-tasked JG 71 and JG 74, especially after Germany accepted the UK vision of Tornado as a long-range all-weather interdictor. With the RF-4E already selected as an RF-104G replacement, the standard F-4E fighter seemed to offer some advantages as an interceptor replacement for the F-104G, and also offered sufficient air-to-ground capability to allow the formation of two ground attack wings, one of which had previously operated F-104s, and one Fiat G91s. The decision to re-equip these six Starfighter wings with Phantoms led to further reductions in the Tornado buy from its original 700-aircraft level, first to 420, and then to 322. Two hundred would be for the Luftwaffe, with the remainder going to the Marineflieger. In the end, the Luftwaffe orders increased to 212, then to 228, and finally to 247, including 35 ECRs.

Economic considerations did result in Tornado deliveries being delayed. Despite plans to increase production from 46 aircraft to 63 aircraft per year between 1981 and 1983, deliveries actually reduced; 44 were delivered in 1981 and 1982, and only 42 in 1983. It had operated F-4 Phantoms since 1971, so the Luftwaffe did have a small cadre of suitably qualified backseaters (known as Kampfbeobachter, literally battle or combat observer), and an established system for training more. Nevertheless, the need to train enough new fast-jet WSOs led to 2./JBG 49 becoming so overstretched that its Alpha Jet pilot conversion task had to be virtually abandoned in order to concentrate on fast-jet familiarisation courses for navigators trained on 3./JBG 49 Skyservants and USAF T-43s.

The Luftwaffe's original four front-line Tornado wings were based in the central and southern parts of Germany alongside the RAF's Tornado wings at Brüggen and Laarbruch in the northwest of the country, with the conversion unit, JBG 38, in the far north at Jever. This geographical distribution left JBG 31 at Norvenich and JBG 33 at Büchel just falling into the area covered by NATO's 2 ATAF, and JBG 32 at Lechfeld and JBG 34 at Memmingen as part of 4 ATAF. Each front-line Geschwader had two Staffelen, for which aircraft were pooled, with centralised servicing at wing level. Aircrew, however, are proud of their individual squadron identities, and often wear Staffel as well as Geschwader flying suit badges. Staffel designations vary, with

some choosing the traditional German style (e.g., 2./JBG 34 for JBG 34's second Staffel) and others choosing European-style designations (e.g., 311 Squadron for JBG 31's first Staffel). Geschwader aircraft establishment was set as 38 aircraft, four with dual controls, except in the case of the single-Staffel training unit, which had 32 aircraft, 14 with dual controls.

Plans to reform JBG 37 at Husum in 1995 with new Tornados were abandoned when Germany cancelled its planned Batch 8 order for 35 IDS aircraft. The unit would have replaced the Alpha Jets of JBG 41. Another inactive Tornado unit is JBG 39, which would activate only in time of tension or war, since it is the shadow unit designation that would be applied to the aircraft and instructors from the German element of the TTTE at Cottesmore. As JBG 39, the unit would be based at Erding, in southern Germany. Two serviceable Tornados are usually on charge with Technischeschule der Luftwaffe 1 at Kaufbeuren, used for technical training of ground crew and engineering personnel. The aircraft are regularly rotated, to ensure even utilisation throughout the fleet.

On 1 April 1994, the Luftwaffe set up a new command structure. The Luftwaffen Führungskommando Süd consisted of 1 Division (HQ Karlsrühe) controlling JBG 32 and JBG 34, while 2 Division (HQ Birkenfeld) controlled JBG 33. Luftwaffen Führungskommando Nord consisted of 3 Division (which had no Tornado units reporting) and 4 Division (HQ Aurich) which controlled JBG 31 and JBG 38. The end of the Cold War and the consequent increase in internationally sanctioned peacekeeping operations led to a reduction in the popular hostility to the deployment of German military units overseas, and to subtle changes to those parts of the constitution which prohibited them. This presented new opportunities for Luftwaffe deployments overseas, and even in the establishment of new units actually based overseas. One was based in Italy for operations over Bosnia, and one in the USA for operational training.

The end of the Cold War and the consequent arms limitation treaties imposed ceilings on the numbers of combat aircraft that could be operated, and Germany decided to reduce the number of

From the outset the Luftwaffe Tornado force was assigned a tactical nuclear strike role, using US-owned B61 weapons.

F-4s in service, rather than getting rid of Tornados. Thus, the last wing of RF-4Es was retired prematurely (its aircraft were to have been upgraded with new EW equipment and sensors) and a new wing of Tornados was formed from aircraft that had been rendered surplus to Marineflieger requirements. There has also been a slight reduction in the overall number of Tornados operated by the Jagdbombergeschwaderen, allowing some aircraft to be redeployed to the USA for training, and for others to be placed in long-term storage in the USAF's 'boneyard', the MADC at Davis-Monthan AFB, Arizona.

Following a constitutional revision, the Luftwaffe established a unit in Italy to aid the peacekeeping operation in former Yugoslavia. ECR and recce aircraft were sent.

Wehrtechnische Dienstelle für Luftfahrtzeuge 61

WTD 61 is the German test and evaluation centre, known until 1987 as Erprobungsstelle (ESt) 61. Based at Manching, the unit has been heavily involved in the Tornado programme from the early days, conducting its initial tests on the prototypes and performing the acceptance trials and initial operational evaluation of the new type.

Since then, the unit has been the prime agency for the integration and testing of all new German Tornado developments, including a wide range of weapon systems and armament trials. Work is undertaken on behalf of both the Luftwaffe and Marineflieger.

Key early programmes were the integration of the MW-1 munitions dispenser and Kormoran anti-ship missile. In the late 1980s the main programme was the upgrade of earlier aircraft to Batch 5 standards with Mil Std 1553 databus and HARM capability. From 1988 WTD 61 was heavily involved in the ECR programme, accepting the first production aircraft on

behalf of the Luftwaffe in 1990. In February 1993 the unit accepted the first 'full-up' ECR with ELS equipment fitted.

In the late 1990s WTD 61 is as busy as ever with new Tornado systems and armament trials. Among the weapons under test are the Apache and KEPD 350 stand-off weapons and Aramis anti-radiation missile. Other tests are aimed at facets of the KWS/KWE upgrade programmes, which include Mil Std 1760 weapons interface, enhanced EW, laser designation pods, steerable FLIR and terrain-referenced navigation systems.

Right and above right: Among the WTD 61 test fleet is this ex-Marineflieger aircraft which has been used for several new-generation stand-off weapons flight tests. These include the DASA KEPD 350 (above right) and the MATRA/BAe Dynamics Apache.

Aufklärungsgeschwader 51 'Immelmann'

During the Starfighter and Phantom era, the Luftwaffe had operated two reconnaissance wings (a third and a fourth were briefly operational with G91Rs during the mid-1960s). The availability of the Tornado ECR, with its IIS and FLIR, gave a measure of reconnaissance capability, and with the end of the Cold War it was decided that a single Tornado-equipped reconnaissance wing (albeit with 40 aircraft, or more) could replace the last two Phantom units, AG 51 'Immelmann' and AG 52. This allowed the RF-4Es to be retired early, reducing front-line aircraft numbers in accordance with CFE treaty obligations and fulfilling public expectations of force reductions. The redundant Phantoms themselves were handed to Turkey, a traditional recipient of redundant Luftwaffe combat aircraft, in a gesture of gratitude for Turkey's contribution to and participation in Operation Desert Storm.

The original AG 51 at Bremgarten closed down in March 1993, following the cessation of flying operations in December 1992. AG 52 at Leck continued in service with RF-4Es until later in 1993. The unit then moved to Schleswig-Jagel, where it changed its designation to AG 51, while retaining its own distinctive panther's head badge in place of the original owl insignia of AG 51. The unit effectively reformed on 21 September 1993, taking over the aircraft of the disbanding MFG 1, which finally ceased

AG 51's aircraft come from both Luftwaffe units and MFG 1, resulting in a range of all four main camouflage schemes being used. This is an ex-MFG 1 aircraft in the later of the two Marine schemes.

operations by deactivating on 1 January 1994. AG 51 had only the most limited reconnaissance capability, taking over only seven former navy MBB/Aeritalia reconnaissance pods with its Tornados. The purchase of 30 more reconnaissance pods (of unspecified type) was funded in 1994, and by 1995 it was reported that 55 pods were on order. The new unit soon began swapping aircraft with other Tornado operators, and even operated some former MFG 2 Tornados armed with HARM missiles during its initial deployment to Piacenza. AG 51 formed the backbone of the German participation in Operation Deny Flight, maintaining a rotational deployment of aircraft with what became Einsatzgeschwader 1 in August 1995, backed up by Tornado ECRs from JBG 32.

This aircraft carries AG 51's panther badge on the fin, but also wears the 511 Squadron diving eagle on the intake. 512 Squadron has a leaping panther as its badge.

Einsatzgeschwader 1

Einsatzgeschwader 1 was established at Piacenza in August 1995 to co-ordinate operations by the six AKG 51 Tornados and eight JBG 32 Tornado ECRs participating in operations over Bosnia (Operation Deliberate Force). A flight of five ECRs flew the unit's first operational sortie on 31 August 1995, an electronic reconnaissance

ECRs from JBG 32 constituted the bulk of EG 1 when it was formed in August 1995, and undertook the unit's first mission. Live HARMs were carried, although none was fired in anger.

sortie over Bosnia. The aircraft flew 811 fighter-bomber missions in support of NATO operations. The ECRs withdrew on 22 November 1996, leaving the reconnaissance aircraft from AKG 51.

The German presence was useful, though restricted, and marked a sea change in German foreign policy. The legacy of World War II (and particularly of Hitler's military expansionism) has been to create a widely held suspicion and distrust within Germany of 'militarism', characterised by an extreme reluctance to deploy German armed forces outside Germany's own borders. Even during the Gulf War, Germany preferred to commit money and material to the coalition effort rather than troops and/or aircraft, and the decision to

actively participate in allied operations in the Balkans was a difficult one for German politicians to make. A senior German officer at NATO's command centre had a veto over any mission assigned to the Luftwaffe detachment, and, as a result, the German Tornados achieved little more than a symbolic presence. No HARM missiles were fired by the ECRs during their time at Piacenza, even though the aircraft participated in the strikes against Bosnian Serb positions in September 1995. The unit's aircraft retained their original fin

markings, but soon received an EG 1 badge on their engine intakes. This consisted of a blue square, with the German tri-coloured flag and the number 1 superimposed, and with the words 'Einsatzgeschwader' and 'Luftwaffe'.

AG 51 supplied reconnaissance pod-equipped aircraft to EG 1, which remained at Piacenza long after the ECRs had departed back to their base at Lechfeld.

Tornado Operators

Jagdbombergeschwader 31 'Boelcke'

It was originally expected that JBG 31 would convert to the Tornado in mid- to late 1981, as the first operational Luftwaffe Tornado unit, with JBG 32, 33 and 34 following in numerical order. In fact, the process of unit conversions was subject to delays (some deliberately specified by the politicians to spread costs over more years).

JBG 31 flew its last F-104G sortie on 30 April 1983, and crews began training at Cottesmore; the first Tornado arrived at Norvenich on 26 July 1983. The wing officially began to transition to the Tornado on 1 August 1983, roughly the date on which the final front-line Tornado unit was to have converted to the aircraft.

JBG 31 received the 100th production German IDS (4400) on 24 August 1983. Five years on, in 1988, this aircraft was especially decorated to celebrate JBG 31's 30th anniversary. The aircraft had a bright blue fin and spine, with a black, red and gold flash superimposed on the fin, and another on the intakes.

As the first Luftwaffe Tornado wing, JBG 31 set many milestones. In May 1986, one aircraft from JBG 31 (with another from JBG 38) deployed across the Atlantic, buddy-refuelling from two pod-equipped JBG 31 Tornados. The aircraft participated

A JBG 31 Tornado demonstrates a PART (Pre-Armed Reverse Thrust) landing with maximum braking.

JBG 31 achieved many firsts for Luftwaffe Tornados, notably Red Flag participation. The two squadrons have badges depicting two mules (311) and a wolf's head, three crowns and a sword (312).

in live drops of the MW-1 at Eglin AFB's ranges and was later displayed at the Andrews AFB open house. After clearing the Tornado to refuel from USAF KC-135s, the unit later deployed nine of its aircraft to Goose Bay, Canada, a six-hour 20-minute ferry flight. In November 1989, the unit became the first German Tornado wing to participate in Red Flag, having amassed 40,000 flying hours on 28 July that year.

Jagdbombergeschwader 32

It had always been intended that the German front-line units would convert to the Tornado in numerical order. Original plans called for JBG 32 to transition to Tornado in mid-1982, but the unit did not fly its last Starfighter mission until 18 April 1984. The wing received its first aircraft on 27 July 1984, and officially reformed on 1 August.

Uniquely among German Tornado wings, JBG 32 has never had a nuclear strike commitment, but has always been closely associated with ECM and EW training. The wing's third Staffel operated Hansa Jets in the ECM training role, and the wing also parented the joint civil/military Gemeinsame Flugvermessungsstelle (GMFS Fachbereich IV), with its calibration BAe 748s and 125s. In 1988, the wing painted up 4450 in a special commemorative colour scheme to celebrate its 30th anniversary. The aircraft had blue and white diamond checkers over the fin, and on bands encircling the wingtips, with a black, red and yellow nose and blue and white flashes on the intakes and underwing

fuel tanks. The words 'Frieden Freiheit' were applied across the undersurfaces of the tailerons.

JBG 32 became the Luftwaffe's second Tornado ECR operator from June 1991, receiving the final 17 Tornado ECRs produced, after the first 18 went to 382 Staffel at Jever. It had originally been predicted that JBG 32's first batch of Tornado ECRs would equip 323 Staffel, displacing that unit's ECM training Hansa Jets. In fact, they were delivered to 321 Staffel, whose standard IDS aircraft were redistributed to other units. JBG 32 formally became the Luftwaffe's only ECR unit on 1

July 1994, when 322 Staffel re-equipped with the Tornado ECRs previously used by JBG 38's second Staffel. The last of JBG 38's ECRs did not arrive at Lechfeld until October 1994. Between August 1995 and November 1996, JBG 32 supplied aircraft and crews to Einsatzgeschwader 1 at Piacenza. The unit's ECRs flew co-ordinated missions with HARM-armed Italian Tornados that lacked an autonomous emitter location system, perhaps presaging combined operations with ALARM-equipped RAF Tornados in the joint Luftwaffe/RAF wing that has been proposed.

Both of JBG 32's constituent squadrons fly the ECR variant with HARM capability. 321 Staffel's badge is a roaring panther, while 322 Staffel uses a dragon and the legend 'Flying Monsters'.

Jagdbombergeschwader 33

Original plans called for JBG 33 to transition to the Tornado in late 1982 or early 1983, but the unit did not relinquish the F-104G until after a final sortie made on 30 May 1985. The first Tornado was delivered to Büchel in August 1985, and the unit had received its full complement by August 1986.

JBG 33 at Büchel is believed to be the Luftwaffe's main nuclear strike unit, being co-located with a USAF weapons support unit. The Geschwader badge depicts a stylised diving eagle with a Tornado plan view superimposed. 332 Staffel employs a red devil on the ace of spades.

Jagdbombergeschwader 34 'Allgäu'

The conversion of JBG 34 to the Tornado was originally scheduled for late 1983, but ran very late, since it was the last German unit to transition to the aircraft, following the second Marineflieger wing, MFG 2. The wing did not fly its last F-104 mission until 16 October 1987, by which time the F-104 was beginning to be regarded with nostalgic affection. As a fighter pilot's toy the F-104 was exhilarating and rewarding, but as a front-line operational aircraft the type was showing its age very badly, and the Tornado marked a massive leap in capability. JBG 34 was declared operational in June 1988, receiving the last of its allocated aircraft in August.

Jagdbombergeschwader 34, the last of the Luftwaffe's Tornado squadrons, is based at Memmingen in the south of Germany, and its badge shows two stylised aircraft overflying mountains, with the four-pointed NATO star in the top left corner.

Jagdbombergeschwader 38 'Friesland'

JBG 38 was the first Luftwaffe Tornado unit to form, since its primary role was the same as that assigned to the RAF's TWCU – weapons and tactical training for aircrew going on to front-line units. At one time it was expected that the unit would take over the designation and traditions of what had been the Starfighter tactical weapons training unit, Waffenschule 10, but instead the unit gained a new designation and was classified as a Jagdbombergeschwader, although initially it had only a single Staffel, and no role apart from training.

Luftwaffenversorgungsregiment 1 (LsVersRgt.1) at Erding was the maintenance unit responsible for the acceptance checking of Luftwaffe Tornados, and an initial weapons training unit was set up as an offshoot of this unit. This was the Waffenausbildungs-komponente (weapons training component), or WaKo, which received its first aircraft on 9 November 1981, formally commissioning on 16 February with nine aircraft on charge, and rapidly working up to its established strength of 16 Tornados. The WaKo Tornados had no unit marking of their own, but did wear the badge of the Technischegruppe 11 on the port side of the fin, with the LsVersRgt.1 badge to starboard. WaKo moved from Erding to Jever on 1 July 1983, where Waffenschule 10 had flown its last F-104 sortie in May. WaKo became JBG 38 on 26 August 1983, by which time 24 Tornados were on charge, and eight more were accepted in subsequent years. WaKo had trained 170 aircrew during five courses, had dropped 4,000 practice bombs and fired 12,000 rounds of 27-mm ammunition. Most of the crews of the first operational German Tornado unit, the navy's MFG 1, were trained at the TTTE and by WaKo, though a handful had been trained by Panavia at Manching.

Newly trained crews from the TTTE at Cottesmore undergo a 30-flying-hour course with JBG 38, learning how to use the Tornado as a weapons system, dropping practice bombs and practising delivery techniques for various weapons, as well as receiving some ACM training. Tornado QFI and QWI instructor's courses are conducted by JBG 38 for the Luftwaffe and Marineflieger, which also runs EW training for all fast-jet types in the Luftwaffe inventory. The unit has occasionally used naval aircraft on loan from MFG 1 and MFG 2.

JBG 38 gained a second, operational Staffel in 1989. This unit was the first to equip with the new ECR variant, and its aircraft began to arrive at Jever in January 1990. 382 Staffel was destined to be short-lived as an ECR unit, however, and transferred its aircraft to JBG 32 during July-October 1994, receiving standard IDS aircraft in return.

JBG 38 performs weapons and tactical training for both Luftwaffe and Marineflieger crews. The badge is virtually the same as that used by WS-10 before it, except that plan views of Tornado, Starfighter and Sabre are incorporated. Before JBG 38 assumed Tornado training, WS-10 had trained Germany's F-86 Sabre and F-104 Starfighter pilots.

Deutsches Ausbildungsgeschwader/German Training Command

A Tornado squadron stood up as part of the German Air Force Training Command at Holloman AFB, New Mexico, on 1 May 1996, after the Luftwaffe spent $44.3 million on improving facilities and infrastructure at Holloman. The unit had an initial establishment of 12 Tornados, which were operated alongside 24 F-4Es (including seven leased from the USAF). The Luftwaffe expected the unit to clock up 2,500 Tornado sorties per annum. The unit will train Tornado instructors, three crews per course, two courses per year. It will also host three-week detachments by eight crews from each Luftwaffe Tornado wing, whose training is hampered by poor weather and a low-level training height limitation of 1,000 ft (304 m). Another 30 Tornados will be added (while the F-4Es will be replaced by Luftwaffe F-4F ICEs) under 'Holloman II', which will be implemented in 1999. Tornado annual flying hours will rise to about 6,000. The enlarged unit may eventually take over basic Tornado type conversion training from the TTTE, and/or tactical training from JBG 38. Tornados assigned to the unit wear a new unit badge, based on the New Mexico state flag.

Deutsches Ausbildungsgeschwader USA is the official title of the Holloman unit, which includes the Tornado Ausbildungsstaffel.

Marineflieger

Like the Luftwaffe, the Marineflieger acquired the Tornado to replace 135 ageing Starfighters operating in the strike, attack, anti-shipping and reconnaissance roles, 25 of which were dedicated RF-104Gs. The more effective (and expensive) Tornado was ordered in slightly smaller quantities, with an initial 110-aircraft requirement translating into eventual orders for 112, including 12 twin-stickers. This allowed each wing to have a nominal strength of 48 aircraft, plus reserves. The relatively small proportion of dual-controlled aircraft reflected the fact that Marineflieger crews were trained as part of the Luftwaffe arrangements at the TTTE.

When it became clear that the Tornado would not be available to replace the first F-104Gs in 1975, the Luftwaffe turned to an interim buy of McDonnell Douglas F-4s to re-equip the two fighter-roled Jagdgeschwaderen and the two reconnaissance units, and to re-equip two Jagdbomber units. The Marineflieger soldiered on with its F-104Gs, and was thus accorded a high priority when the time came to receive Tornados. MFG 1 became a Tornado unit before the first Luftwaffe wing to convert, JBG 31. Marineflieger training and conversion to the Tornado was remarkably rapid, despite the fact that the air arm had never had any fast-jet backseaters.

The Marineflieger took 16 aircraft from Batch 2 (five twin-stickers), 32 from Batch 3 (no trainers), 48 from Batch 5 (five with dual controls), and 24 from Batch 6 (two trainers). All of the Batch 5 aircraft, and the lion's share from Batch 6, went to MFG 2.

The Marineflieger F-104Gs were equipped with AS30 ASMs, and it was clear that a similar, but more modern, missile

would be required for use by the new Tornados. The AS34 Kormoran was selected, and 350 were ordered for DM469 million, with compatibility to be provided on roughly half of the MRCA order. Installation of the Kormoran is remarkably straightforward, and the missile was integrated on the last F-104s in service, and on all Marineflieger Tornados. A total of 174 Kormoran Mk 2s were delivered from 1989, together with AGM-88 HARM missiles. Kormoran 2 is a digital version of the missile, with increased internal volume allowing a heavier 220-kg (485-lb) warhead, compared to the original 165-kg (364-lb) one. A slightly larger boost motor increases

range from 30 to 35 km (18 to 22 miles), while the improved electronics gave better ECCM capabilities and allowed simpler launch procedures, making multiple missile launches a viable proposition. Some 96 Marineflieger Tornados (perhaps all those with MWCS) were equipped to carry Sargent Fletcher 28-300 buddy inflight-refuelling pods, 73 of which are believed to have been delivered.

For the anti-shipping role Marineflieger Tornados routinely employ two specialist weapons: the AGM-88 HARM (above) and the DASA Kormoran 2 (below). The aircraft below wears the original MFG 2 badge which consisted of a weapons sight with the numeral '2' overlaid.

Marinefliegergeschwader 1

A handful of prototype and pre-production aircraft wore Marineflieger colours, and some naval pilots were involved in the project from an early stage, but the first aircraft actually assigned to the Marineflieger was delivered to Schleswig-Jagel on 2 July 1982. MFG 1 had flown its final F-104 mission on 29 October 1981, and stood down while aircrew underwent training with the TTTE at Cottesmore.

The Geschwader was originally classed as the 'naval Tornado conversion and weapon training wing' and formally recommissioned on 2 July 1982, with the delivery of the first four aircraft. The Marineflieger's Tornados were externally identical to those delivered to the Luftwaffe, though they wore an entirely different colour scheme, similar to that applied to naval F-104s and even to the Sea Hawks before them. The aircraft had sea grey upper surfaces and white undersides, with a relatively high demarcation line.

MFG 1 was declared operational on 1 January 1984, and soon proved that the Tornado was a highly effective replacement for the Starfighter in the maritime environment. Its two-man crew and sophisticated radar made it better in adverse weather or at night, while the advanced navigation system eased the task

of finding targets (and indeed the way home) over the featureless sea. The Tornado's long-range, overwater navigation capabilities were demonstrated on 20 July 1984, when two of MFG 1's Tornados flew the 980 miles (1580 km) to the Azores, landing with a navigation system error of only 6 ft (1.8 m).

The first German naval Tornado wing was initially armed with BL755 CBUs, Kormoran ASMs, and a range of bombs. Later, MFG 1 began integrating the AGM-88A HARM missile. The end of the Cold War led to political pressure to reduce the number of Tornado units in service, and it soon became clear that the navy would sacrifice one of its units.

MFG 1 finally deactivated on 1 January 1994, having handed over its remaining aircraft to the Luftwaffe's newly converted AG 51, which moved into its accommodation at Schleswig-Jagel. Some people expressed surprise that MFG 1's identity had not been preserved by redesignating the surviving MFG 2, but in fact both units had formed in the same year (1958) and had enjoyed very similar histories.

The two squadrons of MFG 1 were assigned to maritime strike duties. The Geschwader badge consisted of a sea eagle striking at the water.

Marinefliegergeschwader 2

MFG 2 was the fifth and penultimate front-line German Tornado wing, flying its last Starfighter sortie during May 1987, after receiving its first Tornado on 11 September 1986. MFG 2 was equipped with the 48 HARM-capable Batch 5 Tornados, the AGM-88 being supplied to the unit's second Staffel for use in the anti-shipping role. The Batch 5 naval Tornados were delivered in a new, two-tone wrap-round disruptive camouflage. The first Staffel had a reconnaissance role, using 26 380-kg MBB Aeritalia reconnaissance pods. This task included flying a daily 'Eastern Express' reconnaissance run around the Baltic to monitor and photograph shipping. These sorties provided MFG 2 with many opportunities to see 'enemy' aircraft, since they were sometimes intercepted over

MFG 2 is now the sole navy Tornado unit, although it has adopted the MFG 1 badge. Originally, the Geschwader's 1. Staffel was employed on reconnaissance duties, although these have now been handed over to the Luftwaffe's AG 51.

international waters by Poland-based Russian Su-27s, and by MiG-29s based in East Germany.

When post-Cold War defence cuts dictated that the Marineflieger would lose one of its Tornado units, MFG 2 was the survivor. This was hardly surprising, since the unit fulfilled the same anti-shipping role as MFG 1; its two Staffelen respectively fulfilled the additional roles of tactical

reconnaissance and HARM-shooting, making the wing considerably more versatile. MFG 2 was increased in size following the disbandment of MFG 1, and currently operates about 60 Tornados.

Italy

Aeronautica Militare Italiana

The Italian air force took delivery of 99 production Tornado IDS aircraft, with one pre-production aircraft refurbished to production standards to give a total of 100 aircraft, 12 with dual controls. This gave the AMI an initial front-line strength of 54 Tornados, including 12 dual-controlled trainers earmarked for training and the remaining 34 officially classified as reserves, although they are allocated to units and are not held in store.

Italy took 15 aircraft from Batch 2, five of them with dual controls. The first was MM50000, rolled out on 1 July 1981 and flown on 25 September. Italy took no aircraft from Batch 1, being less ready to receive the Tornado than Britain or Germany. Even when service deliveries began (on 17 May 1982, with MM7003, which went to 1° Centro Manuntenzione Principale), Italy had no trained backseaters for its Tornados, though a number of officers were gaining experience in the backseat environment in the rear cockpits of TF-104s and German Phantoms. Even when Italian aircrew started training with the TTTE, Italy had to leave some of its navigator student slots unfilled; the RAF gleefully took advantage of the situation to train more Tornado navigators. A shortage of navigators was accompanied initially by a shortage of pilots, since poor pay and conditions led to 100 pilots per year leaving the AMI between 1977 and 1980, lured by better-paying civilian jobs. This was more than could be replaced by the output of 50 pilots per year from the flying training schools, especially after instructors had to be posted to reinforce the crumbling front line.

Italy was late in starting to take delivery of its Tornados, but it did not delay deliveries subsequently, unlike both Britain

and Germany who spread deliveries over an extended time in order to reap savings in particular financial years. Italy took 28 aircraft from Batch 3 (five dual-controlled), 27 from Batch 4 (no twin-stickers) and 29 from Batch 5 (two twin-stickers). This gave yearly totals of eight, 23, 24, 23 and 11 during the years 1982 to 1986, respectively. Italian Tornado IDS aircraft are serialled in two blocks: MM7001-MM7088 for the operational IDSs, and MM50000-MM50011 for the twin-stickers. The first batch of leased ADVs are serialled in the range MM7203-MM7211, with twin-stickers MM55056 and MM55057.

Since Italy has no border with a Warsaw Pact nation, its Tornados were thought most likely to have a war role of maritime strike in the Mediterranean, with an overland role supporting any operations in Austria and Yugoslavia if those countries had ever been invaded. With its vital maritime commitment, the Italian Tornado soon received the Kormoran missile (in the shape of about 60 Mk 1 missiles), and the same Sargent Fletcher buddy pod as was used by Marineflieger Tornados. Inflight refuelling has become a more common aspect of Italian Tornado operations since 1990, when the AMI took delivery of its Boeing 707 tankers. Before that, extended overseas deployments (including a June

1987 visit to the USA for an exercise) were supported by RAF VC10 tankers or by using buddy-buddy techniques. The Italian Tornado force soon assumed a NATO nuclear strike commitment, using American B61-M3 nuclear bombs held under a dual-key arrangement, like those used by the Luftwaffe's Tornado fleet. Generally, the Italians treated their entire fleet as a multi-role force, and pilots were trained in all roles, using all weapons, though an element of specialisation has subsequently crept in. The reconnaissance pod, for example, was initially viewed as 'just another store' for use by all of the Italian Tornado squadrons.

The Gulf War saw the adoption of LGBs for precision attack missions, and today the Tornado fleet uses Thomson-CSF CLDPs (Combined Laser Designator Pod). When carried, they are fitted to the port underfuselage 'shoulder' pylon. Other weapons used by the Italian Tornado include the BL755 CBU and the MW-1 dispenser.

In 1995 Italy began operating the Tornado F.Mk 3 to bridge a perceived interceptor gap pending the entry into service of the EF 2000. Here an IDS and ADV from the 36° Stormo fly together.

Italian Tornados serve with four Gruppi (squadrons) within three Stormi. The IDSs wear a disruptive grey and green camouflage on their topsides, with light grey undersides. They have been toned down in recent years, with national insignia and codes being reduced in size and applied in more subdued shades. Gruppo and Stormo markings have been similarly de-emphasised. The Italian ADVs wear their standard RAF-type air defence colour scheme, with toned-down and reduced-size national and unit markings. Each Gruppo is sub-divided into four Squadriglie (flights) for administrative purposes, although they have no autonomous identity or markings.

Right: AMI Tornados have always had a nuclear strike role, thought now to be entrusted to the 6° Stormo at Ghedi. Like the Luftwaffe, the AMI uses US-owned B61-5 thermonuclear weapons.

Below: The Tornado F.Mk 3s leased from the RAF follow AMI tradition in having the Gruppo badge (12°) on the intake and the Stormo (36°) badge on the fin.

Tornado Operators

6º Stormo 'Alfredo Fusca'

154º Gruppo uses the devil badge of its host Stormo (6º Stormo), the emblem previously associated with the Brescia Stormo. The Gruppo's own insignia (an plainly British cockerel being pierced by a red arrow) is not used, for obvious reasons. The Stormo badge is often superimposed on a red fin chevron, while the intakes are left blank. The Gruppo consists of 390ª, 391ª, 395ª, and 396ª Squadriglie. The squadron was the AMI's first Tornado unit, receiving the first aircraft (delivered to Ghedi) in 1982. The Gruppo subsequently acted as Italy's Tornado OCU, training aircrew returning from the TTTE at RAF Cottesmore.

As Italy's operational conversion unit (basic type conversion being handled by the Trinational TTTE at Cottesmore), 154º Gruppo operates the lion's share of the AMI's two-seat Tornados, apart from two with each front-line Stormo and four with the TTTE. 154º Gruppo oversaw the conversion of 156º Gruppo, then 155º, and finally 102º.

155º Gruppo stood down to begin Tornado conversion in September 1984, moving to Ghedi to begin the process on 1 January 1985. When 155º Gruppo finished conversion to the Tornado later in the year, it initially stayed with 6º Stormo, becoming the wing's second Tornado squadron. The new Gruppo was formed from 361ª, 364ª, 365ª and 378ª Squadriglie. Its aircraft wore three blue pennants on the fin (in place of 154º Gruppo's red chevron), but with the same red devil Stormo badge and with the

155º Gruppo panther's head badge on the engine intakes. The squadron transferred to the command of the newly reactivated 50º Stormo on 1 December 1989, and moved to Piacenza the following year.

The Stormo provided aircraft and crews for the Italian contingent in the Gulf War, operating from Aldhafrah in the UAE. 6º Stormo gained a new 'second squadron' in 1993, in the shape of 102º Gruppo from 5º Stormo, which will reportedly undertake the reconnaissance role, and which was once thought likely to receive the new ATARS reconnaissance pod. The new unit wears the 6º Stormo devil badge on the fins of its aircraft, with the Gruppo's flying-suited Donald Duck badge in a black triangle on the engine intakes. The Gruppo consists of 209ª, 212ª, 239ª and 244ª Squadriglie.

Equipment routinely used by the Ghedi-based Tornados includes the Thomson-CSF CLDP laser designator and the MBB/Aeritalia reconnaissance pod. Since September 1995 the Gruppo has mounted rotational deployments at Gioia del Colle for operations over Bosnia, sharing these duties with the AMX-equipped 103º Gruppo at Istrana. The Stormo became the first Italian unit in action over Bosnia on 2 September, when its aircraft conducted an armed patrol. On 7 September aircraft from the same unit bombed Serbian targets using free-fall Mk 83 bombs. 154º Gruppo Tornados have used the MBB/Aeritalia reconnaissance pod over Bosnia, and have reportedly used buddy inflight-refuelling techniques during operations.

Above: 154º Gruppo was the 6º Stormo's original Tornado unit, using a red fin chevron with the original high-visibility markings.

Below: 102º Gruppo is the second Ghedi squadron, its aircraft wearing a Donald Duck badge and, occasionally, a blue lightning flash.

36º Stormo 'Helmut Seidl'

The 36º Stormo's 156º Gruppo converted to the Tornado during 1984, returning to Gioia del Colle in May 1984, and becoming operational in August 1984. The Tornado IDSs of 36º Stormo wear a diving eagle fin badge, superimposed on a yellow lightning flash. They also have red intake lips. The 156º Gruppo lynx's head badge is carried on the intakes, while the stylised initials 'HS' were sometimes applied to the base of the fin. The Gruppo is formed from 381ª, 382ª, 383ª and 384ª Squadriglie. The unit's primary task is maritime strike and interdiction, and it is thus the main user of the MBB AS34 Kormoran anti-ship missile in Italian service. Kormoran-armed 156º Gruppo Tornados flew intimidatory low-level flypasts over Serbian ships during Operation Sharp Guard, the NATO naval arms blockade of Serbia. The 36º Stormo Tornados flew many combat sorties over Bosnia, and have recently flown in support of ground forces involved in Operation Joint Endeavour, acting as a buffer between the belligerents in Bosnia. For these missions the aircraft have tended to carry a pair of 513-kg (1,131-lb) GBU-16 Paveway II LGBs, with another Tornado carrying a Thomson-CSF CLDP (Combined Laser Designator Pod) for designating targets.

The 36º Stormo's second squadron (12º Gruppo) continued to operate the F-104 Starfighter until 1995, when it re-equipped with leased Tornado F.Mk 3s. The unit was the first AMI Gruppo to operate the Tornado ADV, and maintained a flight of MB-339s to keep its backseaters (all but one of them already fully rated pilots) in flying currency until they transition to the front seat after three years. The Gruppo's flights are 73ª, 74ª, 89ª and 90ª Squadriglie. The Gruppo insignia is a black prancing horse, superimposed on a red bow and arrow on a

Above: This Kormoran 1-armed IDS carries the 36º Stormo badge on the fin and an italicised 'HS' at the base (for 'Helmut Seidl').

green disc, though this is not often carried. 12º Gruppo was declared combat ready in February 1995, and began flying CAPs over the Adriatic in support of Operation Deny Flight, alongside RAF F.Mk 3s deployed to Gioia del Colle.

Below: 12º Gruppo Caccia Intercettori switched to ADVs in 1995. The black horse/bow and arrow badge was applied to the intake.

Above: On desert scheme aircraft the unit badges were presented in outline. 156º Gruppo's lynx is on the engine intake.

Below: In 1997 AMI Tornados began appearing in this grey scheme, as displayed by a CLDP pod-equipped 156º Gruppo aircraft.

Left: 155º Gruppo was initially activated under the 6º Stormo at Ghedi, but moved to the new 50º Stormo at Piacenza in 1990. The 50º Stormo badge on the fin consists of a sword crossed with three arrows, flanked by wings.

Below: Low-visibility unit markings accompanied the desert scheme adopted for Operation Locusta. Piacenza-based Tornados have flown missions over Bosnia in company with the co-located EG 1 aircraft.

50º Stormo 'Giorgio Graffer'

50º Stormo was reconstituted at San Damiano-Piacenza on 1 November 1988. 155º Stormo moved from Ghedi to Piacenza on 23 July 1990, transferring from 6º Stormo to the new 50º Stormo. The unit contributed aircraft and aircrew to the Autonomous Flight Detachment A.M. in the Persian Gulf. The winged sword 50º Stormo badge is usually superimposed on the Gruppo's familiar three blue triangular pennants which flow back from the fin leading edge, and Gruppo identity is further proclaimed by the panther's head badge on each intake.

155º Stormo is the AMI's SEAD

specialists, becoming dedicated to the role on 1 April 1994. The squadron received HARM missiles in December 1994. The unit continued to use other types of weapons, including Mk 83 free-fall bombs (used over Bosnia) and perhaps even LGBs. 155º Gruppo will receive the aircraft converted to full ECR standards, when they are ready. From August 1995, the unit was able to study the ECR at first hand, since a deployment of Luftwaffe Tornado ECRs was co-located at Piacenza until late 1996, and the two units often operated together, the German ECRs making up for the Italian IDS's lack of an emitter location system.

53º Stormo

The 53º Stormo's 21º Gruppo (with 73ª, 74ª, 89ª and 90ª Squadriglie) became Italy's second Tornado ADV unit during 1997, following conversion of the second batch of AMI aircrew at the RAF's No. 229 OCU at RAF Coningsby. The unit, based at Novara/Cameri, was a long-time operator of the F-104S Starfighter. The conversion of 21º Gruppo will add another Tornado unit to NATO's collection of 'Tiger Squadrons', joining Germany's JBG 32. The Gruppo badge consists of the fore-quarters of a tiger on a blue disc, with the motto 'Ad Hostes Rugens'. The unit's aircraft will carry the Stormo insignia (a cutlass in a playing card 'ace') on their tailfins.

This F.Mk 3 (with lagging nosewheel) belongs to 21º Gruppo, the second Italian ADV unit. The unit's badge is carried on the auxiliary intake door, while the fin badge is that of 53º Stormo.

Autonomous Flight Detachment AMI

Twelve AMI Tornados were painted in an overall desert sand colour scheme, and were modified for service in the Gulf. Eight were initially deployed to Al Dhafra (Maqatra) in Abu Dhabi from 2 October 1990, being declared operational on 6

October, with two more aircraft arriving later. The aircraft flew 226 sorties in 32 missions and dropped 565 1,000-lb Mk 83 bombs, mainly against airfield targets. Some Italian Tornados flew as buddy-refuelling tankers, since Italian crews were

not familiar with refuelling from USAF KC-135s, and avoided it where possible. One aircraft (MM7074) was lost during the first mission of the war, on 17 January 1991, with its 155º Gruppo crew, Major Mario Betlini and navigator Captain Maurizio Cocciolone, becoming POWs.

A fully armed Locusta Tornado is seen in the Al Dhafra shelter. The aircraft carries a typical warload of five Mk 83 1,000-lb bombs (with chalk messages) and two AIM-9 Sidewinders.

Seen at Gioia del Colle in June 1991, this aircraft had just returned from the Locusta detachment. Political sensitivities in Italy precluded the application of any form of artwork.

Reparto Sperimentale di Volo (311º Gruppo)

The AMI's research, evaluation and development unit is the RSV, which also has the identity of 311º Gruppo, with 535ª and 536ª Squadriglie as its constituent

The RSV usually has one Tornado permanently assigned, augmented by other, borrowed examples. The RSV badge is worn on the fin, consisting of a winged man design, three stars and the unit's name.

flights. Based at Pratica di Mare, the unit has operated a number of Tornados at various times, and during 1996 had three IDS and one ECR Tornado on its books. The unit's aircraft often wear 'RS' codes and carry the RSV shield in silver, white and black on their tailfins. Those operated on loan often wear their own squadron insignia. The 311º Gruppo badge is sometimes applied on engine intakes, and consists of an orange mailed fist holding a tethered black falcon, on a red shield.

Tornado Operators

Saudi Arabia

Al Quwwat al Jawwiya as Sa'udiya

The Royal Saudi Air Force was the first non-Panavia partner to take delivery of Tornados, the first to order the aircraft having been Oman. The Tornado was selected after a long and searching evaluation against a number of competing aircraft types, some of them US teen-series fighters. Selection was a tribute to the Tornado's excellence, but also acknowledged the UK's long and friendly links with the Saudi kingdom. The powerful Jewish lobby in the USA did much to hamper US efforts to sell advanced combat aircraft to Saudi Arabia, insisting on unrealistic basing agreements and objecting strongly to any attempt to sell full-standard versions of current aircraft types.

The Tornado buy (for 48 IDS and 24 ADV aircraft) was part of a much larger package, which also covered the supply of PC-9, Jetstream and Hawk trainers, and significant support contracts for training, support and even the provision of ground and aircrew under contract and on loan. Once Saudi Arabia had signed for the Tornado it wanted early deliveries, and 18 RAF and two German aircraft within Batch 5 were diverted to Saudi Arabia to allow the formation of a first IDS squadron. The 24 Saudi ADVs were similarly diverted from

This unusual scheme of sand, brown and green was applied to all Saudi IDS aircraft, proving effective over the sparsely vegetated desert. Saudi aircraft carry similar weapons to their RAF counterparts.

RAF orders in Batch 6. These aircraft were followed by 28 IDS aircraft built within Batch 7. The first Saudi Tornados allowed the formation of two IDS squadrons, and one ADV squadron (though at one time it seemed as though two ADV units would be established).

The first batch of Saudi ADVs took part in Operations Desert Shield and Desert Storm, sharing the burden of mounting pre-war defensive CAPs with Saudi F-15s, RAF Tornados, and other coalition fighters. Once war had begun, the aircraft mounted both offensive and defensive CAPs, but did not have the opportunity to engage the enemy. The Saudi IDS squadrons also played their part in the Gulf War, though it was largely an unsung part and exact details of what they achieved remain frustratingly difficult to discover. One Saudi Tornado IDS was lost in a non-combat related accident on 19 January, its crew escaping unscathed, but

none fell as a result of enemy action. Their first operation may have been an anti-runway attack against H-3 airfield by four Tornados (probably armed with JP233) on 17 January. This followed an LGB attack by six USAF F-111Fs against ammunition storage facilities at the base, and was covered by the same package of three EA-6Bs, four F-14s and 20 HARM-shooting A-7s from the USS *John F. Kennedy*.

Although delayed on several different occasions, the eventual second Saudi Tornado order resulted in the delivery of 48 additional IDS aircraft, permitting the

formation of two more squadrons. This brought the Saudi Tornado total to 120 aircraft (20 more than Italy received) in five squadrons. Saudi Tornado ADVs wear the same basic colour scheme as their RAF counterparts, with roundels on each side of the forward fuselage above the port wing and below the starboard, and with 'RSAF' above the starboard wing and below the port. 'Royal Saudi Air Force' was applied to the forward fuselage in English and Arabic. Saudi IDS aircraft wear a unique three-tone desert camouflage, in sand, brown and green, and with national insignia in the same positions as on the ADVs.

All Saudi Tornados delivered to date have worn small squadron badges on their tailfins, below the national flag, aft of the serial (presented in English numerals and in Arabic script). On the most recent deliveries (including the ADVs), they were applied at the BAe Warton factory before the aircraft were delivered.

Left: All Saudi ADVs now serve in one squadron. RSAF ADVs flew 451 defensive counter-air missions during Desert Storm.

Below: No. 7 Sqn shouldered the brunt of RSAF combat operations in the Gulf War. Saudi IDS aircraft flew 665 combat sorties, of which 590 were interdiction and 75 were offensive counter-air.

No. 7 Squadron

Between October 1985 and early 1987, Saudi aircrew trained in four courses conducted by a dedicated Saudi Training Flight within the TTTE, and then with the RAF's TWCU. Thereafter, No. 7 Squadron RSAF assumed responsibility for the conversion training of Saudi Tornado IDS crews. The first Saudi aircraft were delivered on 28 March 1986, the same date that Saudi Arabia's first four crews graduated from the TWCU. Four more crews graduated in May 1986, and all eight formed the backbone of No. 7 Squadron and acted as instructors for subsequent Saudi aircrew. The squadron took all 20 of the Batch 5 Tornados (which included six twin-stickers) and four dual-control trainer aircraft from Batch 7. The high proportion of two-seat trainers reflected the squadron's secondary role as a weapons conversion and tactical training unit. No. 7 Squadron was initially based at Dhahran, but a planned move to Taif does not seem to have taken place yet, except briefly during the Gulf War, to make room for other coalition air force units.

No. 29 Squadron

No. 29 Squadron at Dhahran equipped with 12 Tornado ADVs from 20 March 1989, its initial complement including four twin-stickers. All 12 aircraft had been delivered by 20 September 1989. No. 29 Squadron aircraft and crews played their part in Operations Desert Shield and Desert Storm, mainly flying CAPs.

No. 34 Squadron

No. 34 Squadron was the second Tornado ADV squadron, and was initially co-located with No. 29 at Dhahran. It received its first aircraft on 14 November 1989, and had completely re-equipped by mid-1990. Soon afterwards, its aircraft and crews were reabsorbed by No. 29 Squadron, remaining as a cadre within the original unit.

No. 66 Squadron

The second Saudi Tornado squadron formed at Dhahran under the auspices of No. 7 Squadron and was in the process of

Above: No. 7 Squadron was the first Saudi IDS unit, and adopted the training role. This is reflected in the high proportion of 'twin-stickers' attached to the unit.

establishing when the Gulf War broke out. No. 66 Squadron took the second part of the Al Yamamah I batch of IDSs (24 of the 28 Batch 7 aircraft), including four twin-stickers and the six reconnaissance aircraft. The unit was intended to move to Tabuk, but has not done so yet.

No. 75 Squadron

No. 75 Squadron will be the first Saudi Tornado squadron with the new Batch 9 aircraft. It is unclear where it will be based.

No. 83 Squadron

The second Saudi Batch 9 squadron will be No. 83. It may have a reconnaissance and SEAD role.

Above and below: No. 29 was the first Saudi ADV unit, and undertook both training and operations. The second squadron, No. 34, had only a brief career before it was subsumed into No. 29.

Above: No. 66 Squadron operates a mix of 'strike' Tornados and aircraft equipped with the TIRRS system. This 'strike' carries the unit's badge below the tail insignia.

Below: Seen on a pre-delivery test flight from Warton, this is the first aircraft for No. 75 Squadron. This unit was the first to form with the Al Yamamah II Batch 9 aircraft.

Above: No. 83 became the fourth Saudi IDS squadron when it began to take delivery of Batch 9 aircraft. For pre-delivery flying at Warton, the aircraft wear their RAF serials.

US Navy *Warfighters*

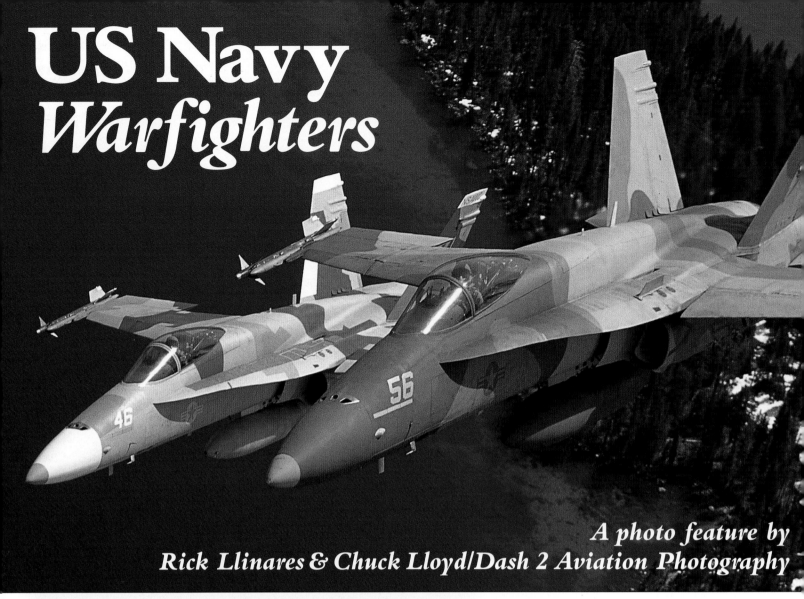

A photo feature by
Rick Llinares & Chuck Lloyd/Dash 2 Aviation Photography

The US Navy has disbanded its acclaimed 'Topgun' Navy Fighter Weapons School and disestablished most of its aggressor training units. However, two aggressor squadrons have survived the cuts, and the functions of 'Topgun', 'Strike U' and 'Top Dome' have now been assumed by the Naval Strike & Air Warfare Center (NSAWC), at NAS Fallon.

Above: These two VFC-12 F/A-18As are pictured over Snow Lake, near Lake Tahoe, 60 miles to the east of NAS Fallon, home of the NSAWC.

Left: Training crews such as these Tomcat flyers from VF-103 'Jolly Rogers' is the task of NSAWC, VFC-12 'Saints' and VFC-13 'Omars'.

Below: This NSAWC Hornet, loaded with two AGM-62 Walleye glide bombs, overflies the Dixie Valley section of the Fallon range.

Above and below: The Naval Strike & Air Warfare Center (NSAWC) combines all previous functions within US Navy aviation training of 'Topgun' (NFWS), Strike Warfare Center ('Strike U') and 'Top Dome' (E-2 school) into a single command. It was established on 11 July 1996, at NAS Fallon, Nevada. The NSAWC mission is one of tactics development, assessment and training standardisation for the entire Navy. The aggressor F/A-18A/B Hornets of VFC-12 'Omars' are heavily involved in training East and West Coast fleet units, working up at NAS Fallon before deployment. VFC-12 is a Reserve unit, based at NAS Oceana, but routinely detaches to other bases to work up with regular squadrons.

Below: NSAWC operates several F-14As, including this splinter camouflaged aircraft seen over the Sierra Nevada mountains; the Tomcats provide dissimilar air combat manoeuvring training for fleet F/A-18 Hornet squadrons. Since the disbandment of dedicated aggressor units such as VF-126/VF-127, the Navy has struggled to retain elements of this essential training mission.

Top: Only two US units still fly the Northrop F-5 Tiger – the Marine Corps' VMFT-401 'Snipers' and the Navy's VFC-13 'Saints', the latter based at NAS Fallon. This two-ship of F-5Es is seen on patrol near the large Carson salt sink flat, north of NAS Fallon. VFC-13 operates approximately 15 F-5s, including several two-seat F-5Fs.

Above: The F/A-18 Hornet is the primary aircraft operated by the Strike & Air Warfare Center. The single-seat F/A-18A and two-seat F/A-18B models are painted in three basic camouflage schemes – splinter blue, multi-tone grey and multi-tone brown.

Left and right: Fleet units preparing for deployment are the regular trade at NAS Fallon. These F-14s are from VF-2 (left) and VF-103 (right). Aircraft from a carrier air wing will train against the F-14s, F/A-18s and F-5s based at Fallon. In addition, the NSAWC has recently established a Combat Search and Rescue (CSAR) school, equipped with SH-60s.

Central America and the Caribbean

Central American nations have long been a byword for instability, and air power has been a small, but important, factor in the history of conflict across Belize, Honduras, Guatemala, Nicaragua and El Salvador. There have always been small spots of security, such as Costa Rica, and today there is an almost universal peace in this once volatile region. The Caribbean is still dominated by Cuba, though it is no longer an exporter of revolution, and its many island neighbours maintain only token air arms.

The Caribbean region is one of major economic and strategic importance, bounded as it is to the west by Mexico and Central America and containing one of the world's two most important inter-oceanic canals. It is particularly important to the United States, which routes 45 per cent of its seaborne trade and 55 per cent of its imported petroleum products through the area, and which has always regarded the Caribbean as its 'back yard'. Although the collapse of the Soviet Union and of the Communist states in Eastern Europe was reflected in the victory of the anti-Communist forces in the Salvadorean civil war and the electoral defeat of the Marxist Sandinista regime in Nicaragua, Fidel Castro's Cuba – for all that it has been deprived of its most powerful supporter and protector – still bays defiance at an increasingly frustrated United States from a mere 90 miles (145 km) off its southern coast.

The US was due to hand over the administration and defence of the Panama Canal to the Republic of Panama on the last day of the present century but, following its invasion of Panama in December 1989 which resulted in the destruction and subsequent abolition of the Panamanian Defence Forces, it now seems that US military forces may remain in Panama well into the 21st century. The US-led invasion of Haiti by the Organization of American States, in 1994, also resulted in the abolition of the grotesquely corrupt Haitian Armed Forces. The air forces of both Panama and Haiti are therefore largely a matter of history.

Several of the tiny island statelets of the Caribbean also maintain minuscule air arms, equipped with one or two aircraft and charged largely with VIP transport and liaison duties. The scope of this study does not extend to such militarily insignificant forces; this principle has been breached only in the case of Belize, because of the lingering possibility of conflict between that country and Guatemala.

Belize

Formerly known as British Honduras, Belize became an independent state in 1981. Guatemala claims the entirety of Belize's territory. Until October 1994 Britain guaranteed Belizean independence by the presence of a small military garrison. Since its withdrawal, Belize has been vulnerable to aggression. Although Guatemala recently came close to renouncing its claim and seemed to be fully occupied in dealing with its own chronic guerrilla insurgency, the recent accord between the Guatemalan government and the various guerrilla organisations means Belize could again become the focus of expansionism.

Belizean Defence Force Air Wing

The Air Wing, which is an integral part of the tiny tri-service Belizean Defence Force, numbers about 50 people and is equipped with two armed Pilatus/Britten-Norman BN-2B Defenders and a single Pilatus/Britten-Norman BN-2A Islander transport. A Slingsby T.67M-200 Firefly was acquired for training, in 1996. In addition to its own fleet, the Belizean government also effectively has the use of two Ayres S.2R Turbo Thrush NEDS aircraft and a Bell UH-1H helicopter of the US Drug Enforcement Administration, which is based in Belize in connection with the campaign against narcotics traffickers.

All aircraft are based at Belize City. Training is undertaken there, with assistance provided by Britain and the US. Airports at Belmopán and Punta Gorda serve as refuelling points for the aircraft of the DFAF, and there are over 30 usable air strips throughout the country.

Permanent British forces have withdrawn, but the UK still maintains a commitment to protect Belize in the event of aggression.

Belizean Defence Force Air Wing

BDF Air Wing
Pilatus/Britten-Norman BN-2B Defender — Belize City
Pilatus/Britten-Norman BN-2A Islander

Costa Rica

The smallest country in Central America, Costa Rica is also the most developed in the region and is referred to as 'The Switzerland of Central America'. Following a bloody civil war in 1948, Costa Rica abolished its armed forces and replaced them with a paramilitary Civil Guard. Although remaining free from internal disturbance, in the context of the instability of its neighbours, particularly Nicaragua, Costa Rica's noble experiment in the abolition of its military forces became progressively something of a pious fraud, as the Civil Guard acquired more and more of the attributes of an army and passed many of its internal security functions to other agencies. It now also includes small but significant coast guard and aviation elements.

Sección Aérea de la Guardia Civil

An Air Section of the Civil Guard (with the full official title of Sección Aérea de la Guardia Civil Costariquense) was established, on a *de facto* basis, during the 1955 invasion of Costa Rica by Nicaraguan-supported expatriates, but most of its aircraft were written off shortly after the termination of hostilities. No further combat aircraft were acquired, although some small transport and liaison types were maintained. This force has recently been expanded, but a CASA C.212 light transport and two Cessna T-41 trainers, reputed to be on order, have not materialised.

The Air Section is an integral part of the Civil Guard and is commanded by a Director of colonel or lieutenant colonel rank. It operates from three bases: Base Aérea Nº 1 (Liberia, Guanacaste), Base Aérea Nº 2 (San José), and Base Aéronaval (Golfito). Each of the first two bases has a permanent staff of approximately 30, the naval air base having a staff of 50. The three Cessna 337s, which are the only combat aircraft operated by the Sección Aérea, are based at the latter installation. Otherwise, flying units are deployed in accordance with operational requirements. In addition to the Cessna 337s, current equipment consists of single examples of the Piper Apache, Aztec and Seneca, two Piper Cherokees, a single

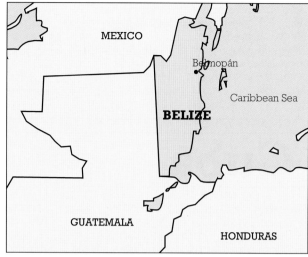

The primary operational type in service with the Belizean Defence Force is the BN-2B-21 Defender (above). Belize is also home to the Turbo Thrush NEDS (Narcotics Eradication Delivery System) aircraft of the US DEA (left).

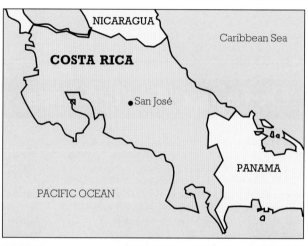

Costa Rica's Public Security Ministry operates a diverse fleet of aircraft and helicopters, including this Cessna U206G (left), MD500E (below left), Piper PA-34 (below centre) and PA-31 Panther Navajo (below right).

...ba's Revolutionary Air Force is easily the most modern ...d best equipped air arm in the entire Central American ...d Caribbean region – at least on paper. Twenty ...G-23MS 'Flogger-Es' (export MiG-23MF 'Flogger-Bs') ... believed to have been supplied by the USSR along ...th R-23 (AA-7 'Apex') missiles – as seen above – and ...0 (AA-8 'Aphid') missiles. For attack missions Cuba ...quired over 40 MiG-23BN 'Flogger-Hs' (right), which ... many years partnered MiG-17Fs in this role.

Aero Commander 680, four Cessna U206Gs, a single Fairchild-Hiller FH-1100 and two Hughes 500Es helicopters.

All personnel receive their basic military training at the National Police School, at San José. Some flying training is carried out by the Air Section but most flying and maintenance personnel have received the bulk of their training abroad, principally in the United States, Venezuela and Germany.

Sección Aérea de la Guardia Civil

Escuadrilla de Comunicaciones   *Liberia/San José*
Aero Commander 680, Cessna U206G, Piper Cherokee, Piper Apache, Piper Aztec, Piper Seneca

Escuadrilla de Helicópteros   *San José*
Hughes 500E, Fairchild-Hiller FH-1100

Escuadrilla de Apoyo a La Guardia Costera   *Golfito*
Cessna 337   *(Coast Guard support flight)*

Cuba

The largest island in the Caribbean, Cuba remained the last major bastion of Spanish power in the Western hemisphere. Independence was finally obtained as the by-product of Spain's defeat by the US in the Spanish-American War of 1898, and Cuba became a republic in 1902. Like Panama, its independence was heavily circumscribed and it remained a virtual protectorate of the United States until the last day of 1958, when a popular rebellion against the corrupt and US Mafia-influenced dictatorship of General Fulgencio Batista installed a left-of-centre nationalist government, led by Dr Fidel Castro. Following the abortive CIA-supported invasion of 1961 (the Bay of Pigs invasion), Castro declared Cuba a Marxist state, aligning himself firmly with the Soviet Bloc. The installation of Soviet strategic missiles in Cuba one year later almost led to World War III but the Soviets backed down at the last minute, avoiding a military confrontation with the United States. Although the disappearance of the Soviet Union and the repudiation of Communism by its former European satellites have deprived Cuba both of the military protection and the heavy economic subsidies which it formerly enjoyed, it remains a heavily militarised Communist state, with an air force that is well equipped and seemingly capable of mounting more than just token operations, despite a severe lack of funds and training. This was evidenced by the co-ordinated shoot-down by a MiG-29 (with a MiG-23) of two Cessna 337 Skymasters belonging to a US-based Cuban exile group, Brothers to the Rescue, in February 1996, outside Cuban territorial boundaries.

Defensa Anti-Aérea y Fuerza Aérea Revolucionaria

In 1915 proposals for the establishment of a military air arm were presented to the Cuban government, and in May 1919 the first squadron of the Cuerpo de Aviación was activated. Following the revolution of 1933, Cuban military aviation was reorganised, being sub-divided into the Aviación del Ejército (Army Air Corps) and Aviación Naval (Naval Air Arm). Cuba's declaration of war on the Axis powers, within days of the Japanese attack on Pearl Harbor, was reflected in a flow of second-line aircraft from the United States under Lend-Lease. Following Cuba's signature of the 1947 Rio Treaty of Mutual Defence, the first modern combat aircraft also began to be received. In 1955 another reorganisation combined both army and naval aviation elements in a semi-autonomous force with the title of Fuerza Aérea Ejército de Cuba (Cuban Army Air Force).

Following the triumph of the revolution in 1959, the name of the force was changed again, to Fuerza Aérea Revolucionaria. The revolutionary government found itself with a motley collection of largely unserviceable aircraft and the Fuerza Aérea Revolucionaria was able to play only a limited part in repelling the Bay of Pigs invasion. Some MiG-15UTI conversion trainers had been presented to the Fuerza Aérea Revolucionaria by the Soviet Union in 1960, and after Castro's unequivocal espousal of Communism these aircraft were followed by large numbers of Soviet combat, transport and training aircraft. The air force, now known as the Defensa Anti-Aérea y Fuerza Aérea Revolucionaria/DAAFAR (Revolutionary Air and Anti-Aircraft Defence Force), remained a semi-autonomous adjunct of the Revolutionary Army until 1972, when it was raised to co-equal status with the army and navy.

Cuban security is both obsessive and all-pervasive, all military units being known almost invariably only by a four-digit 'UM' (Unidad Militar) number. The construction of an accurate and comprehensive order of battle is therefore all but impossible. It is known, however, that the Cuban Revolutionary Air Force divides the country into three territorial commands, known as air zones, and that each of these contains an air brigade made up of a variable number of air regiments and independent squadrons. Each air regiment has a minimum front-line strength of 30 aircraft, the independent squadrons being of variable composition. The Air Force currently numbers approximately 15,000 men and women, operating 530 aircraft. These are estimated to comprise about 300 fighter-bombers, 40 transports, 110 helicopters and 80 assorted trainers. This inventory is estimated to include approximately 20 MiG-15UTIs, 20 MiG 17s, 150 MiG-21s, 20 MiG-21Us, 90 MiG-23s, 10 MiG-29s, eight An-2s, three An-24s, 20 An-26s, two An-32s, two Il-76s, three Yak-40s, 50 Mi-8s, 10 Mi-14s, 10 Mi-25s, 20 L-29Cs and 20 Zlin 326s.

The major bases of the Revolutionary Air Force are San Antonio de los Baños, Havana, San Julián, Santa Clara, Sancti Spiritus, Cienfuegos, Camagüey and Santiago de Cuba.

The Commander of the Revolutionary Air Force and Air Defence Forces (General D. A. Martinez) ranks as a Vice Minister and thus as an equal with the Commanders of the Revolutionary Army and Navy, and reports directly to the Chief of the Revolutionary Armed Forces General Staff. In turn, the Air Force Commander controls the General Staff of the Revolutionary Air Force and Air Defence Forces and a subordinate command structure which largely reflects that of the army and navy.

The Western Air Brigade (designated 'Bay of Pigs Guard Brigade') is believed to consist of two Interceptor Regiments (equipped with MiG-21s), based at San Antonio de los Baños and Baracoa; a Tactical Support Regiment, with MiG-23BNs, based at Guinés; and an independent Fighter Squadron (with MiG-29s), based at San Julián. The latter base also houses all of the training elements of the Revolutionary Air Force. Two Transport Squadrons are based at Havana and San Antonio de los Baños, and there are two general-purpose helicopter squadrons based at Havana.

The Central Air Brigade (designated 'Battle of Santa Clara Guard Brigade') is also believed to contain two MiG-21-equipped Interceptor Regiments, based at Santa Clara and Sancti Spiritus; a Tactical Support Regiment (with MiG-23s), based at Santa Clara; and both a general-purpose and an ASW Helicopter Squadron (equipped with Mi-8s and Mi-14s, respectively) plus a single Transport Squadron, at Cienfuegos.

The Eastern Air Brigade (which may be designated 'Moncada Barracks Guard Brigade') is known to have a single MiG-21-equipped Interceptor Regiment, based at Camagüey; a Tactical Support Regiment (with MiG-23s) based at Holguín; and a single Attack Helicopter Squadron (with Mi-25s), two general-purpose helicopter squadrons (with Mi-8s) and a Transport Squadron, all based at Santiago de Cuba.

Each of the three air zones has an Anti-Aircraft Missile Brigade. There is also an Anti-Aircraft Missile Brigade for the defence of the capital. The Missile Brigades each contain three battalions and comprise about three dozen batteries with SA-3, SA-6, SA-7, SA-9 and SA-13 SAMs. There is also a comprehensive electronic early-warning system.

Operationally, the Interceptor Squadrons are subordinate to Air Defence Command, which also controls the Anti-Aircraft Missile Brigades. The Fighter-Bomber Squadrons are subordinate to Tactical Air Command, which also controls the single Helicopter Attack and Helicopter ASW Squadrons. Transport units are subordinate to Logistic Support Command and training units to Air Training Command.

Most training is carried out at the Aviation Cadet School at San Julián, which offers courses in sophisticated aircraft and missile operation, with specialist technical and flying training

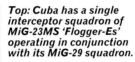

Top: Cuba has a single interceptor squadron of MiG-23MS 'Flogger-Es' operating in conjunction with its MiG-29 squadron.

Above and left: The single-seat 'Floggers' are supported by two-seat MiG-23UB 'Flogger-B' conversion trainers.

Right: Cuba has a large fleet of over 50 Mi-8 and Mi-17 helicopters, spread among several bases.

Above and left: Cuba's MiG-29s were delivered in 1989 and the DAAFAR is believed to operate 10 'Fulcrum-As' and two MiG-29UB 'Fulcrum-Bs' – supplied with R-27 (AA-10) missiles.

Left and right: Cuba operates a mix of MiG-21PFM 'Fishbed-Fs', MiG-21MF 'Fishbed-Js', MiG-21bis 'Fishbed-Ls' and two-seat MiG-21UM 'Mongol-Bs' – totalling over 140 aircraft. A MiG-21bis and a MiG-21UM are seen left, while the aircraft to the right is fitted with a KKR camera pod.

schools. The period of training for officers varies between four and five years according to specialisation. The Instituto Técnico Militar, at Havana, offers comprehensive specialist training in communications, avionics and aeronautical engineering, and for anti-aircraft troops. All flying personnel formerly received part of their training in the Soviet Union, where combat aircrew also received additional advanced training. Officers receive post-graduate training at specific points in their careers at the 'General Máximo Gómez' Academy. This was also formerly supplemented by advanced courses in the Soviet Union. Following the collapse of the Soviet Union, all foreign training assistance to Cuba was withdrawn. The previous dependence of the Revolutionary Air Force on foreign training aid is reflected in its small inventory of training aircraft relative to its overall size. Lack of fuel has all but put an end to flying training and, even without this handicap, the available number of training aircraft would be inadequate to produce a sufficient output of trained aircrew to replace natural attrition from retirement or other causes.

Like the Revolutionary Army and Navy, the Revolutionary Air Force is well trained and motivated. It is also the best-equipped military air arm in Latin America. By its nature, it must, however, be affected to the greatest degree of all the Revolutionary Armed Forces by the current shortage of replacements and spares and the almost total lack of fuel. The latter particularly places a large question mark over its present operational potential and must also have had a highly negative effect on training and morale.

Defensa Anti-Aérea y Fuerza Aérea Revolucionaria – DAAFAR

Brigada de Guardia 'Playa Giron'

21° Regimiento de Intercepción	MiG-21	San Antonio de los Baños
252° Escuadrón de Transporte	An-2, An-26	San Antonio de los Baños
22° Regimiento de Intercepción	MiG-21	Baracoa
24° Regimiento de Apoyo Táctico	MiG-23	Guinés
231° Escuadrón de Caza	MiG-29	San Julián
Escuela de Vuelo de la DAAFAR	MiG-17, MiG-21U, MiG-15UTI, L-39C, Zlin 326	San Julián

251° Escuadrón de Transporte	Il-76, Yak-40, An-32, An-24, An-2	José Martí Intl Airport, Havana
261° Escuadrón de Helicópteros de Propósitos Generales	Mi-8	Havana
262° Escuadrón de Helicópteros de Propósitos Generales	Mi-8	Havana

Brigada de Guardia 'Batalla de Santa Clara'

11° Regimiento de Intercepción	MiG-21	Santa Clara
14° Regimiento de Apoyo Táctico	MiG-23	Santa Clara
12° Regimiento de Intercepción	MiG-21	Sancti Spiritus
162° Escuadrón de Helicópteros de Propósitos Generales	Mi-8	Cienfuegos
161° Escuadrón de Helicópteros de Guerra Anti-Submarina	Mi-14	Cienfuegos
151° Escuadrón de Transporte	An-2, An-26	Cienfuegos

Brigada de Guardia 'Cuartel Moncada'

31° Regimiento de Intercepción	MiG-21	Camagüey
34° Regimiento de Apoyo Táctico	MiG-23	Holguín
361° Escuadrón de Helicópteros de Ataque	Mi-25	Santiago de Cuba
362° Escuadrón de Helicópteros de Propósitos Generales	Mi-8	Santiago de Cuba
363° Escuadrón de Helicópteros de Propósitos Generales	Mi-8	Santiago de Cuba
351° Escuadrón de Transporte	An-2, An-26	Santiago de Cuba

Unit designations should be regarded as notional rather than definitive. Indications are that the current level of serviceability of DAAFAR aircraft is extremely low.

Dominican Republic

The Dominican Republic occupies the eastern two thirds of the island of Hispaniola, which it shares with Haiti. Although the Dominican Republic is both wealthier and more developed than its neighbour, the predominantly mulatto, Spanish-speaking Dominicans have a long-standing wariness of the more numerous, black, French-speaking Haitians who occupied their country twice for a total of 37 years both before and immediately after they declared their independence from Spain. The Dominican Republic was occupied by the United States between 1916 and 1924 and, as in the case of Nicaragua, the paramilitary National Guard set up by the occu-

pation forces produced 31 years of dictatorship from 1930 to 1961. During this period the country was ruled as the personal fief of the self-styled 'Generalissimo' Rafael Leonidas Trujillo, who maintained a powerful army, navy and air force altogether out of proportion to the size and resources of the country and to any perceptible threat. A period of near anarchy quickly followed Trujillo's assassination in 1961 and the USA once more intervened during the civil war of 1965. Since then, the country has been relatively stable and is enjoying a measure of increased prosperity since its discovery in the 1980s as an international tourist destination.

The FAD, which has become largely a counter-insurgency, transport and training force, divides the country into two Air Zones. The Southern and Northern zones have their respective headquarters at San Isidro, to the east of Santo Domingo, and Santiago de los Caballeros, in the northwest. The air force currently has 70 aircraft, manned by approximately 4,200 personnel of all ranks. It is organised into an Air Command, a Base Defence Command, a Combat Support Command and a Maintenance Command.

Air Command is responsible for all flying operations and consists of a Tactical Support Squadron, a Counter-Insurgency Squadron, an Air Transport Squadron, a Communications Squadron and a Helicopter Squadron. There are military air bases at Santiago, Barahona, Puerto Plata, Azua, La Romana, La Vega, Monte Cristi and San Cristóbal, although most aircraft are based at San Isidro (Santo Domingo). Only San Isidro, Santiago and Barahona air bases have permanently deployed operational units, and all training is carried out at San Isidro.

Base Defence Command includes an air defence artillery battalion and a number of parachute infantry squadrons. Combat Support Command controls all base services. Maintenance Command is responsible for the maintenance of all aircraft, vehicles and buildings.

Air Force cadets undergo the first two years of their four-year course at the Military Academy, at Haina, before transferring to the Escuela de Aviación Militar at San Isidro air base, for specialist training. Other ranks receive all-through training at the Escuela de Aviación Militar.

The aircraft inventory includes eight Cessna A-37Bs, six Hughes OH-6As, a few North American T-28Ds, three Douglas C-47s, two Beech Queen Air 80s, one King Air 90, two Aero Commander 680s, single examples of the Piper Navajo, Rallye Commodore, Cessna U206G, Cessna 310 and Mitsubishi MU-2J, 10 Beech T-34Bs, five Cessna T-41Ds, nine Bell UH-1Hs, two Alouette IIs, and single examples of the Alouette III and Dauphin. Most aircraft are based at San Isidro, with detachments to Santiago,

Fuerza Aérea Dominicana

An Aviation Company was formed as part of the Dominican army in 1933 but this remained a very small force, equipped only with second-line aircraft until 1942 when the Dominican Republic began to receive communications and training aircraft under Lend-Lease. In 1947 a well-equipped group of Dominican exiles threatened to invade the Dominican Republic from Cuba, and Trujillo's agents managed to obtain a number of war-surplus combat aircraft in Britain. With this equipment, the Compañia de Aviación expanded to become the Cuerpo de Aviación Militar Dominicana. As a result of the signing of the Rio Treaty of 1947 by the Dominican Republic, the United States also provided some combat and transport aircraft. Further aircraft were obtained from commercial sources, including 42 de Havilland Vampire jets and a similar number of F-51 Mustang fighter-bombers, purchased from Sweden in 1952. By that point, the Cuerpo de Aviación Militar Dominicana had become

independent of the army, as the Fuerza Aérea Dominicana, and had approximately 240 aircraft.

Following the assassination of Trujillo in 1961, the brief golden age of the Dominican Armed Forces came to an end. Funds for the replacement of worn-out material became increasingly scarce and by 1963 the Fuerza Aérea Dominicana had shrunk to 110 aircraft. Nevertheless, 70 of these were combat types and the air force was active in the 1965 civil war: its aircraft strafed Constitutionalist positions in Santo Domingo and two F-51s were lost to ground fire. During the years of democratic rule which have followed the civil war, the Dominican Air Force has continued to decline, aircraft procurement consisting almost exclusively of second-line material.

The Chief of Staff of the Air Force is effectively both its administrative and operational commander. He reports to the Secretary of State for National Defence through the Under Secretary of State for War.

...ove and right: A ...al of eight Cessna ...37B Dragonflys ...s delivered to the ...D between 1984 ...d 1988, replacing ...F-51D Mustangs ...ich were still in ...e with the ground ...ack squadron until ...ey were finally sold ...May 1984.

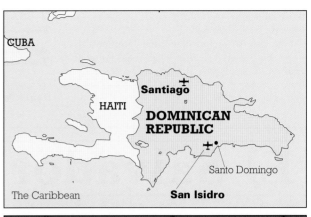

The oldest of the FAD's C-47s was acquired from the USAF in 1954.

Below: Twelve T-34Bs were acquired in the early 1980s and 10 still serve as basic trainers.

Above: Six Hughes OH-6As are believed to be in service with the Escuadrón Contra-Insurgencia, at Santiago.

Left: A single SE.3130 Alouette II light helicopter serves with the Escuadrón de Helicópteros, at San Isidro, the main operational base of the Fuerza Aérea Dominicana.

Above: Dominican T-41Ds were acquired in 1971 and undertake basic training at the EAM.

Below: This Beech 90 King Air is flown by the FAD's liaison squadron.

Above: Eight Bell Model 205A-1s (UH-1Hs) were supplied by the US between 1982 and 1986.

Left: A recent acquisition by the FAD is this Cessna U206G Stationair, which serves alongside a Cessna 210L.

Right: This modified Piper PA-31 Navajo is flown by the San Isidro-based communications squadron.

Barahona and elsewhere, in accordance with operational requirements.

Like the Army and Navy, the Dominican Air Force has suffered from official neglect since the restoration of democratic government and is in urgent need of re-equipment if it is to continue as an effective force.

Fuerza Aérea Dominicana

Escuadrón de Apoyo Táctico	Cessna A-37B	San Isidro
Escuadrón Contra-Insurgencia	Hughes OH-6A,	Santiago
	North American T-28D	
Escuadrón de Transporte Aéreo	Douglas C-47	San Isidro
Escuela de Aviación Militar	Cessna T-41D,	San Isidro
	T-34D	

Escuadrón de Comunicaciones	Beech Queen Air 80, San Isidro
	Beech King Air 90, Piper Navajo,
	Aero Commander 680,
	Rallye Commodore, Cessna 310,
	Mitsubishi MU-2J
Escuadrón de Helicópteros	Bell UH-1H, San Isidro
	Aérospatiale SA 316 Alouette III,
	Aérospatiale SA 313 Alouette II,
	Aérospatiale AS 365 Dauphin

El Salvador

In terms of area, El Salvador is the smallest of the original independent states of Central America. It is also the most densely populated, and demographic pressures contributed in no small measure to the brief conflict with Honduras in 1969. The country is still emerging from the 10 years of bloody civil war which took place from the early 1980s.

Fuerza Aérea Salvadoreña

El Salvador formed a Military Aviation Service in 1922. The Service remained a modest force and the outbreak of World War II cut off the supply of further equipment, although during the closing stages of the war a few training aircraft were transferred from the United States. Following its signature of the Rio Treaty of 1947, El Salvador benefited from the activities of a US Air Mission and increased transfers of aircraft under the Mutual Defence Assistance Program. The Military Aviation Service was renamed the Fuerza Aérea Salvadoreña and acted as an independent component of the Armed Forces. Although the Salvadorean army was clearly superior to that of Honduras during the war of 1969, the inferiority of the Salvadorean Air Force was painfully demonstrated, and its reorganisation and re-equipment was an immediate priority following the close of hostilities. Israel then became a major supplier of aircraft, four Arava transports being delivered in 1974/75, followed by a total of 24 fighter and trainer/light strike aircraft over the next four years.

Following the savage repression of two Communist-led peasant revolts in 1930/31, popular discontent at the gross imbalance of wealth distribution between the tiny wealthy oligarchy and the pauperised peasant majority had been quietly simmering. Although the short conflict with Honduras briefly united the country against a common enemy, upon the 1980 signing of the peace treaty with Honduras the internal situation rapidly became critical and the attentions of the Salvadorean Armed Forces became increasingly focused on internal security.

As already noted, unlike the army, which enjoyed a certain regional primacy which it more than vindicated in the 1969 war with Honduras, the Salvadorean Air Force was among the least significant in Central America. Its performance in the 1969 war was mediocre, although it displayed a certain flair with a pre-emptive strike against the major base of the Honduran Air Force. This was unfortunately largely nullified by defective intelligence which failed to note a radical redeployment of the combat elements of the enemy. In the recent civil war the air force expanded three-fold and performed adequately in support of the ground forces, its own ground troops enjoying a formidable reputation as among the country's most effective counter-guerrilla forces.

Isolated, sporadic guerrilla and terrorist activities which had occurred with increasing frequency from the late 1970s rapidly developed into a full-scale civil war. The anti-government forces soon united under the Marxist-led FMLN (Farabundo Martí Frente de Liberación Nacional), thus guaranteeing the hostility of the United States, and substantial military backing for El Salvador.

Cuban and Nicaraguan support for the FMLN ensured that the Reagan administration poured funding into the El Salvadorean military as part of a misguided policy that led to a secret war fought by proxy by US-trained and -supported Contra guerrillas against Nicaragua. US aid to El Salvador had been forthcoming since the 1970s, but by 1984 it had leaped to $196.6 million. The US supplied six UH-1Hs in 1980 and four in 1981, to be used as gunships. Six of these helicopters, plus four Ouragans and three C-47s, were destroyed during an FMLN guerrilla raid on Ilopango on 27 January 1982. The remaining Ouragans were largely grounded after that.

From February 1982 onwards US aid to the FAS accelerated with the delivery of eight A-37B Dragonflys, 12 Bell UH-1Hs, four Cessna O-2As and three Fairchild C-123Ks. Subsequent UH-1H deliveries brought the air force's operational fleet to approximately 40. Two AC-47s were delivered via the United States, in December 1984, to supplement the three C-47 transports in use.

El Salvador was also a base for US forces engaged in covert operations. These included AC-130s flying night reconnaissance/interdiction missions against arms being flown from Honduras to Nicaragua. Other sources indicate that civilian light aircraft were used for a range of clandestine purposes by the CIA.

Although the civil war ended in a truce of mutual exhaustion in 1990, the Salvadorean Armed Forces remain largely orientated towards internal security.

The Salvadorean Air Force, which currently has a personnel strength of approximately 2,000 people of all ranks, operates 138 aircraft. Only a small proportion of these are serviceable, and are divided between a Fighter-Bomber Group comprising a Fighter-Bomber Squadron and an Attack Squadron; a Transport Squadron; a Helicopter Group; and the Escuela de Aviación Militar. The air force includes a battalion of paratroops and exercises operational control over the army's anti-aircraft battalion. The Air Force Commander is subordinate to the Chief of the General Staff in the overall chain of command but enjoys almost absolute independence in operational matters.

In addition to the main base at Ilopango, there is a new base at Comalapa and air strips at San Miguel, Ahuachapán, Sonsonate, Zacatecoluca, San Vicente, Chalatenango and Usulután. As the air force contracts, on a peace footing, it may concentrate all its forces at these two locations. All training is carried out at Ilopango.

Officer personnel complete the four-year course of the 'Capitán General Gerardo Barrios' National Military Academy, at San Salvador, before commencing flying training at the 'Capitán Reynaldo Cortez' Escuela de Aviación Militar or other specialist training at the Escuela de Especialización de la Fuerza Aérea, both of which are located at Ilopango. There is also an Airborne Forces School at Ilopango. Specialist other ranks receive their training at the Escuela de Especialización. Most officer personnel also pursue additional training abroad.

The current FAS inventory comprises seven unserviceable Dassault Ouragans (18 acquired from the IDF/AF in 1974/75), nine Cessna A-37Bs, 13 Cessna O-2As, single examples of the Fairchild C-123K, Douglas DC-6 and the IAI 201 Arava, two Douglas AC-47s, two Basler T-67s, Fouga CM.170s (nine acquired from the IDF/AF), two Cessna T-41s and three SOCATA Rallye 235Ms. The relatively large helicopter force, most of which is now non-operational, comprises 35 Bell UH-1Hs, 16 UH-1Ms, 11 Schweizer-Hughes 500Ms and four Hughes TH-55s (Schweizer 300Cs), plus three examples apiece of the Aérospatiale (Sud-Aviation) SA 315 and 316. There are also single examples of Cessna 180, 182 and 185 light aircraft which are directly subordinate to air force headquarters and are used for liaison, training and light communications duties.

Fuerza Aérea Salvadoreña

Grupo de Caza-Bombardeo   **Comalapa International Airport**
Dassault Ouragans (unserviceable)

Escuadrón de Ataque   **Comalapa International Airport**
Cessna A-37B, Cessna O-2A

Escuadrón de Transporte   **Ilopango**
Fairchild C-123K, Douglas DC-6, Douglas AC-47, Basler T-67, IAI 201 Arava

Grupo de Helicópteros   **Ilopango**
Bell UH-1H and UH-1M, Hughes (MD) 500M, 4 Hughes (MD) TH-55, Aérospatiale SA 315 Lama, Aérospatiale SA 316 Alouette III

Escuela de Aviación Militar   **Ilopango**
Fouga CM.170 Magister, Cessna T-41, SOCATA Rallye 235M

The A-37B is the front-line combat type of the FAS. The A-37 above is carrying Mk 82 bombs; the aircraft seen left is fitted with an underwing towed target unit.

Below: CM.170 Magisters were acquired from Israel in the 1970s.

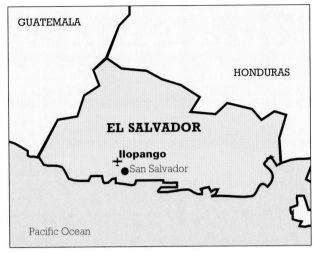

GUATEMALA

HONDURAS

EL SALVADOR

+ Ilopango
● San Salvador

Pacific Ocean

Above: In 1985 the FAS acquired three MD 500MD gunships, armed with 7.62-mm Miniguns.

Below: The high performance of the SE.315B Lama was appreciated by the FAS.

Left: At least one of Salvador's T-67 Turbo Dakotas operates as an AC-47 gunship.

Below left: Gunship-configured Hughes 500D/Ms were supplied by the US in the mid-1980s.

Below: El Salvador still operates a single SA 316B Alouette III.

Below right: The pride of the FAS is this immaculate Douglas C-118A (DC-6).

above: SOCATA Ralleye 235 trainers were delivered 1981, and serve with the EAM.

Above: Several batches of armed Cessna O-2As have been acquired from the United States.

Above: Israel has supplied combat aircraft, jet trainers and IAI 201 Arava transports.

bove: El Salvador's remaining C-123 Providers are ow believed to have been withdrawn from use.

Above: VIP transport is undertaken by specially-adapted Basler T-67 Turbo Dakotas and IAI Aravas.

Above: The FAS operates several VIP-configured UH-1Hs, in addition to utility and gunship versions.

Guatemala

The five original Spanish-speaking countries of Central America (less Panama) formed a single administrative entity under the Spanish colonial empire, and after independence they initially continued to form a single political entity. This, however, rapidly collapsed into mutually antipathetic warring statelets. The ideal of political union does still remain alive and numerous attempts have been made to revive it, usually by the rather counter-productive method of one country attempting to impose its authority over the remainder. Many of these attempts have been under the auspices of Guatemala, the largest state in the region, the most recent being in 1906. From 1931 to 1944, Guatemala was ruled by Jorge Ubico, whose iron dictatorship was aimed principally at the maintenance of favourable conditions for foreign (mainly US) investment. In 1954, an incipiently Marxist-orientated regime,

led by Colonel Jacobo Arbenz Gúzman, was overthrown by an invasion from neighbouring Honduras, by CIA-sponsored anti-Communist Guatemalan expatriates. The political pendulum then swung so far back to the right that the administration of General Miguel Ydígoras Fuentes permitted the CIA to use Guatemalan territory as the main base for the abortive invasion of Cuba by anti-Castro expatriates in 1961. Cuba responded by training and equipping Guatemalan guerrillas, and the country has been wracked by almost incessant guerrilla insurgency ever since. Human rights abuses have sporadically stopped US military assistance and Guatemala, which has claimed the entire territory of neighbouring Belize (formerly British Honduras) since before its independence in 1981, has increasingly turned to Israel for military material and training assistance.

copter Squadron, also based at La Aurora but deployed in elements throughout the country. The Escuela de Aviación Militar is located at Los Cipresales, Guatemala City.

Air force officers receive their basic military training at the Escuela Politécnica, the national Military Academy at San Juan Sacatepéquez, and receive their flying training at the Escuela de Aviación Militar. Most officers also receive advanced training abroad, either in the United States, Mexico or Venezuela. Specialist ground crews and other support personnel receive their training at the Escuela de Aplicación, the army's major technical training centre at Guatemala City, or in the Escuela Técnica de Aviación Militar at Mazatenango.

Most existing aircraft require modernisation and the Guatemalan Air Force is plagued by an endemic shortage of spares. Limited equipment has dictated that the air force confine its recent operations and deployment to the counter-insurgency role. Considering both the scarcity of equipment and the lack of external maintenance support for its existing inventory, the Guatemalan Air Force is nonetheless a remarkably effective counter-insurgency force and presents an object lesson in how to achieve the maximum results with minimum resources.

The current aircraft inventory comprises four Cessna A-37B Dragonflys, four Pilatus PC-7 Turbo Trainers, four IAI 201 Aravas, four Douglas C-47s (of 18 originally acquired), three examples each of the Basler T-67 and the Fokker F27, six Cessna 172K Hawk XPs, two Piper Navajos, and single examples of the Douglas DC-6B (grounded since July 1996), Beech Super King Air 200 (which operates as the Presidential transport), Bellanca Decathalon and Cessna 210. The relatively modest helicopter fleet comprises four Bell 206B JetRanger/206L LongRangers, six Bell 212s, six Bell 412s and four Bell UH-1Hs.

Fuerza Aérea Guatemalteca

A French military aviation mission arrived in Guatemala in 1920 and a flying training school was established, although little progress was made until 1929 when the Cuerpo de Aviación Militar de Guatemala was established. In 1934 the dictator Jorge Ubico decided on a relatively ambitious expansion programme, ordering 30 assorted aircraft in the United States. The outbreak of World War II hindered any further immediate expansion until 1942, when Guatemala began to receive Lend-Lease military assistance. A US military air mission arrived in 1945 and, following Guatemala's signature of the Rio Treaty of Inter-American Reciprocal Assistance in 1947, US military aid again increased considerably. The title of the force was changed to Fuerza Aérea Guatemalteca in 1948.

The hostility of the United States government towards the left-leaning Arbenz Gúzman regime virtually closed off the Guatemalan Air Force's main source of equipment during the period 1951/54. The air force took no part in the coup which overthrew Arbenz in 1954, but aircraft deliveries from the US resumed soon afterwards. Following the suspension of US military aid in 1978 due to Guatemala's human rights record, the country turned to Israel and Argentina as suppliers of defence material. The US had refused to supply six Northrop F-5E/Fs requested in 1978, so the FAH's front-line types remained the survivors of a batch of 13 A-37Bs delivered in 1974/75, and two T-33As. In 1980/81 approximately 10 Bell 212 and 412 helicopters were acquired from civilian sources in the US, but were used for military duties and fitted with weapons. Twelve Swiss-built Pilatus PC-7 Turbo Trainers, bought in 1979/80 ostensibly as trainers, were also used in an armed role. Guatemala had sought to acquire weapons-capable SIAI-Marchetti SF.260W Warriors, but these were embargoed and the PC-7s were acquired instead. Israel supplied 10 IAI Arava transports between 1975 and 1976, several of which were later converted to gunship configuration.

The election of Ronald Reagan as President of the United States (and a 1982 *coup* which brought a more moderate military junta to power) brought with it a mellowing of US foreign policy towards Guatemala, as a direct result of which spares were made available for existing US-built aircraft and some limited deliveries of new material were made. The formal arms embargo was lifted in January 1983. This led to the supply of spares to return nine UH-1s to serviceable condition (with the work undertaken by Taiwanese technicians).

The Guatemalan Armed Forces constitute a single institution with army, navy and air force elements. The air force has a nominal personnel strength of about 700, a figure which is misleading as it refers only to aircrew and personnel directly involved in the operation of aircraft. Taking into account logistic and other support personnel (who are nominally part of the army), air force strength is probably in the region of at least 1,000. To this could also reasonably be added the army's two paratroop battalions and four anti-aircraft artillery batteries, plus the Agrupación Táctica de Seguridad, all of which come under the operational control of the air force. Including these and their logistic support elements, true manpower is probably of the order of 3,000.

The major air bases are La Aurora and Los Cipresales (Guatemala City), San José and Santa Elena, with minor bases at Puerto Barrios, Mazatenango and Flores. There are more than a dozen landing strips suitable for the operation of military aircraft available throughout the country, and most are occupied sporadically.

The air force is organised into two flying wings – Ala Fija (Fixed-Winged Aircraft Wing) and Ala Rotativa (Rotary-Winged Aircraft Wing) – and the Ala de Mantenimiento (Maintenance Wing). The Ala Fija consists of the 'Quetzal' Attack Squadron based at San José, a Tactical Support Squadron based at Santa Elena, and a Transport Squadron based at La Aurora Airport, Guatemala City. The Ala Rotativa comprises the sole Heli-

Fuerza Aérea Guatemalteca

Escuadrón de Ataque 'Quetzal'
'General Felipe Cruz' Air Base, San José, Escuintla
Cessna A-37B Dragonfly

Escuadrón de Apoyo Táctico
'General Danilo Eugenio Henry Sánchez' Air Base, Santa Elena, Petén
Pilatus PC-7, Basler T-67, armed IAI Arava

Escuadrón de Transporte
'La Aurora' Air Base, Guatemala City
Douglas C-47, Fokker F27, armed IAI Arava

Escuadrón de Helicópteros
'La Aurora' Air Base, Guatemala City
Bell 206, Bell 212, Bell 412, Bell UH-1D and H, Sikorsky S-76

Escuadrilla Presidencial
'La Aurora' Air Base, Guatemala City
Beech Super King Air 200, Gulfstream Commander 695/1000, Colemill (PA-31) Panther Navajo, Decathalon, Cessna 210

Escuela de Aviación Militar
'Los Cipresales' Air Base, Guatemala City
Cessna T-37, Cessna 172

The six Aravas, although nominally part of the Transport Squadron, are usually attached to the Tactical Support Squadron. Four Cessna 170s, three 180s and four U206s, together with single examples of the Cessna 310, 182 and 185, which are unattached to any squadron on a permanent basis, rotate between the above bases and the air strips at Retalhuléu, Quezaltenango, Flores and Escuintla as operational necessity demands.

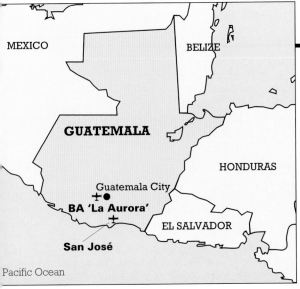

MEXICO
BELIZE
GUATEMALA
HONDURAS
Guatemala City
BA 'La Aurora'
San José
EL SALVADOR
Pacific Ocean

Above: The A-37Bs acquired during the 1970s as part of the Peace Tikal programme are the FAG's only jets.

Left, below left and below: In 1979 Guatemala acquired five Pilatus PC-7s, and more may have been delivered. They operate in a variety of paint schemes.

Above: Between 1975 and 1976, IAI delivered 10 IAI 201 Aravas to Guatemala.

Below: From 1989 onwards Guatemala took (re)delivery of its Basler T-67 conversions.

Above: The FAG operates a single F27-200 (as seen here) and two F27-400Ms.

Below: This Gulfstream Aerospace Commander 1000 is based at Guatemala City.

Above: A mix of UH-1Ds and UH-1Hs were delivered in 1971 and serve with the Escuadrón de Helicópteros.

Left: Some Bell 212s are tasked with VIP transport, and are based at 'La Aurora'.

Above: Six Cessna R172K Hawk XPs are in use with the EAM as basic trainers.

Above: This Colemill Panther Navajo serves with the transport unit based at 'La Aurora'.

Above: A Beech 200 Super King Air is the Fuerza Aérea Guatemalteca's Presidential transport.

151

Haiti

The Republic of Haiti, which occupies the western third of the island of Hispaniola, was the second country in the Americas to become independent, having expelled the French in 1791. Full independence was declared in 1804 but, although Haiti occupied the entire island between 1822 and 1844, it has been chronically unstable throughout almost its entire independent history. Haiti was occupied by the United States between 1915 and 1934, and from 1956 until his death in 1971 was ruled by Dr François ('Papa Doc') Duva-

lier, who used a combination of voodoo and police state terror to consolidate his control. Duvalier distrusted the military and kept the armed forces at a low level of military potential throughout his 15-year reign. He was succeeded by his son Jean Claude ('Baby Doc'), who, although totally corrupt, lacked his father's ruthlessness and was deposed by the army in 1986. The country's first democratically elected President, Jean Bertrand Aristide, was deposed by the military within months of his election in 1991; this action ultimately provoked a US-led invasion to restore him, three years later. Following the restoration of President Aristide, the armed forces were formally abolished and Haiti is now in a stage of transition.

the overall command structure. It consisted of a combat unit, a transport unit and a helicopter unit. Personnel strength was approximately 300 people of all ranks. Bowen Field, Port-au-Prince, was the only permanently occupied base. All officers were trained at the Military Academy at Fréres, NCOs being trained at the Camp d'Application. Flying and specialist training were both carried out at Bowen Field.

The current aircraft inventory, most of which is non-operational, consists of seven Cessna O-2s, three Douglas C-47s, a single Curtiss C-46, a DHC-6, two DHC-2s, single examples of the Beechcraft Baron, Cessna 401 and 402, four SIAI Marchetti SF.260TPs, four Sikorsky S.58s, and a pair each of Hughes 269Cs and 369Cs.

Corps d'Aviation d'Haiti

An aviation section of the Garde d'Haiti, known as the Corps d'Aviation d'Haiti, was established with the help of a US Marine Corps aviation mission in 1943. During the years immediately following World War II, small quantities of second-line types were acquired. In 1950 a US Air Force mission arrived in Haiti and the first combat unit was formed shortly afterwards with four North American F-51D Mustangs. In 1994, following

the US-led OAS invasion and occupation to restore the legitimate President Jean Bertrand Aristide, the Haitian armed forces were formally disbanded. The current status of the former air arm is unknown.

The Corps d'Aviation was an integral part of the Haitian armed forces rather than an independent air force. As such, its Commander was subordinate to the Chief of Staff of the Armed Forces in

Corps d'Aviation d'Haiti

Escadre de Combat   **Bowen Field, Port-au-Prince**
Cessna O-2/337Gs

Escadre de Transport
Douglas C-47, Curtiss C-46, DHC-2, DHC-6, Beechcraft B55 Baron, Cessna 401, Cessna 402

Escadre d'Hélicoptères
Sikorsky S.58, Hughes 269C, Hughes 369C

Ecole Aéronautique Militaire
SIAI-Marchetti SF.260TP, Cessna 150, Cessna 172, Beech Bonanza

Honduras

The least developed country in Central America, Honduras has the distinction of being the birthplace of Francisco Morazán, the apostle of Central American independence and political unity. Due to the country's underdeveloped infrastructure – defective surface communications in particular – air power assumed an unusual importance in Honduras at an early date. While the Honduran army was the last in the region to submit to modernisation and undergo the painful process of transformation from a gang of armed political partisans to a disciplined military force, the air force developed relatively early and established

Honduras as the major air power in Central America. During the 1980s the United States rapidly built up Honduran military power as a counter to that of Nicaragua under its Marxist-orientated Sandinista government and, therefore, it was the only Central American country to receive modern US combat aircraft (F-5s). With the passing of the fancied Sandinista menace, these aircraft were perceived as a major disequilibriant in the regional military balance and the US persuaded the Honduran government to sell at least some of its F-5s to Chile at the beginning of 1995.

stations at Amapala and El Lorque, plus a significant presence at each of its four main bases and small detachments at many of the secondary ones, including those at Dursuna, Jamastrán, Puerto Lempira and Marcala.

All training is nominally carried out at Toncontín but the flying elements of the Escuela de Aviación are regularly deployed to each of the other three main air bases and appear to be currently based at 'Enrique Soto Cano' Air Base, Palmerola. Officers receive their initial training at the Escuela Militar, the National Military College, at Tegucigalpa and their subsequent specialised training at the Escuela de Aviación Militar. Although the flying elements of this institution appear to have moved to Palmerola, various non-flying courses still take place at Toncontín in addition to *ab initio* training for enlisted personnel. Most officer and some selected non-commissioned personnel also receive continuation training abroad.

Fuerza Aérea Hondureña

A military flying school was established in 1921 and expanded to become the Military Aviation Service in 1934. In 1954, the Aviación Militar became independent of the army, as the Fuerza Aérea Hondureña. During the brief Honduras-El Salvador 'Football War' of 1969, Honduras gained complete control of the air at an early stage, although its ground forces had to retreat in the face of the superior Salvadorean army. A considerable build-up, including the replacement with jet aircraft of obsolete piston-engined operational material (mainly Vought F4U Corsairs), took place during the 1970s. Since the early 1980s, the Honduran Air Force has also received considerable material and training assistance from the United States.

The Fuerza Aérea Hondureña currently consists of approximately 1,800 military personnel and

400 civilian employees, manning about 130 aircraft. The force is organised into a Fighter Squadron, a Fighter-Bomber Squadron, a Light Strike Squadron, a Transport Squadron, a Communications Squadron and a Helicopter Squadron. The Commander-in-Chief of the Air Force reports to the Commander-in-Chief of the Armed Forces. The air force has its own General Staff which controls three separate divisions dealing with (i) Personnel, Intelligence, Operations and Technical Support, (ii) Air Bases, and (iii) Training.

The major bases are located at Toncontín, Tegucigalpa; Palmerola, Moncada and San Pedro Sula. There are secondary bases at El Aguacate, Cucuyagua, Dursuna, Jamastrán, Trujillo, Puerto Lempira, San Lorenzo, San Marcos, Marcala and Huanpusipi. The air force also maintains radar

A mystery surrounds the current status of the Honduran Air Force's F-5s, of which it originally operated 10 examples of the E and two of the F variant. A number were delivered by sea to Chile in 1995, but after unloading at Valparaiso disappeared from view. As late as September 1996, at least six were still observed in Honduran service. An unknown number of A-36 Halcóns were obtained from Chile as part of this deal. The remaining inventory of the FAH includes eight non-operational Dassault Super Mystère B.2s (over 20 were acquired from the IDF/AF in 1976), about a dozen Cessna A-37Bs, four Lockheed C-130As, single examples of the Fairchild C-123K, Douglas AC-47, Rockwell 690, Lockheed L-188A, Beechcraft Baron and Piper Navajo, two Cessna 180s, two Cessna 185s, four CASA C.101s, 10 EMBRAER EMB-312 Tucanos and six Cessna T-41s. Helicopter assets include one Sikorsky S.76, four Bell UH-1Bs and seven UH-1Hs, nine Bell 412S and four Hughes 500s.

Above and left: The Fuerza Aérea Hondureña acquired a small number (perhaps as little as four) of ENAER A-36 Halcóns (licence-built CASA 101CCs), which operate alongside the CASA 101BB Aviojet trainers acquired in 1985. The A-36s were delivered, from Chile, in 1996.

Left: The status of Honduras's F-5 force is in doubt, as several aircraft have been transferred to Chile.

Below: This sharkmouthed T-27 (EMB-312) Tucano is one of 12 that had been acquired by 1986.

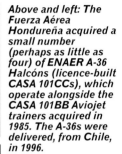

Above: Honduras took delivery of its first C-130A Hercules in 1986 and now operates four.

Below: Only one of the three FAH Aravas is thought to remain operational.

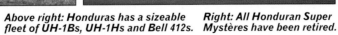

Above: Perhaps five C-47/T-67 conversions remain in FAH service.

Above right: Honduras has a sizeable fleet of UH-1Bs, UH-1Hs and Bell 412s.

Right: All Honduran Super Mystères have been retired.

Left: This Bell 47 is no longer an operational aircraft but is maintained in fully airworthy condition.

Right: MD 500Ds were first acquired in 1977 and four are now believed to be in use.

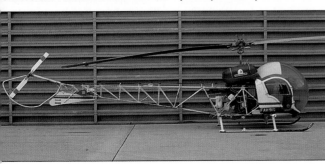

Fuerza Aérea Hondureña

Escuadrón de Caza
Base Aérea 'Coronel Héctor Caracciollo' (Moncada, La Ceiba)
Northrop F-5E and F, Dassault Super Mystère B.2, A-36 Halcón
(The Super Mystères are non-operational)

Escuadrón de Apoyo Táctico
Base Aérea 'Coronel Héctor Caracciollo' (Moncada, La Ceiba)
Cessna A-37B

Escuadrón de Transporte
Base Aérea 'Coronel Armando Escalón Espinal' (San Pedro Sula)
Lockheed C-130A, Fairchild C-123K, Douglas AC-47, Douglas C-47, IAI Arava, IAI Westwind, Aero Commanders, Rockwell 690B, Lockheed L-188A Electra, Cessna 404 Titan

Escuadrón de Comunicaciones
Base Aérea 'Teniente Coronel Hermán Acosta Mejía' (Toncontín, Tegucigalpa)
Cessna 180, Cessna 185, Beechcraft Baron, Piper Navajo

Escuadrón de Helicópteros
Base Aérea 'Teniente Coronel Hermán Acosta Mejía' (Toncontín, Tegucigalpa)
Sikorsky S.76, Bell UH-1B, Bell UH-1H, Bell 412, Hughes 500

Escuadrón de Enseñanza Basica de Vuelo
'Enrique Soto Cano' Air Base, Palmerola
EMBRAER EMB-312 Tucano, Cessna T-41

Escuadrón de Enseñanza de Vuelo Avanzada
CASA C.101

Jamaica

The island of Jamaica, formerly the largest British possession in the Caribbean, became independent in 1962. It maintains a very small tri-service defence force, with a minuscule air arm.

Air Wing of the Defence Force

The Jamaican armed forces are known as the Jamaica Defence Force and comprise land, sea and air elements. An Air Wing was formed in 1963. As an integral element of the Defence Force, the Commander of its land element reports to the Governor-General, via the Minister for Defence. The main bases of the JDFAW are both at Kingston. There is also an air strip at Montego Bay, which is not permanently manned by JDF elements. Limited fixed-wing training is undertaken at Manley International Airport, with helicopter training at Up Park Camp. Most flying and technical personnel receive at least part of their training abroad.

The current aircraft inventory consists of two PBN Islanders, single examples of the Beech King Air 100 and the Cessna 337G, four Bell 206As, three Bell 212s and a single Bell 222.

Air Wing of the Jamaica Defence Force

Fixed-Wing Flight   **Manley International Airport, Kingston**
Britten-Norman Islander, Beech King Air 100, Cessna 337G

Helicopter Flight   **Up Park Camp, Kingston**
Bell 206A, Bell 212, Bell 222

Nicaragua

The largest country of Central America in terms of area, Nicaragua suffered from repeated US military intervention between 1912 and 1927 and was continuously occupied by US Marines from the latter year until 1933. The US occupation forces created an efficient National Guard which combined the functions of defence and internal security, and which provided the power base for the predatory dictatorship of the Somoza family between 1936 and 1979. In 1979, Anastasio Somoza Junior, the third member of the Somoza dynasty, was overthrown by a popular uprising led by the Marxist-orientated Sandinista National Liberation Front. This organisation rapidly gained ascendancy over more moderate centrist elements and thereby incurred the wrath of the US, which attempted to destabilise it through the actions of its surrogate 'Contra' guerrillas throughout the 1980s. In 1990, the Sandinista regime, although still militarily undefeated, succumbed to its own inherent defects and lost an election to a broadly-based centre-right coalition which has since attempted to rebuild a country almost destroyed by 20 years of revolution and civil war.

When asked for assistance with this feature, an official spokeswoman at the Nicaraguan Embassy in London stated, "Nicaragua no longer has an air force as it does not need one."

Fuerza Aérea Nicaragüense

The Fuerza Aérea de la Guardia Nacional was formed in 1938 but little progress was made until the receipt of material and training assistance from the United States, which commenced in 1942. From 1942 small numbers of trainers and light transports were acquired, and by 1945 a total of 20 aircraft was on strength. In 1952 a US aviation mission arrived in Nicaragua and, subsequently, additional quantities of trainers and transports were received, followed by P-38, P-47 and P-51 fighters. For some years to follow, the Nicaraguan Air Force was the strongest in Central America. Many aircraft fell victim to rebel ground fire during the civil war which finally toppled the Somozas, and others were flown into exile by their pilots.

The supply of two SA 316 Alouette III helicopters formed part of a French arms deal of 1981 and, according to repeated reports emanating from official US sources, at least a dozen MiG-23s were to be transferred from Cuba during the same year. Neither these latter aircraft nor the six MiG-21s which were supposed to have been delivered in 1985 ever materialised, although Nicaraguan pilots had undergone training on these types in Bulgaria and Cuba. Material more suitable to Nicaragua's immediate requirements, and which was received from countries of the Eastern Bloc, included numbers of Mil Mi-2, Mi-8 and Mi-24 helicopters, An-2 and An-26 transports and Aero L-39Z trainer/light-strike aircraft. Following the electoral defeat of the Sandinistas in 1990, much of the Eastern European equipment was disposed of, a large proportion of it going to Peru (such as the Mi-25s).

Despite the change of government, the Nicaraguan Air Force retained the title of Sandinista Revolutionary Air Force until 1996, when it reverted to Fuerza Aérea Nicaragüense. It currently numbers 1,200 personnel and possesses approximately 30 aircraft organised into a single Transport Squadron, a Helicopter Squadron, and a Training/Light-Strike Squadron. Most of its aircraft are unserviceable. Following Soviet and Cuban practice, the air force is also primarily responsible for air defence, operating 18 ZU-23 23-mm A/A guns and a similar number of C3-M SAM systems. The Commander of the FAN reports directly to the Commander of the Armed Forces.

The principal base of the FAN is at 'Augusto César Sandino' International Airport, Managua. Other major bases are at Punta Huete, to the northeast of Managua, and Puerto Cabezas, on the Atlantic coast. In addition, there are military airfields at Estelí, Bluefields, Montelimar, La Rosita, El Bluff and Puerto Sandino. Nicaragua is the only country in Central America to have anything approaching an air early-warning system, boasting AEW and intercept control facilities at Masaya, Toro Blanco, Estelí and El Bluff, plus a coastal surveillance radar station at El Polvón.

Personnel receive their basic training in the central school system of the Nicaraguan Armed Forces. The major elements of this are the 'Carlos Agüero Hechevarría' Military Academy; the Centro de Estudios Militares 'Comandante Hilario Sánchez Vázquez', which provides technical and specialised training; and the 'Eduardo Contreras' Basic Military Training School. Under the Sandinista regime this was supplemented by both basic and advanced training in Cuba or Eastern Europe for aircrew and specialists. No alternative source of overseas training assistance appears to have been found to date and there has been no significant resumption of US military aid following the failure of the Sandinistas to win the 1996 elections.

The Sandinista Air Force performed relatively well against the Contra guerrillas but at a heavy cost in attrition of the relatively bountiful inven-

Left: Yellow-painted Cessna T-41Ds serve as basic flying trainers, at Soto Cano.

Above: Hughes TH-55A Osages are used for basic helicopter flying training.

Above left: A single IAI 1124 Westwind is flown as a VIP transport, in Honduras. It was delivered in 1981.

Above right and right: Cessna Model 185s are used for a variety of transport roles and the FAH has several modified Robertson STOL versions (right).

Left: This VIP Piper PA-42 Cheyenne III wears a quasi-civilian registration.

FAH-123

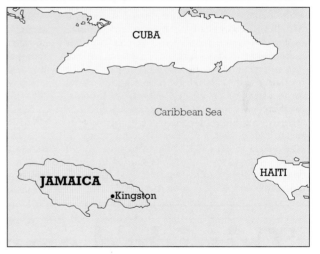

Above: This Piper PA-31 is one of an assortment of light aircraft operated by the transport unit at San Pedro Sula.

Above right: A single Rockwell Commander 690B is in FAH service.

Right: A Gulfstream Aerospace Commander 1000 serves alongside the earlier Commander 690B.

Below: This Cessna 404 has replaced an earlier Cessna 401.

Below right: This Cessna 310 is also based at San Pedro.

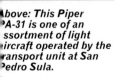

FAH-009

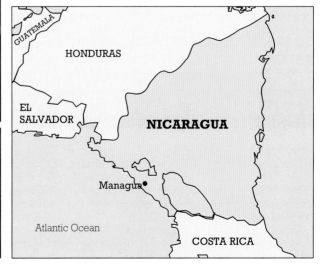

155

tory of aircraft supplied by the Soviet Union and Czechoslovakia. Only a small proportion of its remaining aircraft are still serviceable, and its morale must have suffered a further blow by the 1992 sale to Peru of all seven of its surviving Mi-25s, 12 Mi-8/17s, six P12/19 radars, 30 ZU-23-2 twin 23-mm AA guns and 120 SA-14 and SA-16 missiles. Despite the largesse of the Soviet Union and its satellites, the Sandinista Air Force never received modern combat aircraft and remained deficient in both this area and that of fixed-wing transport and communications aircraft. Its current aircraft inventory, much of it of doubtful serviceability, consists of four An-26s, two An-2s, five L-39Zs, four examples each of the Cessna 337 and SIAI Marchetti SF.260W, small numbers of Cessna 180s, U-7s and T-41s, 15 Mi-8/17 'Hip-Hs' and two Alouette IIIs.

Fuerza Aérea Nicaragüense

Escuadrón de Transporte
An-26, An-2, Cessna 180, Cessna U-7
'Augusto César Sandino' International Airport, Managua

Escuadrón de Helicópteros   Mi-8/17, SA.316 Alouette III

Escuadrón de Entrenamiento y Apoyo Táctico
Aero L-39Z, SIAI Marchetti SF.260W, Cessna 337, Cessna T-41

Panama

Although geographically part of Central America, Panama belongs historically to South America, having been part of Colombia until 1903 when US business interests, anxious to build an inter-oceanic canal through its territory, encouraged secession and the establishment of an independent republic. Although theoretically independent, Panama has remained a virtual dependency of the US whose military occupation of the Canal Zone has always been resented by Panamanians. Under the Carter-Torrijos Canal Treaty of 1979, the United States is supposed to hand over both Canal and Canal Zone to Panama at midnight on 31 December 1999. The Treaty, however, allows the United States to intervene if Panama shows itself to be unable or unwilling to defend the Canal and guarantee its availability to international shipping. The US invasion of 1989, ostensibly to remove the dictator General Manuel Noriega, destroyed the Panamanian Defence Forces; the Panamanian government, which then overrode the will of the majority of the Panamanian people as expressed in a referendum, subsequently formalised the abolition of Panama's military forces. In this context, a US military presence into the 21st century seems increasingly likely.

which its commander reports. It has been effectively reduced to a transport/training force.

The major bases of the Panamanian National Air Service are Tocumen International Airport and Albrook Air Force Base, Panama City. Additional air strips are located at Boca del Toro, David, Santiago, Chitre and La Palma.

Most training is carried out at Albrook Air Force Base. Agreements originally existed whereby all training was carried out by the Colombian and Venezuelan Air Forces, on behalf of the Panamanian government. From the early 1980s until the US invasion, the Panamanian Air Force carried out its own primary training with two Cessna U-17Bs, three 172s and a single 402, single examples of the Piper Cherokee, PA-31 Navajo and PA-31T Turbo Cheyenne II doubling in the liaison/training roles. Both air and ground crew, however, continued to receive their advanced training abroad. This system appears to be still in force.

Servicio Aéreo Nacional de Panamá

In the context of the destruction and subsequent formal abolition of the Panamanian Defence Forces, any description of the Panamanian Air Force is essentially a historical exercise. An air service, established as part of the National Police during the early 1960s, had become known as the Panamanian Air Force in 1969. At the time of the US invasion in 1989, it remained primarily a transport and helicopter force, with a manpower strength of about 500. Its 60 aircraft, none of which were combat types, were organised into a Transport Squadron, a VIP Transport Flight, a Maritime Patrol Flight and a Helicopter Squadron.

The Panamanian Air Force lost a total of 37 aircraft during the 1989 invasion and some of the survivors were transferred to civilian use. The National Air Service, as the former air force is now known, retains a total of only 16 fixed- and rotary-winged aircraft, made up of a single CASA CN.235M, three CASA C.212-300s, two CASA C.212-200s, a PBN BN-2D Islander, four ENAER T-35D Pilláns, three Bell 212s, two 205s and a single UH-1N. A Gulfstream II and Boeing 727-44 are operated as VIP transports, in civilian marks. The Service is an integral part of the new paramilitary police force, known as the Panamanian Public Forces, to the commander of

Servicio Aéreo Nacional de Panamá

Escuadrilla de Patrulla Marítima
CASA CN.235M
Tocumen International Airport (Panama City)

Escuadrón de Transporte
CASA C.212, Pilatus/Britten-Norman BN-2D, Piper Seneca

Escuadrón de Helicópteros
Bell UH-1N, Bell 212, Bell 305

Training/Light Strike Squadron
ENAER T-35 Pillán   Allbrook Air Base

Trinidad and Tobago

The island republic of Trinidad and Tobago lies off the coast of Venezuela and is geographically part of South America. It gained its independence from Britain in 1962 and a republic was declared in 1976. It maintains a very small tri-service defence force with an aviation element of commensurately small size, which initially operated a single Cessna 337 and two SA 341G Gazelles.

copters: two Sikorsky S-76As (acquired in 1981) and two MBB BO 105CBSs (acquired in 1991). The helicopters are operated by National Helicopter Services Ltd, a state-owned quasi-commercial organisation which earns revenue by chartering out elements of its fleet to private users when they are not required by the Air Wing. The revenue earned has permitted the purchase of a fourth helicopter.

Defence Force Air Wing

The armed forces of Trinidad and Tobago form a single entity: the Trinidad and Tobago Defence Force. The Trinidad and Tobago Coast Guard, which was then subordinate to the Ministry for Home Affairs, formed an air element in 1966. In 1977 the Air Wing, although still very small, became an independent element of the Trinidad and Tobago Defence Force. The President is titular Commander-in-Chief of the Defence Force. The Commander of the Air Wing reports to the Prime Minister, as Minister of National Security, via the Chief of the Defence Staff. There are air bases at Piarco (Trinidad) and Crown Point (Tobago). The current aircraft inventory of the Trinidad and Tobago Defence Force Air Wing comprises three fixed-wing aircraft: single examples of the Cessna 402C (acquired 1982), 310R and 172M; and four heli-

Trinidad and Tobago Defence Force Air Wing

Fixed-Wing Flight   **Piarco (Trinidad)**
Cessna 402C, Cessna 310R, Cessna 172M

Rotary-Wing Flight   **Crown Point (Tobago)**
Sikorsky S-76A, MBB BO 105CBS

Adrian J. English

Above: Panama's Servicio Aéreo Nacional has taken the place of the previous formal air force, from which most of its aircraft, such as this **UH-1H**, have been inherited.

Above and top: Eight ENAER **T-35D Pillán** trainers were delivered from **Chile** in 1988.

Above right: This Piper **PA-34 Seneca** is a recent addition to the **SAN**.

Right: VIP transport is the responsibility of this **Bell 212**, one of four originally delivered in 1975.

Above: Panama took delivery of several **CASA C.212- 200/300s** and a single **CN.235.**

Right: A single **BN-2A Islander** remains in use. It was delivered in 1975.

Above: This **Gulfstream II** is the Presidential transport and replaced the **CN.235** in this role.

Above: Panama took delivery of three **CASA 212-300s** in 1988 (foreground) and two **-200s**, in 1982.

The Trinidad and Tobago Defence Force Air Wing maintains a small force of light aircraft and helicopters, split between the two islands. This is one of the two **S-76As** acquired in 1981.

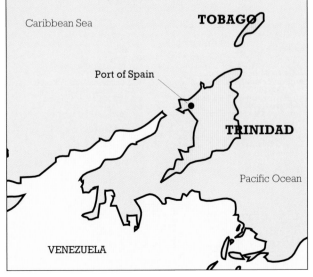

INDEX

INDEX

Picture acknowledgments

Front cover: Rick Llinares/Dash 2. **4:** Erich Strobl, Graham Robson. **5:** Alexander Mladenov, V. Weenen, Gert Kromhout. **6:** Ryszard Jaxa-Malachowski (two). **7:** Christoph Kugler, Robert Hewson. **8:** Robert Hewson, Ryszard Jaxa-Malachowski. **9:** Christoph Kugler, Roberto Yañez, M.J. Gerards. **10:** Kaman. **11:** Kevin Wills, Jim Winchester/Aerospace, Simon Watson. **12:** Simon Watson. **13:** Atsushi Tsubota (two). **14:** Atsushi Tsubota, Cess-Jan van den Ende and Roland van Maarseveen. **15:** Chris Knott (three). **16:** Carey Mavor (two), Jonathan Chuck. **17:** Lockheed Martin (two). **18:** Henry B. Ham, Bob Archer, Teledyne Ryan. **19:** McDonnell, Nate Leong (two). **20-21:** René van Woezik. **22:** Yefim Gordon (two), Victor Drushlyakov. **23-26:** Yefim Gordon. **27:** Victor Drushlyakov, Yefim Gordon. **28:** Wojtek Matusiak, Gert Kromhout. **29:** Gert Kromhout (three). **30:** Gert Kromhout, Wojtek Matusiak (two). **31:** Andrzej Rogucki, Wojtek Matusiak. **33:** Tieme Festner, E.A. Sloot/STAS (four). **35:** Tieme Festner (five), E.A. Sloot/STAS. **36:** Rick Llinares/Dash 2, Jose M. Ramos. **37:** Grumman, Ted Carlson/Fotodynamics. **38:** Ted Carlson/Fotodynamics (two). **39:** Bruce R. Trombecky, Rick Llinares/Dash 2 (two). **40:** Gary Bihary, Grumman, Ted Carlson/Fotodynamics (two), Jose M. Ramos, Matthew Olafsen. **41:** David Donald (two), Northrop Grumman. **42:** Rick Llinares/Dash 2, Carl L. Richards. **43:** Graham Robson, Malcolm Nason, Andrew H. Cline, Rick Llinares/Dash 2, Luigino Caliaro, Matthew Olafsen. **44:** Ted Carlson/Fotodynamics (two), Northrop Grumman, Graham Robson. **45:** Rick Llinares/Dash 2, Matthew Olafsen. **46:** Tadao Imaizumi via Ted Carlson/Fotodynamics, David Donald (two). **47:** Peter Steinemann, Lon Nordeen, Peter R. Foster, Simon Watson. **48-55:** Antoine Roels. **56-57:** Rick Llinares/Dash 2, Ottogalli, Marchetti, Maniago. **58:** Ted Carlson/Fotodynamics, Harry Gann. **59:** McDonnell Douglas, Randy Jolly. **60:** Randy Jolly, Chuck Lloyd/Dash 2. **61:** Rick Llinares/Dash 2. **62:** BAe via Michael Stroud. **63:** BAe via Michael Stroud, Rob Lea. **64:** Cpl John Cassidy/Strike Command. **65:** Rob Lea (two). **66:** Rob Lea. **67:** BAe, Rob Lea (two). **68:** Robert Hewson/Aerospace (three), Rob Lea (two). **69:** David Donald, Rick Llinares/Dash 2 (two). **75:** Cpl John Cassidy/Strike Command (two), Peter R. March (two), Chuck Lloyd/Dash 2, Terry Senior, Salvador Mafé Huertas. **76:** BAe, David Donald (two), Carl L. Richards, Ted Carlson/Fotodynamics, Randy Jolly. **78:** Ted Carlson/Fotodynamics. **79:** Chuck Lloyd/Dash 2, Randy Jolly. **80:** Ted Carlson/Fotodynamics. **82:** Randy Jolly, McDonnell Douglas. **83:** Randy Jolly. **84:** Ted Carlson/Fotodynamics, Bruce Trombecky. **85:** Chuck Lloyd/Dash 2 (two). **86:** Rob Lea (two). **87:** Cpl John Cassidy/Strike Command via Jon Lake, Rob Lea. **88:** BAe via Peter R. March (two). **89:** BAe via Peter R. March, Peter R. March (two). **90:** BAe, Cpl John Cassidy/Strike Command via Jon Lake. **91:** Cpl John Cassidy/Strike Command, Yves Debay. **92:** Yves Debay, Chuck Lloyd/Dash 2. **93:** Chuck Lloyd/Dash 2, Carl L. Richards. **94:** BAe via Salvador Mafé Huertas, Claudio Toselli. **95:** Salvador Mafé Huertas, McDonnell Douglas via Salvador Mafé Huertas. **96:** Luigino Caliaro, Hans Nijhuis, McDonnell Douglas. **97:** BAe via Salvador Mafé Huertas. **98:** Randy Jolly, BAe via Peter R. March. **99:** Peter B. Mersky (three). **100-101:** McDonnell Douglas. **102:** Sgt Rick Brewell/RAF PR, BAe. **103:** Matthew Olafsen, Ted Carlson/Fotodynamics. **104:** Ted Carlson/Fotodynamics, Jamie Hunter. **105:** D. Eklund, Ted Carlson/Fotodynamics (two), Bruce Trombecky, Jamie Hunter, Keith Riddle. **106:** Yves Debay (two), Peter R. Foster, Hans Nijhuis, Carl L/ Richards, Harry Gann, Bruce Trombecky. **107:** Flt Lt Stuart Andrews, Cpl John Cassidy/Strike Command, Kevin Wills (two), Richard Cooper. **108:** Peter R. March, Graham Robson, Alan Key, Richard Cooper, Salvador Mafé Huertas. **109:** E.A. Sloot/STAS, Roberto Yañez, Marco Amatimaggio, Ottogalli, Marchetti and Maniago (two), Kevin Wills. **110:** IAC, Tony Flanagan/IAC (two). **111:** Peter Steinemann, Robert Hewson (two). **112:** IAC, A. Boxman, M.V. Unen, Robert Hewson (two). **113:** Peter Steinemann, Kevin Byrne, IAC. **114:** Peter Steinemann, M.V. Unen (two). **115:** IAC, A. Boxman, Peter Steinemann, M.V. Unen. **116:** CASA via Robert Hewson, IAC (three), Kevin Byrne. **117:** *Irish Times*, Pilatus Britten-Norman, IAC, A. Boxman, Robert Hewson. **118:** Ian Black, Sgt Rick Brewell/RAF PR. **119:** David Donald, Sgt Rick Brewell/RAF PR, Peter R. Foster. **120:** RAF PR, Darron Hall, Ian Black, RAF PR, M. Court. **121:** Kevin Wills, Tim Senior, Darron Hall, RAF PR. **122:** Mike Rondot, BAe, Ian Black, Leen J. Palsroek, Peter R. Foster, Tony Paxton. **123:** Kevin Wills, BAe, Terry Senior, Peter R. March. **124:** Kevin Wills (two), David Donald, Ian Black. **125:** Peter R. March, Peter R. Foster, M. Selbie via P. Spoors, Ian Black. **126:** Stefan Petersen, Paul van Oers, Bob Archer, David Donald. **127:** Peter J. Cooper/Falcon Aviation, Derek Bower, David Donald (two), Kevin Wills, Peter R. Foster. **128:** E.A. Sloot/STAS, Stefan Petersen, F. Lert. **129:** DASA (two), M.D. Tabak, Ralf Hupfeld, David Donald, Marcus Fülber. **130:** Robert Meerding, Ralf Hupfeld, DASA, M.D. Tabak (two), Peter R. Foster. **131:** Matthias Becker, Gert Kromhout, Greg L. Davis. **132:** Kevin Wills, Andreas Jung, Ian Black, Stefan Petersen. **133:** AMI via Luigino Caliaro, Carmine de Napoli and Raffaele Mancini, Cpl John Cassidy/Strike Command via Jon Lake. **134:** Ralf Hupfeld, Frank Smith/VMAS, C. Toselli (two), Ottogalli, Marchetti and Maniago. **135:** Ralf Hupfeld, Frank Smith/VMAS, David Donald, Sergio Bottaro, GRSA Archive, Alan Key. **136:** BAe via Tony Paxton. **137:** Ian Black, via Simon Watson, Terry Senior. **138-141:** Chuck Lloyd and Rick Llinares/Dash 2. **143:** Pilatus Britten-Norman, Jon Lake, Chris Knott (three), Paolo Poggi (all). **145:** Paolo Poggi (all). **147:** Peter Steinemann (seven), Chris Knott (four). **149:** Frédéric Lert (all). **151:** Chris Knott (five), Frédéric Lert (two), Alan Key (six). **153:** US DoD (three), Frédéric Lert (eight). **155:** Frédéric Lert (all). **157:** Chris Knott (six), Alan Key (three), Austin J. Brown/APL.